Palgrave Studies in Economic History

Series Editor
Kent Deng
London School of Economics
London, UK

Palgrave Studies in Economic History is designed to illuminate and enrich our understanding of economies and economic phenomena of the past. The series covers a vast range of topics including financial history, labour history, development economics, commercialisation, urbanisation, industrialisation, modernisation, globalisation, and changes in world economic orders.

More information about this series at
http://www.palgrave.com/gp/series/14632

Luciano Amaral

The Modern Portuguese Economy in the Twentieth and Twenty-First Centuries

palgrave
macmillan

Luciano Amaral
Nova School of Business and Economics
Lisbon, Portugal

Palgrave Studies in Economic History
ISBN 978-3-030-24547-4 ISBN 978-3-030-24548-1 (eBook)
https://doi.org/10.1007/978-3-030-24548-1

Cover illustration: Sean Pavone/Alamy Stock Photo

This Palgrave Macmillan imprint is published by the registered company Springer Nature Switzerland AG
The registered company address is: Gewerbestrasse 11, 6330 Cham, Switzerland

Contents

List of Figures

Chapter 1

Chapter 2

Chapter 3

Chapter 4

Chapter 5

Chapter 6

Chapter 7

Chapter 8

List of Tables

Chapter 7

1

Introduction

The evolution of the Portuguese economy in the twentieth century and in the beginning of the twenty-first century is apparently easy to describe: it started the twentieth century as a relatively poor one but converged afterward to high income levels, in such a manner that it can be classified, since the 1990s, among the club of the richest economies of the world: by 1900, the size of Portuguese GDP was of about 12,000 million EKS 2017 US dollars (in purchasing power parities); by 2017, it was roughly 25 times larger, at 311,120 million, making it rank in 64th position among the economies of the world (corresponding to a fraction of 0.27% of the world's GDP) and place it as the 44th richest one, as measured by GDP per capita (according to the World Bank's World Development Indicators) (Fig. 1). This growth was accompanied by the practical doubling of the population of the country in the same period, from 5.4 million persons in 1900 to 10.3 in 2017, making of Portugal the 89th largest country in the world in population terms (Fig. 2).

The original version of this chapter was revised: Typographical errors were corrected. The correction to this chapter is available at https://doi.org/10.1007/978-3-030-24548-1_9

L. Amaral, *The Modern Portuguese Economy in the Twentieth and Twenty-First Centuries*, Palgrave Studies in Economic History,
https://doi.org/10.1007/978-3-030-24548-1_1

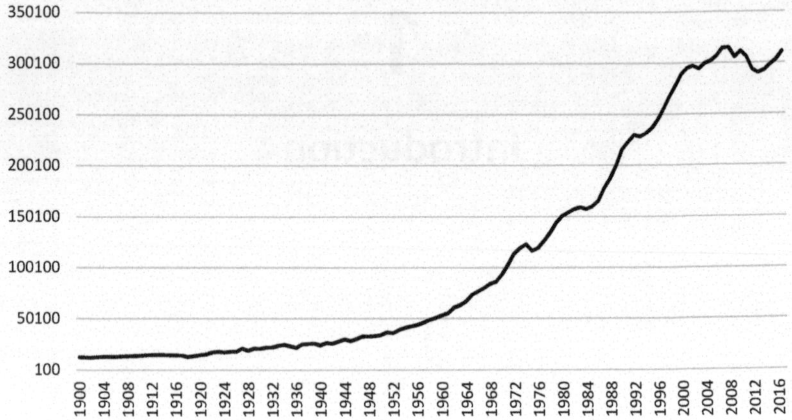

Fig. 1 GDP Portugal (*Source* 1996–2017—The Conference Board, extrapolated backward with Pinheiro [1997] for 1953–1995, Batista et al. [1997] for 1910–1952, and Maddison [2003] for 1900–1909. *Unit* EKS 2017 million US dollars, converted with 2011 PPP)

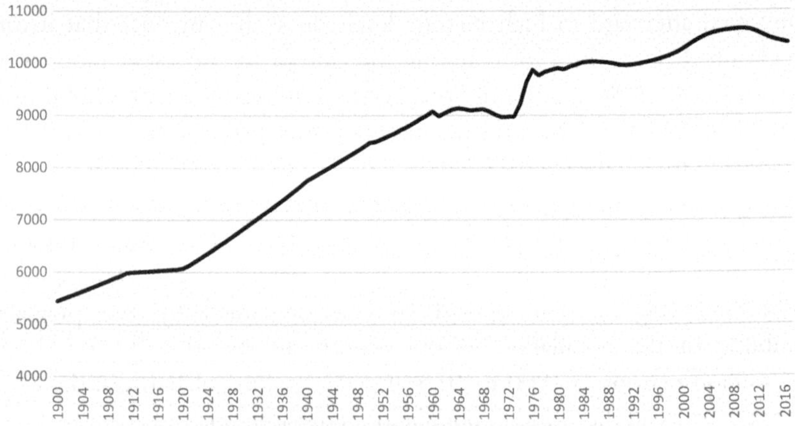

Fig. 2 Population, Portugal (1900–2017) (million persons) (*Source* 1950–2007—Amaral [2009], extrapolated backward with own calculations based on Baganha and Marques [2001] and Henriques and Rodrigues [2009], and forward with INE)

Figures 3 and 4 illustrate the process of convergence of the Portuguese economy with the richest ones: in them, GDP per capita in Portugal is compared with two sets of countries, both of which have also sometimes

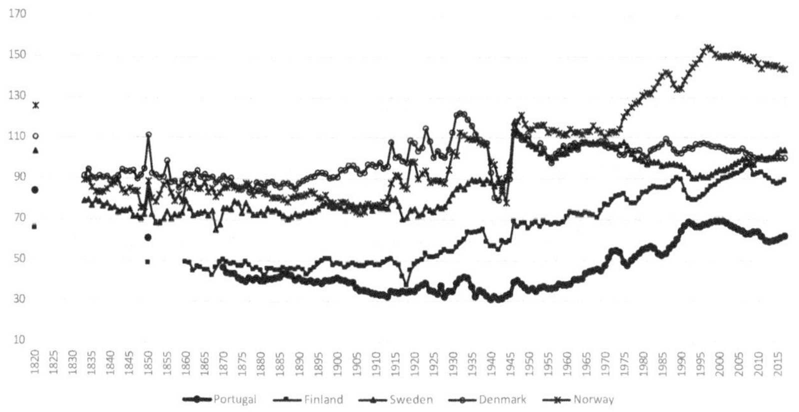

Fig. 3 Portugal and the "northern periphery" GDP per capita as a % of GDP per capita in richer countries (Portugal, Finland, Sweden, Denmark and Norway), 1820–2017 (*Note* Countries represented in the sample: Australia, Austria, Belgium, Canada, Denmark, Finland, France, Germany, Italy, New Zealand, Norway, Sweden, Switzerland, UK, and United States. *Source* Portugal 1820–1910—Maddison [2003]; 1910–1950—Batista et al. [1997]; 1950–2007—Amaral [2009]; 2007–2017—The Conference Board; Spain: Prados, "Contabilidad..."; for the other countries: 1820–1950—Maddison [2003] and 1950–2017—The Conference Board. *Unit* EKS 2017 US dollars, converted with 2011 PPP)

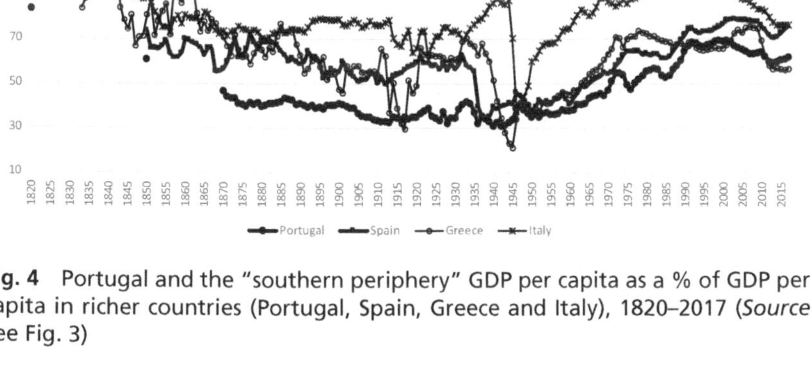

Fig. 4 Portugal and the "southern periphery" GDP per capita as a % of GDP per capita in richer countries (Portugal, Spain, Greece and Italy), 1820–2017 (*Source* See Fig. 3)

been considered to belong to the periphery of economic development in the early twentieth century. GDP per capita in Portugal passed from a level of about one-third of GDP per capita in rich countries (with the lowest point being reached in 1913, when the comparative level was 32%) to 60% one century later (with the highest point having been reached in the very beginning of the twenty-first century, when it got to 70%), i.e., this comparative indicator is now twice as large than one century ago. If the figures are unequivocal in showing catch-up, they also reveal something else, namely that the process was far from linear. For most of the first half of the twentieth century, Portugal was not able to converge. The fact that it did not lose ground was already an improvement in relation to the nineteenth century, when divergence was overwhelming, but actual convergence was only a feature of the second half of the century and, in fact, stopped in the 1990s, i.e., basically for the last thirty years. This means that, if the country can be considered a rich one, it seems to have got stuck, now for more than a quarter of a century, at the bottom of the list of rich countries, and still at a relatively long distance from their average income.

The national and international environment within which Portuguese economic agents operated this transformation had great variations, with some periods being more favorable to economic growth than others. That is what the chapters in this book try to illustrate, according to chronological divisions that are relevant to understand the overall process. The comparison made in Figs. 3 and 4 between, on the one hand, the "northern periphery" and, on the other, the "southern periphery" addresses an issue raised in some literature (Reis 1993, for instance), namely that the peripheral economies of Northern Europe (specifically the Scandinavian countries and Finland), although in similar circumstances to Portugal in the beginning of the nineteenth century, were able to overcome their backward condition in the second half of that century. But Fig. 3 shows that the picture is not that simple: except in the case of Finland, none of these economies was ever as poor as the Portuguese one; Denmark's GDP per capita never fell below levels of 90% of those of the richest countries, and Norway's only briefly fell to something like 75%; Sweden is the poorest performer among the Scandinavian countries and, even in that case, its GDP per capita did not go below 70%. This means that the Scandinavian periphery was never, in reality, as peripheral as

Portugal, leading to the question if these countries can at any moment be classified in the same group as Portugal in the last two centuries. The only economy with an income level and a performance comparable to the Portuguese one is the Finnish, but even then only relatively: Finland was considerably poorer than Portugal in 1820 but never declined nearly as much; except for the period of the Finnish War of Independence, GDP per capita in Finland never went below 50% of the richest countries. When the comparison is made between Portugal and its "natural" companions of the southern periphery, the country's path continues to be idiosyncratic. The performance of the Portuguese economy stands out as especially negative in the second half of the nineteenth century and in the first half of the twentieth century, as GDP per capita in Spain and Greece, except in the catastrophic circumstances of the Spanish Civil War (for Spain) and World War II (for Greece), never went much below 50%, contrarily to Portugal.

A somewhat surprising aspect of the behavior of the Portuguese economy is feeble convergence since the 1980s. The country acquired in that period high-quality institutions, namely those of the European Economic Community/European Union (EEC/EU). In this sense, Portugal converged in institutional terms to the richest countries of the world. The prediction in most common models of growth is that, once institutional differences are suppressed, room is made for market forces to work unhampered and for factors of production to behave strictly along their relative abundance and price. This should allow for efficient allocation of factors, with the consequence of making relatively poorer countries catch-up with relatively richer ones: as returns to capital diminish in richer countries and continue to be higher in poorer ones, and as technical progress increases at the necessarily slow pace of the technological frontier in richer countries, while poorer ones can close the gap by leaping from their lower technological level to that of the frontier, convergence in income levels between richer and poorer countries should take place. The story of the Portuguese economy since joining the EEC/EU does not seem to fit these predictions very well, and the question of why this is so should be raised.

There is one further aspect of the behavior of the Portuguese economy that is worth mentioning at this point: its convergence has been

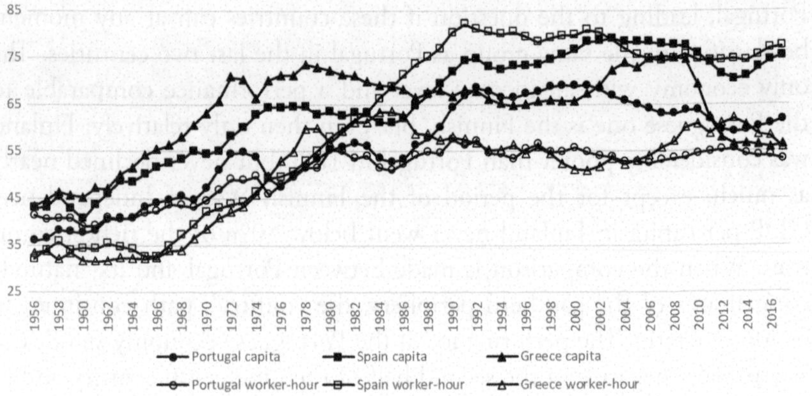

Fig. 5 GDP per capita and GDP per worker-hour in Portugal, Spain and Greece as a % of GDP per capita and GDP per worker-hour in richer countries, 1956–2017 (*Note* Countries represented in the sample: Australia, Austria, Belgium, Canada, Denmark, Finland, France, Germany, Italy, New Zealand, Norway, Sweden, Switzerland, UK, and United States. Source 1950–2007—Amaral [2009]; 2007–2017—The Conference Board; Spain: "Contabilidad…"; for the other countries: The Conference Board. *Unit* EKS 2017 US dollars, converted with 2011 PPP)

higher in terms of GDP per capita than in terms of productivity. Figure 5 shows how the relative level of productivity of the Portuguese economy has stagnated since the early 1980s, at a proportion of 55% of the most productive ones, and how a gap that did not exist before between its relative levels of productivity and GDP per capita opened from the early 1990s onward. This gap started narrowing mildly in the early twenty-first century, thanks to the decline of the relative level of GDP per capita, coinciding with the slowing down of the economy, and practically disappeared after the outbreak of the crisis in 2008, at least until 2014. From then on, it has widened slightly again. This reveals a worrying feature of the recent Portuguese economy, i.e., its difficulty in getting to the same level of efficiency of richer economies. Such difficulty leads, as a consequence, to the conclusion that any past comparative improvements in welfare depended on a growing indebtedness to the outside world. The recent crisis represented essentially a process whereby Portuguese average welfare was made to coincide with the efficiency of the economy. This indicates that, for Portuguese GDP per capita to increase in a relatively balanced way it has to be founded on productivity. Otherwise, the economy will develop an external imbalance. External imbalance (or debt) will not be a major problem as long as foreign creditors believe in the country's repayment capacity. But once they start having doubts, adjustments are inevitable. In this sense, the Portuguese path is similar to that of Greece, which has had a gap between productivity and GDP per capita of the same sort than in Portugal practically for the entire period since the 1950s, with its recent closing coinciding with the latest crisis and being extremely pronounced. Overall, the productivity of the Greek economy is similar to that of the Portuguese one. On the contrary, the productivity of the Spanish economy is much higher and coincides almost fully with GDP per capita, meaning that adjustments in Spain should not be as hard as in the other two countries. Spain, nevertheless, shares a similar worrying aspect with Portugal and Greece: a stagnation of catch-up in productivity persisting basically for the last thirty years.

As is usual in processes of long-run modern economic growth, the structure of the economy changed drastically. The economy started, in the early twentieth century, by being essentially agricultural and rural and, in the early twenty-first century, has transitioned into an essentially service and urbanized one. In between the two extremes, it industrialized, first, and then deindustrialized. That is what Figs. 6 and 7 illustrate: in Fig. 6, we can see how about 65% of active population were employed in agriculture in the early twentieth century, while the remaining 35% were more or less equally distributed between industry and services; when we get to the early twenty-first century, services employ 70% of the active population while industry employs approximately 20% and agriculture has passed to the residual level of 6%. In between the two extremes, employment moved out of agriculture in the direction of industry between the 1930s and the late 1960s/early 1970s and then continued to move out of agriculture mostly in favor of services; from the late 1980s onward, it started moving out of both agriculture and industry in favor of services. Something similar happened with the structure of output (Fig. 7): in the early twentieth century, agriculture and services had the highest weight, each with about 40%, while industry only represented 20%. Then, agricultural output

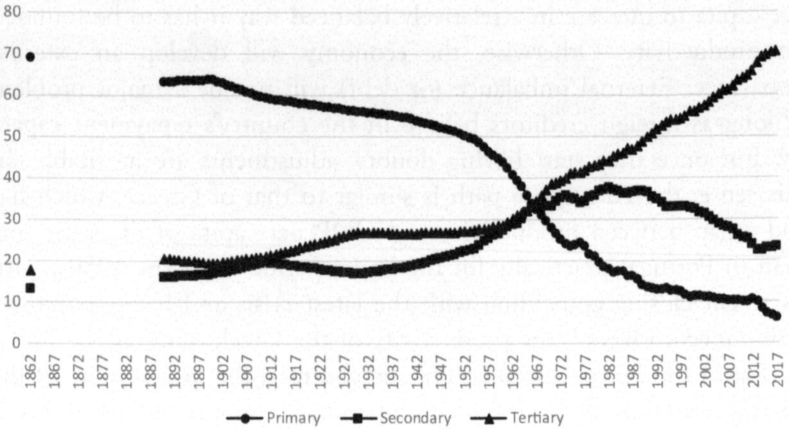

Fig. 6 Structure employment, Portugal, 1862–2017 (% overall employment) (*Source* 1953–1995: Pinheiro [1997], corrected with Amaral [2009], extrapolated backward 1890–1952 using Nunes [2001], and 1862 using Reis [2005], and extrapolated forward using AMECO)

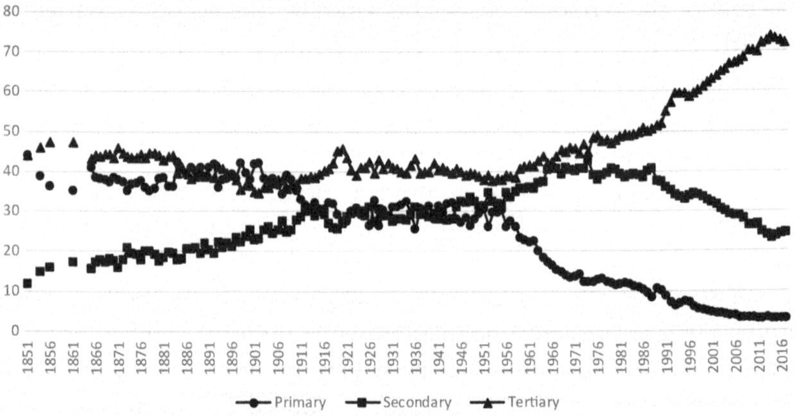

Fig. 7 Structure economy, Portugal, 1851–2017 (% GDP) (*Source* 1996–2017—AMECO, extrapolated backward for 1953–1995 with Pinheiro [1997], for 1910–1952 with Batista et al. [1997] and for 1851–1909 with Lains [2007])

as a proportion of total output declined, first slowly (until the 1950s, when it reached a weight of 30%) and then rapidly (reaching a residual weight of 3% in 2017), while industry gained weight, first slowly (also until the 1950s, reaching then 30%) and then rapidly (until the mid-1970s, reaching 40%), then stopping, to later decline rapidly from the late 1980s/early 1990s onward (25% in 2017). At the same time, services kept a roughly constant share of around 40% until the 1950s and then grew rapidly, representing 73% of output in 2017.

This is in accordance with the famous Colin Clark's (1940) and Simon Kuznets' (1971) three stages of growth, but the Portuguese economy seems to display a few peculiarities. First, we must note that industry was never, throughout all this period, the largest employer nor the largest contributor to GDP. That role was assumed by services, all the time throughout the two centuries in terms of output, and from the 1960s onward in terms of employment. Second, we should also note how the movement out of agriculture somehow stopped from the 1990s until the second decade of the twenty-first century and has only resumed again from then on, and at a rapid pace, now apparently mostly in favor of industry than services. Figure 8 shows this, comparing Portugal with the EU-15 and other peripheral countries, since the 1980s. Finally, we should also note that the transition to a tertiary economy still lags behind the most developed economies today.

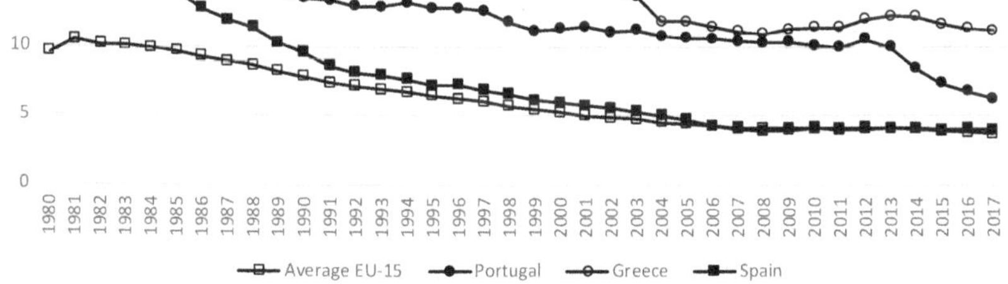

Fig. 8 Employment in agriculture, Portugal, Spain, Greece and EU-15 average, 1980–2017 (% of overall employment) (*Source* AMECO, except Portugal: 1980–1995—Pinheiro [1997], corrected with Amaral [2009], extrapolated forward using AMECO)

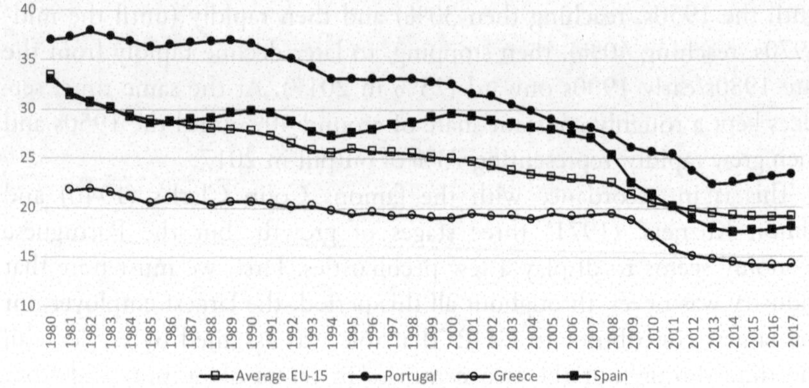

Fig. 9 Employment in industry, Portugal, Spain, Greece and EU-15 average, 1980–2017 (% of overall employment) (*Source* See Fig. 8)

Figures 9 and 10 show the weight in employment of industry and services, respectively, and we can see there that Portugal is still more industrialized than the EU-15 and has a lower weight of services, contrary to Spain, which has fully converged in those respects (Greece has also converged in services, but for a different reason: an exceptionally high relevance of tourism in its economic structure).

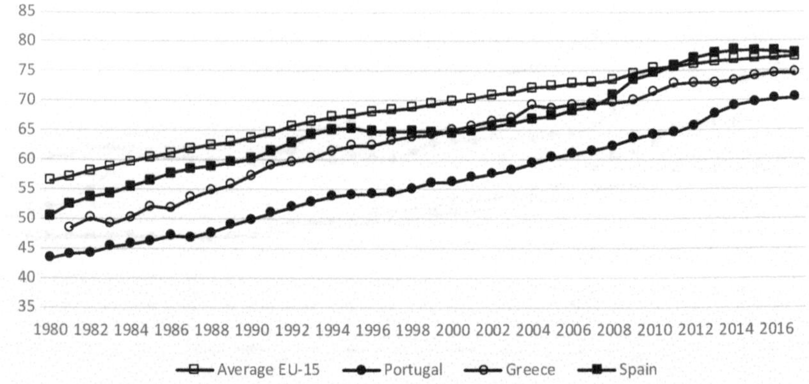

Fig. 10 Employment in services, Portugal, Spain, Greece and EU-15 average, 1980–2017 (% of overall employment) (*Source* See Fig. 8)

This book does not put forward very bold hypotheses or explanations for the behavior of the modern Portuguese economy. It is essentially a state-of-the-art piece of work, presenting the most relevant literature describing and explaining that behavior. In a certain sense, it should be viewed as a sort of textbook, or an introduction to the modern Portuguese economy, useful for both beginners and advanced readers. In another sense, it should be viewed as a sort of bibliographical guide, from which readers can then depart in order to deepen their knowledge of certain periods or details. It covers the entire twentieth century, dividing it into chronological periods defined sometimes by institutional landmarks, sometimes by political landmarks, and sometimes by economic ones: the criteria used for such a division relates with events, shocks or processes that created some sort of essential difference with the immediate past.

Chapter 2 summarizes the fundamental institutional changes brought by the liberal revolution of the early nineteenth century, an event (or rather sequence of events) that changed in a radical manner the way in which economic agents operated in Portugal. The objective of the revolution was the destruction of the political, social, and economic framework inherited from previous centuries and the construction of a new one, inspired by the liberal ideas sweeping the world at the time. The final outcome of the revolution was the creation of a modern State, in the place of the vague administrative structures of the *Ancien Régime*, and of modern private property, replacing the confusing rules of possession typical of that period. The chapter introduces, furthermore, the main aspects of the behavior of the economy during the nineteenth century and the problems both the new institutional framework and that behavior left in inheritance to the twentieth century. It uses the 1891–1892 fiscal, banking, and international payments crisis, which interrupted a certain relationship of the Government with the economy, as a pretext to summarize the changes that occurred during the nineteenth century and set the stage for what followed. This chapter, as well as the remaining ones, always dedicates a section to the economy of the Portuguese Empire, since that empire acquired in the late nineteenth century, and retained until the 1970s, a relatively high degree of relevance for the overall Portuguese economy. Only the last two chapters stop mentioning it, as Portugal lost all of its colonies in the sequence of a revolution that happened in the country in 1974.

Chapter 3 uses World War I as a decisive breaking point for the Portuguese economy. The shock of the war was not specific to Portugal, but we would not be able to understand the evolution of the Portuguese economy in the 1920s without taking it into consideration. The war interrupted for a long time the conditions of international economic liberalism that had defined the Western world in the second half of the nineteenth century, and this created new challenges to all the economies of the world, including, of course, the Portuguese one. Besides direct economic effects, the war was also at the origin of an extremely serious financial and monetary crisis that took more than one decade to be solved. The stabilization policies that were followed to deal with it turned out to be instrumental for the rise to power of an authoritarian regime that would last for almost half a century.

Chapter 4 picks up precisely at the point when this authoritarian regime, the *Estado Novo*, started its life, in 1933. The choice of this breaking point does not relate with the fact that the economy changed drastically its behavior then, but rather with the fact that the new political regime conceived the relationship between the Government and economic agents in a much different manner than the previous ones. The *Estado Novo* was the Portuguese version of the kind of authoritarian or fascist regimes that spread throughout Europe during the 1920s and 1930s, and understood its role in what concerns the economy as based on high interventionism. During the period of its existence, the regime was able to put the economy under a vast set of administrative and bureaucratic mechanisms that limited significantly the freedom of economic agents. Although a lot has been said about this kind of interventionism, the truth is that much of it did not differ much from what regimes contemporary to the *Estado Novo* that retained a democratic form did as well. The main reason for this similarity was the difficulties of the world economy in the interwar period: all Western countries resorted to protectionism, economic nationalism, and Government intervention once they failed to return to the economic liberal order of the nineteenth century and once the 1930s crisis started. The Portuguese *Estado Novo* was one more of them. This time, the world war that started at the end of the 1930s had generally positive effects on the Portuguese economy, mostly on account of the neutrality policy the Portuguese Government was able to keep throughout the entire conflict.

The chronological division introduced in Chapter 5 has fundamentally economic reasons behind it (although some international political and institutional aspects played an important role as well): the political regime installed in the country in the 1930s remained the same and kept its fundamental institutional features, but the economy behaved now in a totally unprecedented manner. The period between the end of World War II and 1973 was the best ever in terms of growth of the Portuguese economy. Growth rates had never been higher and would never be in the future again, at least for such a long period. After more than one century of divergence in relation to the richer economies of the world, the Portuguese economy converged in a consistent manner. This happened despite quick growth in most rich economies as well, as this corresponded to the period that has, since then, received the designation of "golden age of economic growth". High growth in Portugal was accompanied by industrialization, as is usual in processes of the kind: agriculture lost finally its prevalent position in both employment and output, and gave place to the other two sectors, industry and services. Also notable was the abandonment of the country's tradition of protectionism and lack of openness. Up to this period, the Portuguese economy was one of the least open in Europe. It became one of the most open. The fact that the political regime existing in Portugal in the period was an authoritarian one (a survivor from the 1920s and 1930s dictatorial age) did not prevent the country from participating in the process of European integration initiated in the 1950s, accompanying the abandonment of nationalism and protectionism that had been a hallmark of the 1930s.

The reason for the breaking point introduced in Chapter 6 is both political and economic. In political terms, the fundamental event was a revolution that in 1974 abolished the authoritarian regime that had existed in the country for the previous half a century. In economic terms, the fundamental aspect was the interruption of the period of high growth coming from the 1950s. Such an interruption was not limited to Portugal, as all economies of the world also entered into a period of much milder growth. But the association of the political revolution with economic slowdown brought some specificity to the Portuguese case. The revolution involved Portugal in a typical Cold War confrontation, the outcome of which, besides the strictly political dimension, would determine if the country's economy acquired socialist/communist features or remained a fundamentally capitalist one. Even if the institutional framework of the Portuguese economy was substantially transformed during the revolution, in the end the country remained within the capitalist side of the Cold War divide, starting to converge in institutional terms to the sort of solution developed in Western Europe after World War II: political democracy and the Welfare State. The path to this final outcome was not always easy, having led to two interventions by the International Monetary Fund in the country in order to keep the economy afloat.

The last chapter of the book is dedicated to a period that is again defined by a fundamental institutional event, namely the joining of the European Economic Community by Portugal in 1986. Thanks to this step, the Portuguese economy became much more integrated with the other economies of Western Europe, a process that culminated in the adoption of a common currency, the euro, with ten other countries (now nineteen) in January 1999. The process has not been entirely easy: the economy has stopped converging after the early 1990s and had to endure, between 2011 and 2014, its most serious crisis since the nineteenth century. This chapter shows that the Portuguese economy performed poorly almost from the beginning of the participation of the country in the EEC. These difficulties were not immediately visible from the start, thanks to an initial trajectory (between 1986 and 1992) of strong growth. But signs of stress were already visible then, namely in the deterioration of the trade and current accounts. Most of that stress had to do with the adoption of a monetary and exchange rate policy that led to real exchange rate appreciation and, consequently, competitiveness decline. A growing external imbalance developed in the 1990s, which could only be covered by an equivalent external indebtedness in relation to EU countries having external surpluses. Some literature links this process to the adoption of the euro in 1999. This chapter shows that, in reality, it started much before. The Portuguese economic troubles of the last quarter century result from a combination of a specific "Portuguese problem" with a wider "European problem", and the latter did not start with the euro but rather with the early efforts in the mid-1980s of increased economic integration within the EEC.

Two final notes are due. I have signaled throughout the book legal moments that are normally considered to have had important impact on the country's economy. Examples of this sort of moments are the suppression of feudal rights or the abolition of slavery in the empire in the early nineteenth century or the adoption of corporatist institutions in the 1930s or the decrees of nationalization in the 1970s, and I refer to the relevant legal documents in footnotes. The purpose here was to supply a basic guide to students of the Portuguese economy of the most important institutional changes having affected it.

The final note concerns the statistical series used in the book. I have used the existing state-of-the-art historical reconstructions. I have not generated new series, for that was not the purpose of this work, but I have sometimes adapted the existing ones, for the sake of having coherent series for long periods. Those adaptations are duly signaled, whenever they were done.

References

Amaral, Luciano. 2009. Portuguese Population and Employment, 1950–2007: Implications for GDP Per Capita and Labor Productivity. *Análise Social* 193: 767–791.

AMECO. http://ec.europa.eu/economy_finance/ameco/user/serie/SelectSerie.cfm.

Baganha, Maria Ioannis, and José Carlos Marques. 2001. População. In *Estatísticas Históricas Portuguesas*, ed. Nuno Valério, 33–126. Lisbon: INE.

Batista, Dina, et al. 1997. *New Estimates of Portugal's GDP: 1910–1958*. Lisbon: Banco de Portugal.

Clark, Colin. 1940. *The Conditions of Economic Progress*. London: Macmillan.

The Conference Board. https://www.conference-board.org/data/economydatabase/index.cfm?id=27762.

Henriques, Filipe Castro, and Teresa Ferreira Rodrigues. 2009. O século XX: a transição. In *História da População Portuguesa. Das Longas Permanências à Conquista da Modernidade*, ed. Teresa Ferreira Rodrigues, 417–513. Porto: Afrontamento e CEPESE.

INE (Instituto Nacional de Estatística). https://www.ine.pt/xportal/xmain?xpgid=ine_main&xpid=INE.

Kuznets, Simon. 1971. *Economic Growth of Nations: Total Output and Production Structure*. Cambridge, MA: Harvard University Press.

Lains, Pedro. 2007. Growth in a Protected Environment, 1850–1950. *Research in Economic History* 24: 119–160.

Maddison, Angus. 2003. *The World Economy: Historical Statistics*. Paris: OCDE.

Nunes, Ana Bela. 2001. Actividade económica da população. In *Estatísticas Históricas Portuguesas*, ed. Nuno Valério, 149–197. Lisbon: INE.

Pinheiro, Maximiano (ed.). 1997. *Séries Longas para a Economia Portuguesa, Pós-II Guerra Mundial, Vol. I - Séries Estatísticas*. Lisbon: Banco de Portugal.

Prados de la Escosura, Leandro. Contabilidad Nacional Histórica de Espana: Gasto y Producto, 1850–2017. https://espacioinvestiga.org/bbdd-chne/.

Reis, Jaime. 1993. *O Atraso Económico Português em Perspectiva Histórica: Estudos sobre a Economia Portuguesa na Segunda Metade do Século XIX, 1850–1930*. Lisbon: IN-CM.

———. 2005. O trabalho. In *História Económica de Portugal, 1700–2000, Vol. I, O Século XIX*, ed. Pedro Lains and Álvaro Ferreira da Silva, 119–151. Lisbon: ICS.

2
The 1891–1892 Crisis and Beyond

Between 1890 and 1892, Portugal faced a combined fiscal, banking, and international payments crisis, in the sequence of which the Portuguese currency abandoned the gold standard (after almost forty years of membership), and the Government defaulted on its debt. The major consequence of this set of events was the closing of international capital markets to the Portuguese Government. From then on, no longer could the Portuguese Government pursue the policy of the previous half century, consisting in providing the country with such infrastructure as modern roads, railways, or the telegraph.

Sometimes, the 1891–1892 crisis is seen as a major watershed in Portuguese economic history. In fact, its impact was practically limited to the consequences listed above, as the performance and transformation of the economy was little affected. Of much higher relevance was the radical institutional transformation brought by the liberal revolution of the first decades of the nineteenth century: everything started in 1820, but its effects were felt until the end of the century and even the beginning of the next. The objective of this revolution was the destruction of the political, social, and economic framework inherited

L. Amaral, *The Modern Portuguese Economy in the Twentieth and Twenty-First Centuries*, Palgrave Studies in Economic History,
https://doi.org/10.1007/978-3-030-24548-1_2

from previous centuries and the construction of a new one, inspired by the liberal ideas sweeping the world at the time. The final outcome was momentous. Thanks to the liberal revolution, a modern State appeared in the place of the vague administrative structures of the *Ancien Régime*, and modern private property replaced the confusing rules of possession typical of that period. These were the two essential elements for the birth of the modern Portuguese economy. We use the 1891–1892 crisis not as a fundamentally transformative event but rather as a pretext to summarize the changes that occurred during the century and set the stage for the evolution of the Portuguese economy in the twentieth century.

1 First Changes (1820–1834)

Portugal entered into an extremely complex situation when, on 29 November 1807, the royal family, most of the court and a large number of the members of the elite sailed to Brazil (then a Portuguese colony) fleeing from the Napoleonic French revolutionary army. Although the prince regent had left behind a group of regents to rule in his absence, the occupying forces (first French, then British, the latter coming to defend the territory from the former in August 1808) became the true rulers of the country for all practical matters (Ramos et al. 2009). In 1820, thirteen years after his departure, the former prince regent (who had meanwhile become King John VI in 1816) had not yet shown any will to return to Portugal, betting on a sort of "resurrection" of the Portuguese Empire having Brazil as its center. On 24 August 1820, a group of lawyers, magistrates, and military officers organized a movement that claimed for the return of the king to the mainland and for a representative assembly (although still using the traditional name of *Cortes*, in Portuguese, rather than parliament) to be elected in order to draft a Constitution. The *Cortes* started their activity on 26 January 1821 and the king agreed on returning to Portugal, arriving on 4 July (Ramos et al. 2009). It was the beginning of the liberal age in Portugal. But it was also the beginning of an extremely tumultuous political period.

The conflict between the "old order" and the new liberal ideas was the main political and ideological discussion of the day around Europe, after the American and French revolutions, and from then until the mid-1830s it became also the central issue of Portuguese political conflict. Like most of Europe, Portugal was deeply divided over the question, with the two sides (traditionalists and liberals) opposing each other with extreme violence. The *Cortes* were able to produce a Constitution, which was approved on 23 September 1822. Besides the introduction of fundamental political novelties, such as the idea of "national sovereignty" (as opposed to the king's sovereignty, founded on divine delegation), the idea of equality of individuals under the law, and the introduction of an elected representative parliament, the Constitution also brought new economic principles: according to it, private property was a "sacred and inviolable right" of "Portuguese individuals", who could "use [it] [...] according to [their] will, under the limits of the law" (Article 6). This new principle was considerably different from the rules of possession coming from the *Ancien Régime*. Such rules gave the nobility and the Church a certain number of powers that now had to disappear, or at least be reformed. The *Cortes* suppressed some of those powers, such as personal services (the obligation of peasants to perform various temporary services to the lord) and "banal rights" (the obligation of peasants to use—and pay for that use—the lord's capital goods, such as his oven, well, mill or cattle),[1] and reduced to half the tributes to be paid by peasants to the lord on the latter's lands (*direitos de foral*, in Portuguese, or *forais*, as they became known at the time).[2] In addition, the *Cortes* also nationalized the lands owned by the Crown.[3]

But this proved to be just an incomplete revolutionary wave, as in 1823 the king closed the *Cortes*, in a move designed to balance the influence of traditionalists and liberals in the political landscape. Much of the political instability had also to do with the inability to keep

[1]Decree 5 May 1821.

[2]Decree 3 June 1822.

[3]Decree 25 April 1821.

Brazil as a Portuguese colony, when the territory unilaterally declared independence on 7 September 1822. From 1823 to 1826, John VI was able to keep a certain balance, but his death, on 10 March 1826, opened a very complex period that ended with one of the dead king's sons, Miguel, taking the throne and declaring the liberal revolution terminated. Miguel ruled for eight years under traditional institutions. But the liberals were able to organize in exile and gather the support of Miguel's brother, Peter, mounting a military operation to invade the country in 1832. A civil war ensued, lasting until 26 May 1834, when peace was signed, concluding with a liberal victory (Ramos et al. 2009).

This victory did not mean political tranquility, however, as agreement between the different liberal factions was not easy to achieve. Between 1834 and 1851, the country was rocked by several coup d'États, various episodes of political violence, and even two brief civil wars. A persistent constitutional conflict allowed for three different constitutions to prevail: the 1822 Constitution, the 1826 Constitutional Charter (*Carta Constitucional*), and the 1838 Constitution. The conflict drew on the relative powers to be attributed to the parliament and the king, with the most radical revolutionaries asking for the parliament's preeminence and the most conservative ones for a balance between parliament and king. The latter solution allowed for the survival of traditional sovereignty and, consequently, attributed a lesser role to "national sovereignty" as materialized in the parliament. In the end, it was the 1826 Charter, the most conservative among the three documents, that became the lasting constitutional framework from 1842 onward. Some amendments in 1852 made of it a less conservative document, however (Ramos et al. 2009; Fernandes 2012).

2 The Liberal Revolution

Understanding the liberal revolution requires understanding some aspects of the institutions that were abolished. The *Ancien Régime*'s institutional structure differed from that of liberalism in many respects. Concepts that are typical of liberalism and of institutions today and that, consequently, we take for granted did not exist or were not entirely developed during the *Ancien Régime*. This was true of such concepts as the State, civil society, the public sphere, the private sphere, private property, or equality under the law.

A vast plurality of identities existed under the *Ancien Régime* monarchy. The Portuguese were not seen (and did not understand themselves) as individuals that happened to be Portuguese, but as members of particular social groups, which were not informal social groups as we have them today, but defined by particular rights and duties established by the law. They were noblemen, members of the clergy, members of the people, inhabitants of a city, members of a profession, etc., in a vast array of particular social situations (Hespanha 1994; Silva and Hespanha 1993; Xavier and Hespanha 1993). The major subdivision within this framework was the one separating the Clergy, the Nobility, and the People. Being part of these groups implied a particular set of specific rights and duties.

The rights and duties of the different social groups in the *Ancien Régime* meant that there was no clear distinction between the public and private spheres, which also implied the absence of a clear distinction between the State (corresponding to the public sphere) and civil society (corresponding to the private sphere). We can see this in aspects we would call either public or private today. For instance, both the Church and the nobility had powers we would call public. Besides powers of the administrative, judicial, and police type, they also had taxing powers, or, to be more precise, the power to collect compulsory tributes. That is, members of the Church and aristocrats were not simply private individuals pursuing private objectives. They had prerogatives we would call public. The powers of the nobility and the Church to collect tributes were vast. The Church had its own general tribute, to be paid by the population at large, the *dízimos* (equivalent to the English tithe), corresponding to about 10% of personal income. The nobles collected many tributes, some in their own lands, some in lands that had been donated to them by the Crown, some in lands that were possessed by other entities but whose collection of tributes had been granted to them. All these para-fiscal rights were classified as *direitos de foral* (for more details on all of this, cf. Monteiro 1993, 1998).

This means that a typical prerogative of public power today as taxation was disseminated throughout society. The monopoly of taxation, which largely defines the modern State, did not exist. The economic consequences arising from this situation were enormous, especially for the definition of property and of property rights. Due to this structure of collecting powers, private property and property rights in the sense we speak of them today were nonexistent to a large extent, for property was not exactly *private* (it was also *public*) and the rights associated with it did not correspond to the same rights that are associated with it today.

This was particularly visible in the case of the nobility, especially in its relationship with the Crown. From the sixteenth century onward, the Crown created a vast court aristocracy, leading to a substantial change in the nature of the nobility as a social group. Instead of the old military nobility, which had acquired its status in the long war against Islam and had become a landed aristocracy, a vast service nobility (not necessarily landed) and a very restricted court nobility arose, the latter being paid in lands (which worked as a source of rents) and in rents from lands (Monteiro 1993, 1998, 2003). Although this was a process common to all the European monarchies of the day, especially in the seventeenth and eighteenth centuries, there are reasons to believe that it was taken further in Portugal than in other places (de Macedo 1968; Monteiro 1998, 2003). The Crown's major instrument for this transformation was its policy of land donation, or concession of rights to rents to noble houses. In order to best understand this problem, we must have a clearer notion of the structure of land possession during the Portuguese *Ancien Régime*. The largest owners were, first, the king and the Crown or other institutions closely dependent on both: the university, the military orders, and the royal houses; then, there were the many religious institutions (monasteries, convents, churches, and others); and finally, the noble houses. What is interesting here is that a large share of the lands under noble and ecclesiastical control was not of their own property but had its origin in donations made by the Crown (Serrão 1993; Monteiro 1998, 2003).

Not all income coming from the Crown's donations originated in land that had been donated to noble houses. In reality, the largest part of it came from a specific source of income, the *comendas*. The *comendas* were, basically, entitlements to tributes coming from lands of the military orders. The difference with land donations was that the noble houses were not supposed to administer the land but simply appropriate a share of the tributes due to the original owners. This is what has allowed Monteiro (2003) to call the Portuguese aristocracy an "ultra-rentier" class, with a social and economic logic that contrasted heavily with what we might call "entrepreneurial" attitudes.

Also of vast importance were a series of mechanisms restricting the tradability of land. Many lands were completely or partially left out of the market. Some were under perpetual leasing contracts that prevented them from being bought and sold. Others were the lands that the language of the time called *amortizadas*: Church lands, but also *morgados* and *capelas*. *Morgados* were contracts through which the land, by decision of an ancestor, was inherited undivided by the eldest son of a noble house; *capelas* were also lands to be inherited undivided but whose income was to be directed in perpetuity to religious institutions. This implied that lands under *morgadio* or *capela* could not be sold, neither partially nor in their totality. The same occurred with the lands that were donated by the Crown to noble houses.

It was this economic and social structure that the liberal revolutions destroyed, although through a convoluted process that had many stages, each with its own peculiarities. As we have seen, the first stage came with what we might call the first liberal revolution, between 1820 and 1823. At this moment, the new principles of private property were defined by the Constitution and some of the most visible aristocratic prerogatives were abolished, specifically personal services and "banal rights". These were of little importance, however, and their abolition was basically symbolic. More importantly, Crown lands were nationalized, including not only the lands under direct control of the Crown but also those that had been donated. Many problems arose with this, however. The first problem was one of definition: What exactly were Crown lands? Some nobility estates, although not seen as such, had in fact been donated a long time ago, normally in the Middle Ages. This opened a loophole in the nationalizing process, which gave rise to a series of disputes over the date from which donations should be considered irreversible. Another question was that of knowing if the *comendas* could be classified as Crown lands, i.e., if these entitlements were to remain or be abolished and nationalized (Monteiro 2003).

A debate that became very important in the context of the 1820 revolution was the one over the *direitos de foral*. These were seen as separate from Crown lands, for nationalizing lands or leaving them under aristocratic control did not necessarily mean abolishing the tributes paid on them. As a matter of fact, due to the budgetary troubles of those years, many parliamentarians thought of keeping the *forais* on nationalized lands in order to increase the State's receipts. The fact is that, in the first liberal revolution, the *forais* were kept in existence, although reduced by half in their value. The big question here was, of course, to whom should property be attributed following the destruction of the *Ancien Régime*'s rules of possession: Should it be given to the State, transforming all peasants paying tributes into wage earners paid by the Government? To the noble houses receiving the tributes? Or to the peasants, under the idea that tributes were a form of primitive taxes applied to lands that in the end should be seen as owned by them (Monteiro 2003; Bastien 2006)?

In 1832 came the laws that, although still written during the civil war (by the then Minister of Finance in exile, José Xavier Mouzinho da Silveira), were implemented after the 1834 liberal victory and gave the largest blow to the institutional structure of the *Ancien Régime*. The laws abolished the *dízimos* (the tribute paid to the Church),[4] as well as the *comendas*, the *forais*, and the Crown lands themselves.[5] Although extremely important, the law on Crown lands turned out to be very difficult to apply. Three things could happen to the lands affected by it. One, lands could revert to the property of those paying the tributes, normally small peasants. Two, they could revert to the beneficiaries of the donations, that is the aristocratic houses to whom the Crown had donated the lands and whom received the tributes. Third, lands could revert to the State (Fonseca 1989). This indecision opened room for many conflicts. Most noble houses resorted to various judicial methods

[4]Decree 30 July 1832.

[5]Decree 13 August 1832.

in order not to lose their entitlements. One possibility opened by the law was that those affected by it could protest the decision. This judicial device effectively suspended the decision. This meant that, while the question of whom to attribute the land was not resolved, the beneficiary of the donation continued to receive the existing tributes (Silbert 1970). Sometimes, judicial processes were so complicated that they lasted for years, and "in many cases, instead of having to stand long processes, [many of those paying tributes decided to] accept the validity of the *foros*" (Silbert 1970, p. 96). Due to many loopholes in the law, disputes over to whom attribute the ownership of the land continued for a long time.

The transition was made even more complicated thanks to one further process that ran parallel to the one described above. This was the process called, in the language of the time, *desamortização*, which involved the lands of the Church (in particular those of the orders), and the lands under *morgadio* and *capelas*, i.e., those lands that were left out of the market. The lands of the male and military orders were put in the market after 1834, in the sequence of the definite liberal victory in the civil war. This was a particularly brutal process, for it not only involved the nationalization of their lands but also their actual extinction.[6] After being nationalized, those assets were put on sale via public auction. In reality, the whole set of *bens nacionais* (all of the nationalized lands, including the Crown's lands that had been nationalized during the first liberal revolution of 1820 and the ones nationalized in the 1834 wave) were put on public auction. This was an extremely complex process that took decades to come to an end, occupying most of the second half of the nineteenth century and still a bit of the twentieth century. Most of the transactions took place in the twenty years after 1835, but the more complicated ones remained unsolved for many years, and a large number of properties were never bought by private agents: according to Silva (1997), 60% of them, at least between 1835 and 1843.

The process of creation of modern private property would only be concluded with the extinction of the *morgados* and *capelas* after 1861,

[6]Decree 30 May 1834.

and the process of putting these lands on the market lasted the entire second half of the nineteenth century (and part of the twentieth century). As we can see from all this, the passage from *Ancien Régime* to liberalism in Portugal was far from smooth (in reality, it was a true "juridical imbroglio", in the words of Silbert 1978). The Portuguese liberals wanted to apply to the economy and society those categories of interpretation and methods of organization that are typical of liberal societies. But, by doing so, they ended up finding a world of extreme complexity, that was difficult to change and in which it was almost impossible to know how to attribute clear property rights. Still today, Portuguese historiography has not been able to establish clearly who were the new property owners at the end of the process.

Besides these difficulties in the definition of property rights, other aspects of the integration of markets within liberal principles took a long time to come. Although a relatively free labor market was created immediately after the end of the civil war, with the extinction of corporations,[7] the same did not happen with the capital market, which had to wait 34 more years until the 1867 legislation liberated it from *Ancien Régime* restrictions: only from then on could firms be created without arbitrary Government authorization.[8] And the definition of property rights (together with other civil rights) would only become clear in the same year, with the drafting of the first Civil Code.[9]

This institutional revolution was seen by liberals as even more urgent after the loss of Brazil. As Mouzinho da Silveira noted, without Brazil, there would be no other solution for Portugal than to fully explore the economic potential of the mainland, by liberating it of the weight of *Ancien Régime* institutions. Brazil had played a significant role in the Portuguese economy and its loss had a sizable impact (Pedreira 1998). Even if the Portuguese Empire was more than Brazil, extending to

---

[7]Decree 7 May 1834.

[8]Law 22 June 1867.

[9]Law Charter, 1 July 1867.

a relatively large stretch of Africa, what Silveira's and the liberals' position shows is how little developed the African empire was at the time: the Portuguese presence there was very thin, with little in the way of actual colonization, and centering mostly on slave trade. For the Portuguese liberals everything had to start anew, from the mainland to the colonies.

3 A Project to Modernize the Country (1851–1890)

While this long transformative process was taking place, the political situation finally calmed down after 1851, in the sequence of one more coup d'État that took place on 7 April. A long period of political tranquility was then inaugurated, which the successive governments used to implement a certain economic project. The period from 1851 to the 1890s came to be known as "Regeneration" (*Regeneração*, in Portuguese), and its basic political principle was that of "conciliation" between the radical left- and right-wing liberal factions. The idea of the moderates was that political calm would give the opportunity for the economy to grow, with the Government giving decisive assistance through the construction of modern infrastructure, especially means of transportation (Ramos et al. 2009).

The economic idea of the Regeneration was simple: once the hindrances coming from the *Ancien Régime* had been suppressed and free markets been established, there was no reason for Portugal not to reach the levels of wealth typical of such countries as Great Britain, Germany, or France. In order to actualize the potential thus opened, the country only needed to introduce the modern means of communication then spreading in those countries: modern roads (of the Macadam or Telford type), railways, canals, ports, and the telegraph. The Government was to play a fundamental role in the process by subsidizing the construction of the new infrastructure. This should be done, according to the politician most associated with the policy, António Fontes Pereira de Melo, according to certain specific features. First, temporary Government budget deficits should not be seen as a problem: since those were (in the parlance of the day) "reproductive" investments, they should bring growth, leading to higher tax collection and medium- and long-run budget balance. Second, the initial use of debt to put the process in motion should not be seen as a problem either, for the same reason: higher receipts in the medium and long run would allow repayment of debt; debt should be both internal and external, but especially the latter (Ramos 1996; Esteves 2005).

The results of the policy in terms of construction of infrastructure were clear. The first railway line started to be built on 17 September 1853 and was inaugurated on 28 October 1856. From that year until 1890, 2083 km of railways were built, sometimes involving quite spectacular engineering works, such as the bridges over the Douro River in the city of Porto or a succession of bridges and tunnels on the northeast bound line linking Portugal to Spain and France. In the same period, 8696 km of macadam-type roads were built as well as a new artificial harbor close to Porto (Alegria 1990). A telegraph network, including two international connections by submarine cable linking Portugal to Britain and Brazil, was also built (Mata 1988). Table 1 shows the evolution of the Portuguese railway network between 1880 and 1910 and compares it with a series of other European countries: although not reaching the same density as such pioneers of industrialization as the UK, France, and Germany, railway construction in Portugal was perfectly comparable to that of two other equally peripheral, although richer, countries such as Italy and Spain.

Table 1 Railway construction (km/100,000 persons), 1880–1910

Country	1880	1890	1900	1910
UK	84	84	81	79
France	61	87	98	102
Germany	75	87	92	94
Italy	33	45	50	52
Spain	37[b]	50[c]	59	56
Portugal	24[a]	44	47	53

[a]1878; [b]1877; [c]1887
Source Alegria (1990)

The participation of the Government was considerable and took different forms. Sometimes it involved direct subsidies to the companies building the infrastructure, and sometimes it was based on direct ownership. Many times the private companies entered into difficulties and the Government felt the need to take them over. The difficulties were so widespread that, by 1880, half of the railway structure was owned by the Government (Ramos 1996). The economic and fiscal results of the project ended up by being disappointing, however. The problem was that the "Regeneration" fiscal-economic equation never really worked in the manner anticipated by Fontes Pereira de Melo and his peers. First, as we will see below in greater detail, growth was feeble. This meant not only that the expectation that the country would become as rich as the richest European ones never materialized but also that the original assumption that higher growth would mean higher tax receipts failed. Everything was made even more complicated due to the fact that the various governments were unable to modernize the tax structure, despite the abolition of the tributes due to the Church and the noble houses in the *Ancien Régime*. The Government did acquire the monopoly of taxation, but the tax structure remained quite similar to the one inherited from the *Ancien Régime* for a long time. The "continuity" was mostly visible in the large predominance of indirect taxation and, in particular, customs duties (Mata 1993, 2006; Esteves 2005). Attempts at reforming direct taxation faced constant reaction and were the motive of many popular revolts and even a civil war (in 1846–1847) (Mata 1993, 2006; Silva 1994).

Figure 1 shows that the Government grew significantly in size in this period: public spending rose from 3% of GDP in 1852 to 5% by the end of the decade, remaining at about that level until the eve of World War I. But the comparison with other European countries also shown in Fig. 1 reveals that the Portuguese Government remained among the smaller in Europe. Small size did not mean balance, however. That is what Fig. 2 shows: the growth in spending could not be matched by an equivalent growth in receipts, and budget deficits (sometimes sizable) became the norm.

The persistent deficits would feed a growing debt, most of it contracted abroad: various international bonds constituted the bulk of the

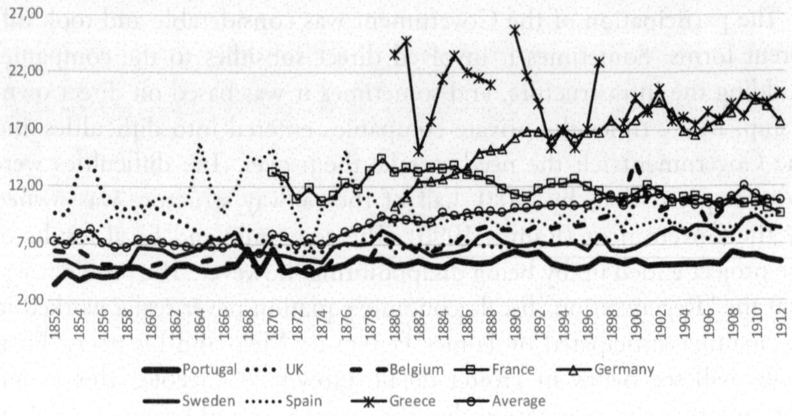

Fig. 1 Public spending, various European countries, 1852–1912 (% GDP) (*Source* Portugal: Mata [2001] and Valério [2001]; for the other countries: Mauro et al. [2013])

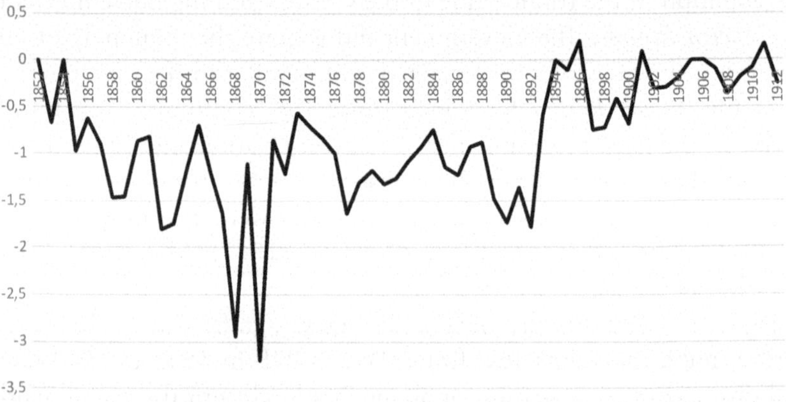

Fig. 2 Government budget deficit, Portugal, 1852–1912 (% GDP) (*Source* Mata [2001] and Valério [2001])

sources that financed public works, with the internal market also playing a role, although smaller (Mata 1993; Ramos 1996; Esteves 2005). The truth is that Portuguese public debt increased persistently from 1852 to the 1880s, from about 30% of GDP in 1852 to 70% in the

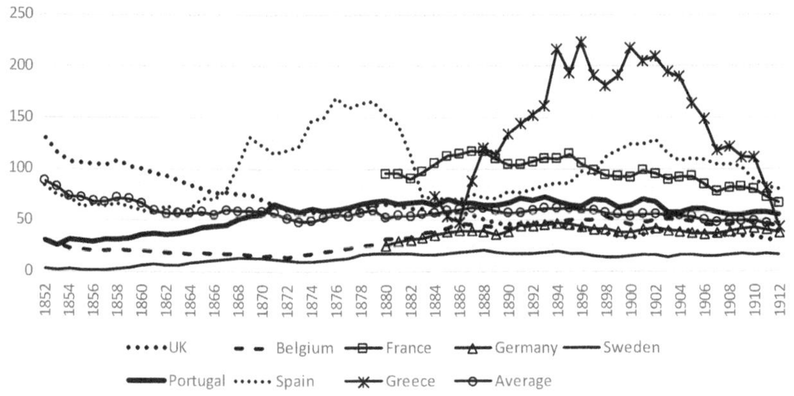

Fig. 3 Gross public debt, various European countries, 1852–1912 (% GDP) (*Source* Same as Fig. 1)

early 1880s: with such a figure, Portugal became one of the most indebted countries of Europe at the end of the century, only below Greece, Spain, and France (Fig. 3). Debt service became the largest item in the Government budget, passing from 15% of total spending in 1853 to around 50% from the 1870s onward (Fig. 4). This raises the question of how it was possible to keep for such a long time an unbalanced situation of that kind. Two further elements explain it.

The first is that the Portuguese currency (the real) joined the gold standard in 1854.[10] In 1854, the gold standard was not yet seen as a "good housekeeping seal of approval", in the expression of Bordo and Rockoff (1996), i.e., it still did not work as a signal to markets that the Government in question was fiscally sound: the doubts concerning gold were many around the world and most rich countries had not yet adopted gold monometallism. Portugal joined mostly for reasons of simplification of the national monetary system (Reis 1996a). But in time this proved to be an asset in the international capital markets, once the gold standard acquired its "seal of approval" functions between

[10]Law 29 July 1854.

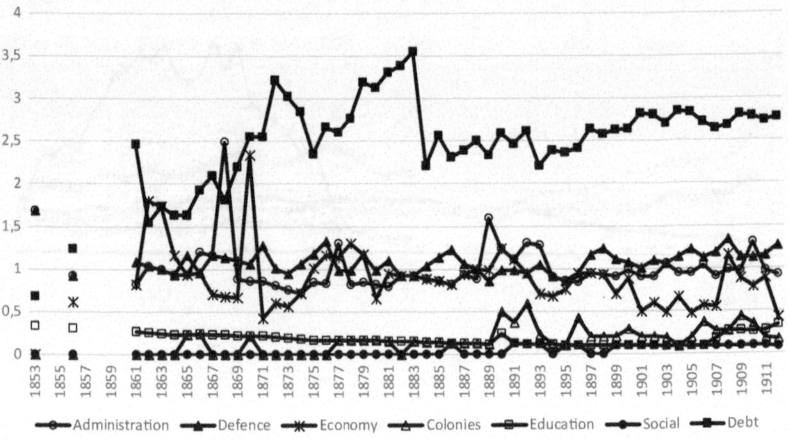

Fig. 4 Structure public spending, Portugal 1853–1912 (% GDP) (*Source* Same as Fig. 2)

the 1850s and the 1870s. Of course, Portugal was far from having sound public finances. But it was able to use the gold standard's signal in such a way as to keep on relying on international capital markets without major problems. Still, the Portuguese real would not have been able to remain in the gold standard if somehow the Government had not been able to pay its debt. This is where the final element of the puzzle enters the picture: emigrant remittances.

From 1836 to 1913, close to 1.4 million persons emigrated from Portugal (Fig. 5). A virtually nonexistent phenomenon in the 1830s, emigration became one of the most important demographic factors in the country, reaching very high figures from the 1850 and 1860s onward. Most of these persons emigrated to Brazil, a country then passing through a typical "New World/Frontier" kind of growth. These emigrants became responsible for an enormous amount of transfers into Portugal. Although we do not have exact figures for these remittances, the existing estimates point to an amount ranging between 2 and 3% of GDP between the 1870s and the 1891–1892 crisis (Esteves and Khoudour-Cásteras 2011; see also Reis 2000; Mata 2002) (Fig. 6, where the amount of transfers should be understood as being roughly

Fig. 5 Emigrants, Portugal, 1836–1914 (*Source* 1836–1854: Rowland [1998]; 1855–1899: Baganha [1991]; 1900–1914: Baganha [1994])

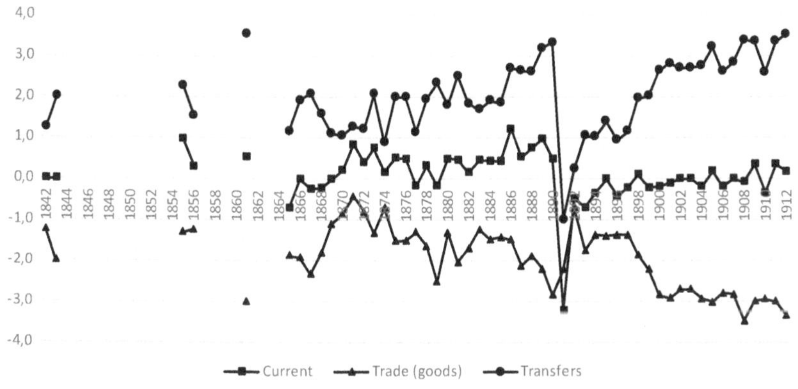

Fig. 6 Balance of payments, Portugal, 1842–1912 (% GDP) (*Source* Fontoura and Valério [2001] and Valério [2001])

equivalent to the amount of emigrant remittances). This volume of capital worked as a vast source of tax receipts as well as an instrument for the acquisition of Government bonds both in Portugal and abroad, especially in London and Paris (Ramos 1996). It was this financial stream that allowed the Portuguese Government to pay its debt on time and be seen as a reliable debtor in the international markets. Doubts about that reliability appeared first only in the 1880s (Esteves 2005).

It was this system that the 1891–1892 crisis destroyed. In April 1890, for the first time in 38 years, the Portuguese Government had trouble placing a loan in the Paris market. At the origin of the difficulties was the Brazilian political situation and its consequences on emigrant remittances: on 15 November 1889, a military coup abolished the monarchy in Brazil, installing a republic in its place; with the depreciation of the Brazilian real, emigrants reduced the volume of their remittances. The absence of remittances from Brazil led to an international payments crisis and to the depreciation of the Portuguese real itself, making it difficult for the Government to respect debt service. Also, we must recall that a large part of the remittances themselves were used directly in that service. Even if the series on remittances in Fig. 6 are not entirely reliable, the movements displayed there give an idea of the shock to the system: They fell about 90% between 1890 and 1891.

The situation was made even more serious thanks to a world crisis that made the traditional broker for the Portuguese Government, Baring Brothers, nearly insolvent in November 1890, as a consequence of an economic crisis originating in Argentina. The Portuguese Government was still able to find a short-run solution through a loan by a financial syndicate involving national and foreign creditors in February 1891, but only in exchange for granting the syndicate the monopoly of tobacco manufacturing (Lains 2008). The amount was enough to cover only the existing commitments until the end of the year. At the same time, due to the international payments crisis, the country was experiencing a process of heavy drainage of gold, putting the Bank of Portugal (BoP) in difficulty to convert its notes into gold. Consequently, the Government determined the suspension of convertibility, first temporarily, in May 1891,[11] later in a definitive manner, in July, in a decree that also gave the BoP the monopoly of money emission in the country.[12] This was how the Portuguese real left the gold

[11]Decree 10 May 1891.

[12]Decree 9 July 1891.

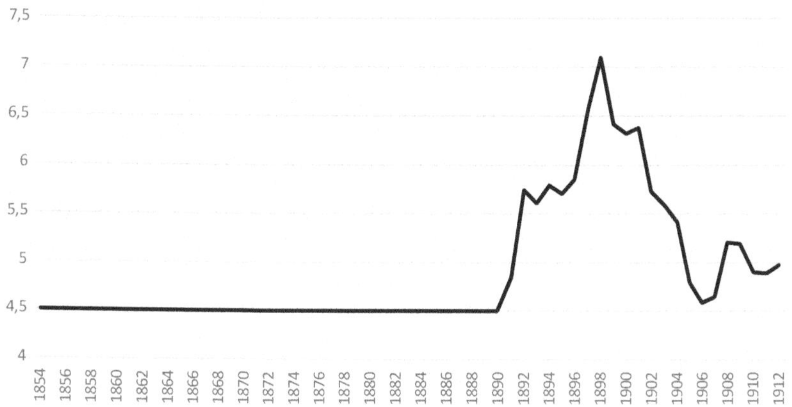

Fig. 7 Exchange rate real/sterling, 1854–1910 (*Source* Mata and Valério [1996])

standard, never to return (except for a brief period of three months in 1931) (Mata 1987). Suspension of convertibility had a double effect: on the one hand, it stopped the gold drainage, although at the cost of a heavy depreciation; the real depreciated 7% in relation to sterling between 1890 and 1891, but the process continued: 22% in 1892, with the peak being reached in 1898, with a 37% depreciation (see Fig. 7). On the other hand, it gave the Government means for its own financing: fiat money printed by the BoP jumped from a share of 7.6% in Portuguese money circulation in 1890 to one of 37% in 1895, and 49% in 1912 (Reis 1990, 1994; Nunes and Valério 2005).

As the Brazilian difficulties and the inability to obtain external loans continued, a new Minister of Finance felt forced to implement an emergency policy package, raising the tax on interest of domestic bonds from 3 to 30%, thus reducing for practical matters their return by one-third.[13] As this was not enough, four months later a similar decision was taken concerning foreign debt: Interest on external bonds was reduced by two thirds.[14] Both represented a form of partial default

[13]Law 26 February 1892.

[14]Decree 13 June 1892.

and the reputational costs for the Portuguese Government were severe: placing loans in the international markets became impossible, as foreign bondholders reacted violently. Negotiations between them and the Portuguese Government lasted for nine years, until finally an agreement was reached in 1902, whereby the capital of all Portuguese debt was reduced by 38% and converted into a new loan to be paid in the next 99 years at an annual interest rate of 3% (Esteves 2005).

The financial crisis had a huge impact on Portuguese public opinion, but this was mostly due to its association with two other separate crises. One was a political crisis, in the sequence of an attempted revolution to abolish the monarchy and proclaim a republic, on 31 January 1891. Even if the event was a failure, it still transmitted a sense of uncertainty over the survival of the constitutional monarchy regime (Ramos et al. 2009). More serious was a colonial crisis: on 11 January 1890, Britain made an ultimatum to Portugal ordering Portuguese troops to be removed from a large stretch of land linking the southwestern and southeastern coasts of Africa. Portugal claimed domination over this territory on the basis of a historical presence on the ground and set the claims in an 1885 document called the "Rose-colored Map". The problem was that these territorial claims clashed with Cecil Rhodes' and Britain's plans to create a corridor linking Cairo to the Cape. Portugal was left with no alternative but to acquiesce to Britain's demands (Ramos et al. 2009).

The British ultimatum must be understood in the context of the Portuguese African empire and the international process known as the Scramble for Africa. Despite having been at the origin of Portuguese expansion in the fifteenth century, Africa had become a progressively neglected part of the empire, with Brazil growing to the status of "jewel in the crown" from the sixteenth century onward (Pedreira 1998). The main function of the African colonies soon became one of provider of labor, in the form of slaves, to help develop Brazil. A system of exclusive trade connections between Brazilian and mainland ports allowed for a close connection between the two territories and between them and the outside world: Brazilian exports (essentially raw materials and agricultural goods) would enter in Portugal to be consumed locally or re-exported to world markets; Portuguese goods (some agricultural, others industrial, most of them unable to compete in the world markets) would be exported to Brazil, and foreign goods in the direction of Brazil would have to pass by the mainland and then re-exported to Brazil (Pedreira 1998). While this system was being built, the former Eastern Portuguese Empire in Asia had also become basically irrelevant, being reduced to a few small outposts: Macau, in China, Goa, Damão and Diu, in India, and Timor, in Indonesia (Newitt 1981; Clarence-Smith 1985; Alexandre 1998a, b, 2005).

This was the situation the new liberal regime found in Africa in the 1830s. But the loss of Brazil fostered some ideas to develop the areas where the Portuguese were present in Africa. A situation made even more pressing thanks to the growing pressures to abolish the international slave trade and even slavery itself, a threat to the essential Portuguese way of life in Africa. Britain had abolished the slave trade within the British Empire in 1807 and signed a treaty with Portugal in 1815, forcing the latter to limit the trade only to the south of the Equator. In 1836, one of the new Portuguese liberal governments abolished the slave trade within the Portuguese Empire itself.[15] The politician responsible for abolition, the Marquis of Sá da Bandeira, abhorred the trade for humanitarian reasons but also because he thought it to be the biggest obstacle to the development of Portuguese Africa: while the trade existed, with its high-profit rates, colonial economic agents would neglect other activities. So, most naturally, abolition of the slave trade was followed by legislation bent on increasing the interconnection between the mainland and Africa: certain foreign imports into the colonies were prohibited, reserving them to Portuguese equivalents, and a rudimentary system of imperial preference was established.[16] The first plans to expand colonization to the African hinterland started appearing in the 1850s and 1860s, but all of this remained essentially modest, due to various reasons: first, because the slave trade continued illegally and in still reasonable numbers (Alexandre 1998a, b, 2005; Pedreira 1998); what is more, even if the slave trade was abolished, the institution of

[15]Decree 10 December 1836.

[16]Decree 17 January 1837.

slavery itself survived in Portuguese Africa, continuing to be legal until 1869, when it was finally abolished, and disappearing completely only in 1878[17]; second, because the "Brazilian connection" (Clarence-Smith 1985) continued even after independence, thanks to Portuguese mass migration, allowing for an economic return that the (then) current development of Africa could not guarantee.

Up to the late nineteenth century, the Portuguese historical territorial claims in Africa were far from clear: the Portuguese were present in significant stretches of coastal lands but their presence inland was very thin. Various local authorities dominated there and the Portuguese had not drawn frontiers or established a colonial administration. They had mere spheres of influence, not even clearly delimited, on the coast of Guinea, in Luanda and its surroundings, in Benguela (both in Angola), on the delta of the Congo River, in the valley of the Zambezi River (in Mozambique), and in the southern tip of Mozambique (Torres 1990; Alexandre 1998a, b). A decisive push to change the situation came with the Scramble for Africa. From the 1870s onward, Africa started to be seen by European countries, especially those lacking an overseas empire, such as Germany or Belgium, as land to conquer and colonize. Much of it, beyond the coast, was practically unknown to Europeans. The only Europeans with some presence in Sub-Saharan Africa (if we except for the British in South Africa) were indeed the Portuguese, although in the relatively informal manner described above. It was this situation, together with the fact that native polities lacked clear borders, that allowed for the Scramble for Africa to begin. In fact, Portugal had, also here, been a pioneer, with the first moves of the 1850s and 1860s, despite its far from outstanding results (Newitt 1981). Then, the other European powers started their own African expansion, with Portugal trying not to lose the train: when king Léopold II of Belgium sent Henry Morton Stanley to explore the region of the Congo (right where the Portuguese presence was stronger) between 1869 and 1874,

[17]Decree 25 February 1869. The measure had been preceded by partial abolition in the Cape Verdean Island of São Vicente in 1855, and in the Angolan provinces of Ambriz, Cabinda and Molembo in 1856; also, a decree of 29 April 1858 set a limit of twenty years for slavery to be completely abolished.

and established the International African Association in 1876; when France sent Pierre Savorgnan de Brazza to explore the same region in 1872–1784; and when the Royal Geographical Society sent Verney Lovett Cameron to assist Livingstone in 1873, in an expedition that would last until 1875 and ended with the first sea-to-sea crossing of equatorial Africa; the Portuguese also set their own exploration missions and institutions: in 1875, the Lisbon Geographical Society (*Sociedade de Geografia de Lisboa*) was founded with the purpose of exploring African territory, leading to various expeditions, the most famous being those of Alexandre Serpa Pinto, in 1877–1879, and Hermenegildo Capelo and Roberto Ivens, in 1884–1885, through vast stretches of the African hinterland between what are today Angola and Mozambique (Newitt 1981; Alexandre 1998a, b).

This is the context in which the question of the Rose-colored Map and of the British ultimatum must be inserted. In the unruly and unsettled environment of the Scramble for Africa, Portugal tried to stick to what it called its "historical rights". The problem for the Portuguese authorities was the lack of the necessary means to enforce their claims, in the face of much more powerful competitors, especially Britain, Germany, and France. Portugal negotiated with all of them in various circumstances and for various purposes, and then tried its luck with the Rose-colored Map, claiming a historical right to territories that had not really been Portuguese. Unable to deal with British power, it had to let go, although still obtaining significant rights in large stretches of the continent (Newitt 1981; Clarence-Smith 1985; Alexandre 1998a, 2005).

4 Dealing with the Crisis: 1890 Onward

During the 1890s, the Portuguese governments did not have the means to continue with the same kind of fiscal policy followed during the Regeneration period: the volume of emigrant remittances, despite some recovery, remained relatively low until 1897 (Fig. 6), while at the same time the default closed access to international capital markets. There was no alternative but to adopt a more disciplined fiscal policy. The success of this reorientation is clear, as large deficits gave place to small ones

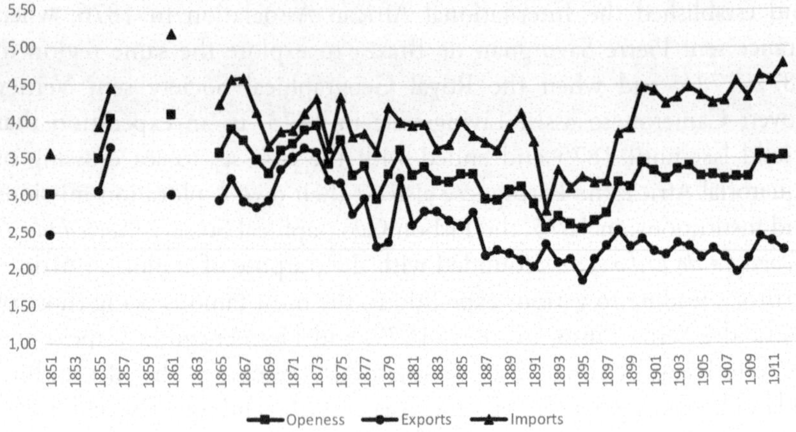

Fig. 8 Exports and imports, Portugal 1851–1912 (% GDP) (Openness = 100 × [(Exports + Imports)/2]/GDP; Current prices; *Source* Author's calculations, based on Fontoura and Valério [2001])

and even some surpluses (Fig. 2). This was achieved mostly by cutting on the kind of expenditure that had been the trademark of the pre-crisis decades: infrastructure and transportation. The pace of construction of roads and railways stagnated during the 1890s. While remittances were scarce, the exchange rate of the real to sterling continued deteriorating. This seems to have played a beneficial role for the growth of Portuguese exports, whose share on GDP grew until the end of the decade. As soon as the volume of remittances returned to pre-crisis levels (Fig. 6), the real re-appreciated (Fig. 7) and the share of exports on GDP stagnated (Fig. 8). This led immediately to the reawakening of the infrastructure programs: railway construction, which had stagnated at around 2300 km between 1892 and 1908, grew to reach 2898 km in 1910 (Alegria 1990). This was accompanied by various programs of urban renewal, affecting mostly Lisbon. Emigration to Brazil reached new records in the first decade of the twentieth century (Fig. 5). Even if the lack of foreign capital forced governments to balance the budget (contrary to what had happened during the Regeneration period), everything could be accommodated thanks to emigrant remittances (Esteves and Khoudour-Násteras 2011).

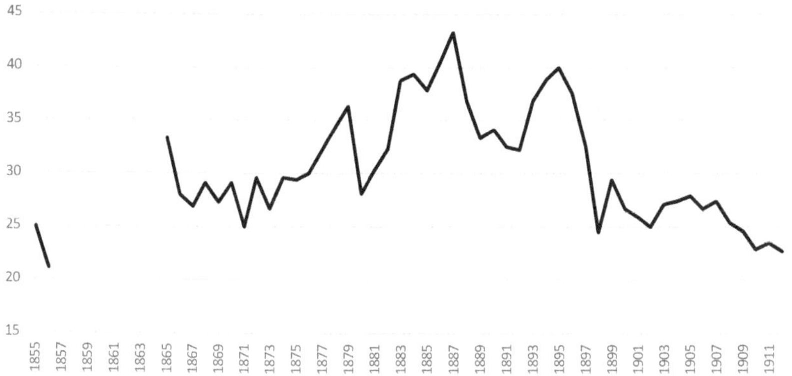

Fig. 9 Average tariffs % of imports, Portugal, 1855–1912 (*Source* Fontoura and Valério [2001])

One further policy instrument adopted by the Portuguese governments in order to deal with the crisis was an increase in the level of protection of the economy, thanks to the elaboration of a new tariff schedule in 1892.[18] Figure 9 shows, however, that, despite some increase in the average weight of tariffs over imports in the years immediately after 1892, the opposite happened from 1895 onward, the responsibility for that being the changes in the composition of trade, leaving many imports outside the effects of the legislation (Labisa 1999). Where the new tariffs seem to have had a more serious effect was in the relationship between the mainland and the African colonies. The 1892 schedule introduced heavy tariffs on foreign goods transported in foreign ships between the mainland and the overseas territories, while at the same time lifting 90% of their weight on Portuguese goods transported in Portuguese ships. The consequence was a visible growth of the exports of Portuguese goods to Africa from 3.3% of total exports in 1890 to 9.5% in 1895 and 17.1% in 1900. Two sectors benefited especially with this transformation: cotton textiles and wine, goods that Portugal had extreme difficulties in placing in the world

[18]Law 10 May 1892.

market, due to their low quality (Clarence-Smith 1985; Pedreira 1998; Alexandre 2005).

These connections were reinforced in 1899, when a new law introduced a more systematic mechanism of imperial preference[19]: according to it, sugar and raw cotton imported from the colonies benefited from a 10-year tariff rebate of 50% in relation to the general tariff, as compensation for the protection given to cotton goods imported from the mainland. In 1901, the period was enlarged to 15 years. At the same time, colonial re-exports to the world market via the mainland acquired some significance in this period, especially concentrated in three goods: cocoa, from São Tomé, and rubber and coffee, both from Angola. Even if these re-exports played a positive role in the balancing of Portuguese foreign accounts (Clarence-Smith 1985; Lains 1998; Alexandre 2005) their contribution, together with the rest of colonial trade, remained negligible for the overall behavior of the economy. This was due not only to the fact that the total amounts involved were small but also to the fact that this activity was accompanied by an increase in public spending, in order to make the Portuguese presence in Africa really effective (Clarence-Smith 1985).

Thanks to the various treaties through which the European powers settled the Scramble for Africa, Portugal ended up by putting large stretches of the African continent under its formal domination, despite its inability to keep the territories disputed with Britain: formal Portuguese rule was thus established in the archipelagoes of Cape Verde and São Tomé e Príncipe, the fortress of São Baptista de Ajudá, and the vast territories of Angola and Mozambique (Ramos 1994). But formal control was not an unqualified blessing, as it led to a series of expenditures (in infrastructure, military expeditions, and regular administrative activity) that limited the return from colonial economic ventures, something that became particularly serious after the 1891–1892 financial crisis. The difficulties in introducing formal rule made then by the Portuguese authorities follow a course of action that ultimately meant alienation of control. While beginning a series of military confrontations with local

[19]Law 17 August 1899.

African powers, the Portuguese also granted large stretches of Angola and Mozambique to chartered companies owned by foreign capital, whose powers ranged from typical sovereign rights (administration, police, military campaigns…) to developmental ones (put land under cultivation, introduce some industries dedicated to transformation of indigenous goods, build such infrastructure as roads or railways…): the Mozambique Company (chartered in 1891 for twenty-five years, later extended to another twenty-five) and the Niassa Company (chartered in 1894 for twenty-five years), in Mozambique, and the Moçâmedes Company (also chartered in 1894 for thirty years), in Angola, were the largest, but many others existed in these and other colonies. Their contribution to local development turned out to be small (Newitt 1981; Clarence-Smith 1985; Alexandre 2005). In the end, although the Portuguese presence did become more effective from the 1890s onwards, it was still limited to only a few pockets inside each of the territories.

5 Economic Growth and Change

The period of the second half of the nineteenth century and the beginning of the twentieth century in Portugal is paradoxical in terms of economic growth and structural change. On the one hand, as stated by Costa et al. (2016), the most important feature of the Portuguese economy in the nineteenth century was its "industrialization", following the path of the newly industrialized economies that entered then in the age of "modern economic growth" (to use Kuznets 1973, terminology). On the other hand, the period was also the one in which the Portuguese economy lost most of the ground to those newly industrialized economies. Figures 3 and 4 of the Introduction to this book show that the Portuguese economy got further and further behind during the entire century, from 1820 to 1913. Even if its expansion allowed for a sizable growth of the Portuguese population (from 2.9 million persons to 5.5 between 1801 and 1911: 2.6 million more—Rodrigues 2009; Henriques and Rodrigues 2009), by the latter year Portugal was the poorest country in Western Europe, with a GDP per capita level that was only 30% of that of the richest economies, coming from about 85% in 1820.

What Figs. 3 and 4 of the Introduction also show is how different the Portuguese path was from those of other peripheral economies. We have already seen in the Introduction that comparing Portugal with Scandinavia is not warranted, despite suggestions by such authors as Reis (1993) that the Scandinavian countries and Finland were in similar circumstances to Portugal at the beginning of the nineteenth century. Figure 3 in the Introduction shows that, except for Finland, none of these economies was ever as poor as the Portuguese one, i.e., the Scandinavian periphery was never, in reality, as peripheral as Portugal.

Even when comparing Portugal with its "natural" companions, that is, the countries of the Southern periphery, the Portuguese path still reveals its singularity. The first thing to note is that we are indeed dealing with a group of countries that declined much more in terms of GDP per capita than the Northern ones. The second is how Italy presents a special path in the southern context, despite the substantial decline until the 1850s: its GDP per capita never went much below 70%, meaning that it should not be classified as a truly peripheral economy. As for Spain and Greece, their decline is much more pronounced. But even in comparison with these poorer performers, Portugal's path stands out as especially negative: they never went much below 50%, contrarily to Portugal.

Figures 3 and 4 in the Introduction also show that the moment for the beginning of catch-up by the Northern economies was the late nineteenth century and the early twentieth century, this time including Finland. Even the Southern economies, although not initiating a consistent catch-up process, were able to sustain decline. Again, this is not true of Portugal, which continued in its downward path. So, the defining feature of the Portuguese economy in the second half of the nineteenth century was its massively negative growth performance, despite participating, at the same time, in the early stages of modern economic growth. Portugal was, thus, an awkward participant in this international process.

It is not easy to find reasons for such a negative behavior, although some description of the economy helps to shed some light on the issue.

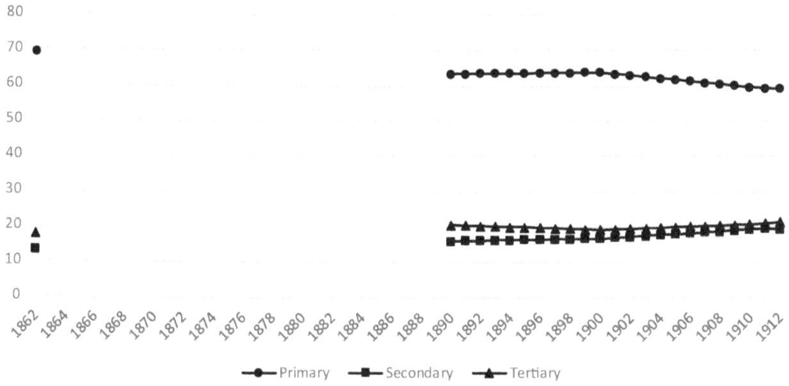

Fig. 10 Structure employment, Portugal, 1862–1912 (% overall employment) (*Source* 1890–1912: Author's calculations based on Nunes [2001]; 1862, extrapolated backward from 1890 using Reis [2005])

Despite industrializing, the Portuguese economy remained one of the most agricultural of Europe during the second half of the nineteenth century: in the mid-nineteenth century about 70% of its workforce was employed in the primary sector; by the early twentieth century, the figure had declined only to 60%; as for industry, the figures were, respectively 13 and 19% and, for services, 18 and 21% (Fig. 10). International comparisons reveal that one part of the problem of slow growth of the economy was its structure. But they also show that structural change (or the lack of it thereof) was not the only issue: slow growth of productivity internal to the sectors played a large role as well (in reality, the most important one). Of course, the structure of the Portuguese economy could not compare with that of the early industrializers by 1870, but that is not the case with other countries. For instance, Sweden had, in 1870, a relative weight of employment in the different sectors that was not too dissimilar with Portugal; but by 1913, the picture was completely different, revealing a much faster process of industrialization (Table 2). This shows that part of the explanation for the divergence between Sweden and Portugal must lie in structural change. But the case of Finland provides a rather different story: the Finnish economy was much less industrialized in 1870 and remained

Table 2 Structure of employment, various European economies, c. 1870–c. 1913 (% total employment)

	Agriculture		Industry		Services	
	c. 1870	c. 1913	c. 1870	c. 1913	c. 1870	c. 1913
Belgium	44.4	20.9	35.0	39.5	33.3	39.6
Denmark	47.8	23.2	37.8	45.5	17.8	31.3
Finland	75.5	69.3	10.1	10.6	30.3	34.2
Netherlands	39.4	28.3	22.4	32.8	38.2	38.9
Norway	49.6	39.6	22.9	25.9	27.5	34.5
Sweden	67.4	45.0	17.4	31.8	15.2	23.2
UK	22.2	11.8	42.4	44.1	35.4	44.1
France	49.8	41.0	28.0	33.1	22.2	25.9
Greece		49.6		16.2		34.2
Italy	61.0	55.4	23.3	26.6	15.7	18.0
Spain	66.3	56.3	18.2	13.8	15.5	29.9
Portugal	69.0	59.0	13.2	19.3	17.8	21.7

Source Broadberry et al. (2010), except Portugal (see Fig. 7)

so in 1913 (Table 2), but this did not prevent it from growing much faster than the Portuguese one. Finally, a comparison with the Southern European countries reveals a structure of the economy that was not excessively different but an overall growth performance that was much worse (Table 2).

In what concerns the relative importance of the sectors in their contribution to GDP (Fig. 11), agriculture kept a weight of about 40% until the early twentieth century; it was only then that it started to decline; as for industry there was consistent but very slow growth: from the mid-1850s to the 1890s, the weight of the sector passed from 15 to 20%; it was only in the last decade of the nineteenth century and the first of the twentieth that this weight jumped to 30%, similar to that of agriculture in 1912. As for services, the weight of the sector was kept at about 45% until the 1880s, but then started declining until reaching 35% in 1912.

The most visible feature of Portuguese agriculture during this period was the expansion of land use. By 1867 close to 45% of arable land was not under use; by 1902, the figure had been reduced to 17% (Lains 2003). This expansion shows how much the *Ancien Régime* institutions had prevented Portuguese agriculture from reaching its full potential.

Fig. 11 Structure economy, Portugal, 1851–1912 (% GDP) (*Source* 1851–1910: Lains [2003]; 1910–1912: Batista et al. [1997])

The process of destruction of those institutions and its replacement by the new liberal ones was essential to allow for the growth of the sector. Portuguese entrepreneurs could finally acquire the property they needed to start using modern methods of production. After the elimination of the restrictions coming from the *Ancien Régime*, land flooded the market, and many new landowners increased significantly its share in their asset portfolio (Fonseca 1996), something that constituted a prior step to the introduction of important innovations: this is clearly exemplified by the cases of the landowners of the Alentejo region (in the South of Portugal), who needed to acquire farms of a certain dimension in order to introduce mechanical harvesters for wheat. Once that happened, the use of those machines spread with relative ease (Reis 1982). The new liberal institutions were, hence, an inevitable prior step to agricultural change, but the process took quite a long time, as it was only concluded during the 1930s, thanks to the juridical complications involving property rights described above.

But the expansion of cultivated land revealed that the problems of Portuguese agriculture went beyond institutional change, many of them having to do with the ecological inadequacy of the territory to adopt the innovations typical of North European countries. Cultivation techniques were much less intensive than in Northern Europe, cattle and fertilizers were scarce, and the capital-labor ratio and land-labor ratio were low (Lains 2003; Costa et al. 2016). The sector was overwhelmingly dominated by the production of cereals and wine, which together represented about 50% of overall production during the second half of the nineteenth century. Animal production (especially meat and wool) reached about 25%, while olive oil, potatoes, and fruit and vegetables represented the remaining 25% (Branco and Silva 2017). As Dennison and Simpson (2010) have shown, the agricultural sectors of Southern Europe passed through deep changes, with considerable innovation, during the nineteenth century. Only these transformations, being different in nature, did not grant them the same pace of growth of productivity as in Northern Europe.

Regional variation within the Portuguese territory was substantial, but productivity was always low (with the partial exception of corn in the Northwest). Cereals, wine, and forestation were the main beneficiaries of the process of expansion of cultivation: in the former case, the most dynamic product was rice, and in the latter cork trees—cork was the fastest growing agricultural product during the period (Martins 2005; Branco and Silva 2017). Most of the production was for internal consumption, with some exceptions in wine, fruit, and cattle (Branco and Silva 2017; Martins 2005). The sector was also marked by a strong asymmetry in the property structure, with very large units (sometimes called latifundia) in a significant part of the South and very small ones (sometimes called minifundia) in the Northwest, and intermediate situations in the rest of the country (Lains 2003).

Between 1860 and 1910, labor productivity in agriculture grew only 0.68% per year, although there were different phases contributing to this overall picture. Between 1860 and 1880, the expansion of agricultural productivity was below the European average, with an annual growth rate of 0.26%. This was essentially due to a long sequence of bad weather conditions affecting mostly cereals but also to the spreading of *oidium* (a disease specific to vines). On the contrary, the 1880–1890 period was positive, with an annual growth rate of 0.9%, allowing for recovery in relation to the previous negative period. The behavior of agricultural productivity was also positive in the following decade, with an annual rate of 0.82%. But the beginning of the twentieth century (1900–1910) was negative, with agricultural productivity displaying a negative rate of −0.25% per year, most probably due to the expansion of cultivation to increasingly marginal lands (Lains 2007). It is the combination of the different periods that results in a picture of very slow overall growth.

Industry did not display impressive productivity growth either: 0.9% per year between 1860 and 1910 (Lains 2007), below the already industrialized countries of Northern Europe (Broadberry et al. 2010). What this shows is that most of the Portuguese industrialization occurred in traditional sectors, with a few exceptions mostly by the end of the nineteenth century and beginning of the twentieth century. Household industry continued to represent the most important part of the sector, with just a few islands of more modern units. Textiles kept an overwhelming weight throughout the period, although declining: about 60% in 1852, and 45% in 1896, with a more or less equi-proportional distribution between cotton and wool; the most important changes in structure came thanks to the growth of the cork and tinned fished industries, the first passing from close to 2% in 1852 to 9.5% in 1896, the second from virtual nonexistence to 10% (Pedreira 2013).

If we except for these two new sectors (cork and tinned fish), most of industry depended on the internal market. This shows how little the industrial sector was able to explore the new conditions of external openness in Europe in the second half of the nineteenth century. And the same goes for the bulk of agricultural goods, since only a few had strong links to the world market. The overall result was a very low degree of openness of the Portuguese economy: the weight of foreign trade oscillated between 2.5% of GDP and 4% between 1851 and 1912, most of the time remaining in the 3.5% mark (Fig. 8). This made of Portugal one of the least open countries of the Western world, with the situation tending to deepen as time passed (Fig. 12): if, in the mid-1850s, Portugal was still accompanied by Spain in its degree of openness, from the 1860s onward Spain clearly converged to the large European countries, while Portugal remained quite far away from the degree of openness typical of small European countries, either relatively rich (Belgium and Denmark) or relatively poor (Finland). And less open

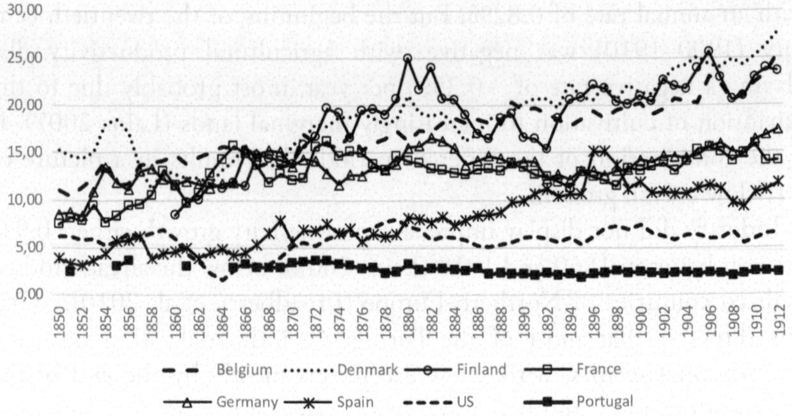

Fig. 12 Openness, various countries, 1850–1912 (exports % GDP) Current prices; (*Source* Federico and Tena-Junguito [2018], except Portugal: Fontoura and Valério [2001])

even than large European countries or even the United States, one of the largest economies in the world.

The pattern of this trade was constant throughout the period: exports of wine represented more than half of total exports, initially with an overwhelming weight of Port wine, but with common wine gaining ground until the end of the period; if we add fruits and vegetables plus cattle we reach a weight of agricultural exports in total exports of about 70%, the remaining exports being mainly of raw materials, with cork growing fast. As for imports, between one-quarter and one-third was made of manufactured goods (especially textiles), another third of agricultural goods, especially grain, sugar, and cod, the remaining third being constituted of raw materials and intermediate goods (Lains 1995).

The Portuguese economy was clearly unable to participate in what is now normally known as the First Age of Globalization, after O'Rourke and Williamson (1999) (see also Federico and Tena 2016). This was a period when Western countries adopted a much more open policy in relation to their mercantilist past, leading to an unprecedented integration of the world economy. Portuguese governments were very reluctant to adopt this kind of policy: a new customs schedule was introduced

Table 3 Level of protection (average tariffs % of imports), various countries, 1875–1914

	1875–1879	1880–1884	1885–1889	1890–1894	1895–1899	1900–1904	1905–1909	1910–1914
Denmark	11.9	11.6	12.6	9.0	9.0	8.1	6.8	5.0
France	5.2	6.0	7.9	9.7	10.4	8.6	8.5	8.9
Germany	3.7	6.1	8.2	8.9	9.3	8.4	7.6	7.0
Italy	7.9	8.3	11.1	9.6	10.2	10.8	11.7	11.7
Norway	10.2	12.6	10.7	11.2	11.6	11.7	11.5	12.8
Sweden	9.7	10.5	4.8	10.7	11.4	10.7	9.5	8.4
UK	5.3	4.8	5.3	4.8	4.8	6.1	5.3	4.8
United States	29.4	29.1	29.9	23.5	22.7	26.8	23.0	18.3
Portugal	32.5	33.8	38.4	34.9	32.8	26.4	26.4	23.2

Source O'Rourke (2000), except Portugal: Fontoura and Valério (2001)

in 1837, reverting relative openness coming from 1810; the schedule would be globally revised twice until the end of the nineteenth century (in 1852 and in 1892), in addition to a series of ad hoc changes during the period (Justino 1989; Labisa 1999; Câmara 2005; Lains 2007), but the level of protection did not fundamentally change: the average level of tariffs in relation to imports was kept at a level oscillating between 25 and 35% (Fig. 9), one of the highest in the world (Table 3). Besides reasons of protection of the economy, fiscal reasons played a role in this as well: tariffs were a source of revenue governments could not dispense with.

According to some literature, namely Bairoch (1989) and O'Rourke (2000), this should have had a positive impact on the growth of the economy, as both authors established a positive relationship between tariff protection and growth. But more recent studies, such as Clemens and Williamson (2001), Tena-Junguito (2010), Lampe and Sharp (2013) or Federico et al. (2017) have questioned this point of view, especially by arguing that the relationship found in the previous literature depended crucially on the choice of country sample: the relationship is only valuable, and only partially, for rich countries; if the sample includes peripheral countries (such as Portugal), the relationship becomes blurred or even disappears completely. The figures presented by Tena-Junguito (2010) show a very clear negative relationship between tariff protection and growth for the European peripheral countries between 1870 and 1913, and Federico et al. (2017) show that there was always a negative relationship between openness and growth in Portugal in the second half of the nineteenth century and early twentieth century. Gains from trade in the sense of Arkolakis et al. (2012) were one of the lowest in the world in Portugal, according to the estimations by Federico and Tena-Junguito (2016).

A final point worth making is that this was the period in which the country also acquired a relatively modern banking system. Before the liberal revolution, there were no banks in the country; by 1891, there were 44 banks of different types, including a prototype central bank, a public savings bank and a bank of issue in the empire (Valério et al. 2006, p. 259). The first bank to be established was the Bank of Lisbon in 1821, which was created for the purpose of lending to the Government in order to help it remove a large amount of paper currency from circulation; this was a privately owned commercial bank with issuing powers. At the time, there was no freedom of establishment of banks, so the next banks being founded, during the 1830s, were directly authorized by the Government; their purposes continued to be to help the Government take paper currency out of circulation, a function they shared with a series of para-banking financial companies also authorized by the Government during the 1840s. In an environment of crisis, one of these companies would merge with the Bank of Lisbon to give birth to the BoP in 1846 (Reis 1996b; Valério et al. 2006). In its original form, the BoP was far from being a modern central bank, but its close connections with the Government prepared the ground for the later evolution. While this was happening, the number of banks started growing, under many governmental efforts to facilitate their creation (Valério et al. 2006). New kinds of banks appeared, such as the savings banks and the banking houses (the latter being non-limited responsibility small institutions personally owned).

Through various crises, the situation by the 1890s corresponded already to a relatively modern banking system: the BoP had become, since 1887, the only bank of issue, a privilege attributed by the Government in exchange for becoming the Treasury's banker; the Government created in 1876 a new institution: the National Savings Bank (*Caixa Geral de Depósitos* [CGD]), having as a function to receive compulsory deposits (for legal processes or other official motives) together with regular deposits—CGD would merge in 1885 with *Caixa Económica Portuguesa*, another public savings bank having as a network the offices of the post system, and assume definitely the nature of a public savings bank; together with this some four dozen banks entered the market, practically all of them concentrated in the two largest cities, Lisbon and Porto. The only bank with a national range was the BoP, which still performed commercial functions. In 1864, a colonial bank was founded, the National Overseas Bank (*Banco Nacional Ultramarino* [BNU]), with issuing powers and a monopoly of banking activities in most of the empire (Valério et al. 2006). Despite such visible growth, financial intermediation was very low (Reis 1990, 1994) and the banking system did not play a large role in the financing of economic activity.

To conclude, we are talking of an economy unable to be at the forefront of modern economic growth. Portuguese economic historians have tried to find explanations for it. According to Reis (1984), the country did not possess the natural resources or a viable specialization pattern through which it could have broken the cycle of backwardness: it did not have coal or iron in sufficient amounts and all expected potential specializations based on the economy's comparative advantages (wine, tinned sardines or cork) were not viable as engines of faster growth. The bleak conclusion from this analysis is that a higher integration with the world market would not have been enough for the country to follow the leading industrialized countries of the period. Lains (1995) proposes a similar, while slightly different, explanation: the economy simply did not possess the potential in the nineteenth century to integrate that group. The most visible sign of this was the lack of industrial development prior to the nineteenth century. The pioneers of the age of modern economic growth had already developed an important industrial sector prior to that age, something very far from having happened in Portugal. Interestingly enough this idea fits well with a recent effort to reconstitute Portuguese GDP from the sixteenth century until the early nineteenth century (Palma and Reis 2018), whereby it is shown that Portugal had a relatively high GDP per capita level in the European context until 1750 (in 1750, its GDP per capita was higher than those of Spain, Germany or Sweden, although lower than those of Great Britain, the Netherlands, or Northern Italy) and how, from that year on, comparative decline started. This suggests that the decline in the nineteenth century was nothing but a continuation of a path reversion coming from the previous century—what these authors have not provided yet is an explanation for this.

Other explanations stress institutional factors. That is the case of Reis (1993), who highlights the very low educational level of the Portuguese population, something that not only implied low productivity but also prevented Portuguese workers from adopting modern machinery or develop new methods of production. According to Table 4, Portuguese educational levels were, indeed, the lowest in Western Europe in the second half of the nineteenth century and early twentieth century, with the initial exception of Finland and Luxembourg (in the latter case, throughout the entire period). The table shows not only the very low level in 1870 but also the extremely slow growth afterward. The average years of schooling of the Finnish population passed from 0.130 in 1870 to 1.630 in 1910, whereas those of the Portuguese population rose only to 0.938 from a higher initial level of 0.267. And other countries with low educational levels in 1870 (although already higher than in Portugal), such as France, Greece, Ireland, or Italy, displayed impressive

Table 4 Average years of schooling for population aged 15–64

Country	1870	1910
Austria	2.163	4.377
Belgium	2.423	3.088
Denmark	2.453	3.169
Finland	0.130	1.630
France	0.715	2.954
Germany	2.223	3.744
Greece	0.783	2.032
Ireland	0.745	2.208
Italy	0.876	1.978
Luxembourg	0.039	0.221
Spain	1.581	3.487
Sweden	3.595	4.502
UK	0.924	3.635
Portugal	0.267	0.938

Source Lee and Lee (2016)

growth. Reis' (1993) explanation for this is twofold: first, Portugal was part of the Catholic South, where education grew slower than in the Protestant North (reading practices in this part of Europe, mostly based on the Bible, helped spread literacy); second, due to precocious political centralization and lack of centrifugal nationalist pressures, the Portuguese Government never felt the need to use education as an instrument of national unification, contrary to other countries of the Catholic South such as Spain or Italy.

Pedreira (1994) is not far either from the previous explanation. According to him, the structure of Portuguese society was simply unfit to adopt modern methods of production, due to a series of social clogs. This goes along well also with an explanation proposed by Amaral (2012), according to whom Portugal had a social and institutional structure prior to the liberal revolution that, contrary to other countries, prevented higher growth before the nineteenth century and, because of that, passed through too lengthy a transition to modern institutions, with the consequence that the nineteenth century represented a long period marked by undefined institutional rules. Dennison and Simpson (2010), precisely, stress the much less clear definition of property rights in countries such as Spain and France, a situation even more clamorous in Portugal's case.

One sort of explanation that has not received much attention is that of the possible effects of participation in the fixed-exchange rate system of the gold standard in the economy's performance. Reis (2000) has shown how the Portuguese economy was surprisingly able to deal with external shocks during this period. But two of the reasons for that should give rise to questions: one reason was that the Portuguese external sector was particularly small, thus having little impact on the overall economy; the other was the role played by emigrant remittances in allowing the Portuguese currency to perform smoothly within the rules of the system. The question this raises is that of knowing if Portugal was not caught, because of these two factors, in an overvaluation trap of the currency, making it very difficult for its exports to rise as a share of GDP, and leading to a sort of perma-slump of the sort predicted for certain areas of monetary unions by such authors as Mundell (1961), Fleming (1962) or Salter (1959). The amount of depreciation of the real in relation to sterling in the 1890s, in the sequence of the 1891–1892 crisis (which reached almost 40% throughout the decade), and of its re-appreciation afterward, as the movement of remittances from Brazil resumed, indicates a possible order of grandeur for this effect. The behavior of exports, accompanying these movements, should make us think of a possible connection. Spanish economic historians have debated strongly the impact of Spanish non-participation in the gold standard, reaching quite different conclusions, with some authors believing that floating rates and inconvertibility were favorable to Spanish growth and with others believing the opposite (for the latest piece in this string of literature, presenting also a summary of the different positions on the topic, cf. Roldan 2018). This is a topic worthy of exploration in Portuguese economic history in the future.

Most probably, the explanation for the Portuguese economic performance in the nineteenth century lies not in one of these various individual explanations but in a combination of many of them. One thing is certain, however: in the first decade of the twentieth century, Portugal was one of the poorest, less industrialized, less educated, and less open countries of Europe, with a long way to follow in order to converge to higher wealth and welfare levels.

References

Alegria, Maria Fernanda. 1990. *A Organização dos Transportes em Portugal. As Vias e o Tráfego*. Lisbon: Centro de Estudos Geográficos.

Alexandre, Valentim. 1998a. Nação e império. In *História da Expansão Portuguesa, Vol. IV – Do Brasil para África (1808–1930)*, ed. Francisco Bethencourt and Diogo Ramada Curto, 90–142. Lisbon: Círculo de Leitores.

———. 1998b. A questão colonial no Portugal oitocentista. In *Nova História da Expansão Portuguesa – O Império Africano, 1825–1890*, ed. Valentim Alexandre and Jill Dias, 21–132. Lisbon: Editorial Estampa.

———. 2005. O império. In *História Económica de Portugal, 1700–2000, Vol. II, O Século XIX*, ed. Pedro Lains and Álvaro Ferreira da Silva, 357–376. Lisbon: ICS.

Amaral, Luciano. 2012. Institutions, Property and Economic Growth: Back to the Passage from Ancien Régime to Liberalism in Portugal. *Análise Social* XLVII (202): 28–55.

Arkolakis, Costas, Arnaud Costinot, and Andrés Rordíguez-Clare. 2012. New Trade Models, Same Old Gains? *The American Economic Review* 102 (1): 94–130.

Baganha, Maria Ioannis. 1991. Uma imagem desfocada: a emigração portuguesa e as fontes portuguesas sobre a emigração. In *Emigración Española y Portuguesa a America*, ed. A. Eiras Roel, 161–175. Alicante: Instituto de Cultura Gil-Albert.

———. 1994. As correntes emigratórias portuguesas no século XX e o seu impacto na economia nacional. *Análise Social* XXIX (128): 959–980.

Bairoch, Paul. 1989. European Trade Policy, 1815–1914. In *The Cambridge Economic History of Europe, Vol. VIII: The Industrial Economies—The Development of Economic and Social Policies*, ed. Peter Mathias and Stephen Pollard, 1–60. Cambridge: Cambridge University Press.

Bastien, Carlos. 2006. Os debates orçamentais nos primórdios da monarquia constitucional. In *Os Impostos no Parlamento Português. Sistemas Fiscais e Doutrinas Fiscais nos Séculos XIX e XX*, ed. Nuno Valério, 13–62. Lisbon: Publicações Dom Quixote.

Batista, Dina, et al. 1997. *New Estimates for Portugal's GDP: 1910–1958*. Lisbon: Bank of Portugal.

Bordo, Michael D., and Hugh Rockoff. 1996. The Gold Standard as a 'Good Housekeeping Seal of Approval'. *The Journal of Economic History* 56 (2): 389–428.

Branco, Amélia, and Ester Gomes da Silva. 2017. Growth, Institutional Change and Innovation, 1820–1930. In *An Agrarian History of Portugal, 1000–2000, Economic Development on the European Frontier*, ed. Dulce Freire and Pedro Lains, 220–224. Leiden: Brill.

Broadberry, Stephen, Rainer Fremdling, and Peter Solar. 2010. Industry. In *The Cambridge Economic History of Modern Europe, Vol. I: 1700–1870*, ed. Stephen Broadberry and Kevin H. O'Rourke, 164–186. Cambridge: Cambridge University Press.

Câmara, Benedita. 2005. Relações económicas com o exterior. In *História Económica de Portugal, 1700–2000, Vol. II, O Século XIX*, ed. Pedro Lains and Álvaro Ferreira da Silva, 337–356. Lisbon: ICS.

Clarence-Smith, Gervase. 1985. *The Third Portuguese Empire, 1825–1975: A Study in Economic Imperialism*. Manchester: Manchester University Press.

Clemens, Michael A., and Jeffrey Williamson. 2001. A Tariff Growth Paradox? Protection's Impact on the World Around 1875–1997. NBER Working Paper, No. 8459.

Costa, Leonor Freire, Pedro Lains, and Susana Münch Miranda. 2016. *An Economic History of Portugal, 1143–2010*. Cambridge: Cambridge University Press.

de Macedo, Jorge Borges. 1968. Nobreza na Idade Moderna. In *Dicionário de História de Portugal, Vol. IV*, ed. Joel Serrão, 388–394. Porto: Figueirinhas Editora.

Dennison, Tracy, and James Simpson. 2010. Agriculture. In *The Cambridge Economic History of Modern Europe, Vol. I: 1700–1870*, ed. Stephen Broadberry and Kevin H. O'Rourke, 147–163. Cambridge: Cambridge University Press.

Esteves, Rui Pedro. 2005. Finanças públicas. In *História Económica de Portugal, 1700–2000, Vol. II, O Século XIX*, ed. Pedro Lains and Álvaro Ferreira da Silva, 305–335. Lisbon: ICS.

Esteves, Rui Pedro, and David Khoudour-Castéras. 2011. Remittances, Capital Flows and Financial Development During the Mass Migration Period, 1870–1913. *European Review of Economic History* 15 (3): 443–474.

Federico, Giovanni, and Antonio Tena-Junguito. 2016. A Tale of Two Globalizations: Gains from Trade and Openness 1800–2010. Universidad Carlos III de Madrid Working Papers in Economic History, No. 16-02.

———. 2018. Federico-Tena World Trade Historical Database. https://www.uc3m.es/ss/Satellite/UC3MInstitucional/es/TextoMixta/1371246237481/Federico-Tena_World_Trade_Historical_Database.

Federico, Giovanni, Paul Sharp, and Antonio Tena-Junguito. 2017. Openness and Growth in a Historical Perspective: A VECM Approach. EHES Working Papers in Economic History, No. 118.

Fernandes, Paulo Jorge. 2012. O Sistema Político na Monarquia Constitucional (1834–1910). In *O Sistema Político Português, Séculos XIX–XXI: Continuidades e Rupturas*, ed. André Freire, 25–49. Coimbra: Almedina.

Fleming, J. Markus. 1962. Domestic Financial Policies Under Fixed and Under Floating Exchange Rates. *IMF Staff Papers* 9 (3): 369–380.

Fonseca, Hélder Adegar. 1989. A propriedade da terra em Portugal, 1705–1850: alguns aspectos para uma síntese. In *Do Antigo Regime ao Liberalismo, 1750–1850*, ed. Fernando Marques da Costa et al., 213–240. Lisbon: Vega.

———. 1996. *O Alentejo no Século XIX. Economia e Atitudes Económicas.* Lisbon: ICS/CM.

Fontoura, Ana Paula, and Nuno Valério. 2001. Relações económicas externas. In *Estatísticas Históricas Portuguesas*, ed. Nuno Valério, 713–739. Lisbon: INE.

Henriques, Filipe Castro, and Teresa Ferreira Rodrigues. 2009. O século XX: a transição. In *História da População Portuguesa. Das Longas Permanências à Conquista da Modernidade*, ed. Teresa Ferreira Rodrigues, 417–513. Porto: Afrontamento e CEPESE.

Hespanha, António Manuel. 1994. *As Vésperas do Leviathan – Instituições e Poder Político: Portugal: Século XVII*. Almedina: Coimbra.

Justino, David. 1989. *A Formação do Espaço Económico Nacional – Portugal 1810–1912*. Lisbon: Vega.

Kuznets, Simon. 1973. Modern Economic Growth: Findings and Reflections. *The American Economic Review* 63 (3): 247–258.

Labisa, António dos Santos. 1999. *A Pauta Aduaneira de 1992*. Lisbon: Banco de Portugal.

Lains, Pedro. 1995. *A Economia Portuguesa no Século XIX: Crescimento Económico e Comércio Externo, 1851–1913*. Lisbon: ICS/CM.

———. 1998. Causas do colonialismo português em África, 1822–1975. *Análise Social* XXXIII (146–147): 463–496.

———. 2003. New Wine in Old Bottles: Output and Productivity Trends in Portuguese Agriculture, 1850–1950. *European Review of Economic History* 7 (1): 43–72.

———. 2007. Growth in a Protected Environment, 1850–1950. *Research in Economic History* 24: 119–160.

———. 2008. The Power of Peripheral Governments: Coping with the 1891 Financial Crisis in Portugal. *Historical Research* 81 (213): 485–506.

Lampe, Markus, and Paul Sharp. 2013. Tariffs and Income: A Time Series for 24 Countries. *Cliometrica* 7 (3): 207–235.

Lee, Jong-Wha, and Hanol Lee. 2016. Human Capital in the Long Run. *Journal of Development Economics* 122: 147–169.

Martins, Conceição Andrade. 2005. A agricultura. In *História Económica de Portugal, 1700–2000, Vol. II, O Século XIX*, ed. Pedro Lains and Álvaro Ferreira da Silva, 219–258. Lisbon: ICS.

Mata, Maria Eugénia. 1987. *Câmbios e Política Cambial na Economia Portuguesa, 1891–1931*. Lisbon: Livraria Sá da Costa Editora.

———. 1988. As três fases do fontismo: Porjectos e realizações. *Estudos em Homenagem a Vitorino Magalhães Godinho*. Lisbon: Livraria Sá da Costa Editora.

———. 1993. *As Finanças Públicas da Regeneração à Primeira Guerra Mundial*. Lisbon: Banco de Portugal.

———. 2001. Finanças públicas e dívida pública. In *Estatísticas Históricas Portuguesas*, ed. Nuno Valério, 657–712. Lisbon: INE.

———. 2002. As crises financeiras no Portugal contemporâneo: uma perspectiva de conjunto. In *Crises em Portugal nos Séculos XIX e XX*, ed. Sérgio de Campos Matos, 38–55. Lisbon: Centro de História da Universidade de Lisboa.

———. 2006. A Discussão Parlamentar dos Orçamentos da Regeneração à República. In *Os Impostos no Parlamento Português*, ed. Nuno Valério, 63–120. Lisbon: Assembleia da República.

Mata, Maria Eugénia, and Nuno Valério. 1996. Monetary Stability, Fiscal Discipline and Economic Performance: The Experience of Portugal Since 1854. In *Currency Convertibility: The Gold Standard and Beyond*, ed. Jorge Braga de Macedo, Barry Eichengreen, and Jaime Reis, 204–227. London: Routledge.

Mauro, Paolo, Rafael Romeu, and Ariel Binderand Asad Zaman. 2013. A Modern History of Fiscal Prudence and Profiglacy. IMF Working Paper, No. 13/5.

Monteiro, Nuno Gonçalo. 1993. Poder senhorial, estatuto nobiliárquico e aristocracia. In *História de Portugal, Vol. IV, O Antigo Regime (1620–1807)*, ed. António Manuel Hespanha, 297–338. Lisbon: Círculo de Leitores.

———. 1998. *O Crepúsculo dos Grandes. A Casa e o Património da Aristocracia em Portugal (1750–1832)*. Lisbon: ICS/CM.

———. 2003. *Elites e Poder. Entre o Antigo Regime e o Liberalismo*. Lisbon: ICS.

Mundell, Robert. 1961. A Theory of Optimum Currency Areas. *The American Economic Review* 51 (4): 657–665.

Newitt, Malyn. 1981. *Portugal in Africa: The Last Hundred Years*. London: C. Hurst.

Nunes, Ana Bela. 2001. Actividade económica da população. In *Estatísticas Históricas Portuguesas*, ed. Nuno Valério, 149–197. Lisbon: INE.

Nunes, Ana Bela, and Nuno Valério. 2005. Moeda e bancos. In *História Económica de Portugal, 1700–2000, Vol. II, O Século XIX*, ed. Pedro Lains and Álvaro Ferreira da Silva, 283–304. Lisbon: ICS.

O'Rourke, Kevin H. 2000. Tariffs and Growth in the Late Nineteenth Century. *Economic Journal* 110: 456–483.
O'Rourke, Kevin H., and Jeffrey Williamson. 1999. *Globalization and History: The Evolution of a Nineteenth-Century Atlantic Economy*. Cambridge, MA: MIT Press.
Palma, Nuno, and Jaime Reis. 2018. From Convergence to Divergence: Portuguese Economic Growth 1527–1850. EHES Working Papers in Economic History, No. 137.
Pedreira, Jorge. 1994. *Estrutura Industrial e Mercado Colonial. Portugal e Brasil (1780–1830)*. Lisbon: Difel.
———. 1998. O fim do império luso-brasileiro. In *História da Expansão Portuguesa, Vol. IV – Do Brasil para África (1808–1930)*, ed. Francisco Bethencourt and Diogo Ramada Curto, 215–227. Lisbon: Círculo de Leitores.
———. 2013. O processo económico. In *História Contemporânea de Portugal: 1808–2010. Vol. 2 - A Construção Nacional, 1834–1890*, ed. Pedro Tavares de Almedia, 111–157. Madrid: Prisa Edições/Fundación Mapfre.
Ramos, Rui. 1994. *A Segunda Fundação (1890–1926)*. Lisboa: Círculo de Leitores.
———. 1996. O sistema fontista. In *Portugal Contemporâneo, Vol. I*, ed. António Reis, 509–530. Lisbon: Publicações Alfa.
Ramos, Rui, Bernardo Vasconcelos e Sousa, and Nuno Gonçalo Monteiro. 2009. *História de Portugal*. Lisbon: A Esfera dos Livros.
Reis, Jaime. 1982. Latifúndio e progresso técnico: a difusão da debulha mecânica no Alentejo, 1860–1930. *Análise Social* 18 (71): 371–433.
———. 1984. O atraso económico português em perspectiva histórica. *Análise Social* 20 (80): 7–28.
———. 1990. *A Evolução da Oferta Monetária Portuguesa, 1854–1912*. Lisbon: Banco de Portugal.
———. 1993. *O Atraso Económico Português em Perspectiva Histórica: Estudos sobre a Economia Portuguesa na Segunda Metade do Século XIX, 1850–1930*. Lisbon: IN-CM.
———. 1994. Aspectos da história monetária portuguesa da segunda metade do século XIX. *Análise Social* 29 (125–126): 33–54.
———. 1996a. First to Join the Gold Standard, 1854. In *Currency Convertibility: The Gold Standard and Beyond*, ed. Jorge Braga de Macedo, Barry Eichengreen, and Jaime Reis, 159–181. London: Routledge.

———. 1996b. *O Banco de Portugal, das Origens a 1914, Antecedentes, Fundação, Consolidação – 1821–1857*. Lisbon: Banco de Portugal.

———. 2000. The Gold Standard in Portugal, 1854–91. In *Monetary Standards in the Periphery, Paper, Silver and Gold, 1854–1933*, ed. Pablo Martin Aceña and Jaime Reis, 69–111. Houndmills, Basingstoke: Macmillan.

———. 2005. O trabalho. In *História Económica de Portugal, 1700–2000, Vol. II, O Século XIX*, ed. Pedro Lains and Álvaro Ferreira da Silva, 119–151. Lisbon: ICS.

Rodrigues, Teresa Ferreira. 2009. O século XIX. In *História da População Portuguesa. Das Longas Permanências à Conquista da Modernidade*, 327–416. Porto: Afrontamento e CEPESE.

Roldan, Alba. 2018. Spain and the Classical Gold Standard: Short- and Long-Term Analyses. Universitat de Barcelona Working Papers, No. 385.

Rowland, Robert. 1998. O porblema da emigração: dinâmicas e modelos. In *História da Expansão Portuguesa, Vol. IV – Do Brasil para África (1808–1930)*, ed. Francisco Bethencourt and Diogo Ramada Curto, 304–323. Lisbon: Círculo de Leitores.

Salter, W.E.G. 1959. Internal and External Balance: The Role of Price and Expenditure Effects. *The Economic Record* 35 (71): 226–238.

Serrão, José Vicente. 1993. O quadro económico. In *História de Portugal, Vol. IV, O Antigo Regime (1620–1807)*, ed. António Manuel Hespanha, 71–117. Lisbon: Círculo de Leitores.

Silbert, Albert. 1970. O feudalismo português e a sua abolição. In *Do Portugal do Antigo Regime ao Portugal Oitocentista*, 85–108. Lisbon: Livros Horizonte.

———. 1978. *Le Portugal Méditerranéen à la fin de l'Ancien Régime, XVIIIe-Début du XIXe siècle, Vol. I*. Lisbon: INIC.

Silva, Ana Cristina Nogueira da, and António Manuel Hespanha. 1993. A identidade portuguesa. In *História de Portugal, Vol. IV, O Antigo Regime (1620–1807)*, ed. António Manuel Hespanha, 18–37. Lisbon: Círculo de Leitores.

Silva, António Martins da. 1994. As finanças públicas. In *História de Portugal, Vol. V, O Liberalismo (1807–1890)*, ed. Luís Reis Torgal and João Lourenço Roque, 381–390. Lisbon: Círculo de Leitores.

———. 1997. *Nacionalizações e Privatizações em Portugal. A Desamortização Oitocentista*. Coimbra: Minerva.

Tena-Junguito, Antonio. 2010. Bairoch Revisited: Tariff Structure and Growth in the Late Nineteenth Century. *European Review of Economic History* 14 (1): 111–143.

Torres, Adelino. 1990. As colónias: da perda do Brasil à luta contra a escravatura. In *Portugal contemporâneo, Vol. I*, ed. António Reis, 137–150. Lisbon: Publicações Alfa.

Valério, Nuno. 2001. Contas nacionais. In *Estatísticas Históricas Portuguesas*, ed. Nuno Valério, 505–535. Lisbon: INE.

Valério, Nuno, Ana Bela Nunes, Carlos Bastien, Rita Martins de Sousa, and Sandra Domingos Costa. 2006. *História do Sistema Bancário Português, Vol. I, Da Formação do Primeiro Banco Português à Assunção pelo Banco de Portugal das Funções de Banco Central, 1822–1931*. Lisbon: Banco de Portugal.

Xavier, Ângela Barreto, and António Manuel Hespanha. 1993. A representação da sociedade e do poder. In *História de Portugal, Vol. IV, O Antigo Regime (1620–1807)*, ed. António Manuel Hespanha, 121–144. Lisbon: Círculo de Leitores.

3

World War I and the 1920s Financial Crisis

The chronology of political events is not necessarily the most adequate to apply to economic events and processes. But that is not the case of the period analyzed in this chapter, as the Portuguese economy was strongly affected by a set of extremely important political events. We should not count among those events the regime change taking place in 1910, whereby the Portuguese monarchy was replaced by a republic. As a matter of fact, the republican revolution, besides the change of nature of the head of state, did not correspond to an institutional transformation of the kind that was operated by the liberal revolutions in the previous century, with paramount effects on society and the economy. There was no abolition of social classes or sweeping redistribution of political power and economic assets to new elites. Replacing the king by a president did not affect the fundamental nature of the relationship between political, social and economic agents: the First Republic inherited without substantial change the principles established by the liberal revolution; we can even look at the period of the existence of the regime (1910–1926) precisely as that of the completion of the most important changes coming from the previous century.

L. Amaral, *The Modern Portuguese Economy in the Twentieth and Twenty-First Centuries*, Palgrave Studies in Economic History,
https://doi.org/10.1007/978-3-030-24548-1_3

The crucial political event impacting the Portuguese economy in this period was World War I. Of course, this was not specific to Portugal, but we would not be able to understand the evolution of the Portuguese economy in this period without taking it into consideration. The magnitude of the war left no country unaffected, participating in it or not. By the end of it, Western elites tried to return to the economic rules of the second half of the nineteenth century, based on free trade and the gold standard, but they soon realized the impossibility of doing so. In the words of David Thomson (1966, p. 601): "modern war is a revolution, and [...], [by 1918], the economic world of 1913 had already passed into history as much as had the Habsburg and Romanoff Empires". As a matter of fact, nothing of the kind had ever been seen: 60 million persons mobilized, 8 million dead, 7 million incapacitated, and 15 million wounded; the end of four empires, three of them having existed for centuries: the German Reich, the Austro-Hungarian Empire, the Russian Empire, and the Ottoman Empire; the first communist regime of the history of humankind, in the territory of the largest of those dead empires; and ten new countries in Europe, many of them without the minimal conditions for political or economic viability. Portugal could not have been left outside of this maelstrom, and the consequences were felt on many economic dimensions.

1 The Course of Political Events: From the Late Nineteenth Century to the Outbreak of the War

The political system of the constitutional monarchy entered into a process of progressive degradation during the last decade of the nineteenth century and the first of the next. Between 1893 and 1906, the Government was, alternatively, in the hands of two parties, one leaning more to the left, the other to the right. This alternation was essentially promoted by the king, who, under the principle of the "moderating power" enshrined in the 1826 Constitutional Charter, was able to systematically depose and nominate governments with a large degree of freedom (Ramos et al. 2009). The political system had a series of structural flaws. The first was that the Government in power always won the elections: the electoral process for the parliament was so marred by fraud that elections did not serve the purpose of making parties alternate in power. Everything depended on the continuous negotiation between the king and the political parties, according to a process that worked more or less as follows: once the king and a certain section of the political class found that the Government in power could not continue, the king would depose the Government, nominate a new one, and ask the new Government to organize parliamentary elections; the new Government would then use a vast array of mechanisms of electoral fraud to win them; and the situation would last until the king deposed again the previously nominated Government and put a new one in its place, thus reinitiating the cycle (Ramos et al. 2009).

Even if the elections were not very meaningful, the franchise was wide between 1878 and 1895. In the former year, a new law enlarged the right to vote to those men that were classified as "heads of family",[1] a condition adding to others coming from previous legislation, which limited the right to vote to literate people having a certain level of wealth. The number of potential voters jumped in that year from 478,509 to 824,726, something that corresponded to roughly 72% of all men of more than 21 years of age (close to universal male voting rights) and made of the Portuguese legislation one of the most open in the Europe of the time (Ramos et al. 2009). But, as seen above, this was not enough to guarantee fair elections. In the sequence of the political, colonial and financial crisis of 1891–1892, the system of understanding between the king and the political class led to an increasingly less transparent situation. For instance, in 1895, the Government in power decided to close the parliament and rule by decree, introducing a series of reforms, including a change in the electoral legislation that restricted again voting rights, by excluding the group that had obtained them in 1878, the "heads of family". The number of potential voters shrank to about 590,000 (Ramos et al. 2009).

[1]Law 8 May 1878.

This was the context in which a republican party appeared in the political scene, offering a "systemic" solution to the country's problems. According to this party, such problems did not depend on any specific Government in power but on the monarchy itself. The Portuguese Republican Party (*Partido Republicano Português*, PRP) was an established reality in the Portuguese political system by the early 1880s. Progressively, the PRP polarized the general disquiet in relation to many aspects of the life of the country. From 1901 onward, the existing traditional parties started to disintegrate in a myriad of factions. In May 1907, the king allowed again the ruling Government to close the parliament in order to operate a series of reforms: it was the second dictatorship in roughly one decade. But on 1 February 1908 the king and his elder son (and natural heir to the throne) were killed in central Lisbon. The period going from then until the republican revolution of 5 October 1910 corresponds to the final disruption of the system of the constitutional monarchy, with the PRP in constant growth (Ramos et al. 2009). Between 3rd and 5th October, a group of military operatives (mostly of intermediate and low rank), together with some members of radical secret societies with close ties to the Freemasonry, organized a rebellion in Lisbon. On the morning of 5th October, they abolished the monarchy. Portugal became one of the only two modern republics in Europe, the other being France (the Third Republic) (Ramos et al. 2009). A provisional Government ruled for practically one year. In May 1911, a parliament was elected to draft a Constitution, which was approved on 18th August of the same year. On 4th September, the provisional Government gave place to the first constitutional Government.

The provisional Government as well as the following constitutional ones was too absorbed with political confrontation to follow clear economic guidelines. Something became clear from the early days of the new regime: the republicans were as divided among themselves as the liberals had been almost one century before. Electoral fraud and political instability became the norm, but now with one major problem in relation to the constitutional monarchy: since the 1911 Constitution had put the parliament at the center of the political system, giving the President only a minor role, no one could exert the "moderating power" that was typical of kings during the constitutional monarchy. This meant that fraudulent elections always resulted in the victory of the faction of the PRP that controlled the mechanisms of fraud (the so-called Democrats). Voting rights were again restricted, with a new electoral law in 1913, amended in 1915[2]: income and wealth restrictions disappeared but literacy became again a requisite. Due to the extremely high level of illiteracy in the country this made the number of voters shrink again, to about 400,000 (Lopes 2012). The consequence of this non-inclusive political system was a spiral of political violence, as the excluded factions tried to find a way of reaching power through revolts or coups d'état. This led to a succession of governments too weak to follow any consistent policy (Ramos et al. 2009).

The most important economic measures taken in the first four years of the regime were few. One was the recognition to workers of the right to strike, a novelty in relation to the constitutional monarchy.[3] But the law was very restrictive, facing strong union opposition. Another important measure was a monetary reform abolishing the Portuguese currency of five centuries (the real) and substituting it with a new one, the escudo. This substitution was little more than symbolic, as the new monetary unit corresponded to the value of 1000 réis while keeping the same definition in gold of the real, 1.626 g.[4] Such as in the case of the real, this corresponded only to the official monetary system, however; parallel to it there was an actual system where the escudo ran initially at a depreciated value of less 15% to the official one (Valério 2001a; Nunes and Valério 2005).

Some attention was also given to public finance: four new decrees in 1911 introduced some mild progressivity in the real estate tax (*contribuição predial*) and in the inheritance tax (*contribuição sucessória*) and abolished some taxes. The extent of the changes was very limited, however (Marques 1978; Mata 2005). Between 1912 and 1914, there was a serious effort of different governments to invert the budget deficits coming from the last years of the constitutional monarchy and the first of

[2]Law 3, 3 July 1913 and Law 314, 1 June 1915.

[3]Decree 6 December 1910.

[4]Decree 22 May 1911.

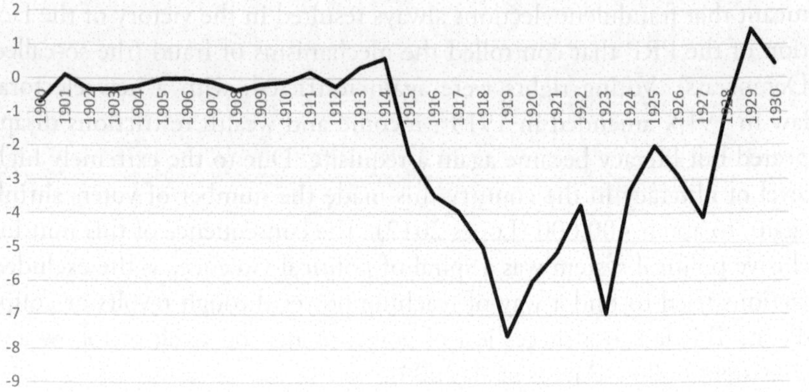

Fig. 1 Government budget deficit, Portugal, 1900–1930 (% GDP) (*Source* Mata [2001] and Valério [2001b])

the Republic. An austerity package that mostly compressed expenditures was able to deliver balance and even surplus, in 1913 (Fig. 1). But the outbreak of World War I would simply destroy all these efforts, besides many other effects.

2 The War and Its Consequences (1914–1922)

Portugal participated in the war as a belligerent but not from the start. When the war broke out between August and September 1914, the Portuguese Government thought of making the country align with the Entente powers, especially Britain. As Spain was then entertaining annexation ideas with respect to Portugal, the Portuguese authorities believed that joining the Entente would be enough to keep the country safe from these threats. But Britain was able to contain initially the belligerent tendencies of the Government, as it did not see any advantage in Portugal's participation. At the same time military activity started in Africa, namely in Angola and Mozambique, where German troops attacked the two Portuguese colonies in 1914, forcing the Portuguese to reply—Germany continued to have plans to annex part or the totality of the Portuguese colonies neighboring their own: Mozambique,

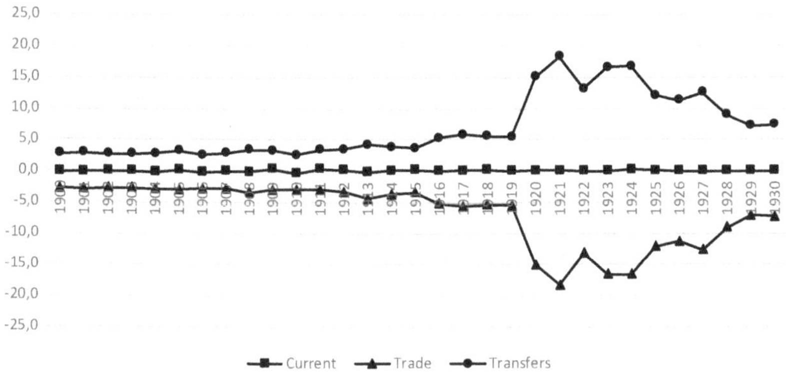

Fig. 2 Balance of payments, Portugal, 1900–1930 (% GDP) (*Source* Fontoura and Valério [2001] and Valério [2001b])

on the southern border of German East Africa (today's Tanzania), and Angola, on the northern border of German South West Africa (today's Namibia). Finally, on 9 March 1916, Germany declared war on Portugal, when the Portuguese Government arrested 70 German ships stationed in Portuguese ports at Britain's demand (Ramos et al. 2009; Oliveira 2010).

Independently of direct participation, the war had many effects on the Portuguese economy, not always in the same direction. On the one hand, it created negative conditions for foreign trade. Especially important were the difficulties in importing essential foodstuffs, such as wheat and cod, leading to various episodes of scarcity. Also important were the limits to imports of fuel and intermediate goods, such as coal, fertilizers, and machinery (Medeiros 1978; Lains 2007). Many exports had difficulties in their traditional markets, but some benefited from war conditions, such as tinned fish, a good in particularly high demand in belligerent countries both for soldiers at the front and civilian populations at home, together with wine, olive oil, and cattle. In the end, despite difficulties with particular goods, the aggregate picture for foreign trade was similar to the past in terms of balance, at least before direct military participation, as the trade deficit remained around the traditional level of 3–4% of GDP until 1918 (Fig. 2): as GDP had a negative behavior, this means that the value of trade also declined.

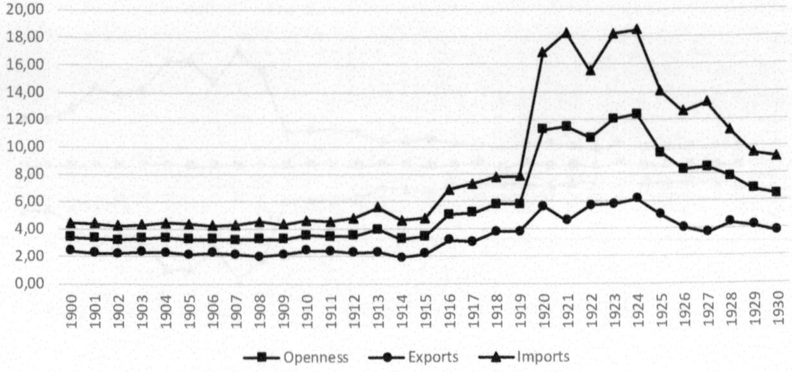

Fig. 3 Exports and imports, Portugal 1900–1930 (% GDP) Current prices; (Openness = 100 × [(Exports + Imports)/2]/GDP. *Source* Author's calculations, based on Fontoura and Valério [2001])

Fig. 4 Emigrants, Portugal, 1900–1930 (*Source* Baganha [1994])

After 1916, there was a slight deterioration of the trade balance, due to the increased import requirements resulting from Portugal's direct participation in the war, with the trade deficit reaching about 5% of GDP (Fig. 2). Figure 3 shows, precisely, the behavior of imports and exports. Another consequence of the war was the collapse of emigration (Fig. 4), with the consequent interruption of the influx of remittances. Re-exports of colonial goods were also negatively affected by the

Table 1 GDP per capita annual growth rates, 1900–1930 (%)

1900–1930	0.74
1910–1914	0.88
1914–1918	−1.64
1918–1923	3.31
1923–1926	−0.13
1918–1930	2.21

Source 1850–1910—Maddison (2003); 1910–1934—Batista et al. (1997)

conditions of the world market (Lains 1998). Even if these two factors had a negative impact on the balance of payments, they ended up by being offset by British loans (of which we will talk more below).

Restricted access to imported fuel and machinery created difficulties to all economic activities. These difficulties were compounded by soldier mobilization, in a number of 80,000 for the whole period of the war, representing about 4% of the male labor force. Labor scarcity generated pressures for higher wages, themselves pressured by higher food prices. Agriculture passed through a particularly difficult phase. Due to the restrictions in importing food products, the wartime governments expected Portuguese agriculture to replace imported goods. But this made life more difficult for farmers, as the Government introduced a system of official prices, which were set constantly below the increased cost of labor and the other inputs. As a large number of producers refused to sell their goods at the official prices, instead channeling them to a growing black market (or simply leaving their land idle), the Government upped the ante by creating a system of compulsory requisitioning and rationing (Pires 2009).

But if agriculture suffered from the war, some other activities derived benefits from it: besides those dedicated to exports in high demand during the period, there were also those thriving under the new conditions of "natural" protection, especially textiles, metals, and machinery (Medeiros 1978; Telo 1980). When adding all positive and negative influences, the final behavior of the economy was far from spectacular, as GDP per capita declined at the rate of −1.6% per year between 1914 and 1918 (Table 1). To this, we must add an extremely serious financial and monetary crisis. One first consequence on public finance

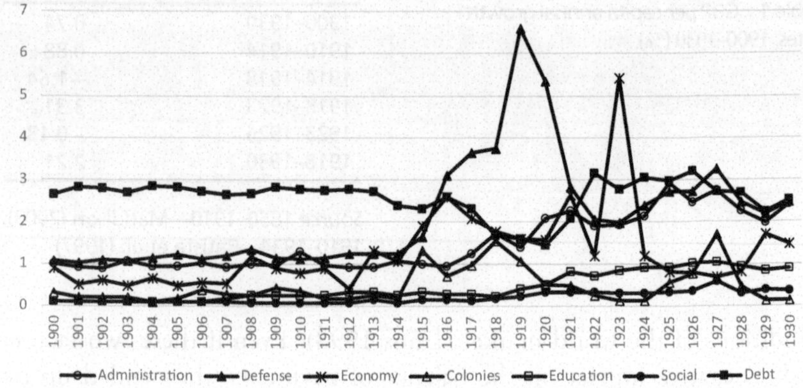

Fig. 5 Structure spending, Portugal 1900–1930 (% GDP) (*Source* Mata [2001] and Valério [2001b])

resulting from the war was to make military spending increase, passing from 1% of GDP in 1914 to 3% in 1916 and almost 7% in 1919. Another consequence was to make the "Economy" item grow as well, mostly because of governmental interventions in the food markets (Fig. 5). Wartime governments tried to obtain without success receipts covering the growth in spending, mostly by increasing existing taxes and imposing surcharges on tariffs (Nunes 2006). As a consequence, budget deficits ballooned: the 1914 surplus was immediately replaced by a deficit of 2% of GDP in 1915, increasing afterward to reach 5% in 1918 (Fig. 1). Thanks to the growth of these various expenditure items, the overall level of public spending expanded from 6% of GDP in 1914 to 10% in 1918 (Fig. 6). To note is the fact that this represented a structural shift, as the level of spending never returned after the war to prewar levels.

About one-third of military spending was financed through loans granted by Britain, amounting to 22 million pounds, thanks to an agreement negotiated in 1916, to be settled between the two countries only at the end of the war (Telo 1980; Valério 1994). But most of the growth in spending and of the budget deficits was financed by debt of the Government with the BoP, something that led to an inevitable expansion of the money supply. Between 1914 and 1923, the BoP's

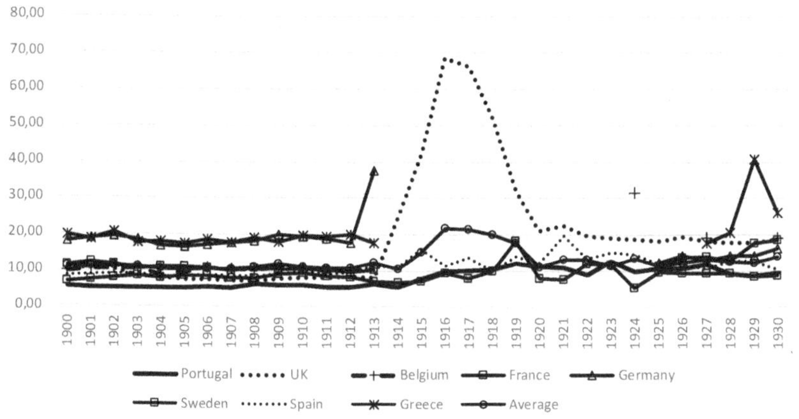

Fig. 6 Public spending, various European countries, 1900–1930 (% GDP) (*Source* Portugal: Mata [2001] and Valério [2001b]; for the other countries: Mauro et al. [2013])

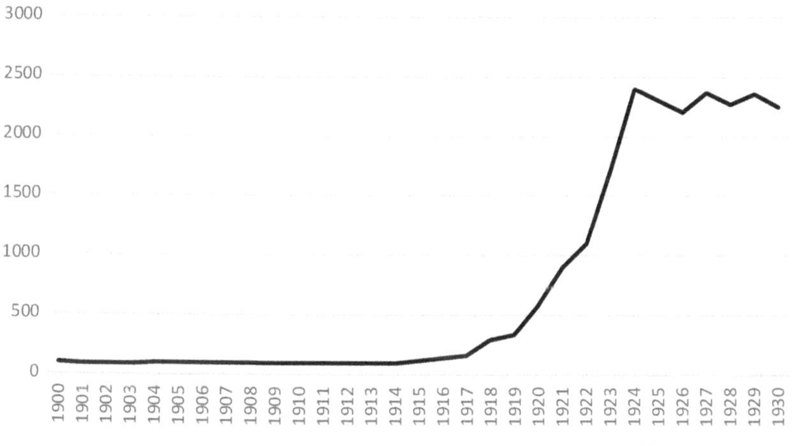

Fig. 7 Consumer price index, Portugal, 1900–1930 (1914 = 100) (*Source* Bastien [2001])

issuing of banknotes passed from 120 million escudos to more than one billion, leading, also inevitably, to an inflationary process (Santos 1996; Carvalho 2001; Valério 2001a) (Fig. 7). Contrary to what might be expected, this situation did not change with the end of the war. In fact, the fiscal and monetary crisis became even more serious then. At the root of this was the continuous deterioration of budget deficits: in 1919, the deficit reached the peak of 8% of GDP; and despite some improvement in the following years, by 1922 it was still 4%, deteriorating again to 7% in 1923 (Fig. 1). The reasons for this persistence were essentially two. From the expenditure side, the Government continued the policy of subsidizing some items fundamental to the general population, such as bread and transportation, to which a new kind of expenditure was added: pensions to war veterans or the families of those deceased in combat.

But the fundamental reason had its origin in taxes. Most existing taxes at the time were set in fixed quantities per good. This meant that their value declined progressively with inflation: by 1920 the value of taxes represented 50% less than in 1914 (Silva and Amaral 2010). Different postwar governments tried to change the situation, but their weakness never allowed them to introduce the proposed reforms (Martins 2012). Monetization of deficits had, thus, to continue, feeding an inflationist spiral. Inflation started immediately in the first year of the war and, by 1918, the general price level was three times higher than in 1914. But the situation became even more out of control in the six years after the end of the war, with prices reaching in 1924 a level 24 times higher than in 1914 (Fig. 7). Only the countries of Central Europe (and Finland) experienced higher inflation than Portugal (Table 2). After a decade and a half of existence, the escudo had lost 96% of its original value, more than its predecessor, the real, throughout its entire existence from 1435 to 1911 (Santos 1996; Nunes and Valério 2005).

Jointly with this crisis there was also an exchange rate crisis, thanks to which the escudo depreciated heavily (Fig. 8). Again, the situation was worse after than during the war, and the explanation lies simply in the continuation of the inflationary process, something that had the effect of, additionally, fueling speculative moves, as investors feared the ability of the Portuguese Government to settle the fiscal crisis. A process of capital flight ensued, making the situation even more serious (Telo 1980; Mata 1987; Santos 1996; Silva and Amaral 2010).

Table 2 Consumer price index, various countries, 1918–1926 (100 = 1914)

	1918	1919	1920	1921	1922	1923	1924	1925	1926
Hyperinflationary countries									
Austria	1163	2492	5115	9981	263,938	76	86	97	103
Germany	304	403	990	1301	14,602	13.2^{10}	128	140	141
Countries where inflation continued after 1920									
Portugal	293	335	580	909	1099	1726	2399	2306	2208
Belgium	1434	344	–	366	340	399	469	498	604
Finland	633	922	889	1055	1033	1033	1055	1100	1078
Italy	289	331	467	467	467	476	481	580	618
France	213	268	371	333	315	344	395	424	560
Countries where inflation was controlled after 1920									
Norway	253	275	300	277	231	218	239	243	206
Sweden	219	257	269	247	198	178	174	177	173
Denmark	182	211	261	232	200	206	216	211	284
UK	200	219	248	224	181	176	176	176	171
The Netherlands	162	176	194	169	149	144	145	144	138

Source Feinstein et al. (1997), except Portugal: Bastien (2001)

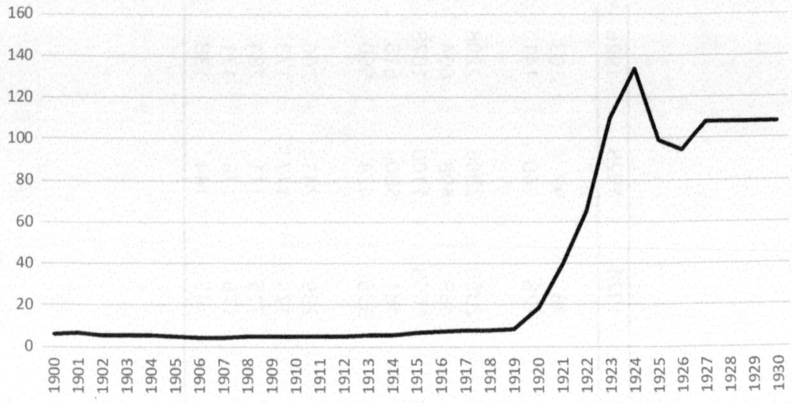

Fig. 8 Index of the exchange rate Real-Escudo/Sterling, 1900–1930 (1914 = 100) (*Source* Mata and Valério [1996])

3 The Stabilization (1922–1930)

Portuguese society and economy mobilized for the war at a considerably lower degree than in other belligerent countries. Portugal entered the conflict only two years after its outbreak, there was no military activity in its territory (if we except for moderate action in Angola and Mozambique), and the country was not a main contender in it. But this sort of reasoning is only valid in relative terms. In absolute and historical terms, the degree of mobilization was unprecedented. The number of soldiers mobilized for the three war fronts was of 80,000: 50,000 to Flanders and France and 30,000 to Angola and Mozambique. As Table 3 shows, this represented 1.4% of the population, a relevant figure, although much lower than in most major belligerents, with the exception of the United States. Spending on defense grew to reach 3.7% of GDP in 1918, again a low figure when compared with the main belligerents, as Table 4 shows, but still significant in historical terms. The number of dead soldiers was of 7000, or 0.1% of total population (Table 5), a figure to be interpreted in a similar manner: low in comparative terms, high in absolute terms.

Once the war was over, the process of dealing with its legacy started. In economic terms, the immediate postwar period was marked by

Table 3 Weight of soldier mobilization on total population (%)

France	11
Germany	7.3
Russia	4.3
UK	7.3
United States	1.7
Portugal	1.4

Source Eloranta and Harrison (2006), except Portugal, author's calculations based on Oliveira (2010) and Henriques and Rodrigues (2009)

Table 4 Military spending % GDP, 1918

France	59.39
Germany	38.80
UK	27.00
US	8.05
Portugal	3.74

Source Blum et al. (2014), except Portugal: Mata (2001) and Valério (2001b)

Table 5 Deaths in combat as % of total population, 1914–1918

France	3.4
Germany	3.0
Russia	1.1
UK	1.6
US	0.1
Portugal	0.1

Source Broadberry and Harrison (2005)

contradictory signs. On the one hand, many of the negative effects of the escudo's depreciation continued to be felt, making most imported goods dearer, from foodstuffs to machines. The difficulties were so serious, especially in what concerns the food supply, that the expression "subsistence crisis" became of current use at the time. Food scarcity, in its turn, led to pressures from labor for higher wages, resulting in one of the periods of stronger labor unrest in Portuguese history. But, on the other hand, exchange rate depreciation also gave a positive contribution, by allowing conditions of "natural" protection and lowering of export prices to persist: some activities thrived, although on the basis of goods of inferior quality, from textiles to tinned fish or even cement and fertilizers (Medeiros 1978; Telo 1980). In the end, the aggregate effect of these contradicting tendencies was positive for economic growth, with the economy growing 3.31% per year between 1918 and 1923 (Table 1).

Despite this positive aggregate behavior, the general feeling was one of crisis. In 1919, a military contingent of monarchical *émigrés* crossing the border from Spain attempted a restoration of the monarchical regime; the main cities were under an apparently perpetual agitation made of strikes and demonstrations, with workers, now inserted in better organized and more radical unions, claiming for higher wages and better working conditions; governments were weak, never surviving more than a few months, despite a constitutional reform in 1919 giving the President a certain moderating power over the parliament and the Government, something that in principle could have allowed for higher party rotation and representativeness of the regime (Lopes 2012). But this never worked well in practice, with the "Democratic Party" continuing to predominate and the opposition having very few expectations of reaching the Government through elections; as a consequence, revolts and coups d'état persisted. Then, on 19 October 1921, the prime minister together with other members of the Government (not belonging to the dominant faction) and revolutionary heroes from the early days of the republic was murdered in an event that passed into history under the name of "Bloody Night", which became a symbol of the lack of political normalcy of the regime (Ramos et al. 2009).

This chaotic environment made the settling of the fiscal and monetary crisis extremely difficult. Many ad hoc tax increases were adopted after 1918, but with no significant results. More thorough fiscal reforms were designed but they were never put in practice, due to governmental instability (Nunes 2006). However, in 1922, better conditions appeared, with a Government that lasted for almost two years. This Government took a series of measures to reduce fiscal spending and terminate excessive money emission. The international situation also helped, when various countries adopted the gold-exchange standard, in the sequence of the 1922 Genoa Conference (Santos 1996). One of the main concerns of the Government was to control the issuing of

Fig. 9 Average tariffs % of imports, Portugal, 1900–1930 (*Source* Fontoura and Valério [2001])

money emission by the BoP. But this required a previous serious effort to balance budgets. The first line of action with respect to the budget was directed at spending: the subsidies still surviving from the time of the war, such as the one dedicated to bread, were eliminated (Medeiros 1978), the admission of new civil servants was suspended, and a recently initiated program of construction of social housing was also terminated (Silva and Amaral 2010).

Then, the Government turned to receipts, initiating a more thorough fiscal reform. Many old taxes, some still coming from the *Ancien Régime*, were abolished. The creation of a modern personal income tax and of a general tax on transactions, together with a new method of collection of the real estate and industrial taxes, based on effective rather than presumed income, was designed (Valério 1994; Santos 1996; Nunes 2006).[5] The reform was complemented by the introduction of a new tariff schedule in 1923, as the value of tariffs had become vastly outdated, again as a consequence of inflation (Fig. 9).[6] The success of the reform was only partial: tax receipts did increase by 8.5% but this was not enough to balance the budget, despite the visible reduction of

[5]Law 1368, 21 September 1922.

[6]Decree 8471, 27 March 1923 and Decree 8747, 31 March 1923.

the deficit (Fig. 1). The policy continued during the following governments, leading to an even stronger reduction in 1924, although this time essentially due to a policy based on the suppression of many public services. But political and social turmoil never allowed for much governmental stability, transforming these measures only into incomplete steps to the full resolution of the crisis.

Even if incomplete, the reduction of the budget deficit was enough for the Government to finally stop asking the BoP the same amounts of fresh money as before. The 1922–1923 Government had still used this resource, but the 1924 one interrupted it altogether. The end of the monetization of budget deficits let inflation slow down and even stop: in 1924 prices stabilized (Fig. 7). This was an inevitable condition to settle the persistent external depreciation of the escudo. The 1922–1923 Government decreed that exporting companies should deposit in the BoP 50% of the foreign exchange obtained with their activities, thus allowing for a reinforcement of the BoP's reserves. In the sequence of this measure, the BoP initiated a systematic policy of intervention in the exchange market through open market operations. On the other hand, the Government used the returns of a sale of silver by the BoP to create a fund dedicated to intervene in the market, also with the purpose of stabilizing the value of the escudo (Santos 1996). The 1924 Government reinforced these measures with the adoption of a policy of paying the interest on Portuguese debt with a fixed escudo/sterling exchange rate (Mata 1987; Nunes and Valério 2005). Finally, emigrant remittances reanimated, thanks to the resumption of the traditional emigration flows to Brazil (Fig. 4).

Currency and price stabilization was essentially concluded in 1924, even if some difficulties resurfaced in 1926. The escudo sustained its fall in relation to sterling, and even experienced some re-appreciation in 1925 (Fig. 8), although this was not enough for the Government to feel confident enough to reinsert the escudo in the gold standard—something that a number of currencies did between 1924 and 1926 (Silva and Amaral 2010). There were many reasons for this. First, governmental instability continued, raising doubts over the consistency of the policy initiated in 1922. Second, despite reduction, deficits did not disappear, still reaching 3.3% of GDP in 1924 and 2% in 1925—and debt was still at 75% of GDP in 1924. In 1925, there was a major episode of banknote falsification, introducing one more ad hoc element of uncertainty (Silva and Amaral 2010).

Uncertainty increased further after a military revolution deposed the First Republic regime and initiated a Military Dictatorship on 28 May 1926. The deficit rose again, reaching 4% of GDP, and the Government failed to obtain a loan from the League of Nations in 1927 (Valério 1994). This was the pretext António de Oliveira Salazar used to appear in 1928 in the political scene as the man capable of definitely solving the financial crisis. Salazar reached the position of Minister of Finance in April 1928 and applied a thorough fiscal reform, although incorporating some measures taken by his predecessor (who, in turn, had himself incorporated measures proposed by a commission for fiscal reform presided by Salazar),[7] reaching a close to balanced budget in 1928 and a surplus one in 1929 (Fig. 1). Much of this reform was based on the reversion of the 1922–1924 fiscal reform. One aspect of this reversion was the return to presumed income as a basis for tax collection, rather than real income. Another was the abolition of the income tax introduced in 1922, substituting it with a series of disaggregated taxes: a reformed real estate tax (*contribuição predial*), a reformed industrial tax (*contribuição industrial*), a new wage tax (*imposto profissional*), a reformed capital tax (*imposto sobre a aplicação de capitais*) added with a new tax applied to overall income (*imposto complementar*), and a public salvation tax (*imposto de salvação pública*) to be collected from civil servants. *Imposto complementar* allowed for some progressivity: the tax was collected over the sum assessed in all other income taxes, with progressive rates being applied. In addition, tariffs were reinforced in 1929.[8] From the side of spending, there was not much change, even if some new principles were introduced, especially a right of veto attributed to the Minister of Finance over the spending of the other ministries, a method that has received the label of Salazar's "financial dictatorship" (Valério 2006; Silva and Amaral 2010).

[7]Decrees 15,288, 15,289, 15,290, 15,291, and 15,292, all from 30 March 1928; Decrees 14,465, 14,466, and 14,467, all from 14 May 1928; and Decree 16,731, 13 April 1929.

[8]Decree 17,823, 31 December 1929.

Thanks to such kind of procedures, Salazar was able not only to balance the budget but to reduce public debt as well: short-term external debt was entirely repaid, part of internal short-term debt was also fully repaid while another part was converted into long-term debt (Valério 1994; Santos 1996). As the exchange rate with sterling stabilized (Fig. 7), Salazar saw this as the opportunity to insert the escudo in the gold-exchange standard, something that happened on 9 June 1931: the escudo was defined as having a weight of 0.0739 g in gold with a purity of 900/1000, corresponding to a parity with sterling of 110 escudos (Valério 1984).[9] This represented a slight depreciation, meaning that Salazar opted to incorporate the previous devaluation of the currency, mostly with the objective of preserving some exporting competitiveness. Membership of the gold-exchange standard would only last for three months; however, as on 21 September the Government decided to remove the escudo from the system, pegging it to sterling and the US dollar instead: the escudo would remain primarily pegged to the British currency but, in case the latter reached the value of 3.33 US dollars, it would then be pegged to the American currency (Valério 1984). This time the problem was not the Portuguese currency's weakness but rather sterling's, which abandoned then the gold standard for good. Independently of this, the gold standard was then collapsing, with the different currencies aligning under different currency blocs (Eichengreen 1996).

The fiscal and monetary stabilization strategy followed by the Portuguese authorities did not differ much from that followed by other European governments. At the end of the war all countries had to face a similar dilemma: either adopt a deflationary policy in order to restore prewar financial balance and reintroduce the currency in a fixed exchange rate system, or rely on an inflationary policy (with exchange rate depreciation), assuming the impossibility of returning immediately to the pre-war situation. As John Maynard Keynes said in his 1923 *A Tract on Monetary Reform*, the inflation ravaging various countries in the early 1920s was not the result of bad monetary policy but rather

[9]Decree 19,869, 9 June 1931.

of a way of distributing the costs of the war and transferring resources between different social groups. An inflationary policy with depreciation imposed a toll on those whose savings or income was fixed but prevented a sudden stop of economic growth as well as the eruption of serial bankruptcies and high unemployment. The opposite was true of a deflationary policy. The Portuguese authorities followed the two alternatives in different moments. In a first moment, until 1922–1924, they opted for the inflationary method. In a second moment, from 1924 onward, they opted for the deflationary method. This was not original in the European context, as it corresponded to the same sequence of events happening in the famous cases of postwar hyperinflation—Germany, Austria, Hungary, Czechoslovakia, and Poland—as well as in those of more moderate inflation—France, Belgium, or Italy (Aldcroft 1977; Eichengreen 1996); on the contrary, this was not the solution adopted by the countries that proceeded immediately to stabilization after the war, suffering consequently the inevitable deflationary effects (Silva and Amaral 2010) (Table 2).

In the end, Portugal had one of the most successful stabilization programs of the period, although only completed in 1931, by the Military Dictatorship, with Salazar in the position of Minister of Finance: from then on, the country acquired consistent monetary and financial credibility, inaugurating a period of almost forty years of balanced budgets (only interrupted during World War II) (Silva and Amaral 2010). As in the case of the countries of the first group mentioned above, Portugal had an episode of strong economic growth during the inflationary years and another of contraction during the deflationary ones: GDP per capita grew at 3.3% a year between 1918 and 1923, and at −0.13% between 1923 and 1926. The overall 1918–1926 period, however, turned out to be positive, with a rate of growth of 1.81% a year (Table 1).

The war represented a structural break in terms of the weight of the Portuguese Government on economic activity (Fig. 6). Responsibility for this has to be attributed, first, to spending on defense, which jumped from about 1% of GDP before the war to about 2.5% during the 1920s (after a massive increase during the war), but also to general public administration, which followed a similar path. Debt service remained at

Table 6 Structure of public spending (some items), various countries, 1913–1920 (% GDP)

	Education 1913	Defense 1920	Debt 1920	Social 1920
Belgium	–	2.4	6.6	0.5
France	1.3	1.9	4.5	0.6
Germany	2.7	0.9	–	–
Italy	0.6	2.7	4.4	–
Spain	0.4	5.8	2,3	0.4
Sweden	–	2.0	1.0	1.1
UK	1.1	2.6	5.7	1.4
Portugal	0.5	5.4	1.4	0.3

Source Tanzi and Schuknecht (2000), except "Social": Lindert (2004), and Portugal: Mata (2001) and Valério (2001b)

a high level as well. A lower contribution was given by spending in the colonies (and only in the years between 1924 and 1927) and education, passing from around 0.2 to 0.3% of GDP in the final years of the monarchy and the early days of the republic to 1% from the 1920s onward (Fig. 5). In comparative terms, the size of Portuguese Government converged slightly to the European average but remained among the smallest (Fig. 6). The growth of the weight of administration on GDP in Portugal parallels that witnessed in other countries and is explainable by the fact that Government interventionism in markets increased in all countries during the war, breaking with the traditional liberal framework coming from the nineteenth century: the responsibilities governments acquired in the control of foreign trade, in the setting of prices (and their enforcement), in food rationing or in various instances of requisition of private resources made of them a more permanent presence in the economy (Broadberry and Harrison 2005; Pires 2009). As for military spending, Portugal seems to have converged much strongly to the European norm than in other respects (Table 6). This seems to reveal a higher difficulty of Portuguese governments to demobilize after the war. The growth of spending in education reflects the relevance attributed by republican governments to the issue of literacy and education in general (Magalhães 2010). Republican governments blamed the monarchy for the lack of investment in the sector, something that was reflected in appalling levels of illiteracy, and proposed to invert the situation. The republican regime created a Ministry of Education and expanded the number of schools and teachers. But in the end the effort was low by European standards (Palma and Reis 2018).

The very slow growth of social spending made by the Government, again below the European average (Table 6), does not reveal lack of interest of republican authorities on the issue but rather a certain inefficiency in implementing the policies designed. Many republican politicians and intellectuals had followed with interest the rise of public schemes of social protection in various Western countries, especially those involving compulsory social insurance. As a consequence, they tried to introduce a similar system in Portugal (Cardoso and Rocha 2009). A Ministry of Labor was created in 1916 as well as an Institute for Compulsory Social Insurance and General Welfare (*Instituto de Seguros Sociais Obrigatórios e Previdência Geral*, ISSOPG) in 1919.[10] The objective of the program was to replace various voluntary institutions that had appeared during the nineteenth century. But its implementation failed, especially due to the difficulties of the various governments to square the fiscal and financial crisis with the necessary spending to make the program operative. In 1925, the experience of the Ministry of Labor was terminated and the ISSOPG entered into a sort of limbo (Cardoso and Rocha 2009).

4 The Empire

Despite the "national humiliation" of the 1890 British Ultimatum, Portugal was still able to put a significant amount of African territory under its formal rule in the sequence of the scramble for Africa, something quite remarkable for a country with so little international power (Alexandre 2000). Table 7 puts the Portuguese Empire in perspective: although it was clearly the smallest in comparison with the other European imperial powers, the figures were still relevant in absolute terms; and in what concerns the area under Portuguese control, it was

[10] Decree 5640, 10 May 1919.

Table 7 Colonies: population and land surface, 1913

	1913	
	Population (millions)	Land surface (million km²)
British dominions	19.9	19.5
British colonies	380.1	13.5
French colonies	48.4	10.7
Dutch colonies	44.1	2.1
Portuguese colonies	7.2	2.1

Source Eloranta and Harrison (2010), except Portugal: Valério and Tjipilica (2006)

at least the same as the one amassed by the Dutch. But control over this large landmass and population did not mean easy access to assets. The vast territories over which Portugal established its formal sovereignty were subject to different kinds of pressures, some external others internal. Externally, the pressures came from the remaining European imperial powers. One of the reasons Portugal had been able to acquire those territories was, paradoxically, its international weakness. Such aggressively expansionist powers as Britain and Germany preferred many times to let Portugal rule certain areas of the African continent than conceding them to each other. But they never really stopped coveting the Portuguese territories. In 1898, for instance, Britain and Germany signed a secret agreement whereby Angola and Mozambique should be divided between British and German areas of influence. Although the agreement was not immediately put in practice, it was reanimated later, on the eve of World War I, in 1912 and 1913, as an instrument to diffuse the tensions between the two countries (Newitt 1981; Alexandre 1993, 1998). Another example of these international pressures was the case of the campaigns against the labor conditions of the indigenous populations in the Portuguese colonies, one in the 1890s, another in the 1920s. These campaigns were understood both in Portugal and outside of Portugal as an instrument to delegitimize Portuguese colonial rule, thus opening the way for a possible expropriation of the newly acquired empire. They resulted from a new perspective on European colonialism after World War I, where a supposed "civilizing mission" associated with European domination replaced the former, more predatory, approach (Newitt 1981; Alexandre 1993, 1998).

But internal pressures were equally serious. The Portuguese African territories were not coherent units in geographical, ethnic, or economic terms. They had been assembled as a consequence of diplomacy in order to define spheres of influence of European imperial powers and had not taken into consideration the local realities on the ground. What is more, formal rule did not mean actual rule. The latter would only be achieved, and even then in an imperfect manner, after practically half a century of confrontation between the Portuguese colonial authorities and different indigenous groups, in so-called campaigns of "pacification" (Oliveira 2014). In the words of Newitt (1981, p. 49): "almost every year from 1875 to 1924 saw military expeditions undertaken in all three of their mainland colonies, and 'police' operations were still needed in the years that followed". According to Clarence-Smith (1985), by 1910, the Portuguese controlled only about 10% of the populations of Angola, Guinea, and Timor; by 1920, the situation was altogether another one, with only some remote areas outside Portuguese control. Inside each of the territories, there were dozens of different ethnic groups, many conflicting with each other, with some having better relations with the Portuguese than others. The life of Portugal as a colonial power in Africa in this period consisted basically in trying to impose actual rule while putting in motion a sort balance of power between the different African groups through a combination of military force and diplomacy (Newitt 1981; Alexandre 1998). Portugal did not even make a significant effort to colonize these territories with mainland white settlers, which remained residual throughout the period. The two colonies with a larger white contingent were Angola, where they represented 0.4% of the overall population in 1900 and 0.9% in 1930 (Pimenta 2005) and Mozambique, where proportions were similar (Castelo 2007).

But not even full formal rule made these Portuguese territories economically coherent, and many times Portuguese colonial rule fragmented them even further. The 1892 tariff tried to establish a system of imperial preference, but tariffs were never uniformly applied throughout the colonies: "in Mozambique a separate commercial agreement with the Transvaal allowed free trade between the two countries; the chartered companies in Mozambique were allowed to set their own tariffs; in Angola the northern Congo district had a separate tariff regime"

(Newitt 1981, p. 73). And beyond tariffs, the economies of each of the territories could be seen as a collection of different and separate economic areas.

The Mozambican economy consisted first of a southern tip, where the capital Lourenço Marques was located, functioning as a sort of annex to the neighboring mining economy of the Rand. The essential economic activity in this area was the export of labor to the gold mines on the other side of the border. A railway line opened in 1895 with the main purpose of transporting this labor back and forth between Mozambique and the Rand. These workers were the source of a large volume of remittances, which the Portuguese authorities taxed heavily. The number of workers involved in the process is difficult to establish, but estimates point to something like 100,000 per year in the early twentieth century (Newitt 1981, 1995; Neves 2001). The free trade agreement signed with the Transvaal in 1868 made of this part of the country mostly an economic region of Transvaal/South Africa (Newitt 1981, 1995).

To the north of this region, most of the territory had been leased to various entities. These concessions arose, precisely, out of the difficulty of Portuguese authorities to establish a formal rule. The concession entities were mostly foreign, with sovereign powers, exerted through their own armies and police forces. They collected taxes and imposed their own economic rules. The charter of the Mozambique Company was in place between 1891 and 1941, for a vast area between the Zambezi river and the 22nd parallel. Its developmental successes were very meager, consisting basically of the operation of the railway linking the coastal city of Beira to Rhodesia, of the collection of taxes over the indigenous population, and of the recruitment of cheap (or even free) labor to various employers; in a later moment, the company sub-leased parts of its concession to third companies that became quite successful, such as Sena Sugar Estates (Newitt 1981, 1995; Clarence-Smith 1985). Further north, another vast area of the territory between the rivers Rovuma and Lurio was conceded to the Niassa Company, with a charter running from 1894 to 1929. The successes of this company were even more modest than those of the Mozambique Company; with its activity consisting essentially of tax collection through various means, the development of a few plantations for cotton, sugar, tea, or sisal was not enough to change the nature of the economy of the area, which remained essentially under traditional native activities based on such goods as bee wax, cashew, coffee, banana, beans, corn, or manioc, as well as some fishing (Newitt 1981, 1995; Clarence-Smith 1985; Neves 2001).

Between the two companies lay the territory of the "prazos". These were also generalized concessions that had been operative since the seventeenth century and given to different persons, mostly of Indian and Portuguese origin. In the late nineteenth century and the early twentieth century, there were about 140 of these concessions. The success of these "prazos" was also very limited, consisting again essentially on tax collection and recruitment of labor. Only in the early twentieth century, some plantations started appearing in a few of the "prazos". The system ended in 1930 (Newitt 1981; Dias 1998).

At the same time this was happening, and in a manner largely independent from Portuguese policy, traditional economic activities and trade connections continued and sometimes even intensified. This happened, for instance, with the Angolan rubber boom of the late nineteenth century and early twentieth century, a boom that was accompanied by the growth of the exports of wax, groundnuts, and sesame. The link between hinterland producers and the coastal exporters was established by a kind of caravan trade that had existed for centuries (Newitt 1981).

The economy of Angola, despite not being legally divided in concessions, as in the case of Mozambique, was equally fragmented in economic terms. The only chartered company operating in the territory was the Moçâmedes Company, occupying a large area in the south, close to the border with German South West Africa. But this company was very different from those operating in Mozambique. As it did not have the same kind of sovereign rights, it could not simply live out of tax collection and labor mobilization. Consequently, it ended up by promoting some cattle ranches and cotton plantations, besides building the Benguela railway line (Newitt 1981). Another company established in Angola was Diamang, created in 1917 with the objective of exploring the diamond deposits existing in the northwestern region of the Lunda. Diamang did not have any kind of sovereign rights, but was exonerated from taxation in Angola; its owners were mostly foreign, first Belgian, then German (with some French, Portuguese and American partners), and a significant fraction of the profits were handed to the Portuguese colonial authorities (Newitt 1981; Clarence-Smith 1985; Pedreira 1998). The rest of the economy was based on the traditional economic activities of the indigenous population, based on such goods as peanuts, palm oil, bee wax, or ivory, except for some coffee plantations run by white Portuguese in the Cazengo Highlands close to Luanda (in the northwest of the country) and some coffee and cotton plantations in the Huila Plateau in the south, mostly run by Boers and Madeirans (Newitt 1981; Freudenthal 2001).

Outside the big territories of Angola and Mozambique, in the small units of Guinea, Cape Verde, and São Tomé, the Portuguese economic approach varied. In Guinea, it never went much beyond a coordinating role of the marketing of the indigenous production of groundnuts and rice, never trying to interfere much with traditional methods of production or to establish large-scale plantations (Newitt 1981; Silveira 1998). In Cape Verde, a ten-island archipelago subject to frequent episodes of drought, most economic activity was of the traditional, subsistence kind, based on fishing, corn, beans, potato, or manioc, with some exports of salt, coffee, sugar, and fodder crops. The strategic location of the territory on the west coast of Africa allowed some of its islands to specialize in shipping services. The repetition of the drought episodes and the difficulties with some of the export markets created a vast migratory movement of Cape Verdeans in the direction of the United States and South America (Newitt 1981; Estêvão 1998; Reis 2001). As for São Tomé e Príncipe, the two-island archipelago gave birth to one of the biggest successes of the Portuguese Empire: cocoa exports. The amount of cocoa exported from São Tomé to world markets made quick fortunes, mostly of Portuguese capitalists investing in plantations on the island. Coffee also contributed to the export mix of the territory. Cocoa production became embroiled in an international controversy over the forced labor used in the plantations. The Portuguese plantation owners were accused of using forced workers imported from other colonies, especially Angola, with the collaboration of colonial authorities. Some truth seems to have existed in these accusations, and the Portuguese colonial authorities felt the need to change the contract system in the early twentieth century. From the 1920s onward, cocoa production declined massively, due to a bush-killing disease, never to recover (Newitt 1981; Nascimento 1998, 2001).

The lack of resources to develop seriously this variegated collection of economic areas made of the Portuguese African empire in this period essentially a structure to harness African labor (Jerónimo 2010). This was a natural extension of its slave-trading past. The most important pieces of colonial legislation were dedicated to manage this resource. In 1899, a comprehensive labor code was introduced, being reformed in 1914, although without significant change,[11] and in 1901 the same was done for land.[12] The labor code essentially legalized forced labor. According to it, "indigenous" peoples had an obligation to work, either through a recognized profession or by cultivating their land. Failing these conditions, they had to contract themselves to an employer and, failing the latter, they could be forced to do it by the colonial administration. Furthermore, the indigenous population could at any moment be called to work for the administration, either in public works, in the police or as carriers. In practice, this regulation led the Portuguese authorities to use their powers in order to supply forced labor to both public and private employers (Newitt 1981). The famous example of forced labor in the São Tomé plantations was a result of the corrupt manner in which the labor code was implemented, the same going for the Cazembo and Huila plantations. Of course, not all labor was used in this manner and Portuguese authorities were probably most of the time able to implement the legislation in the correct manner (which, nevertheless, always implied some degree of forced labor) (Newitt 1981). Who was an "indigenous" or a "civilized" person (the two categories in which the population of the colonies was classified) was not clearly defined, but the 1914 Organic Law of the Portuguese Empire established that "natives" were not subject to Portuguese law but to their own customary one. "Civilized" were all those persons that were able to

[11]Decree of 9 November 1899 and Decree 951, 10 October 1914.

[12]Law 9 May 1901.

Table 8 Weight of colonial trade, 1890–1930 (% total trade)

	Imports from colonies (final use in mainland)	Exports to colonies (includes re-exports foreign goods)	Reexports (% of total) From the colonies	Reexports (% of total) To the colonies
1890	2.0	3.3	56.3	33.9
1895	2.8	9.5	55.7	17.2
1900	2.6	17.1	71.0	17.0
1905	2.9	16.8	71.6	13.5
1910	3.6	17.1	70.2	16.5
1915	5.0	19.5	66.9	17.8
1920	4.6	13.1	48.0	14.5
1925	6.8	12.6	49.4	8.0
1930	7.9	11.8	40.6	36.3

Source Pedreira (1998)

speak Portuguese (rather than only a "native" language), that had a regular income and that conformed to certain vague cultural traits.[13]

The regulation of labor and land allowed for the survival of much of the traditional subsistence agricultural activities but it also led, progressively, to the creation of a cash-oriented section of the economy. The 1901 land law recognized the right of the indigenous populations to own their lands. Again, here, the practice sometimes contradicted the law, something visible in the case of the Cazembo plantations, during the installation of which many indigenous populations were expropriated in favor of white settlers (Newitt 1981).

Despite all the difficulties, there is no doubt that Portugal was increasingly able to put its African empire to economic use from the late nineteenth century to the 1930s. Table 8 shows the growing importance of colonial trade: imports for consumption in the mainland grew from 2% of total imports in 1890 to close to 3% in the beginning of the twentieth century, to 7% in 1925 and 8% in 1930; but the growth of exports was even more noticeable: 3% in 1890, to reach a peak of 19.5% in 1915; afterward there was a certain decline, but, by 1930, they still represented 12% of the total of mainland exports. As noted

[13]Law 277, 15 August 1914.

by Pedreira (1998), this made of Portugal the country having a higher share of colonial trade in its total foreign trade, with the exception of Britain. Imports ranged from tropical goods to raw materials: coffee, cocoa, sugar, tobacco, cotton, rubber, or wax; exports were concentrated in a very narrow number of products, especially wine and cotton textiles, activities that desperately needed the colonies due to their difficulties to compete in the world market. Also important was the prosperous re-export trade, especially of African goods to the world, making of Lisbon a dynamic shipping platform. Table 8 shows again the importance of this trade, which also gave a contribution for the mainland's balance of payments: according to Lains (1998), the importance of colonial re-exports was in certain years equivalent to that of emigrant remittances.

All of this was compounded by the creation of an overseas banking system in 1864, which, in practical terms, corresponded to a monopoly, granted to *Banco Nacional Ultramarino* (BNU, National Overseas Bank): BNU was given a fifteen-year monopoly over banking and the issuing of money in all the colonies, except Macau and Timor (Clarence-Smith 1985; Valério et al. 2006). The bank operated from Luanda, but opened various branches in the mainland and throughout the empire in the following years, being responsible for financing some important projects in the colonies. BNU lost its monopoly status as a commercial bank in 1901 but retained it in money issuing. Other banks were allowed to enter the colonial market, but only Portuguese ones. Foreign banks, except in Mozambique, where the BNU monopoly had also disappeared earlier, in 1891, were not. In practical terms, BNU continued dominating the market (Clarence-Smith 1985; Valério et al. 2006).

During the 1920s, the republican authorities tried to implement a program of devolution of power in the large colonies of Angola and Mozambique, with the purpose of creating a special model of development. The plans ended in failure, but we will assess why in the next chapter, when analyzing the transition between the colonial rule of the First Republic to that of the following authoritarian regime.

Although the Portuguese African empire of the late nineteenth century and early twentieth century has acquired a certain "bad press", in fact its differences with the other European empires were not too vast.

The main difference resulted from the fact that Portugal was too poor to be an effective investor overseas, giving rise to an "imperialism of beggars", in the famous expression of Lenin. The fact that Portuguese exports had more trouble penetrating the world market made of the empire a much more important market than for the remaining European imperial powers—even if Britain, the most productive economy of the day, relied even more on colonial markets than Portugal. Otherwise, despite the rhetoric of the "civilizing mission" after World War I, we can find features similar to those found in the Portuguese Empire elsewhere, even if perhaps in different proportions: forced labor, chartered companies and effective little concern for "native" welfare, independently of the specific administrative format adopted. After all, even if they had more means, these richer European imperial powers never invested much in their empires (Porter 1994).

5 Economic Growth and Change

In the period under analysis, the Portuguese economy continued growing based on the structures developed during the nineteenth century, which were described in the previous chapter. But the period was also marked by the particularly difficult international context resulting from World War I and the troublesome reconstruction of the 1920s. The overall period is marked by a suspension of the divergence with richer economies coming from the nineteenth century. This corresponds to the initial stages of a long period of roughly one hundred years during which the economy was able either to keep the distance or to actually catch up (Figs. 3 and 4 of the Introduction). Population grew 1.4 million between 1900 and 1930, from 5.4 million to 6.8 million. This was the beginning of the demographic transition for the Portuguese population, a phase when birth rates are still high and death rates start to decline (although infant mortality in Portugal was among the highest in Europe: between 130‰ and 140‰ throughout the period). Life expectancy increased a few years between 1900 and 1930: from 37 years to 47, equally very low by European standards (Henriques and Rodrigues 2009). Population grew despite the impact of the war and the "Spanish flu", the latter leading to a peak in the death rate in 1919 and 1920. Portugal started its demographic transition later than most rich countries of Europe, where it began in the nineteenth century.

Despite the fact that these were the first steps of a long period of suspension of divergence, the performance of the Portuguese economy was still not very impressive when compared to that of other peripheral economies. Figure 3 of the Introduction shows how Finland, whose GDP per capita was similar to the Portuguese one in the late nineteenth century, entered into a consistent catch-up process in the 1920s, at a pace Portugal was not able to replicate. This was also the period in which the Scandinavian economies reached their core position. If the comparison is made with the companions of the southern periphery, the result is a bit more flattering for the Portuguese economy but still far from impressive: its performance was never comparatively better than theirs (Fig. 4 of the Introduction).

This general picture hides some differences during the war and postwar periods. Growth was negative during the war: GDP per capita declined −1.6% per year between 1914 and 1918 (Table 1). But, since Portugal was not alone in these difficult circumstances, most of the richer economies felt similar effects—or even stronger. Consequently, Portuguese divergence was only mild (Figs. 3 and 4 of the Introduction). The immediate postwar period, on the contrary, brought positive growth, with a 3.3% rate of GDP per capita between 1919 and 1923 (Table 1), although soon followed by a new negative period, after 1922–1924, bringing again divergence. The picture for the whole period is, however, one of stability in the distance to the richest economies, something that is explained by the general lackluster performance of the latter during the interwar period (Ritschl and Straumann 2010). The Portuguese economy conformed now perfectly with the picture of lack of convergence in Europe (Roses and Wolf 2010).

The structure of the economy continued to be very traditional. Agriculture did lose weight both in terms of employment (Fig. 10) and production (Fig. 11), but at a still very slow pace, especially in what concerns employment, which passed from a share of 64% in 1900 to one of 56% in 1930, still among the highest in Europe; as for GDP, the share of agriculture declined from 40% in 1910 to 30% in 1930,

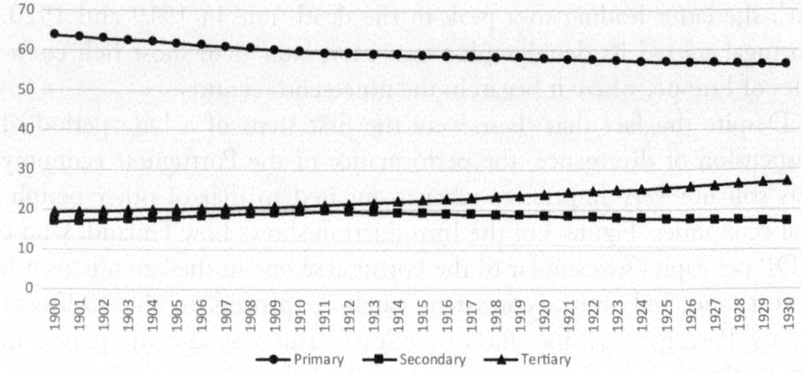

Fig. 10 Structure employment, Portugal, 1900–1930 (% of overall employment) (*Source* Nunes [2001])

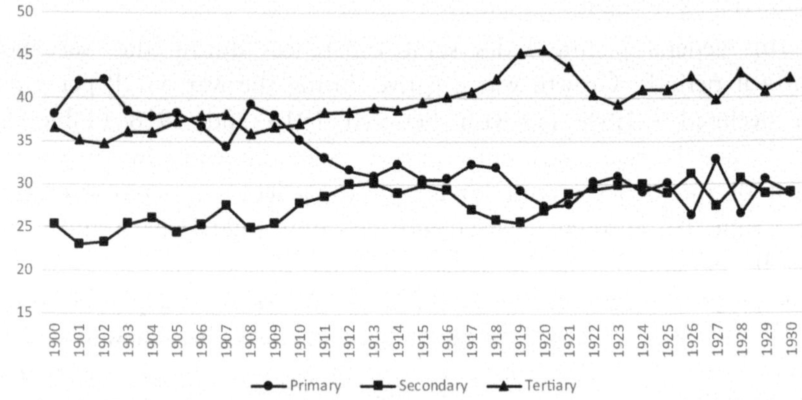

Fig. 11 Structure economy, Portugal, 1900–1930 (% GDP) (*Source* Author's calculations based on Lains [2007] for the period 1900–1910 and Batista et al. [1997] for the period 1910–1930)

also among the highest in Europe. An interesting aspect of this decline is how it benefited mostly services rather than industry: employment in industry kept the same proportion, at roughly 17% of overall employment, but the services sector passed from 20% in 1910 to 29% in 1930; as for GDP, services became the most important sector of the economy, passing from a proportion of around 35% to roughly 43% in the same

Table 9 Structure of employment, various European economies, c. 1870–c. 1913 (% total employment)

	Agriculture		Industry		Services	
	c. 1913	c. 1930	c. 1913	c. 1930	c. 1913	c. 1930
Belgium	23.2	17.7	45.6	46.4	31.3	35.9
Denmark	43.1	35.8	25.0	27.5	31.9	36.7
Finland	78.5	69.8	12.0	15.9	9.5	14.4
The Netherlands	28.6	20.8	33.1	36.8	38.3	42.3
Norway	40.0	35.6	26.2	26.6	33.8	37.8
Sweden	48.3	36.3	26.9	32.3	24.8	31.5
UK	10.2	6.0	45.1	46.5	44.7	47.5
France	41.0	35.6	33.1	33.3	25.9	31.1
Greece	57.1	61.1	18.7	18.0	24.2	20.9
Italy	55.7	46.8	26.8	30.8	17.5	22.4
Spain	66.6	45.5	16.3	26.5	17.0	28.0
Portugal	59.0	56.1	19.3	16.9	21.7	26.9

Source Buyst and Franaszek (2010), except Portugal (see Fig. 9)

dates. Industry also increased its weight, but only from 25 to 30%. Table 9 provides international comparisons, revealing Portugal to be the most agricultural country of Western Europe and the least industrialized one, except for Greece and Finland. Countries such as Italy and Spain, which by 1913 still had a similar distribution of employment, show a quick process of industrialization until 1930 when compared to Portugal.

The growth of agricultural productivity was very slow in this period, putting its performance among the worst in Europe (Branco and Silva 2017), a somewhat surprising result, as Portugal was spared the direct impact of the war, unlike most European countries from France to the East (Federico 2005; Buyst and Franaszek 2010). This poor performance is mostly due to the fact that the sector suffered very few transformations. Final occupation of the territory with agricultural activity was concluded in this period, especially in the first decades of the century (Lains 2003a), but the land-labor ratio continued to be one of the lowest in Europe (only Greece and Belgium had lower ones) (Federico 2005). The asymmetric structure of land ownership identified in the previous chapter was consolidated in this period, with very large properties in the southern region of Alentejo and very small ones in the northwestern region of Minho, with the other regions in intermediate positions. Some innovations were felt, such as the quick introduction of steam harvesters in Alentejo and of modern fertilizers in Alentejo and Ribatejo (the latter a fertile agricultural region of large farms just north of the country's capital, Lisbon) (Lains 2003a; Branco and Silva 2017). But the overall rate of technological innovation was low and international comparisons are very unfavorable, as capital intensity and the use of fertilizers expanded much quicker around Europe in this period than in Portugal (Federico 2005).

In terms of relative weight, cereals continued to be the largest production, with a growing share, thanks to a policy of systematic tariff protection, especially dedicated to wheat: new legislation introduced in the last decade of the nineteenth century (in 1889 and 1899) allowed for wheat to expand massively in the largely uncultivated lands of the Alentejo region (Reis 1979). Thanks to it, the weight of wheat in agricultural output passed from around 11% at the turn of the century to about 18% in the early 1930s. Cattle and animal production (meat, dairy, and wool) continued to be the second most important branch in the sector, expanding slightly its share from 23% at the turn of the century to 28% in the early 1930s, but still remaining low by European standards (Branco and Silva 2017). Wine was next, although strongly losing weight, from 23 to 14% in the same dates, whereas fruits and vegetables kept their relative importance, at around 6 to 7%, which was again small by European standards. Rice and potatoes also increased their share in the product mix, from 0.7% in 1900 to 1.5% in the early 1930s in the former case, and 4.5 and 9% in the latter for the same dates. As for forest, its importance increased, especially due to the expansion of cork trees (data from Lains and Sousa 1998; Baptista 1993; Lains 2003a).

In what concerns industry, the general picture is one of only moderate change: textiles continued to be the largest branch, although declining, from 45% of overall industrial production in 1896 to 36% in 1929; textiles were followed in relative importance by food and beverages, which kept their share at around 24%, in a branch where tinned fish and milling displayed fast progress. Wood and cork kept their contribution at around 10%, despite some strong oscillations, while chemicals passed from a share of around 11% in 1910 to one of about 14% in 1930. At a much lower level but with an interesting contribution we have paper and paper pulp, cement and metalworking, although only the latter reached the 5% share in 1930 (Aguiar and Martins 2005). This is the period sometimes labeled internationally as the "Second Industrial Revolution", coinciding with the development of branches such as chemicals, electricity or metalworking, the latter associated especially with car production or various electrical and telecommunication appliances (Buyst and Franaszek 2010). Despite the appearance of some new industrial units in Portugal comparable in modernity and scale to those existing in richer economies, most of the industrial sector remained traditional and based on units of very small scale (Lains 2003a; Castro 1973; Medeiros 1978). Modern units could be found mostly in chemicals, especially due to the fertilizer company Companhia União Fabril (CUF), which was created in 1898 and became the largest business group in the country in the following decades (Silva et al.

2016; Mateus 2005; Pereira 2005; Castro 1973; Medeiros 1978). Another modern branch was cement, whose first factories appeared in the first two decades of the twentieth century, although still at a small scale. More traditional branches such as cotton and wool textiles, tinned fish, glass, and milling also developed some modern units in this period (Mateus 2005; Castro 1973; Medeiros 1978). But such modern units continued to be few, existing alongside a multitude of traditional ones, making of the Portuguese industrial sector one of the least developed in Western Europe. Electricity, which spread quickly around Europe and North America in this period, expanded very slowly in Portugal: despite some examples of early use of this energy source in the last decades of the nineteenth century (some industries, public lightning: Matos et al. 2004; Mateus 2005), the profile of the sources of energy in the country reveals again a very traditional picture, with most of energy still originating in organic sources such as firewood and animals, at a time when fossil fuels and, increasingly, electricity started to be adopted elsewhere (Henriques 2011; Henriques and Sharp 2019).

As for the services sector, it remained a mostly traditional one, based on wholesale and retail trade, although with some growth of public services. The most dynamic branches, such as finance, telecommunication, or transportation, remained very small, a picture much divergent with richer countries, where the growth of the sector was precisely concentrated in the new branches (Buyst and Franaszek 2010).

The protectionist tradition of Portuguese trade policy did not change in the period. In addition, the war and the subsequent inflationary process created conditions of implicit protection. When the stabilization policy of 1922–1924 was implemented, a revision of the level of tariffs became necessary, due to the effect of inflation: this was done in 1923, through a new schedule (Fig. 9). The Portuguese economy remained one of the least open in the Western world: Fig. 12 shows the collapse of openness during the war but a return to prewar levels afterward. The degree of openness in Europe was, by 1929, a third higher than in 1913 (Federico and Tena-Junguito 2016). Portugal increased its exports as a share of GDP during the war, but remained far from being an open economy. Most economic activities continued to live under a high wall of protection, sparing them international competition. Whereas

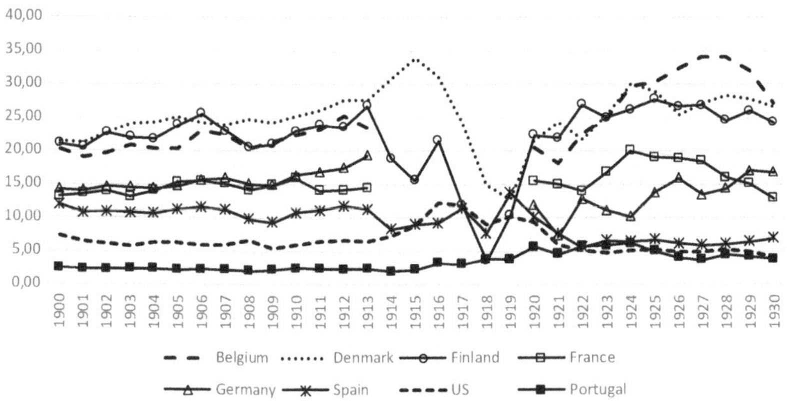

Fig. 12 Openness, various countries, 1900–1930 (exports % GDP) Current prices; (*Source* Federico and Tena [2018], except Portugal: Fontoura and Valério [2001])

for the nineteenth century there is a discussion over the possible benefits of protectionism on growth, the discussion does not exist for the period of the 1920s: the relationship between protection (or the lack of it) and growth is totally absent, as growth rates simply became uncorrelated with the levels of protection (Clemens and Williamson 2001). Portuguese growth was better in comparative terms in this period but there is no relationship between this fact and the level of protection: the overall growth rate of the Portuguese economy was still not impressive; the difference now lay in the fact that most European countries had relatively bad performances as well.

Portuguese trade was concentrated in a small number of products. Exports were essentially agricultural, with the largest share belonging to wine, initially mostly Port but progressively including the common variety as well. Port was exported fundamentally to Europe, with the UK being the largest buyer; common wine was exported fundamentally to the colonies, as its low quality prevented it from penetrating the world market. Colonial re-exports represented an important share of exports as well, although not as large as wine (Lains 1998). Tinned fish was another export item and one of the few able to compete internationally. Overall, food, beverages, and tobacco represented about 60% of the totality of exports between 1910 and 1930 (Afonso and Aguiar 2005).

Textiles had also an important weight: about 10% between 1910 and 1930 (Afonso and Aguiar 2005), but they were mostly directed to the colonies. The remaining sectors had a much lower participation, with cork representing a share of about 5% between 1910 and 1930. As for imports, 60% of them were concentrated in intermediate goods; these were mostly constituted by raw materials and equipment (Lains 2007). The second largest share was food, beverage, and tobacco, resulting mostly from imports of cereals and codfish (Lains 2007).

The banking system continued to grow in this period, despite having been very seriously affected by the financial crisis and the economic circumstances of the period. The sector was marked by strong volatility up to 1925, as many banks tried to profit from the quasi-hyperinflation business environment and the speculative incentives resulting from rising public debt and monetary lack of discipline. This led to a significant number of banks sprouting until 1925, but also to almost as many closing, sometimes just after a few months of activity: for an initial total of 23 incorporated banks, 17 new ones appeared until 1925, while 16 went bankrupt (Reis 1995a; Valério et al. 2006). The streak of bankruptcies led to three serious banking crises, in 1920, 1923, and 1925. Such an unreliable behavior of commercial banks was responsible for the public's lack of trust in them, something that favored the concentration of deposits in the National Savings Bank (*Caixa Geral de Depósitos*, CGD) and the BoP (Reis 1995a).

The second half of the 1920s was different. The successful monetary and fiscal reforms of 1922 and 1924 were instrumental in this respect, by bringing high inflation to an end. The population of commercial banks remained virtually the same from 1925 to 1929, and the confidence in them was reflected in the growth of deposits, even if the CGD retained a massive presence and the BoP remained among the largest commercial banks in the country (Reis 1995a). A new banking law, the purpose of which was to bring higher solidity to the sector, was also crucial.[14] The law had a series of prudential, competition, and specialization features: capital requirements were raised; the opening of banks was

[14]Decree 10,634, 20 March 1925.

Table 10 Sources of growth, Portugal, 1910–1934

	GDP	Labor	Capital	Human capital	TFP
Silva and Lains (2013)	2.2	0.1	1.7	–	0.4
Lains (2003b)	2.2	0.3	0.4	0.7	0.7

Source Silva and Lains (2013)

made dependent of authorization by the Minister of Finance, as well as mergers and acquisitions (for further considerations on the new legal framework, see Reis 1995a; Valério et al. 2006; Amaral 2013).

The CGD was also reformed, in 1929, although already inserted within Salazar's general fiscal and monetary reforms. A new legislative package changed its name into *Caixa Geral de Depósitos, Crédito e Previdência*, creating annex to the CGD itself two new institutions, a National Investment Bank (*Caixa Nacional de Crédito*) and a National Social Security Bank (*Caixa Nacional de Previdência*). The latter should manage the pension funds of various types of public servants, and the former should act as an investment bank, using the CGD funds for that purpose (for all these aspects, see Reis 1995b).[15] The completion of legislative change in the banking sector came with a reform of the BoP.[16] This reform was an integral part of the more general fiscal and monetary reform mentioned above and which we will discuss in higher detail in the next chapter. Its main purpose was to make of the BoP a "true central bank".

To sum up, in terms of economic growth and convergence, the period was a mixed one. On the one hand, the Portuguese economy interrupted the divergence process coming from the beginning of the nineteenth century but on the other it continued to be the worst performer in the European periphery. In what concerns explanations for this mixed behavior, we lack works that are specifically dedicated to the period. But some positive and negative factors can be pointed out. On the positive side, there was the conclusion of the process of institutional change inaugurated by the liberal revolution, allowing economic agents

[15]Decrees 16,665, 16,666, 16,667, and 16,668, all from 27 March 1929.

[16]Decrees 19,869 and 19,870, both of 9 June 1931.

to deal with property rights that were more clearly defined (Amaral 2012). This probably explains the strong capital accumulation that a recent growth accounting exercise (Silva and Lains 2013) has identified for the period, as economic agents became more certain of appropriating the full return to investment (Table 10). Freitas (2005) also shows how the investment rate jumped from about 2.5% in the second decade of the century to more than the double in 1930: 7.5%; still low by the standards of richer economies but marking a clear change with the past. On the negative side, there was the persistent difficulty in changing the structure of the economy, which, as we have seen above, was one of the slowest to industrialize. The same growth accounting exercise attributes very little weight to total factor productivity, something that weak structural change certainly helps to explain: Aguiar and Martins (2005) show structural change giving a residual contribution to productivity growth in the 1910–1950 period.

Another contribution to low TFP came certainly from the equally persistent low educational standards of the Portuguese population. The regime of the First Republic paid considerable lip service to the need of improving those standards but achieved little in practical terms. The regime created for the first time in 1911 a ministry especially dedicated to Education (*Ministério da Instrução Pública*) and made access to primary education free for all children while also making the first three years of schooling compulsory, later to be extended to five in 1919 (Amaral 2002).[17] Spending on teachers and schools increased, especially during the 1920s, which explains why the Education item in public expenditure reached a level close to 1% of GDP (Fig. 5). In international terms this was not very high, however, as Table 6 shows, so that the final outcome was modest: school enrollment progressed very slowly and was still dismally low in 1930 (Table 11); the Portuguese situation is to be contrasted with that of Finland, for instance, a country starting with a lower level of schooling in 1900 but that had practically converged to those with higher levels of education in 1930. In the end, the educational effort of this regime did not achieve much. Although the

[17]Decree 29 March 1911.

Table 11 School enrollment (students enrolled in primary schools as a percentage of the 5–14 age group) (%)

	1900	1910	1920	1930
Portugal	19.41	20.31	21.25	26.07
Italy	38.96	44.59	50.56	59.92
Spain		35.34	38.85	44.83
Belgium	59.25	61.65	72.56	73.07
Denmark	71.76	68.70	64.84	67.37
Finland	18.84	26.54	38.82	51.85
France	85.53	85.33	71.86	78.99
Germany	73.23	72.01	87.20	68.73
Netherland	66.37	70.30	70.64	74.17
Norway	66.80	68.55	69.42	71.63
Sweden	68.90	69.88	60.82	62.80
Switzerland	72.66	70.74	70.99	70.13
UK	69.15	74.55	71.61	76.87

Source Mitchell (2013), except for Portugal: Amaral (2002)

relatively low and late amount of public spending dedicated to it might be a reason for the relative failure, recently Palma and Reis (2018) have added one possible further explanation: that the educational programs designed during the period were too progressive for the conservative tastes of the population, who resisted the introduction of modern schools.

A possible source of technological improvement might have been foreign direct investment (FDI), but this seems to have been very low, although we lack any figures (Silva 2016). Despite many examples in mining, public transportation in the two largest cities in the country (Lisbon and Porto), telecommunication (telegraph and telephones), agriculture and fishing (cork and tinned fish), and various public works projects (Castro 1973), the aggregate picture was not impressive: foreign investors simply did not look at Portugal as an interesting destination during the period (Silva 2016).

An increasingly more important development in Western countries in the first decades of the twentieth century was the growth of social spending by the Government (Tanzi and Schuknecht 2000; Lindert 2004). Portugal did not follow the trend. As Table 12 shows, social spending emerged in a few Western countries, at still very low levels

Table 12 Public social transfers, 1880–1930 (% of GDP)

	1880	1900	1910	1930
Belgium	0.17	0.26	0.43	0.56
Denmark	0.96	1.41	1.75	3.11
Finland	0.66	0.78	0.90	2.97
France	0.46	0.57	0.81	1.05
Germany	0.50	0.59	–	4.82
Sweden	0.72	0.85	1.03	2.59
UK	0.86	1.00	1.38	2.24
Spain	–	–	0.02	0.07
Portugal	0.14[a]	0.10	0.09	0.36

[a]1888
Source Lindert (2004), except for Portugal: Mata (2001)

from 1880 onward, but Portugal was not among them. The forces stimulating such sort of spending, which, according to Lindert (2004), were political voice (through the expansion of voting rights), aging, and economic growth (associated with industrialization and the expansion of the industrial labor force), were not present in Portugal. Besides the early and tenuous efforts of poor relief by church organizations having existed for centuries, the first systematic steps of social support appearing in Portugal date from the nineteenth century. But Government efforts were minimal, meaning that, whatever existed in this respect resulted essentially from scattered voluntary associations in certain professions (Pereira 1999). After World War I, political authorities considered creating a compulsory social insurance system modeled on similar ones appearing then in countries such as the UK or Germany, but the outcome was basically a failure. Five decrees covering various social relief dimensions were issued on 10 May 1919, but their implementation, due to lack of public resources devoted to them and poor organization, was virtually nonexistent (Cardoso and Rocha 2009).[18]

This leads to the question of knowing if the First Republic could have evolved in such a manner as to approach the kind of social-democratic experiences then happening in Scandinavia, Germany, or the

[18]Decrees 5636, 5637, 5638, 5639, all of 10 May 1919.

UK, where traditionally liberal regimes tried to accommodate labor in a relatively peaceful way. During the Constitutional Monarchy, there had been a close connection between republicans and labor organizations. Striking was formally forbidden since 1886 (by a *Penal Code* published in that year), even if sometimes tolerated, and the creation of unions was authorized in 1891, but with several limitations: they should be restricted to the simpler professional level and their boards had to be approved by the Government.[19] This was later reformed to abolish the governmental authorization of boards in 1907,[20] but the truth is that unions continued to grow at a slow pace, on account of the low industrial development of the country, and remained few and fragmented. By 1905, there were 161 unions, by 1910 there were 223 (Freire 1992, p. 122). Additionally, for a long time they remained estranged from the actual interests of workers on the ground. Most unions originated in a romantic streak of socialism or in anarchism, both having more of an individualistic and philosophical nature. Marxism or social-democracy had a very weak penetration in the Portuguese labor movement (Telo 1980; Cabral 1988; Freire 1992). To a large extent, the nature of the Portuguese labor movement was a reflection of the level of development of Portuguese industry.

This started to change some years before the war but mostly during the war. The difficulties in imports and the inflationary process in the period, which continued in the postwar period, created serious problems of scarcity leading unions to adopt a more forceful approach in such issues as wages or working times (Medeiros 1978). The number of unions practically doubled, from 223 in 1910 to 420 in 1915; there was some decline in 1920, when the number of unions reached 334, but then a recovery followed, and their number reached 507 in 1925 (Freire 1992, p. 122). Anarchistic unions became more combative and a communist party was created in 1921, inspired and sponsored by the Soviet revolution (Telo 1977). But the Republic dealt with this reinforced labor movement through heavy repression rather than

---

[19]Decree 9 May 1891.

[20]Law 14 February 1907.

accommodation. What had been a close relationship between republicans and unions before 1910 was progressively transformed into a bitter one. In 1919, an attempt was tried at mending this relationship, when the Government proposed the new social insurance legislation mentioned above, together with legislation establishing the working time at eight hours a day and 48 h a week in industry and wholesale and retail trade (Medeiros 1978; Telo 1980; Patriarca 1995).[21] This continued with the approval of new legislation allowing union federations, rather than just isolated unions, to negotiate collective agreements.[22] But the tensions arising from the inflationary process and the inability of the Government to implement the social programs did not allow for pacification (Pereira 1999). The tensions ended with the labor movement asking, together with business and other political forces (including right-wing ones), for the demotion of the regime in 1926. No embryonic Welfare State or social-democratic regime could blossom from such a situation. The truth is that most republican leaders still viewed Government functions in a typical liberal and minimal manner, something that prevented them from adopting other solutions for public spending. This inability of Portuguese governments to have a closer relationship with labor was also decisive to give strength to the latter's revolutionary and non-reformist currents, furthering the chasm between the movement and the regime: the labor movement was itself divided between a reformist and a revolutionary wing and was not able to present a clear position when bargaining with the republican governments.

If the relationship with labor was so conflictive, one might expect the opposite to happen with business. But that is not the case. The first business associations in the country had appeared during the nineteenth century, initially still regulated in an incomplete manner. The first to be created was the Lisbon Commercial Association (*Associação Comercial de Lisboa*, ACL) in 1834 (under the name of Associação Mercantil Lisbonense, changing to its final name in 1903), followed by the Porto Commercial Association (*Associação Comercial do Porto*,

[21]Decree 5516, 7 May 1919.

[22]Decree 10,415, 27 December 1924.

ACP) in the same year. Industrial associations appeared slightly later: the Portuguese Industrial Association (*Associação Industrial Portuguesa*, AIP) was created in Lisbon in 1837 and the Porto Industrial Association (*Associação Industrial Portuense*, AIPortuense) in 1852. An agricultural association was created in 1860: Central Association of Portuguese Agriculture (*Associação Central da Agricultura Portuguesa*, ACAP, called *Real Associação Central da Agricultura Portuguesa* between 1878 and 1911). Regulation of these associations would only come in 1891, with the same legislation that allowed for the creation of unions. From then on, a myriad of smaller associations at the professional level were also created (Cerdeira and Padilha 1998). These were the main business actors in the relationship with Government during the period of the Republic, and that relationship deteriorated especially during and after the war: the switch from an inflationary policy to a deflationary one, the increase in tax rates during the various fiscal reforms, the hesitations in the relationship with labor (sometimes repressing it with violence, sometimes accommodating its demands), created an instability to business conditions that did not allow for a good relationship with political power. The interventions in the markets for agricultural goods, together with the circulation of some ideas of "agrarian reform", created also an uncomfortable relationship with large landowners. By 1925, the business representative associations began maneuvering, together with some conservative politicians and military operatives, to overthrow the regime (Medeiros 1978; Madureira 2002).

References

Afonso, Óscar, and Álvaro Aguiar. 2005. A internacionalização da economia. In *História Económica de Portugal, 1700–2000, Vol. III, O Século XX*, ed. Pedro Lains and Álvaro Ferreira da Silva, 305–341. Lisbon: ICS.

Aguiar, Álvaro, and Manuel M.F. Martins. 2005. A indústria. In *História Económica de Portugal, 1700–2000, Vol. III, O Século XX*, ed. Pedro Lains and Álvaro Ferreira da Silva, 185–226. Lisbon: ICS.

Aldcroft, Derek H. 1977. *From Versailles to Wall Street, 1919–1929*. London: Penguin.

Alexandre, Valentim. 1993. Ideologia, economia e política: a questão colonial na implantação do Estado Novo. *Análise Social* XXVIII (123–124): 1117–1136.

———. 1998. Nação e império. In *História da Expansão Portuguesa, Vol. IV – Do Brasil para África (1808–1930)*, ed. Francisco Bethencourt and Diogo Ramada Curto, 90–142. Lisbon: Círculo de Leitores.

———. 2000. O império africano (séculos XIX e XX) – as linhas gerais. In *O Império Africano (Séculos XIX e XX)*, ed. Valentim Alexandre, 11–28. Lisbon: Edições Colibri/IHCUNL.

Amaral, Luciano. 2002. *How a Country Catches-Up: Explaining Economic Growth in Portugal in the Postwar Period (1950s–1973)*. Doctoral dissertation, European University Institute, Florence.

———. 2012. Institutions, Property and Economic Growth: Back to the Passage from Ancien Régime to Liberalism in Portugal. *Análise Social* XLVII (202): 28–55.

———. 2013. Imperfect but True Competition: Innovation and Profitability in Portuguese Banking During the Golden Age (1950–1973). *Financial History Review* 20 (3): 305–333.

Baganha, Maria Ioannis. 1994. As correntes emigratórias portuguesas no século XX e o seu impacto na economia nacional. *Análise Social* XXIX (128): 959–980.

Baptista, Fernando Oliveira. 1993. *A Política Agrária do Estado Novo*. Porto: Afrontamento.

Bastien, Carlos. 2001. Preços e salários. In *Estatísticas Históricas Portuguesas*, ed. Nuno Valério, 615–655. Lisbon: INE.

Batista, Dina, et al. 1997. *New Estimates for Portugal's GDP: 1910–1958*. Lisbon: Bank of Portugal.

Blum, Matthias, Jari Eloranta, and Pavel Osinsky. 2014. Organization of War Economies. 1914–1918 Online—International Encyclopedia of the First World War. https://encyclopedia.1914-1918-online.net/article/organization_of_war_economies.

Branco, Amélia, and Ester Gomes da Silva. 2017. Growth, Institutional Change and Innovation, 1820–1930. In *An Agrarian History of Portugal, 1000–2000, Economic Development on the European Frontier*, ed. Dulce Freire and Pedro Lains, 220–244. Leiden: Brill.

Broadberry, Stephen, and Mark Harrison. 2005. The Economics of World War I: An Overview. In *The Economics of World War I*, ed. Stephen Broadberry and Mark Harrison, 3–40. Cambridge: Cambridge University Press.

Buyst, Erik, and Piotr Franaszek. 2010. Sectoral Developments. In *The Cambridge Economic History of Modern Europe, Vol II: 1870 to the Present*, ed. Stephen Broadberry and Kevin H. O'Rourke, 208–231. Cambridge University Press: Cambridge.

Cabral, Manuel Villaverde. 1988. *Portugal na Alvorada do Século XX, Forças Sociais, Poder Político e Crescimento Económico de 1890 a 1914*. Lisbon: Editorial Presença.

Cardoso, José Luís, and Manuela Rocha. 2009. O seguro social obrigatório em Portugal (1919–1928): acção e limites de um Estado previdente. *Análise Social* XLIV (192): 439–470.

Carvalho, Vasco. 2001. Answers to a Puzzle: Monetary Regimes and Macroeconomic Performance in the Portuguese 20s. Working Paper, Department of Applied Economics, University of Cambridge, Cambridge.

Castelo, Cláudia. 2007. *Passagens para África. O Povoamento de Angola e Moçambique com Naturais da Metrópole (1920–1974)*. Porto: Afrontamento.

Castro, Armando de. 1973. *A Economia Portuguesa do Século XX, 1900/1925*. Lisbon: Edições 70.

Cerdeira, Maria da Conceição, and Maria Edite Padilha. 1998. *O Movimento Associativo Patronal Português, de 1834 a 1994*. Lisbon: Ministério do Trabalho e Solidariedade Social.

Clarence-Smith, Gervase. 1985. *The Third Portuguese Empire, 1825–1975: A Study in Economic Imperialism*. Manchester: Manchester University Press.

Clemens, Michael A., and Jeffrey Williamson. 2001. A Tariff Growth Paradox? Protection's Impact on the World Around 1875–1997. NBER Working Paper, 8459.

Dias, Jill. 1998. Guiné. In *Nova História da Expansão Portuguesa – O Império Africano, 1825–1890*, ed. Valentim Alexandre and Jill Dias, 319–556. Lisbon: Editorial Estampa.

Eichengreen, Barry. 1996. *Globalizing Capital: A History of the International Monetary System*. Princeton University Press: Princeton.

Eloranta, Jari, and Mark Harrison. 2006. Correlates of Mobilization in the Two World Wars. Paper to XIV International Economic History Congress, Helsinki.

———. 2010. War and Disintegration, 1914–1950. In *The Cambridge Economic History of Modern Europe*, ed. Stephen Broadberry and Kevin O'Rourke, 133–155. Cambridge: Cambridge University Press.

Estêvão, João. 1998. Cabo Verde. In *Nova História da Expansão Portuguesa – O Império Africano, 1825–1890*, ed. Valentim Alexandre and Jill Dias, 167–210. Lisbon: Editorial Estampa.

Federico, Giovanni. 2005. *Feeding the World: An Economic History of Agriculture, 1800–2000*. Princeton: Princeton University Press.

Federico, Giovanni, and Antonio Tena-Junguito. 2016. A Tale of Two Globalizations: Gains from Trade and Openness 1800–2010. Universidad Carlos III de Madrid Working Papers in Economic History, 16-02.

———. 2018. Federico-Tena World Trade Historical Database. https://www.uc3m.es/ss/Satellite/UC3MInstitucional/es/TextoMixta/1371246237481/Federico-Tena_World_Trade_Historical_Database.

Feinstein, Charles H., Peter Temin, and Gianni Toniolo. 1997. *The European Economy Between the Wars*. Oxford: Oxford University Press.

Fontoura, Ana Paula, and Nuno Valério. 2001. Relações económicas externas. In *Estatísticas Históricas Portuguesas*, ed. Nuno Valério, 713–739. Lisbon: INE.

Freire, João. 1992. *Anarquistas e Operários. Ideologia, Ofício e Práticas Sociais: o Anarquismo e o Operariado em Portugal, 1900–1940*. Porto: Afrontamento.

Freitas, Miguel Lebre de. 2005. O capital. In *História Económica de Portugal, 1700–2000, Vol. III, O Século XX*, ed. Pedro Lains and Álvaro Ferreira da Silva, 91–124. Lisbon: ICS.

Freudenthal, Aida Maria. 2001. Angola. In *Nova História da Expansão Portuguesa – O Império Africano, 1890–1930*, ed. A.H. de Oliveira Marques, 259–467. Lisbon: Editorial Estampa.

Henriques, Filipe Castro, and Teresa Ferreira Rodrigues. 2009. O século XX: a transição. In *História da População Portuguesa. Das Longas Permanências à Conquista da Modernidade*, ed. Teresa Ferreira Rodrigues, 417–513. Porto: Afrontamento e CEPESE.

Henriques, Sofia Teives. 2011. *Energy Transitions, Economic Growth and Structural Change: Portugal in a Long-Run Comparative Perspective*. Lund: Lund University.

Henriques, Sofia Teives, and Paul Sharp. 2019. Without Coal in the Age of Steam and Dams in the Age of Electricity: An Explanation for the Failure of Portugal to Industrialize Before the Second World War. EHES Working Paper, No. 148.

Jerónimo, Miguel Bandeira. 2010. *Livros Brancos, Almas Negras. A "Missão Civilizadora" do Colonialismo Português c. 1870–1930*. Lisbon: ICS.

Lains, Pedro. 1998. Causas do colonialismo português em África, 1822–1975. *Análise Social* XXXIII (146–147): 463–496.

———. 2003a. New Wine in Old Bottles: Output and Productivity Trends in Portuguese Agriculture, 1850–1950. *European Review of Economic History* 7 (1): 43–72.

———. 2003b. Catching Up to the European Core: Portuguese Economic Growth, 1910–1990. *Explorations in Economic History* 40: 369–386.

———. 2007. Growth in a Protected Environment, 1850–1950. *Research in Economic History* 24: 119–160.

Lains, Pedro, and Paulo Silveira e Sousa. 1998. Estatística e produção agrícola em Portugal, 1848–1914. *Análise Social* XXXIII (149): 935–968.

Lindert, Peter H. 2004. *Growing Public: Social Spending and Economic Growth Since the Eighteenth Century, Vol. I—The Story*. Cambridge: Cambridge University Press.

Lopes, Fernando Farelo. 2012. Concorrência partidária e processo político-constitucional na I República. In *O Sistema Político Português, Séculos XIX-XXI: Continuidades e Rupturas*, ed. André Freire, 65–85. Coimbra: Almedina.

Maddison, Angus. 2003. *The World Economy: Historical Statistics*. Paris: OCDE.

Madureira, Nuno Luís. 2002. *A Economia dos Interesses – Portugal entre as Guerras*. Lisbon: Livros Horizonte.

Magalhães, Justino. 2010. *Da Cadeira ao Banco. Escola e Modernização (Séculos XVIII-XX)*. Lisbon: Educa.

Marques, A.H. de Oliveira. 1978. *História da Primeira República Portuguesa. As Estruturas de Base*. Lisbon: Iniciativas Editoriais.

Martins, Guilherme d'Oliveira. 2012. Notas sobre finanças públicas na I República. Orientações e tendências. In *Congresso Internacional I República e Republicanismo. Atas*, ed. AAVV, 221–228. Lisbon: Assembleia da República.

Mata, Maria Eugénia. 1987. *Câmbios e Política Cambial na Economia Portuguesa, 1891–1931*. Lisbon: Livraria Sá da Costa Editora.

———. 2001. Finanças públicas e dívida pública. In *Estatísticas Históricas Portuguesas*, ed. Nuno Valério, 657–712. Lisbon: INE.

———. 2005. A discussão Parlamentar dos Orçamentos da Regeneração à República. In *Os orçamentos no Parlamento Português, Sistemas Fiscais e Doutrinas fiscais nos séculos XIX e XX*, ed. Nuno Valério et al., 63–120. Lisbon: D. Quixote.

Mata, Maria Eugénia, and Nuno Valério. 1996. Monetary Stability, Fiscal Discipline and Economic Performance: The Experience of Portugal Since 1854. In *Currency Convertibility: The Gold Standard and Beyond*, ed. Jorge Braga de Macedo, Barry Eichengreen, and Jaime Reis, 204–227. London, Routledge.

Mateus, Abel. 2005. A tecnologia. In *História Económica de Portugal, 1700–2000, Vol. III, O Século XX*, ed. Pedro Lains and Álvaro Ferreira da Silva, 125–156. Lisbon: ICS.

Matos, Ana Cardoso de, Fátima Mendes, Fernando Faria, and Luís Cruz. 2004. *A electricidade em Portugal. Dos Primórdios à II Guerra Mundial*. Lisbon: EDP.

Mauro, Paolo, Rafael Romeu, Ariel Binderand, and Asad Zaman. 2013. A Modern History of Fiscal Prudence and Profligacy. IMF Working Paper, 13/5.

Medeiros, Fernando. 1978. *A Sociedade e a Economia Portuguesas nas Origens do Salazarismo*. Lisbon: A Regra do Jogo.

Mitchell, Brian R. 2013. *International Historical Statistics, 1750–2010*. London: Palgrave.

Nascimento, Augusto. 1998. São Tomé e Príncipe. In *Nova História da Expansão Portuguesa – O Império Africano, 1825–1890*, ed. Valentim Alexandre and Jill Dias, 269–318. Lisbon: Editorial Estampa.

———. 2001. S. Tomé e Príncipe (1890–1926). In *Nova História da Expansão Portuguesa – O Império Africano, 1890–1930*, ed. A.H. de Oliveira Marques, 201–258. Lisbon: Editorial Estampa.

Neves, Olga Iglésias. 2001. Moçambique. In *Nova História da Expansão Portuguesa – O Império Africano, 1890–1930*, ed. A.H. de Oliveira Marques, 469–584. Lisbon: Editorial Estampa.

Newitt, Malyn. 1981. *Portugal in Africa: The Last Hundred Years*. London: C. Hurst.

———. 1995. *A History of Mozambique*. Bloomington and Indianapolis: Indiana University Press.

Nunes, Ana Bela. 2001. Actividade económica da população. In *Estatísticas Históricas Portuguesas*, ed. Nuno Valério, 149–197. Lisbon: INE.

———. 2006. A reforma fiscal de 1922. In *Os Impostos no Parlamento Português. Sistemas Fiscais e Doutrinas Fiscais nos Séculos XIX e XX*, ed. Nuno Valério, 121–160. Lisbon: Publicações Dom Quixote.

Nunes, Ana Bela, and Nuno Valério. 2005. Moeda e bancos. In *História Económica de Portugal, 1700–2000, Vol. III, O Século XX*, ed. Pedro Lains and Álvaro Ferreira da Silva, 227–263. Lisbon: ICS.

Oliveira, Pedro Aires. 2010. A República e a guerra, 1914–1918. In *Outubro: a Revolução Republicana em Portugal (1910–1926)*, ed. Luciano Amaral, 185–225. Lisbon: Edições 70.

———. 2014. Um império à medida das possibilidades (c. 1890–1910). In *História da Expansão e do Império Português*, ed. João Paulo Oliveira e Costa, 409–446. Lisbon: A Esfera dos Livros.

Palma, Nuno, and Jaime Reis. 2018. Can Autocracy Promote Literacy? Evidence from a Cultural Alignment Success Story. EHES Working Papers in Economic History, No. 127.

Patriarca, Fátima. 1995. *A Questão Social no Salazarismo, 1930–1947*. Lisbon: Imprensa Nacional-Casa da Moeda.

Pedreira, Jorge. 1998. Imperialismo e Economia. In *História da Expansão Portuguesa, Vol. IV – Do Brasil para África (1808–1930)*, ed. Francisco Bethencourt and Diogo Ramada Curto, 268–301. Lisbon: Círculo de Leitores.

Pereira, João Martins. 2005. *Para a História da Indústria em Portugal, 1941–1965. Adubos Azotados e Siderurgia*. Lisbon: ICS.
Pereira, Miriam Halpern. 1999. As origens do Estado-Providência em Portugal: as novas fronterias entre público e privado. *Ler História* 37: 45–61.
Pimenta, Fernando Tavares. 2005. *Brancos de Angola. Autonomismo e Nacionalismo*. Coimbra: Minerva.
Pires, Ana Paula. 2009. *Portugal e a I Guerra Mundial. A República e a Economia de Guerra*. Lisbon: Caleidoscópio.
Porter, Andrew. 1994. *European Imperialism, 1860–1914*. London: Palgrave.
Ramos, Rui, Bernardo Vasconcelos e Sousa, and Nuno Gonçalo Monteiro. 2009. *História de Portugal*. Lisbon: A Esfera dos Livros.
Reis, Célia. 2001. Cabo Verde. In *Nova História da Expansão Portuguesa – O Império Africano, 1890–1930*, ed. A.H. de Oliveira Marques, 95–144. Lisbon: Editorial Estampa.
Reis, Jaime. 1979. A'Lei da Fome': as origens do proteccionismo cerealífero (1889–1914). *Análise Social* XV (60): 745–793.
———. 1995a. Portuguese Banking in the Inter-war Period. In *Banking, Currency and Finance in Europe Between the Wars*, ed. Charles H. Feinstein, 472–501. Oxford: Oxford University Press.
———. 1995b. The National Savings Bank as an Instrument of Economic Policy: Portugal in the Interwar Period. In *The Evolution of Financial Institutions and Markets in Twentieth Century Europe*, ed. Youssef Cassis et al., 163–186. London: Scholar Press.
Ritschl, Albrecht, and Tobias Straumann. 2010. Business Cycles and Economic Policy, 1914–1945. In *The Cambridge Economic History of Modern Europe, Vol II: 1870 to the Present*, ed. Stephen Broadberry and Kevin H. O'Rourke, 156–180. Cambridge University Press: Cambridge.
Roses, Joan, and Nikolaus Wolf. 2010. Aggregate Growth, 1913–1950. In *The Cambridge Economic History of Modern Europe, Vol II: 1870 to the Present*, ed. Stephen Broadberry and Kevin H. O'Rourke, 181–207. Cambridge University Press: Cambridge.
Santos, Fernando Teixeira dos. 1996. Last to Join the Gold Standard. In *Currency Convertibility: The Gold Standard and Beyond*, ed. Jorge Braga de Macedo, Barry Eichengreen, and Jaime Reis, 182–203. London: Routledge.
Silva, Álvaro Ferreira da. 2016. Multinationals and Foreign Direct Investment: The Portuguese Experience (1900–2010). *Journal of Evolutionary Studies in Business* II (1): 40–68.

Silva, Álvaro Ferreira da, and Luciano Amaral. 2010. A economia portuguesa na I República. In *Outubro: a Revolução Republicana em Portugal (1910–1926)*, 257–298. Lisbon: Edições 70.

Silva, Álvaro Ferreira da, Luciano Amaral, and Pedro Neves. 2016. Business Groups in Portugal in the *Estado Novo* Period (1930–1974): Family, Power and Structural Change. *Business History* 58 (1): 49–68.

Silva, Ester Gomes da, and Pedro Lains. 2013. Capital Formation and Long-Run Growth: Evidence from Portuguese Data, 1910–2011. Paper Presented at Iberometrics III, Zaragoza University.

Silveira, Joel Frederico da. 1998. Guiné. In *Nova História da Expansão Portuguesa – O Império Africano, 1825–1890*, ed. Valentim Alexandre and Jill Dias, 211–267. Lisbon: Editorial Estampa.

Tanzi, Vito, and Ludger Schuknecht. 2000. *Public Spending in the Twentieth Century: A Global Perspective*. Cambridge: Cambridge University Press.

Telo, António José. 1977. *O Sidonismo e o Movimento Operário Português. Luta de Classes em Portugal, 1917–1919*. Lisboa: Ulmeiro.

———. 1980. *Decadência e Queda da Primeira República Portuguesa*. Lisboa: Regra do Jogo.

Thomson, David. 1966. *Europe Since Napoleon*. London: Penguin.

Valério, Nuno. 1984. *A Moeda em Portugal, 1913–1947*. Lisbon: Livraria Sá da Costa Editora.

———. 1994. Valério. In *As Finanças Públicas Portuguesas entre as Duas Guerras Mundiais*. Lisbon: Cosmos.

———. 2001a. *O Escudo - A Unidade Monetária Portuguesa, 1911–2001*. Lisbon: Banco de Portugal.

———. 2001b. Contas nacionais. In *Estatísticas Históricas Portuguesas*, ed. Nuno Valério, 505–535. Lisbon: INE.

———. 2006. Os debates das leis de autorização das receitas e despesas. In *Os Impostos no Parlamento Português. Sistemas Fiscais e Doutrinas Fiscais nos Séculos XIX e XX*, ed. Nuno Valério, 161–178. Lisbon: Publicações Dom Quixote.

Valério, Nuno, and Palmira Tjipilica. 2006. Economic Activity in the Portuguese Colonial Empire: A Factor Analysis Approach. Paper Presented at the International Economic History Congress, Helsinki.

Valério, Nuno, Ana Bela Nunes, Carlos Bastien, Rita Martins de Sousa, and Sandra Domingos Costa. 2006. *História do Sistema Bancário Português, Vol. I, Da Formação do Primeiro Banco Português à Assunção pelo Banco de Portugal das Funções de Banco Central, 1822–1931*. Lisbon: Banco de Portugal.

4

The *Estado Novo* Period: The 1930s and World War II

Political chronology is again relevant to understand the Portuguese economy from the 1930s onward. Not because the economy changed drastically its behavior, but because the political regime that was installed in the country after 1933, the *Estado Novo*, conceived the relationship between the Government and economic agents in a much different manner than the previous ones. The *Estado Novo* was the Portuguese version of the kind of authoritarian or fascist regimes that spread throughout Europe during the 1920s and 1930s, and understood its role in what concerns the economy as based on high interventionism. During the period of its existence, the regime was able to put the economy under a vast set of administrative and bureaucratic mechanisms that limited significantly the freedom of economic agents. Although a lot has been said about this kind of interventionism, the truth is that much of it did not differ much from what regimes contemporary to the *Estado Novo* that retained a democratic form did as well. The main reason for this similarity was the difficulties of the world economy in the interwar period: all Western countries resorted to protectionism, economic nationalism, and Government intervention once

L. Amaral, *The Modern Portuguese Economy in the Twentieth and Twenty-First Centuries*, Palgrave Studies in Economic History,
https://doi.org/10.1007/978-3-030-24548-1_4

they failed to return to the economic liberal order of the nineteenth century and once the 1930s crisis started. The Portuguese *Estado Novo* was one more of them.

1 The Course of Political Events

The essential political problem of the regime of the First Republic continued to be, to its end, the inability to have a peaceful rotation of political personnel through Government. The main faction of the regime (associated with the Portuguese Republican Party, PRP) continued to dominate the levers of Government for all practical purposes, despite some reforms at the end of World War I, especially designed to give the President of the Republic a "moderating power" that should have allowed him to become a sort of umpire of the system. In the sequence of the 1921 "bloody night", there was a serious attempt to reform the system: a sort of two-party mechanism was created, in order for the Government to be held, in alternate fashion, between a moderate left-wing party and a moderate right-wing one. But the practice was always far from these intentions, as the diverse rivalries within the political personnel of the regime finished by immersing them in an environment of mistrust. In the end, rather than a center-right and a center-left party, two left-wing factions emerged, one moderate and the other radical. When, on June 1925, the moderate faction was able to manipulate elections in such a manner as to humiliate the radical faction, the fate of the First Republic was sealed: from then on practically everyone, including now the radical left-wing forces, became enemies of the regime (Ramos et al. 2009).

The fact that the Army had become a constant public presence after Portugal's participation in the war made all factions opposing the regime turn to the military. The size of the Army had more than doubled during the war, and the weak republican governments were unable to demobilize it: the share of defense on public spending continued to be one of the highest in Western Europe. In a country with such low human capital, the Army represented a sort of technocratic elite whose supposed efficiency contrasted with the supposedly cynical and unstable traditional political elite. Furthermore, the Army was then conflicting with political power over the issue of their pay: during the inflationary period, until 1922, military wages had lost value and, after that, their level had been virtually frozen during the fiscal reforms of 1922 and 1924. Consequently, dissatisfaction with the republican governments was generalized also among the military (Ramos et al. 2009).

Various military revolts erupted during the 1920s, but most of them failed. Until one succeeded, on 28 May 1926, giving birth to the regime of the Military Dictatorship (*Ditadura Militar*): the parliament was shut down and the military started ruling by decree. This regime was as chaotic as the First Republic, however, as very few things unified the winners of 28 May, except opposition to the First Republic. What is more, public finances began to deteriorate again, something that had been one of the few partial successes of the traditional republican political class since 1922 (Ramos et al. 2009; Silva and Amaral 2010). This is precisely the moment when António de Oliveira Salazar appeared in the political scene, with strong ideas about how to definitely solve the fiscal and monetary crisis. Salazar had acquired a strong technical reputation as an economist, but his political origins were in the catholic, right-wing forces of the political spectrum. He was able to reinforce his reputation with the fiscal reforms of 1928 and 1929, analyzed in the previous chapter, and used it as the base to conquer power. Once there, he was able to harness a vast range of political factions (from right to left), under a political formula inspired in the sort of authoritarian regimes that had started appearing in Europe in the sequence of the fascist Italian experience of 1922 (Ramos et al. 2009).

In 1932, Salazar proposed a new constitution and organized a popular plebiscite to approve it. The plebiscite took place on 19 March 1933. The Constitution of 1933 marked the end of the Military Dictatorship and gave birth to an authoritarian regime, based on strong nationalism and a corporatist institutional framework. In itself, the Constitution was an eclectic text lumping together demo-liberal and corporatist sources: it recognized all typical liberal rights, such as the right to vote, the right to associate in a party, the right to express opinion freely, as well as protection against arbitrary imprisonment. This occurred, however, simply in the realm of principles. The actual limits to those freedoms were, according to the constitution, to be codified in ordinary law. It so happens that ordinary law set those limits in a very strict way, leaving, furthermore, a large role for arbitrary decisions on the part of administrative or police authorities (Lucena 1976; Cruz 1988). Despite the constitutional guarantees, the truth is that the creation of consistent political parties or movements was forbidden for any practical purposes, freedom of expression was vastly limited by a systematic use of censorship, and political crimes were exempted from general law, so that all guarantees against arbitrary imprisonment could be ignored by the political police (Lucena 1976; Cruz 1988; Ó 1999; Ribeiro 2000).

Despite all of this, a simulacrum of parliamentary representation survived under the regime. Legislative power was held by a representative chamber, formed every four years in the sequence of national elections. To these elections only the candidates of the single party, the National Union (*União Nacional*), could run. The President of the Republic (at least until 1959) was also elected by the population in general. The elections were run under very harsh restrictions: the franchise was limited, although larger than under the First Republic—the new 1933 to 1935 legislation gave the right to vote to all literate men over 21 years of age (as in the Republic), enlarging it also to illiterate ones having an income high enough to pay taxes, and to women having a secondary or university degree (both groups constituting extremely small minorities within the population of the country).[1] The number of voters passed from 545,192, or 9% of the population, in 1925, to 743,930, or 11% of the population, in 1938 (Cruz 1988, p. 196). Since, in addition to this, there were no organized legal opposition parties, the significance of the electoral procedures was, hence, rather limited. In the new regime, parliamentary representation should be complemented by corporatist representation. Corporatism was seen by the *Estado Novo*'s political elite as a "third way" between liberalism and socialism: the relationship between the Government and civil society should overcome both the extreme individualistic atomization of liberalism and the excessive centralization

[1] Decree-law 23,406, 27 December 1933, Decree-law 24,631, 6 November 1934, and Decree-law 23,897, 10 January 1935.

of State socialism (Lucena 1976; Brito 1989). The State should, hence, no longer look to individuals simply as such but rather as members of what were then called "intermediate corps", e.g., the family, the union, or the corporation. In those corps, individuals should cooperate toward a common goal and the corps themselves should cooperate with each other toward larger but still common goals. A Corporatist Chamber, complementary to the National Assembly (or parliament), was created, although only with consultative powers, and a vast set of corporatist organisms were put in place in the first decades of the regime (Schmitter 1999; Cruz 1988).

2 The *Estado Novo* and Economic Interventionism

This institutional setting put the *Estado Novo* in a class of authoritarian and corporatist regimes that became frequent in Europe in the 1920 and 1930s (Payne 1995; Cardoso and Mendonça 2012). All of them relied on a large number of methods of intervention in the economy. But they were not alone, for democratic regimes also developed similar methods, essentially in response to the course of world economic events. The ideal structure of the Portuguese corporatist regime was a sort of pyramid, set up in a document having a para-constitutional nature called National Labor Statute (*Estatuto do Trabalho Nacional*).[2] At the basis of this pyramid, there were the primary organizations. These received the name of unions (*sindicatos*), for employees in industry and services, and guilds (*grémios*), for employers in both activities plus in agriculture and fisheries. In agriculture and fisheries, two other kinds of organizations were created: the houses of the people (*casas do povo*, in agriculture) and the houses of the fishermen (*casas dos pescadores*, in fisheries). Above these primary organizations, there should be a set of secondary organizations, federating the primary ones, precisely called federations. Finally, towering the whole edifice, corporations

[2]Decree-law 23,048, 23 September 1933.

should be established (Lucena 1976; Freire and Ferreira 2019). Despite being apparently designed in a clear way, this structure was, in reality, subject to various exceptions, essentially for two reasons. The first reason is that, in addition to these properly speaking corporatist organizations, there were other organizations created by the *Estado Novo*, having been defined as "para-" or "pre-corporatist", where the Government and the different agents of a specific market interacted in order to define various aspects of the functioning of that market. These were called organisms for economic coordination (*organismos de coordenação económica*) and had vast powers: they set prices, quantities to be produced, margins of operation of the agents in the market as well as a vast array of regulatory principles (Lucena 1978, 1979; Freire and Ferreira 2019). The second reason complicating the picture is that some of the corporatist organizations were compulsory while others were voluntary and that some were the sole representatives of the agents in a certain market while others shared that role with other non-corporatist organizations (Lucena 1976; Freire and Ferreira 2019).

Ideally, for the *Estado Novo*, the corporatist organizations should arise out of the spontaneous interest in their creation of economic and social agents. In practice, some were born in that manner but most were created by the Government (Lucena 1976; Freire and Ferreira 2019). These organizations, from unions to guilds, had very little autonomy. The 1891 and 1924 legislation on unions was replaced, in September 1933, by the National Labor Statute and three more pieces of legislation, one of them dedicated to employers in all three sectors of the economy,[3] another one to workers in the secondary and tertiary sectors,[4] and still one more dedicated to rural workers.[5] Existing unions were asked to adopt the new corporatist format or dissolve until the end of the year. As for guilds, they were given until 1938 to convert to the new corporatist format or disappear. But even after that the largest traditional employers' associations survived: the Central Association of Portuguese

[3]Decree 23,049, 23 September 1933.

[4]Decree 23,050, 23 September 1933.

[5]Decree 23,051, 23 September 1933.

Agriculture (ACAP), the Portuguese Industrial Association (AIP), the Industrial Association of Porto (AIPortuense), the Commercial Association of Lisbon (ACL), and the Commercial Association of Porto (ACP) (Cerdeira and Padilha 1998). The new legislation forced unions to be small, representing workers only at the level of the profession and of the region (they could not represent workers at the national level). The Government intervened in almost every aspect of their life, monitoring elections (and arbitrarily accepting or rejecting their results), sanctioning statutes, and constantly interfering in the bargaining process between workers and employers (Lucena 1976; Patriarca 1995). What is more, the Government was given the power to set wages independently of the bargaining process.[6] All of this in a context where striking was forbidden[7] and little employment protection existed: reasons for firing workers established in labor law were many and vague, and easy to be invoked by employers.[8] No generalized unemployment benefit existed. Legal conditions were, thus, generally unfavorable to workers, even if many times employers also disliked their corporatist organizations and the constant intervention of the Government in the bargaining process, especially because officials many times decided in favor of workers (namely on the issue of wages, where the Government's capacity to set by decree the wage level was used frequently) (Patriarca 1995).

Many authors note that the theoretical corporatist structure proposed by the *Estado Novo* was never really established in practice (Lucena 1976; Garrido 2016). But this did not prevent the regime from relying on the incomplete structure of organisms that were effectively created to implement a vast apparatus with which to intervene systematically in the economy. And we still need to take into consideration the purely governmental organizations, adding to an institutional paraphernalia that was used to impose various limits to the free functioning of markets. This started with prices, which, for most goods, were controlled at

[6]Decree 25,701, 1 August 1935, Decree 29,006, 17 September 1938, and Decree 32,749, 15 April 1943.

[7]Decree-law, 23,870, 18 May 1934.

[8]Law 1952, 10 March 1937.

various levels of the economic cycle (in production, consumption, and sale); it continued with the regulation of markets, where sale conditions and margins were also imposed, and was complemented by a series of other instruments such as tax incentives, ad hoc tariff exemptions or special credit instruments, designed to affect the structure and behavior of the economy.

One of the fundamental reasons why these mechanisms of Government intervention in the economy existed was the general distrust of the regime about competition (Lucena 1976; Rosas 1986; Brito 1989). This lack of trust was particularly visible in the case of industrial licensing, where the main instrument of policy was something called industrial conditioning (*condicionamento industrial*). The new legislation was put in place between 1931 and 1937 and made the opening and restructuring of factories, as well as purchases of industrial inputs and capital goods in the world market subject to a strict bureaucratic and arbitrary process: requests to install a factory had to be evaluated by the Government, whose decision was discretionary, after consultation with the firms already existing in the market; the same applied to the restructuring of factories and even to imports of certain materials. In certain branches, once a factory was installed or restructured, the Government also had the power to impose prices by decree. In other branches, the discretionary decisions of the Government were subject to general rules, so that if a certain industrial project fulfilled certain requirements, it would be licensed. But it was always possible for the Government to reject the project on some arbitrary grounds. Only the so-called household industries (*indústrias domésticas*) were exempted from the system: these were very small firms whose dimensions were never clearly defined. It is very difficult to know the exact coverage of industrial conditioning. We know that in 1960 it covered about 30% of the existing firms (Loureiro 1991, p. 142). What we do not know is the evolution through time as well as what part of industrial output or value added they represented, but it should be more than 30%, as all firms above a certain dimension were subject to the regime. The stated objectives of this system were to prevent the negative effects of "excessive competition" and the "de-nationalization" of the Portuguese economy, i.e., an "excessive" presence of foreign capital. This means that industrial conditioning was also a mechanism to control foreign investment, i.e., it was an instrument to limit both internal and external competition (for detailed studies on *condicionamento industrial*, see Brito 1989; Loureiro 1991; Confraria 1992).[9]

The Government developed other forms of intervention. One of them was a primitive version of central planning, in a law called "Law of Economic Reconstitution" (*Lei de Reconstituição Económica*), of 1935.[10] The law was essentially a list of investment expenditures to be made for a period of 15 years (1935–1950), based on the availability of resources resulting from the policy of budget balance followed by the regime since 1928. The amounts involved in this list of expenditures corresponded to roughly 3.5% of GDP, and about half of the resources were used in the re-equipment of the Portuguese Armed Forces, the other half being dedicated to the following items: agriculture, especially reforestation and irrigation schemes, and public works, especially ports, roads, airports, and social housing. To note is the small amounts dedicated to electricity and also to colonial investment (Nunes and Valério 1983).

Another form taken by Government intervention was the direct participation in the ownership of various companies. Although never becoming the exclusive owner of firms, the Government became a significant partner in public–private joint ventures (such as in aerial, maritime, and rail transportation, electricity, and oil refining), and this gave it an important influence on various investment decisions. This made of the Government one of the largest stock owners in the country, although having a scattered portfolio.

All of this was compounded with the continuation of protectionism inherited from previous periods. As we have seen in Chapter 3, the revision of the general level of tariffs was part of Salazar's fiscal reforms in December 1929. But new measures were taken during the 1930s. In the beginning of 1932, the general level of tariffs was again increased by 20%, while at the same time more products were put under tariff

[9]Decree 19,354 14 February 1931, and Law 1,956, 17 May 1937.

[10]Law 1,914, 24 May 1935.

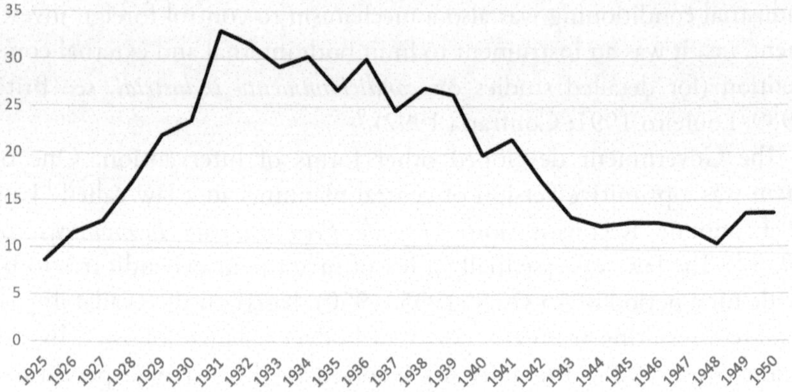

Fig. 1 Average tariffs % of imports, Portugal, 1925–1950 (*Source* Fontoura and Valério [2001])

protection (Rosas 1986).[11] To this we must add the introduction of quantitative restrictions. These became quite common in international economic relations during the 1930s, as countries resorted to "beggar-thy-neighbor" policies in order to protect their economies. Portugal followed the trend, something that was accompanied by the signing of various clearing agreements with different countries, another common practice in those years (Rosas 1986). Figure 1 shows the weight of tariffs over imports growing in the sequence of the 1923 tariff schedule and, again, after the 1929 one, but then stabilizing or even declining mildly afterward. But, as we have just seen, protection took increasingly other forms during the 1930s. Portugal continued to be one of the most protectionist countries in Europe and one of the least open: Fig. 2 shows the decline of openness in the 1930s across the Western world; even if the weight of exports declined on practically all countries presented in the graph, Portugal remained the least open among them.

Agriculture was a particularly protected sector. This had certainly to do with pressures from agricultural interest groups but also with the notion that the "beggar-thy-neighbor" policies adopted throughout the

[11] Decree 20,935, 26 February 1932.

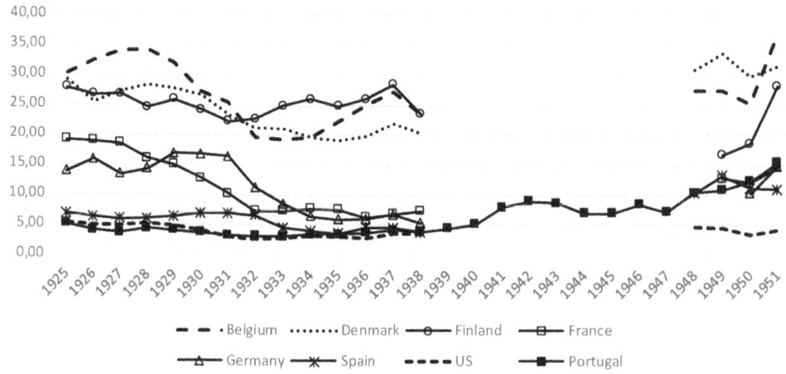

Fig. 2 Openness, various countries, 1925–1950 (exports % GDP) Current prices; (*Source* Federico and Tena [2018], except Portugal: Fontoura and Valério [2001])

world should not leave Portugal without a response: the country had to be as self-sufficient in foodstuffs as possible. To this must be added the idea that the overpopulation of the countryside had to be dealt nationally, once the traditional escape route of emigration had been closed, due to the international crisis. Protection through tariffs, quantitative restrictions, and various support mechanisms (from prices to different subsidies and other instruments) was especially felt in grain (mostly wheat), olive oil, wine, wool, rice, milk, and meat. One of the most famous policies of the period was the "Wheat Campaign", initiated in 1929 and where all the above-mentioned instruments were used to expand massively the production of wheat (Baptista 1993; Amaral and Freire 2017).

But besides protection, the *Estado Novo* also held some ideas of structural improvement for agriculture. One of them, shared by some members of the political personnel and technocrats (although not all of them), was that of "agricultural reform". Many of these ideas had already circulated during the period of the First Republic but had never passed into actual policy, mostly on account of the weak nature of the republican governments. These were particularly difficult policies, as they involved meddling with property rights. But as a large number of the republican elites transited into the new regime, many of their ideas were given a new lease of life during the *Estado Novo*. "Agricultural reform" implied mostly the modification of the property structure, by dividing the southern latifundia into smaller plots and by grouping the northern minifundia into larger plots. Due to the limited rainfall in the southern part of the country, this should be accompanied by the irrigation of the new smaller plots. The whole process implied a vast transfer of population between the "overpopulated" north and the "sub-populated" south, something the politicians of the time called "internal colonization". The new southern farms should, additionally, replace the traditional dryland crops (wheat, olive oil, cork, and cattle) with new ones, especially fruit and vegetables. Finally, vast stretches of the territory, either in public or communal lands (especially in the north), should be converted to forest. The final social outcome of the process was the creation of a strong agricultural middle class (Baptista 1993; Amaral 2000; Freire 2011; Amaral and Freire 2017). In 1936, an Internal Colonization Board (*Junta de Colonização Interna*) was created, in order to study the implementation of plans for population resettling,[12] and in 1937 the Government was given powers to expropriate certain agricultural properties for purposes of internal colonization.[13] In 1930, an Agricultural Board for Irrigation Projects (*Junta Autónoma das Obras de Hidráulica Agrícola*) was created and, in 1937, this board produced an irrigation plan to be put in place in the next 12 years. The plan was approved the following year, and various irrigation projects were built from its first year onward (Baptista 1993). In 1938, a Forestation Plan (*Plano de Povoamento Florestal*) for the next 30 years was approved and began to be implemented in 1940.[14] In the latter case, there was a link with industrial policy, as it should be connected with the development of two modern industries: paper and paper pulp, and resinous products (Baptista 1993; Branco 2011; Amaral 1994, 2000; Amaral and Freire 2017; Branco and Neves 2018). Ideas of reform gained particular strength as, especially after the Wheat Campaign, the entirety of the Portuguese territory fit for agricultural use had finally

[12]Decree 27,207, 16 November 1936.

[13]Law 1,949, 15 February 1937.

[14]Law 1,971, 15 June 1938.

been put under use. Agricultural output could not increase anymore out of simply putting more land under cultivation—the matter was now one of productivity (Baptista 1993; Amaral 1994, 2000; Branco 2011; Amaral and Freire 2017).

In what concerns industry, the regime's policy in the 1930s was subject to two sometimes contradictory main principles, both based on protection and Government support. One was import-substitution, implying an idea of industrialization based on branches that were considered to be "fundamental". This is the case of chemicals, oil refining, cement, machinery and equipment or paper and paper pulp (Rosas 1986; Confraria 1992; Branco and Neves 2018). The other principle was protection across the board, without distinction between branches, size, or efficiency of firms, in the name of preventing bankruptcies and unemployment (Rosas 1986; Confraria 2005). The Government's approach respecting industrial relations should also be seen as part of industrial policy, as the generally unfavorable attitude toward labor developed by the Government was an instrument to keep wages low.

Fiscal and monetary policy also had an impact on the behavior of the economy. Between 1928 and 1931, Salazar, as Minister of Finance, put in practice a series of fiscal and monetary reforms aimed at, in the short run, solving the financial troubles generated by World War I and its aftermath, and, in the long run, producing the conditions for the growth of the economy. His actions revealed a commitment to fiscal balance and stabilization of prices. The 1929 fiscal reform was described in the previous chapter, but we should add to it a very strong commitment to long-run budget equilibrium, through its transformation into a constitutional principle (Article 66 of the 1933 Constitution), as well as by denying the ersatz parliament of the regime the ability to propose and vote the annual budget, thus keeping it under the iron fist of Salazar's "financial dictatorship" (Lopes 2005). These authoritarian methods did indeed allow for budget balance to be respected throughout the 1930s, as shown in Fig. 3.

This approach allowed for monetary discipline as well. The 1931 monetary reform reinserted the escudo into the gold standard (now the gold-exchange standard), with a value of 65.51 mg of fine gold, and made the Bank of Portugal's (BoP) notes and coins fully convertible.

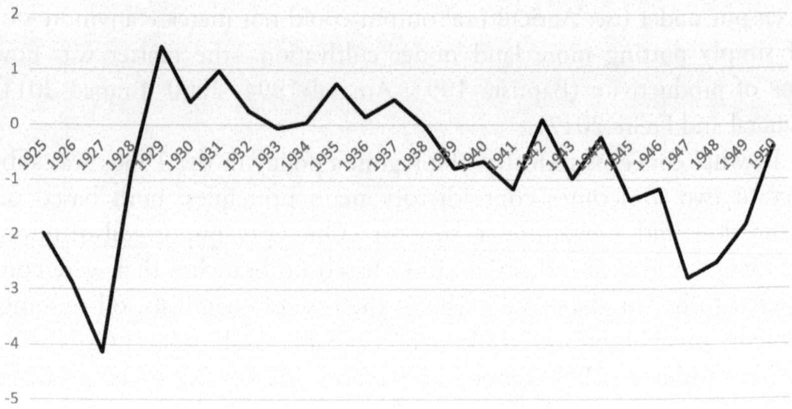

Fig. 3 Government budget deficit, Portugal, 1925–1950 (% GDP) (*Source* Mata [2001]; Valério [2001])

Following the recommendations of the 1922 Genoa Conference, convertibility was indirect, through sterling. In this new monetary regime, the BoP was assigned the task of keeping the parity of the escudo with gold. In principle, this should have been enough to control inflation, but the Government went beyond it, forcing the BoP to adopt an ultra-cautious stance: the bank should keep reserves in gold, foreign currency convertible in gold, and public debt of countries in the gold-exchange standard in a proportion of at least 30% of its sight liabilities (notes and deposits) and, independently of this reserve, could not issue more than 2.2 billion escudos in notes without full backing with gold reserves (bullion or coins).[15] Thus, the BoP should not use discretion but simply follow the rule of indexing money issuing to the amount of gold and foreign reserves in its hands. This amount depended on the international payments position of the country. Due to the traditional pattern of this payments position, which was one of constant struggle to achieve balance, this indexation was supposed to allow for low inflation. If that proved insufficient, there was the

[15]Decrees 19,869 and 19,870, 9 June 1931.

additional 2.2 billion escudos limit for notes without full gold backing (Valério 1984; Amaral 2018).

This reform, however, came at the same time as the virtual end of the gold standard, when sterling abandoned the system in September 1931 (Eichengreen 1996). For the sake of realism, due to the special trade connections between Portugal and Britain, the Portuguese authorities decided to follow the step. The escudo abandoned the gold standard a mere three months after having returned to it. In doing so, Portugal became one of the two dozen countries that suspended convertibility and depreciated until the end of 1932, leaving only seven European countries in the gold standard (France, Belgium, Switzerland, the Netherlands, Czechoslovakia, Poland, and Romania) (Eichengreen 1996). The Portuguese currency remained pegged to sterling, although conditionally: in case of what the Portuguese monetary authorities considered to be "excessive" depreciation of sterling, they pegged it to the US dollar instead (which remained in the gold standard until 1933). Despite all of this, the BoP kept on acting *as if* inserted in the gold standard. Thanks to this monetary setting, price and exchange rate stability were a hallmark of the period (Figs. 4 and 5).

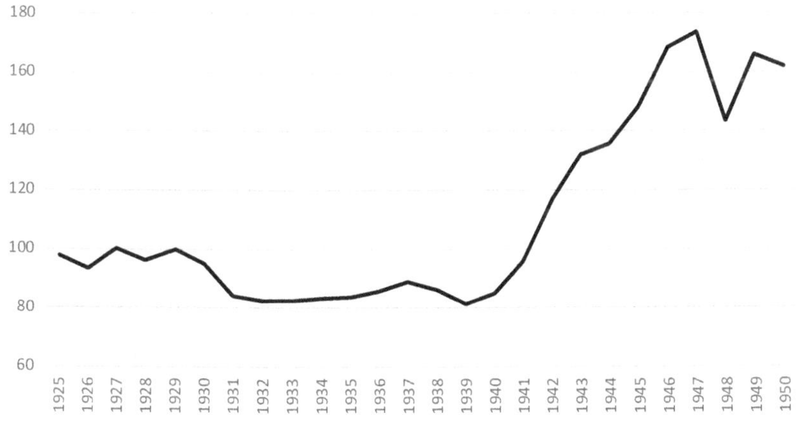

Fig. 4 Consumer price index, Portugal, 1925–1950 (1929 = 100) (*Source* Bastien [2001])

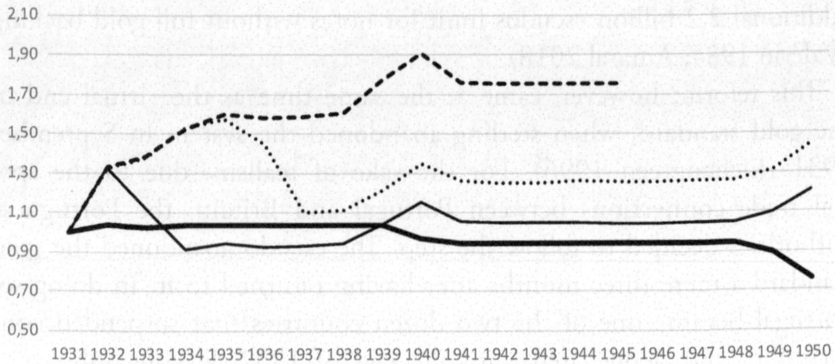

Fig. 5 Index of the exchange rate of the escudo versus main currencies, 1931–1950 (1939 = 1) (*Source* Amaral [2018])

Besides discipline, the governments of the authoritarian regime kept also a low level of public spending, as shown in Fig. 4: the Portuguese Government remained the smallest in Europe, only closely followed by that of Sweden and Spain. A significant part of the explanation for the low level of spending has to do with the decline of the amounts dedicated to debt service, as a consequence of the systematic efforts to balance the budget, with the exception of a few years between 1934 and 1936 (Valério 1994) (Fig. 6). Apart from this, the structure of expenditure remained roughly stable, with the largest items being dedicated to the Armed Forces and general administrative services. The relatively high level of military spending was rather common in Europe at the time; Table 1 shows that the proportion of public spending dedicated by Portugal to defense was similar to that of most other European countries. A certain change is observed in the expenditures devoted to the economy, essentially as a consequence of investment on public works, under the heading of the Law of Economic Reconstitution (see above): still the amounts were relatively low, passing from 1% of GDP in 1928 to 2% in 1939. Control of spending was especially visible in the case of the colonies (never going beyond 0.2% of GDP), social items (always around 0.4% of GDP), and education (stable at around 1% of GDP) until 1939. In the latter two cases, the behavior of the Portuguese Government diverges from that of most other European

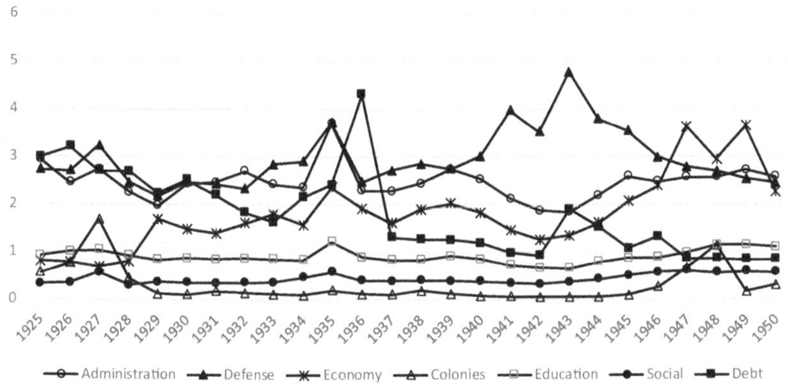

Fig. 6 Structure spending, Portugal 1925–1950 (% GDP) (*Source* Mata [2001])

and North American countries, where public spending on social items started increasing decisively during the 1920s and 1930s (Lindert 1994) (Table 1).

The impact of spending on public works was visible in the period. Most of the effort was dedicated to the construction of new ports and renovation of the old (almost 80% of the overall spending on public works) (Nunes and Valério 1983; Rosas 1986). But the amounts spent on the construction of new roads and in the restructuring of the preexisting road network were also important: 500 kilometers of new roads were built between 1930 and 1939, besides the construction of new

Table 1 Structure of public spending (some items), various countries, 1930–1937 (% GDP)

	Defense 1937	Education 1937	Social 1930
France	5.5	1.3	1.0
Germany	9.6	2.8	4.8
Italy	9.9	1.6	0.1
Spain	3.8	1.6	0.1
Sweden	1.6	–	2.6
UK	5.3	4.0	2.2
Portugal	2.7	0.8	0.4

Source Tanzi and Schuknecht (2000), except "Social": Lindert (2004), and Portugal: Mata (2001) and Valério (2001)

concrete bridges (replacing many old wooden ones) and the substitution of the surface of many existing roads. The first motorway in the country was built, and various other spectacular projects were part of the overall plan, such as a famous coastline road north of Lisbon (Costa 2012; Sousa 2016). The number of persons transported and the volume of merchandise carried had a strong expansion during the period (Vieira 1980; Rosas 1986; Henriques 1999). The third largest volume of spending was dedicated to school construction. This was especially true after 1941, when the Government adopted a plan of mass construction of new primary schools for the next ten years (Beja et al. 1996; Gomes and Machado 2019). About 2000 new schools were built until 1950. Although less important than these items, some spending was also dedicated to social housing and various urban improvements (Ferreira 1983; Pereira 1999).

Much less impressive was the volume of resources the Portuguese regime dedicated to social items, against the trend then starting in many European countries (and the United States), as a side effect of the 1930s crisis. As stated by Tanzi and Schucknecht (2000, p. 9), "by the late 1920s many European countries had introduced rudimentary social security systems, and the Depression resulted in a wave of expansionary Government expenditure policies including social programs, [...] [while] the United States introduced major public expenditure programs with the New Deal". The Portuguese regime did have a social policy, but the Government was not supposed to play a big role in it. The Portuguese social security system (or *Previdência*, in the jargon of the time) was an integral part of the new corporatist organisms of the regime. According to the Constitution and the National Labour Statute, all unions and entrepreneurs' associations should bargain to define working conditions, wages, and social security benefits in collective contracts, but the state would have no direct participation in the process (Lucena 1976). The role of the state in this context was simply one of legally approving, supervising, and coordinating the social security institutions created by the corporatist labor organizations. Funds for the *previdência* institutions were to be obtained through contributions coming from workers and entrepreneurs (5.5% of the workers' income, 15% of the employers'). The Government would give no financial help.

In 1933, the Institute for Compulsory Insurance and Social Protection that had been created in 1919 was replaced by the National Institute of Labor and Social Protection (*Instituto Nacional do Trabalho e Previdência*, INTP)[16] and in 1935 the first social security law was published.[17] According to it, the Government recognized only four types of institutions devoted to social security activities. First, there were those of the unions, those of the *Casas do Povo* (the rural workers corporatist associations), and those of the *Casas dos Pescadores* (the fishermen corporatist organizations). Second, there were those spontaneously created by the workers or professionals' associations outside the corporatist structure but that were recognized by the Government. Third, there were those of civil servants. Finally, there were the private associations of "mutual support" (Maia 1985; Carreira 1996). The social security institutions created by the corporatist organizations were named *Caixas Sindicais de Previdência* (CSP, the unions' social insurance associations), *Caixas de Previdência das Casas do Povo* (CP, the rural workers' social insurance associations),[18] and *Casas dos Pescadores* (CPe, the fishermen corporatist organizations). Those created outside the corporatist system were named *Caixas de Reforma* (CR, pensions associations), and *Caixas de Previdência* (CPre, social insurance associations). Civil servants had a variety of institutions, and private mutual support associations were named *Associações de Socorros Mútuos* (ASM) (Maia 1985; Carreira 1996).

Enrollment in CSPs, CPes, CRs, CPres, and some of the civil servants' associations was compulsory. In CPs, ASMs, and some of the civil servants' associations, enrollment was free. CSPs covered manufacturing and services' workers through a system of compulsory insurance in sick pay, incapacity to work, unemployment, and old age. CRs and CPres also covered manufacturing and services' workers in sick pay, incapacity to work, and old age, but unemployment was excluded.

---

[16]Decree-law 23,035, 23 September 1933.

[17]Law 1,884, 16 March 1935.

[18]These were to be extinguished in 1940. Whereas according to the 1935 law members of *Casas do Povo* were free to join a *Caixa de Previdência*, from 1940 onward membership of *Casas do Povo* implied automatic social security coverage.

Funds for CSPs, CRs, CPres, and civil servants' associations came, as we know, from the contributions of entrepreneurs and workers (or of the Government and workers, in the case of civil servants). CPs covered rural workers in various (and variable) cases. Depending on the financial health of the CPs, coverage could be restricted to medical assistance or, otherwise, be extended to birth-, death-, incapacity-subsidies, and pensions. The amounts involved were, nevertheless, very small when compared to services and manufacturing institutions. CPes covered fishermen in medical assistance and also conceded them incapacity- and death-subsidies (Maia 1985). Funds for CPs and CPes came from their members (which included the whole social spectrum of rural and fishing activities) (Maia 1985). The number of people covered by at least one of the systems was very low, ranging between 5 and 10% of the population in the last years of the 1930s (Carolo and Pereirinha 2010).

In what concerns education, the *Estado Novo* did not allocate large amounts of public money to it, but this does not mean that it did not attribute importance to the topic. In this respect, the new regime did not differ from the First Republic. The differences were visible less in the realm of principles than in the methods used. The *Estado Novo* presented itself as more pragmatic and hence able to use more expedient methods to solve some of the educational problems of the country. Together with that went a slight reordering of priorities. In what concerns literacy and primary education, the Republic proposed a complex and expensive system, whereas the *Estado Novo* proposed a cheaper and simpler one. In what refers to secondary education, the Republic improved the public system, while hampering the development of the private sector; the *Estado Novo*, on the contrary, kept the standards of the public system at the same level but, additionally, promoted the expansion of private schools. In what concerns university, the First Republic expanded significantly the system, whereas the *Estado Novo* had a more Malthusian approach. No doubt the regime's greatest success was in literacy and primary education (Amaral 2002, 2005).

There are three big moments in the *Estado Novo*'s educational policy concerning primary education. The first moment precedes the beginning of the regime itself, coinciding with the final years of the Military Dictatorship. The legislation enacted in that period would remain, nevertheless, of the utmost importance for the development of primary education throughout the following decades. Its starting point was a general critique of the educational methods used during the First Republic. The main lines of that legislation were the reduction of the period of compulsory education, the simplification of educational programs, and the increase in the supply of public teachers and schools. In 1927, compulsory schooling was reduced from five to four years,[19] and in 1928 to three (even if the primary cycle continued to have four years).[20] In 1930, primary education was divided into two levels, the first one corresponding to the first three years of schooling, the second corresponding to the fourth year.[21] Compulsory schooling was limited to the first (3-year) level. In 1931, teaching posts (*postos de ensino*) were created.[22] This was presented as a major step toward the reduction of illiteracy, since there was no need for school posts to have neither a proper building nor a fully prepared teacher. School posts should be installed in remote villages of small population and could operate in any place (a private house, the church, the main square of the village, etc.). Teaching in school posts was handed to persons whose minimum requirements were the ability to read and write (Rias 1997). The second big moment in educational reform took place between 1936 and 1938. The prior policy steps were consolidated and complemented. Additionally, policy acquired a more ideological tone. In 1936, a single compulsory book was adopted for all schools in the country.[23] Teaching posts changed their name to school posts (*postos escolares*), but that did not correspond to any change of substance of the institution. In 1938, all these reforms were consolidated.[24] The division of

[19]Decree 13,619, 17 May 1927.

[20]Decree 14,900, 16 January 1928.

[21]Decree 18,140, 22 March 1930.

[22]Decree 20,604, 30 November 1931.

[23]Law 1,941, 11 April 1936.

[24]Law 1,969, 20 May 1938.

Table 2 Yearly rate of growth of enrollment in the Portuguese schooling system, 1919–1949

	Primary	Secondary		University
		General	Professional	
1919–1929	1.64	2.14[a]		2.71
1930–1939	4.1	7.12	6.24[b]	3.79
[a]1940–1949	1.03	2.84	2.69	4.16

Notes [a]1918–1929 [b]1929–1940
Source Amaral (2002)

primary education into two levels was kept, the first three years corresponding to what was then called elementary education and the fourth one to what was called complementary education. Compulsory education was kept restricted to the elementary level. Teachers were divided into three categories: teachers properly, with a full preparation, and which were able to teach both in elementary and complementary schools; certified regents, with a less comprehensive preparation than the former, and that could only teach in elementary schools; and school regents, whose required preparation was the simple ability to read, in a first phase, and to read and write in a second phase, which could only teach in school posts. Primary education was to be supplied by the Government free of charge. This policy lowered the cost for households of primary education. In a country with so little urbanization (where the population was, hence, scattered all over the country in small communities), with an extremely thin road network and with poor transportation, the encroaching of the schooling system on the most remote parts of the country had a positive impact. Thus, even if the volume of spending did not change much, continuing to be among the lowest in Western Europe (Table 2), the number of students in primary schools increased significantly: Table 3 presents the growth rates of the number of students enrolled in the various educational levels and we can see that the period under study (from the 1930s onward) corresponded to an acceleration in relation to previous periods. In the 1930s, the number of students enrolled in primary schools rose 4% a year (1.64% in the 1920s), although the war, as expectable, brought a relative slowdown.

Table 3 GDP per capita annual growth rates, 1930–1950 (%)

1930–1935	1.306
1935–1939	−0.001
1939–1945	0.626
1930–1939	1.414
1930–1945	1.134

Source Batista et al. (1997)

The overall behavior of the economy in this period was not very impressive, as shown in Table 3: GDP per capita grew at 1.4% in the 1930s, with a visible slowdown in the second half of the decade, during which growth was even mildly negative. Figure 7 shows that the country was able to resist better the pressure of imports during the 1930s, as they declined from around 15% of GDP in 1925 to around 7% in 1931, where they stayed until the outbreak of World War II. At the same time, the composition of imports also changed, with foodstuffs declining and machines and equipment rising (Lains 2007), indicating both a substitution of foreign agricultural goods with national ones and a process of industrial import-substitution.

Agriculture performed better than industry: between 1930 and 1940, agricultural productivity grew almost twice as fast as industrial productivity

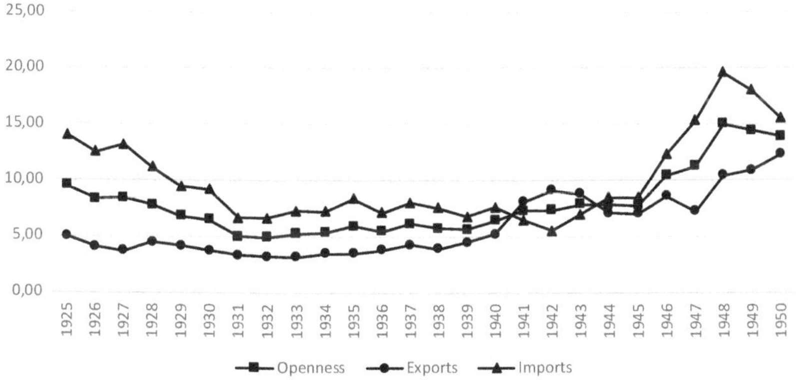

Fig. 7 Exports and imports, Portugal 1925–1950 (% GDP) Current prices; (Openness= 100 × [(Exports+Imports)/2]/GDP. *Source* Author's calculations based on Fontoura and Valério [2001], for the period 1925–1947, and Pinheiro [1997], for the period 1948–1950)

(Lains 2007). Within agriculture the largest contribution came from wheat, showing the effectiveness of the Wheat Campaign: as many new soils were then put under cultivation, the first years of their use corresponded to an explosion of productivity—but soon this effect would die out (Lains 2003a; Soares 2005). Rice also gave a contribution to improved agricultural productivity, but most other productions did not perform that well (Rosas 1986; Lains 2003a). As for the plans for agricultural reform, practically nothing went beyond preparatory studies (Baptista 1993; Branco 2011). In fact, many aspects of agricultural policy were contradictory with those plans: the clearest example was precisely that of wheat; the plans for structural reform would have implied dividing the latifundia of the southern drylands, colonizing the new farms with people from the north, irrigating them and introducing new cultures, especially fruit and vegetables. The Wheat Campaign meant the exact opposite: keep latifundia as they were, undivided, without artificial irrigation and without any crop substitution. Still, some governmental projects went ahead, although disconnected from change in property structure: both the Irrigation and Reforestation plans started to be implemented in the late 1930s and early 1940s, certainly contributing to agricultural productivity.

As for industry, most of the little growth that was registered was due to the new branches, profiting from the closing of the world market and the import-substitution policies: chemicals, machinery and equipment, cement, and paper pulp. New factories appeared, dedicated to fiber-reinforced cement, light bulbs, radios, batteries, various electrical machinery, mechanical production of glass, different fertilizers and chemicals, metalworking or oil refining, but their weight in the industrial structure remained small (Rosas 1986; Mateus 2005). Some of the most traditional and larger branches such as textiles, wood and cork, and food and beverages had a negative performance (Aguiar and Martins 2005). Some activities benefited from policies that were not specifically dedicated to them: chemical equipment industries benefited from the protection to wheat and rice, by supplying fertilizers and agricultural machines; cement benefited from the program of public works; paper and paper pulp from the reforestation program.

Figure 7 shows that exports had a good behavior during the 1930s. Decline was only mild in the first years of the 1930s crisis, from about

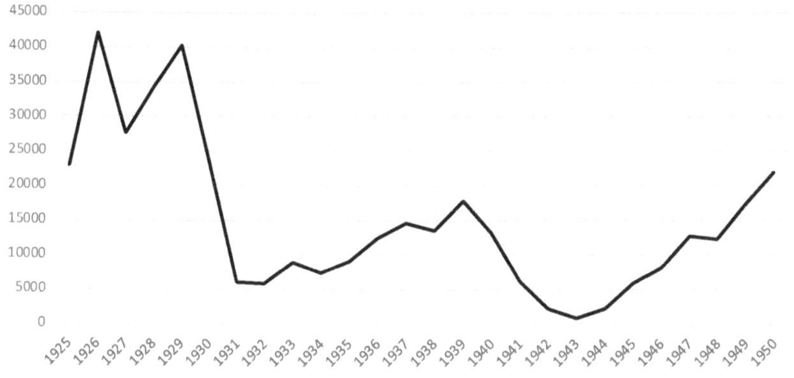

Fig. 8 Emigrants, Portugal, 1925–1950 (*Source* Baganha [1994])

5% of GDP to about 3%, in contrast to the heavy fall of imports. This means that the Portuguese export sector was able to sustain the worst effects of the international crisis. A lot of this had to do with the preservation of competitiveness under the pragmatic exchange rate policy (leading to the abandonment of the gold standard). It had also to do with the fact that there were not that many other suppliers in the world market for some of the goods exported by Portugal. But the impact was differentiated depending on the branches. Most of the traditional exports such as wine (especially Port), raw cork, and tinned fish were strongly affected in the first years of the 1930s, but not manufactured cork and resinous products; and, after an initial impact, soon tinned fish had a fast recovery (Rosas 1986).

The combination between the good performance of exports and the ability to protect the national market from imports led to the halving of the trade deficit, from roughly 10% of GDP to 5% in the early 1930s (Fig. 7). This helped to keep external balance, precisely in a period where the traditional source for current account balance, emigrant remittances, was faltering, thanks to the fall of emigration, again as a consequence of the crisis: such traditional outlets for Portuguese emigrants as Brazil or the United States were then closed to new immigrants. The number of emigrants declined to very low levels by historical standards (Fig. 8). Even if they recovered in the second half of the 1930s, they were comparable to the low levels of the 1890s crisis. But other sources of foreign exchange appeared in the period, especially tourism, which had its first big spurt in Portugal in the 1930s, mostly concentrated in the beach areas close to Lisbon. We cannot yet talk of mass tourism, quite on the contrary, as it was directed at the luxury end of the market (Cadavez 2017), but it still played an important role in the rebalancing of Portuguese international payments.

3 The Effects of World War II

World War II was another global shock with heavy impact on the Portuguese economy, although not entirely negative. Portugal remained neutral throughout the conflict. In fact, the Portuguese authorities never declared explicitly the country's neutrality but remained generally faithful to its practice, although with some attitudes verging on belligerence, always on the allies' side (Telo 1987, 2000). Portugal's neutrality was understood by all participants in the war as generally "aligned" with Britain. The two occasions in which Portugal was close to direct participation in the war were in the allies' favor. The most important of them was through the concession of Portuguese territory for the installation of an air base in the Azorean islands in 1944. Although allowing the allies to install such a base was still short of a declaration of war, it nevertheless showed a clear alignment. The other occasion was when, in 1945, Portugal offered a military contingent to help the allies liberate the Portuguese Asian colony of Timor from Japanese occupation.

This general Portuguese pro-allied stance had, however, to be tempered. First, although "collaborative neutrality" was in Britain's (and the US's) interest, it was not in Germany's interest. A hypothetical German invasion of the Iberian Peninsula was never entirely dismissed until the end of the war; and the threat of a Spanish invasion with German support survived until 1943 (see Rosas 1988; Telo 2000). Portugal felt, thus, the need to "keep Germany satisfied", and trade was a very important instrument for that. We are, of course, talking of a period when trade was a heavily politicized issue, put under close direction of national authorities. This had already been true before the war, when the trade wars of the 1930s pushed countries to abandon free trade and even protection by tariffs, adopting bilateral agreements with various direct physical restrictions instead. The situation was, of course, even more restrictive during the war. Additionally, Britain adopted an economic blockade, conducted by the new Ministry of Economic Warfare, through which it used a series of instruments to avoid neutrals to trade with Germany (Milward 1976). The British Government was aware of most trade relations between Portugal and Germany and even tolerated it (on the verge of fomenting it) precisely in order to, in Churchill's own words, "keep the Germans quiet" (quoted in Leite 1999b), even if Portugal sometimes went beyond what was British toleration and knowledge.

That leads us to a second reason why Portugal wanted to have trade with Germany even within a general alignment with the allies' side. The reason was that such trade was sometimes absolutely indispensable to the Portuguese economy. Britain was the main traditional supplier of a series of essential goods. But it was now imposing various restrictions on its own exports, as many of them were needed for the country's war effort. Germany, in need of many Portuguese exports, tried to replace Britain in the supply of such goods (Rosas 1990). One final reason for trade with Germany was the fact that it was extremely favorable to the country in terms of its international payments position. Germany's demand of certain Portuguese products was very high, and there was no reason for Portugal to lose the opportunity. Of course, this had always to be done with enough care not to trigger Britain's ire (Rosas 1990; Leite 1999b; Louçã 2000; Telo 2000).

The Portuguese Government, hence, played its neutral position in order to benefit from trade with both sides of the conflict. From the start the war created various difficulties in terms of the external supply of fundamental goods for the Portuguese economy. This was especially felt in fuel (coal and oil), foodstuffs (wheat and cod), raw materials (cotton and different minerals, such as copper and iron), fertilizers, and equipment (Rosas 1990). The reaction of Portuguese authorities was to introduce a series of measures (through subsidies and guaranteed prices) officially to stimulate national production, in order to replace the faltering foreign goods, from agriculture to mines. The few goods that had not been subject to administrative prices were now included and the

Government started running a centralized system of marketing, something that included rationing. Administrative prices were always kept below the increase in costs. Together with the complicated marketing systems put in place by the Government, this led to the natural creation of a vast black market, with prices many times above the official ones (Rosas 1990).

On the other hand, various Portuguese goods were heavily demanded by the two belligerent sides. Some traditional Portuguese exports were now highly valued, such as cork and tinned fish. But even some goods in which Portugal was notoriously inefficient such as wool, cotton clothing, glass, porcelain, beer, or shoes were being exported to the belligerents. And, most of all, certain raw materials were strategic for both sides' war effort: tin and, above all, tungsten (Rosas 1990; Telo 2000; Nunes 2010). The latter was in high demand from both sides, as it was essential for armament. But until 1941 most of the demand came from Britain, as Germany was able to get most of its supply from China, profiting from the 1939 non-aggression pact with the USSR. After that year, however, when Germany declared war on the USSR, that was no longer an option. Germany looked then desperately for other suppliers. Portugal was a natural choice. A sort of wolfram fever then swept the country, particularly in areas where it was abundant. Farmers abandoned the toil of the land to try their fortune in improvised wolfram pits. Fortunes were made (and lost) from one day to the next during this period (Nunes 2010).

It is not surprising that the behavior of the Portuguese economy was not exactly spectacular during the war: GDP per capita grew at 0.6% between 1939 and 1945 (Table 3). But the different sectors had quite varied performances: productivity in agriculture grew practically two times quicker than in manufacturing, and productivity in services declined. The growth of agricultural productivity was not achieved through traditional crops, the productivity of most of which declined, but to a recomposition of the structure of production, in the direction of higher-productivity crops such as rice, maize and fruits and vegetables, besides cattle (Lains 2007). This was largely achieved thanks to the fact that many irrigation projects started operating during the war (Baptista 1993; Amaral and Freire 2017). Forests also increased their share in output, in the sequence of the Forestation Plan (Branco 2011). The slow growth of industry is explained by the fact that, despite the appearance of some new modern sectors, the conditions of extreme protection and scarcity of fundamental industrial goods allowed for the survival of all kinds of small, antiquated, and inefficient firms (Rosas 1990; Lains 2007). As for services, the sector suffered a lot under the bureaucratic complications created by the marketing mechanisms designed by the Government (Rosas 1990).

The pattern of international transactions during the war created a very unusual situation for the Portuguese balance of trade. Traditionally a deficit country that paid its excess imports with emigrant remittances, Portugal reduced significantly its trade deficit and even attained surplus for three years, between 1941 and 1943, as shown by Fig. 9. Deficits returned after 1944, when Portugal aligned more closely with the allies (a step that was sealed with the concession of an air base in the Azores) and restrained its trade with Germany (Rosas 1990; Louçã 2000). In addition to trade, Portugal's external position improved markedly in terms of other forms of payment. Again, neutrality was crucial for this result. Portugal became a safe haven for refugees fleeing either from the war or from Nazi persecution in Germany and its occupied territories. These refugees, many of them of high social standing, arrived in Portugal, either in transit (mostly to America) or to remain permanently in the country, bringing with them their savings, which they deposited in national banks (Rosas 1990). Many aid agencies (especially from the United States) made transfers in their favor (Pimentel 2006; Milgram 2010). Also important were the freight and carry payments on Portuguese ships, again an absolutely new situation for the country. Portugal was now a neutral port at the head of Europe and its ships had not been mobilized to contribute to the war effort. Refugees, most of them Jewish, arrived in Portugal in a number estimated at between 50,000 and 100,000 for the whole war period. Finally, although reduced, the traditional flow of emigrants' remittances kept on arriving in the country. As Fig. 9 shows, the invisibles balance had in some years an even higher importance in quantitative terms than the trade one.

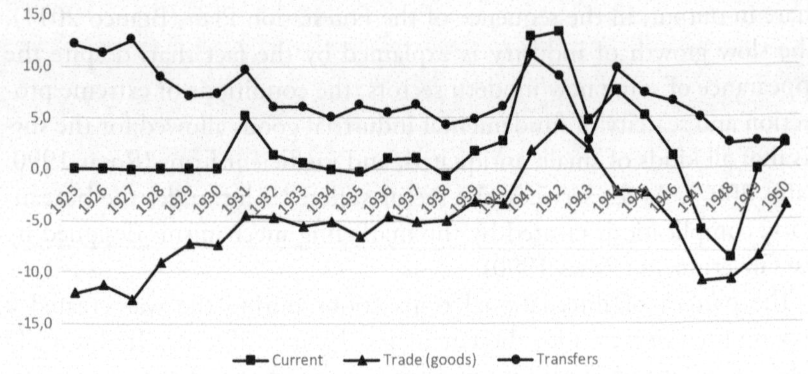

Fig. 9 Balance of payments, Portugal, 1925–1950 (% GDP) (*Source* 1925–1947: Fontoura and Valério [2001]; 1948–1950: Pinheiro [1997])

A series of very restrictive agreements framed trade relations between Portugal and the belligerents, especially Britain and Germany. Also of relevance were the payment agreements between Portugal, on the one side, and Britain and Germany on the other. The 1940 payments agreement with Britain was particularly important. The agreement offered rather favorable conditions to Britain, as it allowed for virtually unlimited credit in trade relations with Portugal for the duration of the war. According to this agreement, the Bank of England (BoE) opened a special account in pounds at the BoP, and the latter a special account in escudos at the BoE. All official trade in goods and services between the two countries was to be settled through these accounts. There was no limit to the amount of escudos the BoP could sell to the BoE at the fixed exchange rate of 100.2 escudos per pound. The debt was to be settled only at the end of the war. Britain was given five years after the end of the war to repay the debt. The debt was "guaranteed" in gold (that is, it had to be repaid in gold). Also, the BoE promised to find profitable uses for the sterling balances accumulating in London. Thanks to this agreement, Britain accumulated a sizeable debt (£76 million), which was of much help in its military efforts (Abreu 2014; Amaral 2018).

The situation created various challenges to the Portuguese authorities. One had to do with the escudo's exchange rate. Since the collapse of the gold standard in 1931, the BoP and the Government had essentially pegged the escudo to sterling, changing to the dollar or the French franc in case of "excessive" depreciation of the British currency (Valério et al. 2010). In the month the war started, September 1939, Britain introduced exchange controls and the pound embarked on a trend of persistent depreciation. The BoP's initial reaction was to combine depreciation with a certain preservation of the external value of the escudo, first by making it depreciate only in a proportion of 90% of the successive pound depreciations, and later by pegging the escudo to the dollar (Fig. 5). These decisions combined an anti-inflationary stance with concerns about competitiveness.

However, in July 1940, the United States and the UK signed a payments agreement pegging the dollar and the pound to each other in order to help the British war effort, and the picture changed. In the sequence of the agreement, in the same month, the BoP and the BoE signed the payments agreement mentioned above pegging the escudo to sterling at the value of 100.20 escudos per pound (thus incorporating a depreciation of the British currency). This rate was to prevail until the end of the war (and beyond) (Fig. 5). However, as Portuguese exports were in high demand and both the British and American governments imposed restrictions on their own exports, this led to an increasingly positive payments balance between Portugal and the two allies. Also, the payments agreement between the BoP and the BoE, signed in 1940, allowed the UK to accumulate a virtually infinite debt. This meant that the escudo became more and more undervalued as the UK debt increased and the balance with the United States became favorable.

Payments with Germany were never on an equally favorable footing, as Germany had to find immediate ways of paying for its imports from Portugal, in the form of either gold or foreign currency (particularly Swiss francs). Trade with Germany had been regulated since 1935 by a clearing agreement according to which the imports from Portugal had to be paid in Reichsmark in a special account of the BoP in the German Clearing Chamber (*Deutsche Verrenschnungkasse*), and the amounts there deposited could only be used by Portuguese importers of German goods in order to clear the balance between the two countries (Leite 1999b; Telo 2000). But, as a trade surplus grew in Portugal's favor in the first years of the war, a new settlement had to be reached: in 1941 and 1942 some German payments were made in Swiss francs, but in 1942 the Portuguese Government refused continuing the practice and demanded the trade exchanges to be exclusively settled in gold, although shipped from the Swiss National Bank only (Leite 1999b; Telo 2000). Even if these agreements did not include any clause pegging the exchange rate of the escudo to the Reichsmark and the Swiss franc, the truth is that (as in the case of sterling and the dollar) stability basically prevailed (Fig. 5). However, this also corresponded, as in the case of sterling and the dollar, to an increasing undervaluation of the escudo in relation to the Reichsmark.

The second challenge faced by Portuguese authorities during the war was inflation (Fig. 4). By boosting exports and favoring the introduction of large means of payment in the country, the exchange rate policy was not helping, but the (mostly political and strategic) constraints did not allow for anything substantially different. The problem now was that the 1931 rule of indexing money emission to the BoP's holdings of gold and foreign currency was also unhelpful. The rule had been conceived in the expectation of a strong foreign constraint from the international payments position of the country and of a fixed exchange rate between the escudo and sterling, but the war completely reversed the situation. This was at the origin of something the BoP called at the time a "monetary plethora" (Amaral 2018). Portuguese authorities dealt with this "plethora" in different ways. The BoP used a series of non-conventional policies to control money issuing. According to the 1931 automatic rule, the BoP was meant to translate the availability of gold and foreign currency into emission and sight deposits. However, the BoP chose to keep its sight liabilities below what the rule would have allowed, thus "sterilizing" the availability of reserves, complementing this with the reception of vast amounts of reserves from commercial banks (Amaral 2018).

But there was some Government action too, mostly visible in the issuing of public debt: budget deficits appeared during the period, even if small (Fig. 3); this was not in accordance with the general fiscal stance of the Government, but the situation should be understood as "contingent", that is, related to exceptional wartime spending. The Government sterilized these deficits by issuing public bonds in excess of its needs (Amaral 2018).

4 The Empire

The fundamental piece of colonial legislation of the *Estado Novo* was the Colonial Act, of 8 July 1930.[25] This was no ordinary piece of legislation, as it was meant to be a part of the constitutional order of the new regime: once the new Constitution had been approved (something that eventually happened in 1933), the Colonial Act should stand alongside it as a part of the constitutional framework of the regime. The general idea of the Colonial Act was that there should be a stronger integration between the mainland and the colonies on various dimensions. This had been partly spurred by the renewal of the attempts by the other colonial powers to strip Portugal off its colonies. Besides Germany and Britain, now Italy and South Africa joined the group of candidates to carve up and get a piece of the Portuguese Empire (Alexandre 1993; Léonard 1999). The essential aspects of the Colonial Act were felt on three topics. The first concerned the relationship between the colonial authorities and the local populations. The second concerned the relationship between the Government of the mainland and those of the colonies. The third concerned the economic relationship between the mainland and the colonies (Silva 1989; Leite 1999a).

In what refers to the relationship between the colonial authorities and the local population, the Colonial Act essentially reinstated the principles developed since the labor code of 1899 and the land code of 1901. These principles were also unified in a more systematic document. That document was the Political, Civil, and Criminal Statute of the Indigenous Peoples (*Estatuto Político Civil e Criminal dos Indígenas*), from 1929,[26] which divided the population of the empire into two categories: the civilized (*civilizados*) part and the indigenous (*indígenas*) part. *Civilizados* were all white people plus all creole people and the members of the indigenous part of the population that had successfully gathered the requisites to become *civilizado*. The statute did not apply to the territory of Cape

[25]Approved by Decree 18,570, 8 July 1930.

[26]Decree 16,473, 6 February 1929.

Verde, meaning that regular Portuguese law applied to all inhabitants of the archipelago (the reason for this being the overwhelmingly creole nature of its population). The indigenous populations lived under African customary law and under the authority of a traditional tribal chief. Besides having access to communal land, they were forced to pay the native tax. In order to pay it, they would have to have a profession or work on their own plot of land. If missing any of these conditions, they would have to supply their labor under contract to any hiring entity (public or private). If unable to do it, they could be forcibly contracted by the administration and work as carrier and in public works, or serve with the police (Newitt 1981; Clarence-Smith 1985). Some of the most iniquitous situations in the Portuguese Empire involved these workers under contract, in cases sometimes amounting to true forced labor: until 1928, administrative officials could forcibly recruit indigenous workers in order to supply the labor needs of private companies; in 1928, this form of forced labor was forbidden, with the issuing of the Code of Indigenous Labor (*Código do Trabalho Indígena*),[27] even if it continued for practical matters, due to difficulties of enforcement (Bailey 1969). The conditions for an indigenous to reach the status of "*assimilado*" ("assimilated") were: to have more than 18 years of age, to be able to express himself correctly in Portuguese, to have a recognized profession, to be able to provide for his own needs and of his family, and not to have deserted from conscription. Having gathered these conditions, the candidate not working in public administration would need to apply and expect for the Portuguese Government to accept his case (those working in public administration did not need to apply and would be automatically given the statute once gathering the necessary requirements). Even if a lot has been said about this legislation and the issue of forced labor in the Portuguese colonies, the fact is that other colonial empires had similar legislation and similar practices (Newitt 1981; CEAUP 2006).

Complementary to the above aspects but equally important in terms of the management of African labor was "compulsory cultivation". The

[27] Decree 16,199, 6 December 1928.

system had been roughly copied from equivalent German and Belgian practices and was first introduced in the final years of the Republic, being fully developed by the *Estado Novo*: it consisted in dividing the colonies into "zones of influence", each of which was then attributed to concessionaires. In those zones, the concessionaires would be given the right to market certain goods. The guaranteed prices offered by the corporatist colonial organisms were strong incentives for the concession companies to try and disseminate various crops, especially cotton, to serve as raw material for the mainland textile industry (Newitt 1981; Clarence-Smith 1985). "Cotton campaigns" promoted by these companies became famous, whereby they would clear vast stretches of land, divide them in small units, and then gather the natives of the region, giving them weeds to plant and buying the cotton at extremely low prices, thus obtaining a sizable margin when selling to the colonial cotton board. Some estimates point toward about 800,000 people involved in this scheme in Mozambique at its peak in 1944 (Newitt 1981, p. 122). The system also existed in Angola but on a much smaller dimension. Without the same relevance, other crops were also inserted in this system, especially rice (Rosas 1990).

In what concerns the relationship between the Government of the mainland and those of the colonies the main idea was to put the latter under the strict control of the former. The function of high commissioner was abolished and replaced by that of a Governor and the budgets of colonial governments had to be approved by the Minister of Colonies in the central Government, who also could legislate by decree and ratify colonial concessions. The purpose here was to deal with the legacy left by the First Republic. In 1919, at the end of World War I, the Republic decided to put in practice the principles of autonomy of Government introduced by the 1914 Organic Law of the Colonial Empire: two high commissioners were appointed, one for Angola, the other for Mozambique, with large autonomous powers. Local budgets were to be elaborated and approved locally as well as the most important aspects of economic policy. The action of the two high commissioners became famous, especially that of general José Norton de Matos in Angola. Matos had a vast plan for the territory, including the rationalization of its administrative structure, its effective colonization with population coming from the mainland, the expansion of its infrastructure (ports, railways, roads, telegraph, and telephone), and the final eradication of all forms of forced labor (Alexandre 1993, 1998). Matos' rule lasted only four years (1920–1924), with just a fraction of the initial plans having been achieved, but leaving behind total financial chaos. The achievements, although incomplete, were not negligible: the road network indeed expanded and became one of the best in Africa, the railway network doubled in extension, ports and airports started to be built, and the white population practically doubled—from about 20,000 in 1920 to roughly 36,000 in 1924 (still an insignificant fraction of the overall population, however: 1%) (Alexandre 1998; Freudenthal 2001). These plans led to a growing tension with the National Overseas Bank (*Banco Nacional Ultramarino* [BNU]), as the issuing authority and practical monopolist of banking activity. The result of the crisis was the creation, through a long period between 1923 and 1926, of a new bank (issuing and commercial) for the colony, the Bank of Angola (*Banco de Angola*) (Valério et al. 2006). Another price of Matos' plans was the spiraling of budget deficits and debt, leading to a pre-default situation in the early 1920s. Manuel Brito Camacho's rule as high commissioner in Mozambique was less ambitious but equally flawed, as Camacho was incapable of dealing with a territory fragmented between various interests irresponsive to the colonial Government: chartered companies, "prazos" or Transvaal (Newitt 1981). By 1929, when Salazar became Minister of Finance, this was the situation still prevailing in both colonies, and it was to deal with it that the Colonial Act stripped colonial governments of all autonomy. Through sometimes very brutal policies, the fact is that budget balance was achieved during the 1930s (Newitt 1981).

In what concerns the relationship between the economy of the mainland and those of the colonies the essential idea was to create a higher integration between them, under strong protection and mechanisms of imperial preference (Newitt 1981). The Colonial Empire was to play two fundamental roles: the colonies should provide foreign exchange to help balance the mainland's balance of payments, and the mainland's and the colonies' economies should be functionally integrated. The colonies should supply raw materials for manufacturing as well as agricultural and tropical goods; industrialization was to remain a prerogative of the mainland (Clarence-Smith 1985; Ferreira 2005). The essential idea behind this sort of policy was to help Portugal fight the world economic crisis. In this sense, the Portuguese policy was not much different from the ones followed by Britain, France, or the Netherlands (Léonard 1999). The instruments to implement this policy were, first, the 1929 tariff schedule, a system of prices set by the administration and a mechanism of preferences that was based on quotas and discriminatory tariffs (certain colonial goods would benefit from rebates to general tariff levels), as well as exchange controls, now managed by the same kind of corporatist institutions that had been created for the mainland. Raw cotton for the textile factories of the mainland, sugar, coffee, and palm oil were the colonial goods mostly affected by the new mechanisms created in the 1930s (Newitt 1981; Clarence-Smith 1985). The system of "forced cultivation" played an important role in this context.

On the other hand, the colonies were to be the recipients of mainland industrial goods, as well as some agricultural ones (especially wine). Manufacturing in the colonies was subject to the same industrial conditioning principles existing in the mainland, although with special provisions.[28] One of the most important of those special provisions was that no factories could be installed in the colonies in sectors also existing in the mainland and where current production was below installed capacity. This limited severely the number and type of industries being developed in the colonies. These involved mostly simple processing activities of indigenous staples, such as crushing, decorticating, and cleaning, with some slightly more complex but still simple activities as match production, soap, tobacco, alcohol, and others. On the contrary, the colonies were important markets for mainland cotton textiles, shoes, and food products. An example of the effectiveness of imperial industrial conditioning is the fact that only in 1944 was the first cotton mill installed in the colonies (Newitt 1981).

[28]Decree 26,509, 11 April 1936, later reformed through 33,924, 5 September 1944, without changing the main principles.

There is no doubt that, under the Colonial Act, there was both an increase in the integration between the mainland economy and those of the colonies. This happened in a moment when the Portuguese authorities could finally claim true formal rule overseas. The share of colonial trade in total Portuguese trade rose from 10% in the 1920s to 20% at the end of World War II (Clarence-Smith 1985, pp. 230–231). And the special conditions of World War II were relevant to deepen this relationship (Rosas 1990).

In terms of effective Portuguese rule in the colonies, the end of the concessions to the chartered companies (except for Diamang, in Angola) and the "prazos" was decisive: thanks to it, Mozambique could finally be seen as a unified territory, at least in administrative terms—in economic terms it continued to be largely fragmented (including the continuation of the export of labor from its southern region to the gold mines of the Rand). The charter of the Niassa Company had already finished in 1929, but that of the Mozambique Company ended only in 1941. None of them was renewed. The "prazos" system ended in 1930 (Newitt 1981; Léonard 1999). The disappearance from the colonial landscape of the foreign capital associated with these companies opened the colonies to Portuguese mainland capital (Rosas 1990).

Not everything in the Portuguese colonies was forced labor and compulsory cultivation. In fact, despite the fact that they were widespread, only a minority of the indigenous population was affected by them. Most Africans were involved essentially in free peasant activities and a growing minority started participating in urban free wage-earning activities. Peasants were essentially involved in coffee, maize, tobacco, and groundnuts cultivation in different points of the colonies. Wage earners started concentrating in the most important cities, as the colonial economies grew and urbanized (Newitt 1981). In the end, although at a very low level, the approach of the *Estado Novo* to the empire delivered some growth and development in the colonies. That is why, by 1950, Mozambique ranked in eight position in GDP per capita among 45 countries of sub-Saharan Africa, and Angola 13 (Prados de la Escosura 2012, p. 36).

5 Economic Growth and Change

The economic growth record of the Portuguese economy in this period was modest: GDP per capita grew at 1.1% per year between 1930 and 1945, with some years of mildly negative growth in the second half of the 1930s (Table 3). But since most developed economies were affected by the difficulties arising from the 1930s crisis, the Portuguese economy continued suspending divergence in relation to them, a process that had already started in the second decade of the century (Chapter 3 and Figs. 3 and 4 of the Introduction). When compared to other peripheral economies, this behavior was not special: the Scandinavian economies continued their process of convergence until the outbreak of World War II, and among them Sweden was even able to continue beyond it, thanks to neutrality during the conflict. We already know that these economies cannot be classified in the same peripheral category as Portugal, but Finland, the one northern economy comparable to Portugal, also continued its convergence, reaching a GDP per capita level of 70% of the richest economies of the world in 1945, whereas Portugal remained at only 40% (Figure 3 of the Introduction). The behavior of the other countries of the southern periphery (Spain and Greece) was closer to the Portuguese one but these countries were directly affected by two tragic military events that determined a collapse of their GDP per capita levels in the 1930s and 1940s: the 1936–1939 civil war in Spain and World War II in Greece, with a succession of foreign occupations: Italian, German, and British (Fig. 4 of the Introduction). So, in the end, this was a positive period for the Portuguese economy, despite its relatively slow growth.

There was very little change in the structure of the economy in this period, both in terms of employment and in terms of output. The output shares of agriculture, manufacturing and services remained practically unaltered from 1925 to 1950 (Fig. 10): agriculture and industry at around 30%, services at around 40%. This is certainly related with the indiscriminate protectionism adopted by Portuguese authorities, which allowed all economic activities to remain sheltered from foreign

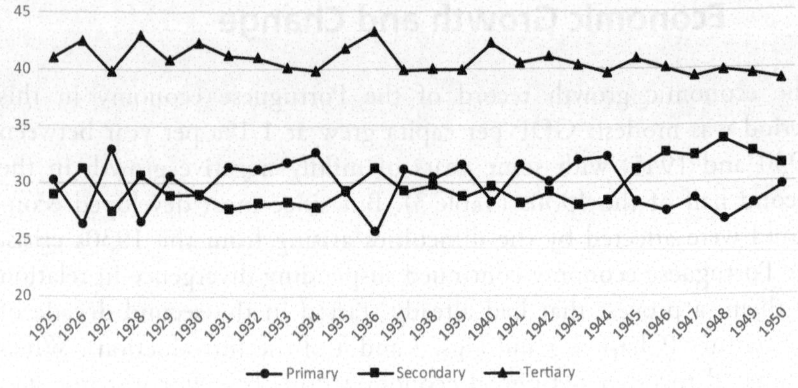

Fig. 10 Structure economy, Portugal, 1925–1950 (% GDP) (*Source* Author's calculations based on Batista et al. [1997])

competition during the 1930s crisis: most traditional and labor-intensive activities were able to survive. When referring to employment, we can notice some movement out of agriculture and into industry, but at a very slow pace: employment in agriculture dropped from 57% of overall employment in 1925 to 51% in 1950; this drop worked in favor of industry, where employment rose from 18% of total employment in 1925 to 22% in 1950; and it worked also in favor of services, where the numbers are 25% in 1925 and 27% in 1950 (Fig. 11). Thanks to this structure, Portugal remained one of the least industrialized countries of Europe (Table 4).

The sector that performed better was agriculture, whose productivity increased at 1% per year between 1930 and 1940 and at 2.2% per year between 1940 and 1950. This was not due to the performance of the traditional crops but to the replacement of some of them by new ones. Wine kept its share of about 13% in agricultural output between 1935–1939 and 1954–1958. But the share of cereals declined from roughly 30 to 20%, even if the share of wheat increased, as a result of the Wheat Campaign and the various systems of support to the crop—this means that other cereals, especially rye, declined in importance. The growth of labor productivity in wheat production had a strong initial jump, due to the fact that many lands that had been left idle for centuries were put to

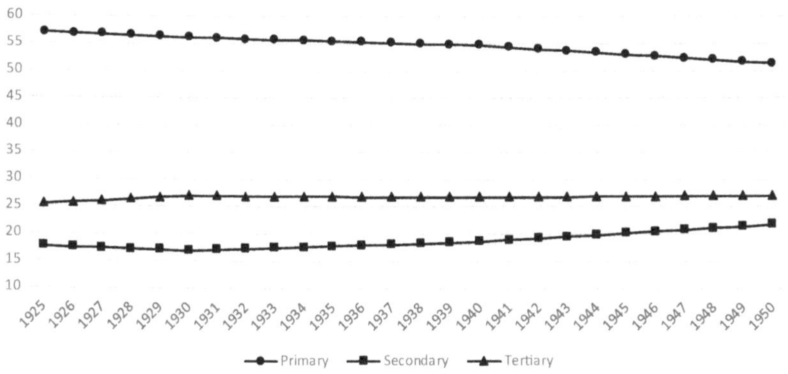

Fig. 11 Structure employment, Portugal, 1925–1950 (% of overall employment) (*Source* Author's calculations using Nunes [2001])

Table 4 Structure of employment, various European economies, c. 1930–c. 1950 (% total employment)

	Agriculture		Industry		Services	
	c. 1930	c. 1950	c. 1930	c. 1950	c. 1930	c. 1950
Belgium	17.7	12.5	46.4	48.7	35.9	38.8
Denmark	35.8	25.4	27.5	33.7	36.7	40.9
Finland	69.8	46.6	15.9	28.1	14.4	25.3
Netherlands	20.8	19.6	36.8	30.7	42.3	43.0
Norway	35.6	26.1	26.6	36.6	37.8	37.3
Sweden	36.3	20.5	32.3	41.1	31.5	38.4
UK	6.0	5.1	46.5	49.1	47.5	45.8
France	35.6	31.8	33.3	32.8	31.1	35.3
Greece	61.1	51.3	18.0	20.7	20.9	28.0
Italy	46.8	42.2	30.8	32.1	22.4	25.7
Spain	45.5	49.6	26.5	25.5	28.0	24.9
Portugal	56.1	51.3	16.9	21.7	26.9	27.0

Source Buyst and Franaszek (2010), except Portugal—1953–1995: based on Nunes (2001), extrapolated from Pinheiro (1997), corrected with Amaral (2009)

use after 1929. But their intrinsic bad quality meant that, after the initial years, productivity started declining. Rice was the only cereal whose productivity expanded in a consistent manner. This was very much associated with the construction of the first irrigation schemes promoted by the *Estado Novo* (Amaral and Freire 2017). The productivity of most other traditional products, from maize to potato, was negative (Lains 2003a). This was compensated, however, with the doubling of the share of fruits and vegetables, from 6.5% in 1935–1939 to 12.7% in 1954–1958, and of animal products, from 28% in 1935–1939 to 35.9 in 1954–1958, both having higher productivity than the more traditional crops and also dependent of the new irrigation projects. Forests increased their share as well, mostly thanks to the governmental efforts dedicated to reforestation, thus also contributing to the productivity of the sector (Lains 2003a).

Productivity in industry grew at about half the rate than in agriculture and most of such growth did not depend of a change in weight between the different branches, which kept their relative importance throughout the period, despite the direct Government efforts to introduce new industries—one of the most famous examples was that of the installation of an oil refinery on the outskirts of Lisbon between 1937 and 1940, a public–private joint venture where the Government held 33% of the capital (Castaño et al. 2017). Textiles remained the largest branch (with a share in output of about 40%), followed by food and beverages (20%), chemicals (20%), wood and cork (also 20%), and the others with much smaller shares (Aguiar and Martins 2005). Services also retained their traditional profile (Pinheiro 1997).

The protectionist tradition of the country survived in this period and actually increased, thanks to the adoption of quantitative restrictions. This time, however, something new happened: on the one hand, many other countries, traditionally more open, closed their economies as well during the 1930s crisis and World War II, making of Portugal less of an outcast; on the other, Portugal doubled its degree of openness during the war (with exports passing from 5% of GDP to 10%) and keeping that position after the war (Fig. 2). Anyway, in a period of systematic closing of the world economy, the association between openness and growth was nonexistent (Federico et al. 2017). Still, the composition of Portuguese exports changed, with food and beverages declining from 60 to 30% between 1930 and 1950, and textiles and wood and cork passing from 5 to 15% (Afonso and Aguiar 2005). Even if textiles continued to rely heavily on colonial markets they were also able to conquer other markets during the war. As for imports they kept the path coming from the previous period and largely associated with the import-substitution process, as consumption goods declined and transport equipment, raw materials and fuel increased (Lains 2007).

The Portuguese banking system passed through a stable phase in the 1930s, in spite of the international crisis. The legislative framework designed between 1925 and 1929 described in the previous chapter, and the relatively tranquil economic situation of the country allowed for that. Some banks were forced to shut down during the decade, but only in small numbers (Reis 1995). In a sense this worked as a means to clean up the market of some of its unhealthier institutions. Those that resisted were more apt at survival. As the number of banks remained unaltered and deposits grew throughout the 1930s, commercial banks increased their size and became more stable. This in turn increased the public's confidence in them, leading to further depositing (Reis 1995). In 1939, at the start of the war, the Portuguese banking system comprised 22 incorporated commercial banks, 20 non-incorporated banking houses, and 13 savings banks (Valério et al. 2010). Most of the savings banks were of small size, with the exception of the National Savings Bank (*Caixa Geral de Depósitos* [CGD]) which was the largest financial institution in the country: at the start of World War II, the CGD was still larger than all commercial banks combined. There were also 10 credit (or mortgage) companies, among which only one was of significant size, the *Companhia Geral de Crédito Predial Português* (known as *Crédito Predial Português* [CPP]). Then there was the BoP, increasingly assuming the role of central bank, although still in an incomplete way. Thus, in 1939, the banking system was on the way to acquire a clearer functional definition but the process was to be completed yet: the BoP still played an important role as a commercial bank; the CGD still had an overwhelming presence in the market and still attracted a large number of bank's reserves, but played a crucial role as an investment bank through its National Investment Bank (*Caixa Nacional de Crédito*) branch; and the commercial banking sector still had a relatively small presence in the market. The World War II period was decisive to help complete the process.

Table 5 Sources of growth, Portugal, 1934–1947

	GDP	Labor	Capital	Human capital	TFP
Silva and Lains (2013)	2.1	0.6	2.8	–	−1.3
Lains (2003b)	2.2	0.4	1.3	0.4	−0.1

Source Silva and Lains (2013)

So, the Portuguese economy continued behaving in this period in the mixed manner identified in the period analyzed in Chapter 3: slow growth but still allowing for the distance to the richest economies of the world to be kept at the same level. In what concerns explanations for this behavior we can again start by resorting to growth accounting. The existing exercises (Table 5) point to a double phenomenon: strong growth of capital and strong decline of TFP. The growth of capital might be explainable by the institutional conditions of the *Estado Novo*, which favored investment: repression of labor and organization of markets and sectors under the corporatist organizations signaled protection of property rights. This might indeed explain why the investment rate passed from 7.5% in 1930 to more than 10% at the end of the war (Freitas 2005).

As for the bad performance of TFP, one first obvious explanation is the lack of structural change, which would have meant the passage of resources from less efficient sectors to more efficient ones. According to Aguiar and Martins (2005), the switch of resources between sectors gave a contribution of only 10% to productivity growth, while the contribution internal to the sectors amounted to 85%—and the interaction between the two to only 5%. Other explanations might come from the indiscriminate protection of all economic activities in the context of the world crisis and World War II, allowing for the survival of a large number of inefficient units. They might also come from the bureaucratization of the economic process, with the constant Government presence in markets and industrial licensing. The same instruments giving confidence to investors may have also imposed a bureaucratic burden slowing down economic activity. Brito (1989),

Loureiro (1991), and Confraria (1992) show the complex intricacies of the industrial conditioning processes, concluding by the existence of a true bureaucratic cost. Confraria (1992) shows, additionally, how, out of the combination of the strategies of entrepreneurs and the Government, a persistent problem of excess capacity in many industries developed, imposing a cost on efficiency. Governmental strategies diverged with respect to different markets and through time, but in many circumstances they allowed for the existence of monopolies and oligopolies, while in other circumstances they allowed for the opposite: the survival of a large number of firms, independently of their efficiency (Confraria 1992). As the weight of foreign direct investment continued to be small, under the strict conditions imposed by industrial conditioning, this was another potential source of technology that remained virtually closed (Silva 2016).

As for the behavior of human capital, a large role in its relatively positive behavior has to be attributed to the educational policy of the regime, that, by lowering the cost of primary schooling for families, promoted the expansion of education in the country. This brings us back to an old discussion concerning the relative weight of supply and demand factors in the growth of education. Reis (1993) and Ramos (1988, 1993, 1998) stress that the main cause of the historical slow growth in literacy was due to lack of demand. But in doing this, both authors seem to separate the supply of schools and teachers from the household decision of sending children to school. However, the low demand for schooling may have been closely dependent on the low supply of schools and teachers. Low supply made the return from schooling too small to be rewarding. Low demand for schooling may have been, hence, not simply dependent on too few job opportunities for educated people (a factor that must have been present too) but also on the fact that education was too expensive, even when supplied by the Government. In fact, the two things are not separable, for the cheaper and more accessible Government schools became, the higher the rate of return from education was, and hence the larger the stimulus to go to school became as well.

References

Abreu, Marcelo de Paiva. 2014. A 'Blank Cheque'? Portuguese Second World War Sterling Balances, 1940–1973. *Economic History Review* 67 (2): 535–555.

Afonso, Óscar, and Álvaro Aguiar. 2005. A internacionalização da economia. In *História Económica de Portugal, 1700–2000, Vol. III, O Século XX*, ed. Pedro Lains and Álvaro Ferreira da Silva, 305–341. Lisbon: ICS.

Aguiar, Álvaro, and Manuel M.F. Martins. 2005. A indústria. In *História Económica de Portugal, 1700–2000, Vol. III, O Século XX*, ed. Pedro Lains and Álvaro Ferreira da Silva, 185–226. Lisbon: ICS.

Alexandre, Valentim. 1993. Ideologia, economia e política: a questão colonial na implantação do Estado Novo. *Análise Social* XXVIII (123–124): 1117–1136.

———. 1998. Nação e império. In *História da Expansão Portuguesa, Vol. IV – Do Brasil para África (1808–1930)*, ed. Francisco Bethencourt and Diogo Ramada Curto, 90–142. Lisbon: Círculo de Leitores.

Amaral, Luciano. 1994. Portugal e o passado: política agrária, grupos de pressão e evolução da agricultura portuguesa durante o Estado Novo (1950–1973). *Análise Social* XXIX (128): 889–906.

———. 2000. Reforma agrária. In *Dicionário de História de Portugal, Suplemento P/Z, Vol. IX*, ed. António Barreto and Maria Filomena Mónica, 212–213. Porto: Livraria Figueirinhas.

———. 2002. *How a Country Catches-Up: Explaining Economic Growth in Portugal in the Postwar Period (1950s–1973s)*. Doctoral dissertation, European University Institute, Florence.

———. 2005. O trabalho. In *História Económica de Portugal, 1700–2000, Vol. III, O Século XX*, ed. Pedro Lains and Álvaro Ferreira da Silva, 65–90. Lisbon: ICS.

———. 2018. A Monetary Plethora and What to Do with It: The Bank of Portugal During the Second World War and the Postwar Period. *Economic History Review* 71 (3): 795–822.

Amaral, Luciano, and Dulce Freire. 2017. Economic Policy, Growth and the Demise, 1929–2000. In *An Agrarian History of Portugal, 1000–2000: Economic Development on the European Frontier*, ed. Dulce Freire and Pedro Lains, 245–276. Brill: Leiden.

Baganha, Maria Ioannis. 1994. As correntes emigratórias portuguesas no século XX e o seu impacto na economia nacional. *Análise Social* XXIX (128): 959–980.

Bailey, Norman F. 1969. Education, Health and Social Welfare. In *Portuguese Africa: A Handbook*, ed. David M. Abshire and Michael A. Samuels, 178–201. London: Pall Mall Press.

Baptista, Fernando Oliveira. 1993. *A Política Agrária do Estado Novo*. Porto: Afrontamento.

Bastien, Carlos. 2001. Preços e salários. In *Estatísticas Históricas Portuguesas*, ed. Nuno Valério, 615–655. Lisbon: INE.

Batista, Dina, et al. 1997. *New Estimates for Portugal's GDP: 1910–1958*. Lisbon: Bank of Portugal.

Beja, Filomena, Júlia Serra, Estella Machás, and Isabel Saldanha. 1996. *Muitos Anos de Escolas, Vol. II—Anos 40-Anos 70*. Lisbon: Ministério da Educação.

Branco, Amélia. 2011. El Plan de Repoblación Florestal (1938–1968): una medida del Estado Novo por evaluar. In *Agriculturas e Innovacíon Tecnológica en la Península Ibérica (1946–1975)*, ed. Daniel Lanero and Dulce Freire, 135–165. Madrid: Ministerio de Medio Ambiente y Medio Rural.

Branco, Amélia, and Pedro Neves. 2018. From Backward to Modern: The Adoption of Technology by the Pulp Industry in Portugal, 1891–2015. In *Technological Transformation in the Global Pulp and Paper Industry*, ed. Timo Särkkä, Miguel Gutiérrz-Poch, and Mark Kuhlberg, 1800–2018. Cham: Springer Nature Switzerland.

Brito, José Maria Brandão de. 1989. *A Industrialização Portuguesa no Pós-Guerra (1948–1965)*. Lisbon: Publicações D. Quixote.

Cadavez, Cândida. 2017. *A Bem da Nação. As Representações Turísticas no Estado Novo entre 1933 e 1940*. Lisbon: Edições 70.

Cardoso, José Luís, and Pedro Mendonça. 2012. Corporatism and Beyond: An Assessment of Recent Literature. ICS Working Papers, nº 1.

Carolo, Daniel, and José A. Pereirinha. 2010. The Development of the Welfare State in Portugal: Trends in Social Expenditure Between 1938 and 2003. *Revista de História Económica — Journal of Iberian and Latin American Economic History* 28 (3): 469–501.

Carreira, Henrique Medina. 1996. As políticas sociais em Portugal. In *A Situação Social em Portugal, 1960–1995*, ed. António Barreto. Lisbon: ICS.

Castaño, David, Ana Mónica Fonseca, Pedro Lains, and Daniel Marcos. 2017. *Os Petróleos em Portugal. Do Estado à Privatização*. Lisbon: ICS.

CEAUP (Centro de Estudos Africanos da Universidade do Porto). 2006. *Trabalho Forçado Africano. Experiências Coloniais Comparadas*. Porto: Campo das Letras.

Cerdeira, Maria da Conceição, and Maria Edite Padilha. 1998. *O Movimento Associativo Patronal Português, de 1834 a 1994*. Lisbon: Ministério do Trabalho e Solidariedade Social.

Clarence-Smith, Gervase. 1985. *The Third Portuguese Empire, 1825–1975, a Study in Economic Imperialism*. Manchester: Manchester University Press.

Confraria, João. 1992. *Condicionamento Industrial, Uma Análise Económica*. Lisbon: Direcção-Geral da Indústria.

Confraria, João. 2005. Política económica. In *História Económica de Portugal, 1700–2000, Vol. III, O Século XX*, ed. Pedro Lains and Álvaro Ferreira da Silva, 397–421. Lisbon: ICS.

Costa, Sandra Vaz. 2012. *O País a Régua e Esquadro. Urbanismo, Arquitetura e Memória na Obra Pública de Duarte Pacheco*. Lisbon: IST Press.

Cruz, Manuel Braga da. 1988. *O Partido e o Estado no Salazarismo*. Lisbon: Editorial Presença.

Eichengreen, Barry. 1996. *Globalizing Capital: A History of the International Monetary System*. Princeton: Princeton University Press.

Federico, Giovanni, and Antonio Tena-Junguito. 2018. *Federico-Tena World Trade Historical Database*. https://www.uc3m.es/ss/Satellite/UC3MInstitucional/es/TextoMixta/1371246237481/Federico-Tena_World_Trade_Historical_Database.

Ferreira, Manuel Ennes. 2005. O império e as relações económicas com África. In *História Económica de Portugal, 1700–2000, Vol. III, O Século XX*, ed. Pedro Lains and Álvaro Ferreira da Silva, 343–371. Lisbon: ICS.

Ferreira, Vítor Matias. 1983. A Lisboa do império e o Portugal dos Pequeninos: estrutura fundiária e política urbana de Lisboa, anos de 1930–1940. *Análise Social* XIX (77-78-79): 693–735.

Fontoura, Ana Paula, and Nuno Valério. 2001. Relações económicas externas. In *Estatísticas Históricas Portuguesas*, ed. Nuno Valério, 713–739. Lisbon: INE.

Freire, Dulce. 2011. Ensayos de Ingeniería Social: reforma agraria y modernización de la agricultura en las últimas décadas del Estado Novo (1954–1974). In *Agriculturas e Innovacíon Tecnológica en la Península Ibérica (1946–1975)*, ed. Daniel Lanero and Dulce Freire, 213–242. Madrid: Ministerio de Medio Ambiente y Medio Rural.

Freire, Dulce, and Nuno Estêvão Ferreira. 2019. A construção do sistema corporativo em Portugal (1933–1974). *Tempo* 25 (1): 256–277.

Freitas, Miguel Lebre de. 2005. O Capital. In *História Económica de Portugal, 1700–2000, Vol. III, O Século XX*, ed. Pedro Lains and Álvaro Ferreira da Silva, 91–124. Lisbon: ICS.

Freudenthal, Aida Maria. 2001. Angola. In *Nova História da Expansão Portuguesa – O Império Africano, 1890–1930*, ed. A.H. de Oliveira Marques, 259–467. Lisbon: Editorial Estampa.

Garrido, Álvaro. 2016. *Queremos uma Economia Nova! Estado Novo e Corporativismo.* Lisbon: Círculo de Leitores.

Gomes, Pedro, and Matilde Pinto Machado. 2019. Literacy and Primary School Expansion in Portugal, 1940–1962. Universidad Carlos III de Madrid Working Paper, 2019-07.

Henriques, Maria Carlota de Sales. 1999. Estradas. In *Dicionário de História de Portugal, Suplemento A/E, Vol. VII*, ed. António Barreto and Maria Filomena Mónica, 684–685. Porto: Livraria Figueirinhas.

Lains, Pedro. 2003a. New Wine in Old Bottles: Output and Productivity Trends in Portuguese Agriculture, 1850–1950. *European Review of Economic History* 7 (1): 43–72.

———. 2003b. Catching Up to the European Core: Portuguese Economic Growth, 1910–1990. *Explorations in Economic History* 40: 369–386.

———. 2007. Growth in a Protected Environment, 1850–1950. *Research in Economic History* 24: 119–160.

Léonard, Yves. 1999. O império colonial salazarista. In *História da Expansão Portuguesa, Vol. V – Último Império e Recentramento (1930–1998)*, ed. Francisco Bethencourt and Kirti Chaudhuri, 10–30. Lisbon: Círculo de Leitores.

Leite, Joana Pereira. 1999a. Colonial, Política. In *Dicionário de História de Portugal, Suplemento A/E, Vol. VII*, ed. António Barreto and Maria Filomena Mónica, 352–361. Porto: Livraria Figueirinhas.

Leite, Joaquim da Costa. 1999b. *Relatório da Comissão de Investigação sobre as Transacções de Ouro Efectuadas entre as Autoridades Portuguesas e Alemãs durante o Período compreendido entre 1936 e 1945*. Lisbon, manuscript.

Lindert, Peter H. 1994. The Rise of Social Spending, 1880–1930. *Explorations in Economic History* 31 (1) (January): 1–37.

———. 2004. *Growing Public: Social Spending and Economic Growth Since the Eighteenth Century, Vol. I—The Story*. Cambridge: Cambridge University Press.

Lopes, José da Silva. 2005. Finanças Públicas. In *História Económica de Portugal, 1700–2000, Vol. III, O Século XX*, ed. Pedro Lains and Álvaro Ferreira da Silva, 265–304. Lisbon: ICS.

Louçã, António. 2000. *Hitler e Salazar, Comércio em Tempos de Guerra, 1940–1944*. Lisbon: Terramar.

Loureiro, João Adolfo. 1991. *Economia e Sociedade. A Indústria no Após-Guerra.* Lisbon: Edições Cosmos.

Lucena, Manuel de. 1976. *A Evolução do Sistema Corporativo Português, Vol. I - O Salazarismo*. Lisbon: Perspectivas & Realidades.

———. 1978. Sobre a evolução dos organismos de coordenação económica ligados à lavoura (I). *Análise Social* XIV (56): 817–862.

———. 1979. Sobre a evolução dos organismos de coordenação económica ligados à lavoura (II). *Análise Social* XV (57): 117–167.

Maia, Fernando M. 1985. *Segurança Social em Portugal. Evolução e Tendências.* Lisboa: IED.

Mata, Maria Eugénia. 2001. Finanças públicas e dívida pública. In *Estatísticas Históricas Portuguesas*, ed. Nuno Valério, 657–712. Lisbon: INE.

Mateus, Abel. 2005. A tecnologia. In *História Económica de Portugal, 1700–2000, Vol. III, O Século XX*, ed. Pedro Lains and Álvaro Ferreira da Silvam, 125–156. Lisbon: ICS.

Milgram, Avraham. 2010. *Portugal, Salazar e os Judeus*. Lisbon: Gradiva.

Milward, Alan S. 1976. *War, Economy and Society, 1939–1945*. Berkeley: University of California Press.

Newitt, Malyn. 1981. *Portugal in Africa: The Last Hundred Years*. London: C. Hurst.

Nunes, Ana Bela. 2001. Actividade económica da população. In *Estatísticas Históricas Portuguesas*, ed. Nuno Valério, 149–197. Lisbon: INE.

Nunes, Ana Bela, and Nuno Valério. 1983. A Lei de Reconstituição Económica e a sua execução: um exemplo dos projectos e realizações da política económica do Estado Novo. *Estudos de Economia* III (3): 331–359.

Nunes, João Paulo Avelãs. 2010. *O Estado Novo e o Volfrâmio (1933–1947)*. Coimbra: Imprensa da Universidade de Coimbra.

Ó, Jorge Ramos do. 1999. *Os Anos de Ferro, O Dispositivo Cultural durante o Estado Novo, 1933–1949*. Lisbon: Editorial Estampa.

Patriarca, Fátima. 1995. *A Questão Social no Salazarismo, 1930–1947*. Lisbon: Imprensa Nacional-Casa da Moeda.

Payne, Stanley. 1995. *A History of Fascism, 1914–1945*. London: University College London Press.

Pereira, Miriam Halpern. 1999. As origens do Estado-Providência em Portugal: as novas fronterias entre público e privado. *Ler História* 37: 45–61.

Pimentel, Irene Flunser. 2006. *Judeus em Portugal durante a II Guerra Mundial: Em Fuga de Hitler e do Holocausto.* Lisbon: Esfera dos Livros.

Pinheiro, Maximiano, ed. 1997. *Séries Longas para a Economia Portuguesa, Pós-II Guerra Mundial, Vol. I - Séries Estatísticas*. Lisbon: Banco de Portugal.

Prados de la Escosura, Leandro. 2012. Output Per Head in Pre-Independence Africa: Quantitative Conjectures. *Economic History of Developing Regions* 27 (2): 1–36.

Ramos, Rui. 1988. Culturas da alfabetização em Portugal: uma introdução à história da alfabetização no Portugal contemporâneo. *Análise Social* XXIV (103–104): 1067–1145.

———. 1993. O método dos pobres: educação popular e alfabetização em Portugal (séculos XIX e XX). *Colóquio Educação e Sociedade* 2: 41–68.

———. 1998. 'O chamado problema do analfabetismo': as políticas de escolarização e a persistência do analfabetismo em Portugal (séculos XIX e XX). *Ler História* 35: 45–70.

Ramos, Rui, Bernardo Vasconcelos e Sousa, and Nuno Gonçalo Monteiro. 2009. *História de Portugal*. Lisbon: A Esfera dos Livros.

Reis, Jaime. 1993. O analfabetismo em Portugal no século XIX: uma interpretação. In *O Atraso Económico Português em Perspectiva Histórica: Estudos sobre a Economia Portuguesa na Segunda Metade do Século XIX, 1850–1913*, 227–253. Lisbon: Imprensa Nacional/Casa da Moeda.

———. 1995. Portuguese Banking in the Inter-War Period. In *Banking, Currency and Finance in Europe Between the Wars*, ed. Charles H. Feinstein, 472–501. Oxford: Oxford University Press.

Rias, Ana Paula Lopes de Oliveira Andrade. 1997. *Regentes Escolares, 'Colaboradores Benévolos' ao Serviço da Educação Nacional*. Masters' thesis presented at the Faculdade de Ciências Sociais e Humanas of the Universidade Nova de Lisboa, Lisbon.

Ribeiro, Maria da Conceição. 2000. *A Polícia Política no Estado Novo, 1926–1945*. Lisbon: Editorial Estampa.

Rosas, Fernando. 1986. *O Estado Novo nos Anos Trinta, Elementos para o Estudo da Natureza Económica e Social do Salazarismo (1928–1938)*. Lisbon: Editorial Estampa.

———. 1988. *O Salazarismo e a Aliança Luso-Britânica: Estudos sobre a Política Externa do Estado Novo nos Anos 30 e 40*. Lisbon: Fragmentos.

———. 1990. *Portugal entre a Paz e a Guerra, 1939–1945. Estudo do Impacte da II Guerra Mundial na Economia e na Sociedade Portuguesas*. Lisbon: Editorial Estampa.

Scmitter, Philippe C. 1999. *Portugal: Do Autoritarismo à Democracia*. Lisbon: Imprensa de Ciências Sociais.

Silva, Álvaro Ferreira da. 2016. Multinationals and Foreign Direct Investment: The Portuguese Experience (1900–2010). *Journal of Evolutionary Studies in Business* II (1): 40–68.

Silva, Álvaro Ferreira da, and Luciano Amaral. 2010. A economia portuguesa na I República. In *Outubro: a Revolução Republicana em Portugal (1910–1926)*, 257–298. Lisbon: Edições 70.

Silva, António E. Duarte. 1989. Salazar e a política colonial do Estado Novo: o Acto Colonial (1930–1951). In AAVV, *Salazar e o Salazarismo*, 101–152. Lisbon: Publicações D. Quixote.

Silva, Ester Gomes da, and Pedro Lains. 2013. Capital Formation and Long-Run Growth: Evidence from Portuguese Data, 1910–2011. Paper Presented at Iberometrics III, Zaragoza University.

Soares, Fernando Brito. 2005. A agricultura. In *História Económica de Portugal, 1700–2000, Vol. III, O Século XX*, ed. Pedro Lains and Álvaro Ferreira da Silva, 157–183. Lisbon: ICS.

Sousa, Maria Luísa. 2016. *A Mobilidade Automóvel em Portugal, 1920–1950*. Lisbon: Chiado Editora.

Tanzi, Vito, and Ludger Schuknecht. 2000. *Public Spending in the Twentieth Century: A Global Perspective*. Cambridge: Cambridge University Press.

Telo, António José. 1987. *Portugal na Segunda Guerra*. Lisbon: Perspectivas & Realidades.

———. 2000. *A Neutralidade Portuguesa e o Ouro Nazi*. Lisbon: Quetzal.

Valério, Nuno. 1984. *A Moeda em Portugal, 1913–1947*. Lisbon: Livraria Sá da Costa Editora.

———. 1994. *Valério, As Finanças Públicas Portuguesas entre as Duas Guerras Mundiais*. Lisbon: Cosmos.

———. 2001. Contas nacionais. In *Estatísticas Históricas Portuguesas*, ed. Nuno Valério, 505–535. Lisbon: INE.

Valério, Nuno, Ana Bela Nunes, Carlos Bastien, Rita Martins de Sousa, and Sandra Domingos Costa. 2006. *História do Sistema Bancário Português, Vol. I, Da Formação do Primeiro Banco Português à Assunção pelo Banco de Portugal das Funções de Banco Central, 1822–1931*. Lisbon: Banco de Portugal.

———. 2010. *História do Sistema Bancário Português, Vol. II, Da Assunção pelo Banco de Portugal das Funções de Banco Central à União Monetária Europeia*. Lisbon: Banco de Portugal.

Vieira, António Lopes. 1980. Os transportes rodoviários em Portugal (1900–1940). *Revista de História Económica e Social* 5: 57–94.

5

The *Estado Novo* Period After World War II: The Golden Age of Economic Growth

The period between the end of World War II and 1973 was the best ever in terms of growth of the Portuguese economy. Growth rates had never been higher and would never be in the future again, at least for such a long period. After more than one century of divergence in relation to the richer economies of the world, or at best non-divergence, the Portuguese economy converged in a consistent manner, with a particularly strong pace during the 1960s. This happened despite quick growth in most rich economies as well, as this corresponded to the period that has, since then, received the designation of "golden age of economic growth". High growth in Portugal was accompanied by industrialization, as is usual in processes of the kind: agriculture lost finally its prevalent position in both employment and output and gave place to the other two sectors, industry and services. Also notable was the abandonment of the country's tradition of protectionism and lack of openness. Up to this period, the Portuguese economy was one of the least open in Europe. It became one of the most open. The fact that the political regime existing in Portugal in the period was an authoritarian one

L. Amaral, *The Modern Portuguese Economy in the Twentieth and Twenty-First Centuries*, Palgrave Studies in Economic History,
https://doi.org/10.1007/978-3-030-24548-1_5

(a survivor from the 1920s and 1930s dictatorial age) did not prevent the country from participating in the process of European integration initiated in the 1950s. Growth would come to a sudden stop in 1974, at the same time as in the rest of the world, in the sequence of the 1973 "oil shock". In Portugal, however, the interruption of growth went hand in hand with a political revolution that abolished the authoritarian regime and substituted it with a democracy. The combination of the two facts brought special challenges to the Portuguese economy, as we will see in the next chapter.

1 The Course of Political Events

The fact that World War II was fought in the name of democracy on the part of the Allies gave rise to expectations that the Portuguese authoritarian regime might fall after 1945. But soon those expectations waned, as it became clear, on the one hand, that the notion of democracy sustained by the USSR corresponded to the sovietization of the countries under its domination and, on the other, that the United States would tolerate authoritarian regimes as long as they retained their anti-communist character. The latter was the case of the Portuguese regime, which, as the Cold War started, was able to find shelter within the Western-capitalist side of the confrontation (Ramos et al. 2009). In order to at least superficially conform to the formal democratic principles purported by its international patrons, the *Estado Novo* embarked on some cosmetic changes that, in fact, did not alter its fundamentally authoritarian nature. It also participated in the movements of European integration spurred by the Marshall Plan: Portugal was a founding member of the Organization of European Economic Cooperation (OEEC) in 1948 (the institutional structure whose fundamental function was to manage Marshall Aid and promote trade liberalization in Europe) and of the North Atlantic Treaty Organization (NATO) in the same year, the defense umbrella for the countries aligning with the United States in the Cold War. Acceptance in the United Nations (UN) took a little longer, due to the opposition of communist and newly independent countries, but eventually happened in 1955. And as the movement of European integration persisted throughout the 1950s and 1960s, Portugal became also a founding member of the European Free Trade Association (EFTA), together with the impeccable democracies of the UK, Switzerland, Sweden, Denmark, Norway, and Austria (Ramos et al. 2009).

A new challenge to the regime came in 1961, when, on 15 March, a group of Angolan nationalists attacked in northern Angola. There was some expectation over dictator Salazar's reaction to the events: if he would respond with military action or start decolonizing, following the attitude of the remaining European imperial powers. Decolonization was the rule in the early 1960s, after some hesitation in the 1940s and 1950s, when some of those empires had been involved in confrontations with independentist movements overseas. In the end, Salazar decided to take a military response, thus initiating a fourteen-year-long conflict that came to be known as the Colonial War (Oliveira 2014). After Angola in 1961, a new front was opened in Guinea in January 1963 and another one in Mozambique, in September 1964 (Cann 1997). The political elite had started to divide in the 1950s over the need to reform the regime in order to make it converge to the liberal democracies then becoming the norm in Western countries as well as over the response to give to the African nationalists: a military coup almost dethroned Salazar in April 1961, but failed; Salazar gained the upper hand and continued to control the levers of the regime until his incapacitation in August 1968 (followed by his death on 27 July 1970). There was a new expectation of reform at the time of his death. His successor, Marcello Caetano, became prime minister on 27 September 1968, carrying with him a reformist aura. Some initial indications went in that direction, but in the early 1970s Caetano pedalled back and, by 1974, the regime not only was fundamentally unreformed but continued embroiled in an apparently never-ending war overseas. The regime would fall on 25 April 1974, under a military coup led by a mix of senior and junior officers having as their main purpose, precisely, to disengage from the war (and the empire) in Africa (Ramos et al. 2009).

2 Transition to Normalcy and Economic Growth

Once World War II was over, the unusual position of the Portuguese balance of payments quickly reversed. Portuguese exports that had been in such high demand during the war (especially wolfram) collapsed. Also, those goods that Portugal had not been able to import due to various restrictions suddenly became available and abundant in the world market. These natural circumstances were aggravated by the Government's deliberate policy of using the reserves accumulated during World War II, as well as the bilateral trade agreements inherited from the 1930s and the war, to promote a massive wave of low-priced imports in order to crush the black market that had spread through the country then (Rosas 2000; Amaral 2018). The immediate consequence was a swelling of the trade deficit (Fig. 1).

The reserves accumulated during the war were put under pressure, and the risk of deflation became real. The BoP and the Government seem to have anticipated this and changed the money emission rule in 1946: now the BoP's notes in circulation plus its other sight liabilities had to be backed in a proportion of 50% by gold and foreign exchange

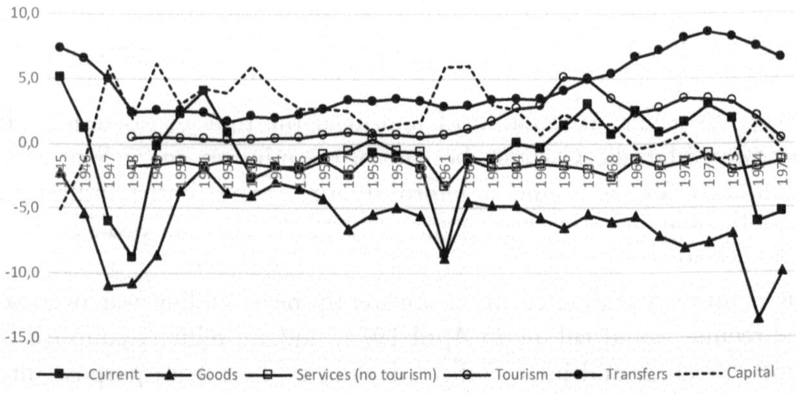

Fig. 1 Balance of payments, Portugal, 1945–1975 (% GDP) (*Source* Pinheiro [1997])

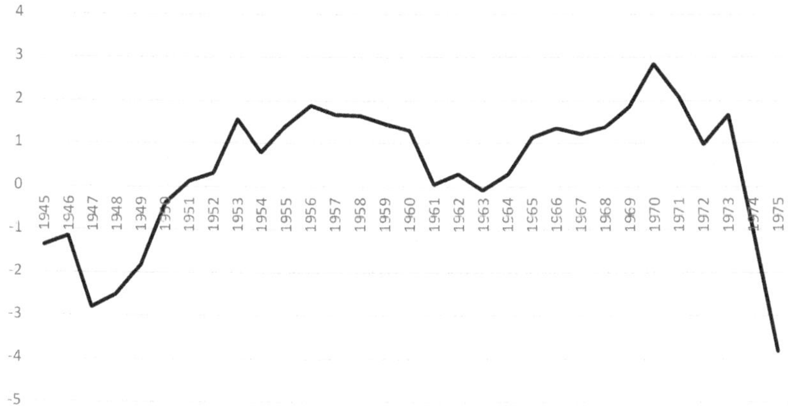

Fig. 2 Government budget deficit, Portugal, 1945–1975 (% GDP) (*Source* 1945–1952—Mata [2001]; 1953–1975—Pinheiro [1997])

reserves, half of them in gold.[1] The element of flexibility introduced by the new rule came with the dropping of the additional condition present in the 1931 rule of having to fully back with gold any amount of notes beyond 2.2 billion escudos. The BoP used various instruments to deal with the threat of deflation and was helped by the Government, which accepted a few budget deficits, despite its orthodox stance and the constitutional principles of the regime (Fig. 2) (Nunes and Valério 2005; Amaral 2018). But the amount of reserves accumulated during the war proved to be more than enough for the BoP to deal with deflation and still retain an amount that more than covered the notes in circulation.

This persistent abundance of reserves certainly provides an explanation for why the Portuguese Government and the BoP did not feel the need to devalue the escudo despite the pressure from the drain on reserves. However, the question of the escudo's exchange rate should be viewed as part of the wider issue of the international monetary system to be adopted after the war. The blueprint for such a system had

[1]Decree-law 35,575, 3 April 1946.

been basically designed during the war, in a meeting held by the allied countries at Bretton Woods in July 1944. The resulting proposals led to a system defined by Bordo as "a weak variant of the gold standard" (Bordo 1993, p. 19). This was to be a multilateral, full-convertibility system with fixed exchange rates, and with the US dollar as its nominal anchor, which should retain a price of $35 per ounce of gold. The whole system was to be managed by an international fund—which became the International Monetary Fund (IMF) in 1945—dedicated to the monitoring of national policies and endowed with resources to help countries in duress (Eichengreen 1996).

Although this blueprint remained the ultimate objective to be achieved, the countries that committed to it soon realized that its immediate implementation was impossible, due to the problems inherited from the wartime period. Two major problems overwhelmed the various countries: the first was a string of bilateral agreements and of trade and exchange controls originating in the previous decades. Most countries soon understood that they could not adopt immediately multilateralism and full convertibility, mostly on account of an acute shortage of international reserves. That was, precisely, the second problem: two-thirds of the world's gold reserves had accumulated in the United States by 1945 (Bordo 1993), and most of the countries did not have, and could not acquire, enough dollars to face the world market confidently. Most of the large European countries had overvalued currencies and had accumulated large current account deficits. They needed dollars but had no means to obtain them (Bordo 1993; Eichengreen 1996).

The problems of the immediate postwar period became tragically clear in 1947, when the United States and the UK decided to make sterling convertible in dollars again. In a matter of weeks, the reserves at the Bank of England evaporated, and the experiment was immediately halted. It became obvious that sterling was highly overvalued and that it could not become a reference for the international monetary system again (Eichengreen 1996). Most other currencies were also overvalued, with the exception of those of neutral countries (such as Portugal, Switzerland, or Sweden). The beginning of relief came with the Marshall Plan in 1948, followed by the 1949 devaluations of most European currencies (Bordo 1993; Eichengreen 1996).

Portugal was in a relatively comfortable position, although it faced some uncertainties. The Portuguese authorities decided not to participate in the foundation of the IMF. The reasons for this have yet to be understood, but, as Valério et al. (2010, p. 97) remarked: "the generality of the European members of the fund were ... [then] much farther from complying with the ideal rules of the organization than Portugal". The country was sitting on a heap of international reserves and did not have the kind of shortage plaguing most other European countries. The composition of those reserves was, however, problematic, being essentially composed of sterling (Amaral 2018). In a context of exchange inconvertibility, bilateral trade agreements, increased weakness of sterling, and strength of the US dollar, this was a reason for concern. Bilateral trade and currency inconvertibility meant that exchanges in one currency area could not be settled with exchanges in another.

As a result of the "sterling problem" inherited from the war, Portugal had thus a vested interest in the return of sterling not only to convertibility but to its position as a reserve currency too. It is in this context that Portugal's initial rejection of the Marshall Plan must be viewed. Since, contrary to most European countries, Portugal was not starved of reserves, what it needed most was the return to multilateral trade and currency convertibility, in order to use its accumulated reserves freely. As the original scheme of the Marshall Plan involved a set of bilateral agreements with the United States, Portugal decided to reject it in the first instance (in January 1948), despite participating in all institutions related to it, including the OEEC.

Between 1948 and 1950, this complex set of problems was progressively solved. First, there were various efforts at the international level to reinstitute convertibility of current account transactions (trade and transfers). After some incipient agreements, a new organization was created in 1950 making international payments easier: the European Payments Union (EPU). The EPU functioned as a clearinghouse, settling payments for current account transaction purposes made in different currencies (Bordo 1993; Eichengreen 1996). The creation of the EPU was preceded by a series of currency depreciations, the most relevant of which was that of sterling, which depreciated 30.5% in relation to the dollar in 1949. The combination of depreciation with ease of payments considerably improved the international payments position of these European countries. Portuguese authorities had again to take an important decision concerning the escudo's exchange rate. In the end, the Government and the BoP decided to revalue the escudo by 25% in relation to sterling, which implied depreciation of about 15% in relation to the US dollar. A new peg of 1 dollar = 28.75 escudos was thus established. As in 1931, this decision was influenced by a desire to both preserve the external value of the escudo (by appreciating it in relation to sterling) and keep competitiveness (by depreciating it in relation to the dollar). These were the exchange rates with which the escudo became fully convertible 10 years later, together with the other European currencies, under a system called European Monetary Agreement (Amaral 2018).

The EPU, which was supposed to last for only two years, remained active until 1958, something that reveals the difficulties experienced by these countries in returning to full-convertibility and multilateral payments. Portugal joined the EPU at its creation in 1950 with a debtor position calculated on the basis of its 1948 balance of payments. However, the Portuguese position had begun to change by 1949, mostly due to the end of the import program of the previous two years (Fig. 1). In 1950, another event would further improve Portuguese international payments: the outbreak of the Korean War. For the three years of the duration of the war, there was a new boom in demand for Portuguese wolfram as well as for some raw materials produced in the colonies. Additionally, Portugal started receiving Marshall Aid, once the latter acquired a more multilateral nature, even if the amounts were small (Rollo 1994). The fact is that soon the payments position of the country returned to balance. The expectation when Portugal joined the EPU was that it would continue to face an international payments deficit, but quite early in the life of the organization the country acquired a creditor position (Amaral 2018). An essential contribution to the success of this policy was the quick return to budget balance once the deflationary context passed (Fig. 2), a stance that was kept until the end of the regime.

Salazar preserved throughout the postwar period a non-Keynesian approach to budgetary and monetary matters, even when that approach became the rule in most Western countries (Battilossi et al. 2010). Demand management through fiscal policy was not part of the acceptable policy arsenal of Portuguese authorities: budgets were to be balanced in an "orthodox" manner, a principle that remained enshrined in the Constitution. Consequently, the BoP could continue following the principle of letting the money supply depend on a rule. This was quite original in the postwar period, during which most Western countries resorted to some sort of discretion (Lopes 1996; Amaral 2002). As we can see in Fig. 2, between 1951 and 1973, the Government's budget had only one minor deficit in 1963, in the specific context of the outbreak of the Colonial War. After the initial shock, comfortable surpluses returned from 1964 onwards, at around 1–2% of GDP.

A tax reform was implemented in the first half of the 1960s, in part as a response to higher spending caused by the Colonial War, in part to make the Portuguese tax structure approach those of richer European countries. The outbreak of the war led to the creation of a few ad hoc taxes, the most important of which was a "tax for the defense and valorization of the Overseas Territories" in 1962: this was a special tax applied over the profits of firms with preferential (and protected) relations with the overseas territories (Valério 2006).[2] But there were other, more thorough changes: in 1962, the existing wage tax (*imposto profissional*) was reformed, in order to be applied to real income rather than presumed income (a principle still coming from the 1928–1929 fiscal reform) while at the same time making its progressivity clearer (although also milder).[3] Reliance on real profits rather than presumed ones was introduced as well in the case of the industrial tax (*contribuição industrial*) in 1963.[4] And the same principle was introduced in the non-wage tax (*imposto complementar*) in 1963.[5] The other fundamental piece

---

[2]Law 2,111, 21 December 1962.

[3]Decree-law 44,305, 27 April 1962.

[4]Decree-law 54,103, 1 July 1963.

[5]Decree-law 45,399, 30 November 1963.

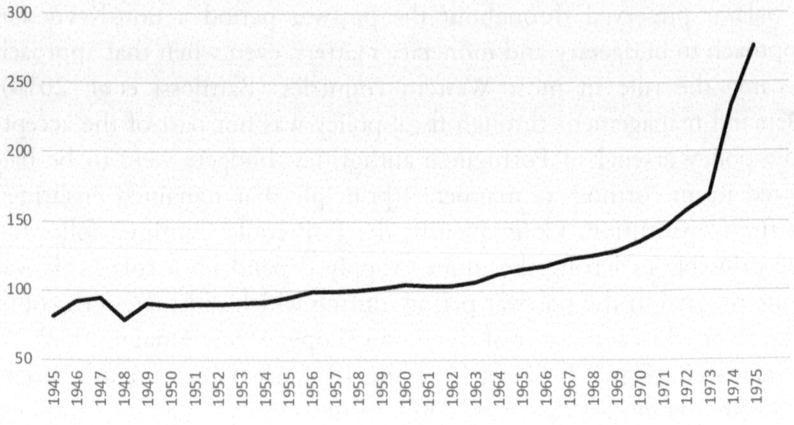

Fig. 3 Consumer price index, Portugal, 1945–1975 (1958 = 100) (*Source* Bastien [2001])

of reform was the creation in 1966 of a transactions tax (*imposto de transacções*) to be applied at the level of wholesale transactions (a move sometimes seen as a first step toward the creation of a value-added tax: Valério 2006).[6] Besides these big changes, some other minor ones were also implemented, and the overall package corresponded to a clear modernization of the tax system, making it approach the European norm (Valério 2006).

The "orthodox" stance of the regime allowed for low inflation, at least until 1965 (Fig. 3). From that year onward, inflation changed its behavior. But this transformation was not connected with fiscal policy but rather with the external payments position of the country: from then on, a vast influx of external means of payment took place (for reasons to be detailed below), leading to an expansion of monetary circulation, thanks to the existing money emission rule. The consequences on prices were inevitable.

The non-Keynesian approach of Portuguese authorities did not simply imply fiscal balance but also a low level of public spending. That is

[6]Decree-law 47,066, 1 July 1966.

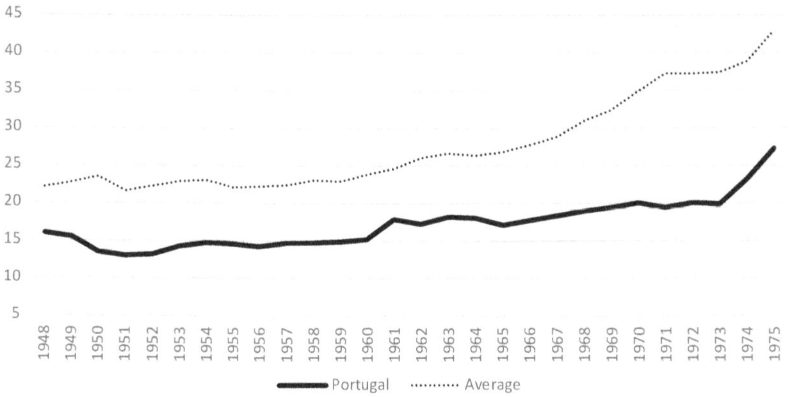

Fig. 4 Public spending, Portugal vs. average European countries, 1948–1975 (% GDP) (*Source* 1953–1975—Pinheiro [1997] spliced with Mata [2001] for 1948–1952)

what Fig. 4 shows, where we can see how the Portuguese Government's level remained considerably below the European average until 1973. The differences lay not only in size but in structure too (Fig. 5). The main difference between Portugal and most other West European countries resulted from the low level of spending on social items, on

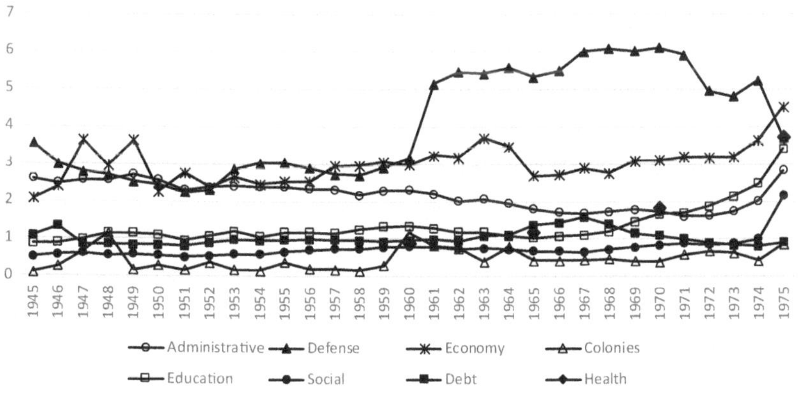

Fig. 5 Structure public spending, Portugal 1945–1975 (% GDP) (*Source* Mata [2001])

Table 1 Structure of public spending (some items), various countries, 1960–1970 (% GDP)

	Defense		Education		Health		Social	
	1960	1970	1960	1970	1960	1970	1960	1970
France	6.3	4.1	3.4	5.0	2.5	4.3	4.8	3.5
Germany	4.0	3.2	2.4	4.0	3.1	4.2	5.0	4.4
Italy	2.7	2.3	3.7	4.5	3.2	4.8	4.2	3.4
Sweden	2.8	3.4	4.6	6.2	3.4	6.2	2.8	4.0
UK	6.4	4.6	3.6	5.3	3.4	3.9	2.5	3.6
Portugal	3.0	6.1	1.3	1.7	0.4	1.8	0.8	0.9

Source Defense: World Bank Open Data; All others: OECD (1985), except Portugal: Mata (2001) and Carreira (1996) for Health

education and on health care: 0.5–0.75% of GDP on social programs until the late 1960s, 1% on education and 1% on health care. In the late 1960s, there was a certain change in this structure, with spending on education and health jumping to 2.5–3% of GDP until the end of the regime, and social items to 1%. But these were still low levels by European standards (Table 1).

Most of Europe embarked then on the construction of a state-provided welfare framework, but not Portugal, at least not on the same scale, either because the regime considered some social problems to be irrelevant or because it tried to find private or semi-private (corporatist) solutions to them. But things changed somehow in time. In principle, social security issues should be part of the corporatist institutions. According to the 1935 social security law, the Government gave civil society the initiative to create corporatist social security institutions. Its role was simply that of authorizing their creation and approving (or not) their statutes and boards. In 1943, however, a new piece of legislation gave the Government the possibility to create them, especially in circumstances where the corporatist organizations did not reveal any interest in doing so.[7] The Government used this power abundantly from then on, meaning that, despite its anti-statist rhetoric, it ended up by being responsible for creating many of those institutions. In 1962,

[7]Decree-law 32,674, 20 February 1943.

Table 2 Social security beneficiaries as a percentage of active population, 1953–1972

	Total	Total minus ASM
1953	50.76	35.71
1960	72.18	56.90
1966	79.26	63.48
1972	93.32	78.43

Source Amaral (2002)

a new social security law was enacted, enlarging insurance to maternity protection and (in certain circumstances) unemployment, while at the same time making enrollment in the rural institutions compulsory.[8] In 1969, coverage by social security was enlarged for the generality of rural population (and not only the members of *Casas do Povo*) and the number of eventualities insured for the rural population increased.[9] Financial management of social security institutions continued to be based essentially on capitalization, relying on the contributions of both employers and employees, but some institutions started adopting different methods throughout time (Carreira 1996; Amaral 2002; Carolo and Pereirinha 2010). What most of these changes suggest is a progressive abandonment on the part of the *Estado Novo* of its initial strict corporatist approach to one where, even if still in incipient manner, a large role was also recognized to the Government, more in line with what was common in the European welfare states of the time (Cardoso and Rocha 2003).

Not surprisingly, the social security system expanded vigorously. As Table 2 shows, the number of beneficiaries had a spectacular increase between the 1950s and 1972: in 1953, beneficiaries (including those of private mutual support associations, ASMs) as a proportion of total active population were roughly 51%; in 1972, coverage was almost universal: 93%. Even if we exclude ASMs from the count, the figures are still impressive: 36% of active population in 1953, 78% in 1972. If we count overall population rather than just active population, the numbers are less impressive but still show growth: 20% in 1956

[8]Law 2,115, 18 June 1962.

[9]Law 2,144, 25 May 1969.

Table 3 Social security spending by type of institution, 1960–1970 (% GDP)

	Corporatist	ASM	Government	Total
1960	1.86	0.09	0.70	2.65
1970	3.36	0.08	0.67	4.11

Source Carolo and Pereirinha (2010)

and 42% in 1973 (Carolo and Pereirinha 2010). Not only the number of beneficiaries grew, but the amounts spent did too. If we add Government spending to that made by the corporatist institutions and ASMs, we get relatively high figures: in 1953, expenditure by social security institutions including ASMs corresponded to 2.3% of GDP, and in 1973 to 5.6% (Table 3). Still, the amounts remained smaller in Portugal than in the rest of Europe (Table 1).

The semi-private/semi-public approach of the Portuguese regime was also visible in the case of health care services. Most of these services depended on a set of private institutions called *Misericórdias*, founded in the fifteenth century. These were private organizations, funded and run by laymen of religious orientation and dedicated to charity, but in close connection with political power (Sá and Lopes 2008; Campos and Simões 2011). Throughout time they were able to create a relatively vast network of health establishments dedicated to assistance to poor people. In the first decades of the twentieth century, most existing hospitals in Portugal were run by the *misericórdias*. Government hospitals were concentrated in the large cities (Lisbon, Porto, and Coimbra) and were only a handful. Their specialty was also assistance to poor people. Most of the Government's action was devoted to sanitation (having epidemics in mind) or certain psychiatric conditions (Carreira 1996; Campos 2000).

Compulsory insurance included some health protection but functioning within the system of the corporatist organizations, without much Government responsibilities. Health was essentially a private issue, for which individuals should (or not) take personal provisions or rely on their private or corporatist organizations (Campos and Simões 2011). Financial means and coverage diverged vastly depending on the specific organization. Even when the Government decided, in 1946, to promote the construction of a large number of hospitals around the country,[10] these were handed in to the *misericórdias* (Carreira 1996). But some change started to appear: still in 1946, a national federation of *Caixas de Previdência* (the private voluntary social security associations) allowed the range of health protection for their members to be enlarged. By the early 1970s, health coverage was wide but uncoordinated: poor people used the medical assistance provided either by the *misericórdias* or the few public services (there were then 350 *misericórdias* spread around the country: Sá and Lopes 2008); about 80% of the population was covered in some manner by their corporatist or private systems of social protection, and civil servants had their own system (Carreira 1996). Finally, in 1971, a reform increased the direct responsibility of the Government in the provision of health care, with the immediate consequence of a series of health centers being built.[11] There was also an agreement between the public hospitals and the *previdência* institutions, making access of the members of these institutions to hospitals easier: health care insurances passed from covering 52% of the population in 1970 to 69% in 1972 and 89% in 1974 (Campos 2000). Population coverage and Government spending increased, passing from about 1% of GDP in 1965 to 2% in 1970 (Fig. 5), but continued to remain much below the European norm (Table 1). Also, the fragmentation between the various subsystems persisted.

In what concerns education, the regime continued with its efforts to expand schooling, although always within very tight budgetary guidelines. In 1941, the Government launched a 10-year plan (updated in 1955 and 1961) to build 6082 schools, corresponding to 9314 new classrooms (Gomes and Machado 2019; Beja et al. 1996): in fact, by 1951, only half of the amounts initially proposed had been spent and only 2883 classrooms had been built (Ramos 1999). But in 1952, a new Popular Education Plan was designed (renovated in 1954), proposing to apply a "shock therapy" to the problem of illiteracy, with a vague inspiration coming from similar experiences in Brazil and Mexico

---

[10]Law 2,011, 2 April 1946.

[11]Decree-law 413/71, 27 September 1971.

(Ramos 1999).[12] The plan aimed explicitly at the final eradication of illiteracy and involved a new spurt in the supply of teachers as well as the launching of a National Campaign for Adult Education. By the early 1950s, school regents (the low-skilled teacher category created in 1931—see Chapter 4) were still responsible for a vast part of primary education (Rias 1997). By 1962, 7000 more new teachers and 3000 new regents had been put in the system (Rias 1997), and 5000 new schools had been built (Gomes and Machado 2019, p. 6). This effort was complemented with a series of other measures: in 1956, compulsory education was enlarged to four years, although exclusively for male children[13]; in 1960, the distinction between elementary and complementary primary education that had been established in 1930 was eliminated, and compulsory education was enlarged to four years for female children as well[14]; in 1964, compulsory education was enlarged to six years,[15] and in 1973 to eight years (Ramos 1999; Amaral 2002).[16] In 1973, school posts were suppressed, remaining operative only until new local schools had been built to replace them.[17] According to Amaral (2002) and Gomes and Machado (2019), the Government's efforts to increase schooling were decisive to change the literacy and schooling levels of the Portuguese population, by lowering the cost of acquiring formal education by families. The effectiveness of the 1950s plan seems to be confirmed by a clear jump in the number of students concluding the primary level of education during that decade (Amaral 2005).

Until the 1960s, the *Estado Novo*'s policy concerning secondary education aimed at restricting access to public general secondary education (*ensino liceal*) while promoting it in the private sector. This only changed from 1967 onward. In 1967, the Government created

[12]Decree-law 38,968 and Decree-law 38,969, 27 October 1952.

[13]Decree-law 40,964, 31 December 1956.

[14]Decree-law 42,994, 28 May 1960.

[15]Decree-law 45,810, 9 July 1964.

[16]Law 5/73, 25 July 1973.

[17]Decree-law 67/73, 26 February 1973.

a Preparatory Cycle for Secondary Education.[18] The Preparatory Cycle merged the first two years of general and vocational secondary schooling into a single course. Before that, the separation between students finishing primary education and following general secondary education and those following vocational education had to be made at the start of secondary schooling. With the new legislation, that separation occurred two years later. This was inserted into the general policy of enlarging the period of compulsory schooling from four to six years and was accompanied by the construction of a large number of new public secondary schools (Amaral 2002). It is consequently not surprising that spending on education increased decisively in those years (Fig. 5). The low level of resources spent on secondary schooling did not prevent the growth of students at that level, especially from the 1950s onward (Amaral 2002, 2005). The volume of resources dedicated to university was also low, and this meant very slow growth of students at that level, except in the final four years of the regime (Amaral 2002, 2005). Despite all this, the Portuguese figures for spending in education remained much below the European norm (Table 1).

The biggest shock to public spending in this period was the Colonial War: because of it, military expenditure passed from about 3% of GDP in 1960 to about 5–6% from 1961 onward. Such a weight was very unusual in the Western context, except in those countries with a more active role in the Cold War: the United States (8.6% of GDP in 1960 and 7.7% in 1970), the UK (6.4 and 4.6% in the same dates), and France (6.3 and 4.1%) (World Bank Open Data), the latter two on a declining trend. All other West European countries had much lower levels, between 1 and 3%. The combination of increased military spending with the expansion of social, health and education programs led to the growth of the general level of public spending, with one first jump in 1961 and persistent growth in the late 1960s and early 1970s (Fig. 4). Still, this was not enough to make it converge to what was common in the rest of Western Europe. Quite on the contrary, the Portuguese

[18] Decree-law 47,480, 2 January 1967.

Government diverged from most European countries, as they were expanding social programs very quickly.

Besides public spending, the instruments the *Estado Novo* used to intervene in the economy were the same coming from the 1930s: corporatism, industrial conditioning, administrative prices, subsidies, strategic tax breaks, protectionism, or reserved markets. But this set of instruments, which had been designed in the context of the international closure of the interwar period, had to adapt to the conditions of the 1960s openness. Openness challenged not only the traditional protectionist policies of the regime (of all Portuguese regimes since the nineteenth century, in fact: see Chapters 2 and 3) but some of its other policies too. The path was somewhat convoluted, however.

In the mid-1940s, the Government adopted finally in an explicit manner an import-substitution industrialization policy (Confraria 2005). From that moment on, protection of agriculture became much less pronounced. Quite on the contrary, crushing the prices of some traditional crops, such as wheat, maize, or olive oil, became a deliberate effort (Mendes 1983; Confraria 2005; Soares 2005). As this policy only affected the prices directly set by the Government, all others increased quite fast (Lains 2009). Therefore, incentives for farmers to switch between crops grew, from traditional to modern ones, such as fruits and vegetables, meat, dairy or forest.

The agrarian reform plans for rebalancing the farm structure ended up by never being implemented (Baptista 1993). But some of their parts, although decoupled from the redefinition of property structure, went forward. This is the case of the Forestation Plan, advancing from the 1950s onward more or less on schedule, with 76% of the projected area in place by 1973 (Branco 2011, p. 154). This plan had close connections with the paper and paper pulp industry, something that led, from the 1950s onward, to a switch in the preferred species to be planted, from pine trees to eucalyptus (Branco 2011; Branco and Neves 2018). Another aspect of structural reform that went forward was irrigation, with some projects being concluded and a new irrigation plan, only for the Alentejo region (*Plano de Rega do Alentejo*), starting in the 1960s. Both aspects led to widespread replacement of crops in the large farms of southern Portugal, from wheat and olive oil to fruits, vegetables, and rice (and eucalyptus too, although with no connection to irrigation) (Baptista 1993; Amaral and Freire 2017). Irrigation, which was conceived initially as an instrument to allow for property restructuring, had the opposite effect, as it helped the large southern farms to modernize. Another instrument designed by the Government to support the agricultural sector was a set of subsidies, introduced from the 1950s onward, for agricultural inputs, especially fertilizers, tractors, cattle, or fodder (Baptista 1993; Amaral and Freire 2017).

The import-substitution policy was based on two laws: the Electrification Law and the Law of Industrial Development and Reorganization, from 1944 and 1945, respectively.[19] Import-substitution was to happen through two essential means: the promotion of electrical projects (mostly hydro-electric) and of new industries (in order to diversify the country's industrial structure). This should be complemented by efforts to increase concentration and scale in existing industries. The policy instruments the Government preferred were trade protection, industrial conditioning, labor repression (in order to keep wages low), and low prices of agricultural goods (savings and labor were to be transferred from agriculture to industry, so that investment in the latter sector expanded). The Government was to participate directly in the effort. The means for that were various: participation in the capital of chosen companies, bonds issued in order to be used in industrial investment or underwriting of industrial loans in the capital market. The favorite new sectors were chemicals (fertilizers), steel, shipbuilding and repair, paper and paper pulp, and electricity (Loureiro 1991; Confraria 2005).

A new instrument created by the *Estado Novo* in the 1950s became a very important part of the regime's package to intervene in the economy: a series of development plans (*Planos de Fomento*). These were four-year plans, which never became as heavy as in socialist countries, or as in some capitalist countries such as Nazi Germany or even postwar France. But a growing number of important investment decisions were taken under their heading. Five such plans were designed:

[19]Law 2,002, 26 December 1944 and Law 2,005, 14 March 1945.

the first development plan, for the period 1953–1958, the second, for the period 1959–1964, the intermediate development plan (*Plano Intercalar de Fomento*), for the period 1965–1967, the third plan, for the period 1968–1973, and the fourth, for the period 1974–1979 (although the latter was never implemented as it coincided with the fall of the regime). The plans grew in complexity with time: the first was still essentially a list of public investment projects in infrastructure and "fundamental" industries, but from then onward, they became increasingly more comprehensive and complex (Lains 1994; Lopes 1996).

The amount of investment inserted in the development plans grew from 14% of gross fixed capital formation (GFCF) in the first (2.4% of GDP), to 20% in the second (4% of GDP), 43% in the intermediate plan (10% of GDP), and 39% in the third (10% of GDP) (Lains 1994, p. 928). However, we must note that the amounts involved were simply indicative for private investors and compulsory only for the Government. But the weight of public investment under the heading of the plans was always lower than that of private investment, except in the first. This means that the direct influence of the Government was much lower than the numbers above might indicate: perhaps somewhere between 10 and 15% of GFCF (Lains 1994). However, if we take into consideration the fact that many of the private projects were jointly financed by the Government, a relevant indirect impact must be considered too. Various activities became substantially dependent on Government investment, such as the steel, paper and paper pulp, or oil refining industries, as well as the modern hydro-electric infrastructure. The development plans were complemented by the creation of a National Development Bank (*Banco de Fomento Nacional*) in 1958, the first investment bank in the country, again a public–private joint-venture: the Government shared the capital with the remaining banks in the Portuguese financial system (Valério et al. 2010).

Although this was an impressive apparatus, the intensity of the *Estado Novo*'s presence in the economy did not differ much from the one existing in the new demo-liberal regimes of Europe. In almost every one of them, the strong influence of left-wing parties (social-democratic or communist proper) opened the way for heightened Government interventionism. In France, for instance, the whole of the energy sector (electricity, gas, and coal), most of the insurance and banking sectors and some specific companies (such as Renault, Berliet, and Air France) were nationalized at the end of World War II, something that amounted to roughly one-fifth of industrial production (Van der Wee 1986). In Britain, around 20% of British industry came under Government control after the war, plus the Bank of England, the airline companies, the airports, and road haulage. Government also bought a significant number of shares in various companies, among them BP, Rolls Royce, and Upper Clyde Shipbuilders (Van der Wee 1986). In Italy, the Government-controlled holding *Istituto per la Ricostruzione Industriale* (IRI) became the largest employer and industrial owner in the country. The *Estado Novo* never nationalized any company, but this did not prevent the Government from becoming the largest stock owner in the country, thanks to a vast, although scattered, portfolio in industries considered to be "strategic" (Pinho 1976). Even when the issue is corporatism, the differences between Portugal and the other countries are again not too stark. To take a few examples, Sweden, the Netherlands, Austria, and Belgium developed after the war institutions of a corporatist nature, whereby investment decisions, wage, and price levels came to be decided through various central-consultation institutional mechanisms (Van der Wee 1986; Faxén 1982).

This kind of interventionism was, however, accompanied by a progressive return to a freer international trade environment. In fact, the postwar period is defined by relatively free trade within European regional blocs combined with internal interventionist policies at various levels (Coppolaro and Lains 2013). The Portuguese Government also followed the free trade trend. The country participated in all major events and organizations of international cooperation put in place in the postwar period: the Marshall Plan (Rollo 1994) and OEEC, of which it was a founding member, both in 1948. The main purpose of the OEEC was to slash, or even eliminate, the quantitative (i.e., non-tariff) restrictions dating from the 1930s and World War II, substituting them with tariffs. Portugal eliminated around 90% of its quantitative restrictions to trade in non-agricultural products with the European countries, the United States and Canada until the end of the 1950s, making of it one of the countries more thoroughly complying with the principles of the OEEC (Macedo et al. 1988; Lopes 1996). The country also participated in the EPU, the international mechanism created in 1950 to facilitate payments between the participant countries.

Most importantly, Portugal was a founding member of the EFTA, together with Britain, Switzerland, Austria, Denmark, Norway, and Sweden, in 1960. The reasons for participating in EFTA rather than in the European Economic Community (EEC), which was founded in 1958, were many. The Portuguese authorities were skeptical about the kind of supra-national integration (pointing to a possible future political unification) put in motion in the first half of the 1950s by France, Germany, Italy, Belgium, the Netherlands, and Luxembourg (the core six countries of EEC) (Leitão 2007). A position in which they were not alone: the British authorities, for instance, were not only skeptical about these efforts but entirely against them. Throughout the 1950s, the UK tried systematically to put forward an alternative vision of integration, based simply on free trade and intergovernmental cooperation, without any pretense of political unification. But when these efforts failed and the "core six" founded the EEC in 1958, the British authorities were left with a dilemma: either to follow them or be left outside of European cooperation. As an alternative, they initiated a process including the European countries not included in the EEC: the creation of EFTA in January 1960, through the Stockholm Convention, was its outcome (Milward 1992).

Besides being more satisfying for the principles espoused by the Portuguese authorities, EFTA had three further advantages over EEC: one, it did not imply the participant countries to be political democracies (a criterion Portugal could not satisfy at the time); second, it allowed member countries to retain systems of preferential trade, such as the one existing within the Portuguese Empire (a point also shared by Britain): the EEC included a common tariff for all participants while EFTA allowed its participants to establish freely the level of protection in relation to third countries (Leitão 2007; Cunha 2015); third, the free trade principles of EFTA covered only manufacturing, excluding agriculture, something the Portuguese authorities saw as advantageous taking into consideration the inefficiency of the country's agriculture by comparison with those of the other West European countries (Lopes 1996).

Portugal was able to negotiate a particularly favorable status within EFTA, as the other member countries accepted the idea that its lower level of economic development deserved special treatment: on the one hand, Portugal was able to obtain from the organization the classification of tomato pulp and tinned fish as industrial goods; these were goods for which there was no competition from the remaining countries, thus opening entirely the EFTA market to Portuguese exports; on the other hand, the Stockholm Convention included an annex (called Annex G), establishing that the reduction of Portuguese tariffs should proceed at a slower pace than elsewhere, and also that some infant industries (such as steel production and car assemblage) could have even longer transition periods: the total dismantling of tariffs for the participating countries was of six years, but Portugal obtained an initial period of twenty years, which was later postponed many times. Only in the goods for which there was no national production was the elimination of tariffs immediate (Lopes 1996). The special status obtained by Portugal is reflected in the fact that 87% of Portuguese exports were immediately affected by the common rules of the association but only 23% of the imports from the other member countries were affected in the Portuguese market. In order to make the process even less shattering to protected Portuguese economic activities, the general tariff level was raised on the eve of the signing of the Stockholm Convention, with the approval of a new schedule.[20] Additionally, Portugal was able to retain a discretionary import licensing system, named import register bulletin, created during World War II (Macedo et al. 1988).

Joining EFTA implied joining also the General Agreement on Trade and Tariffs (GATT), the platform dedicated to the reduction of protectionism at the world scale. Portugal became a member in 1961, something that implied further trade liberalization, now with respect to some extra-European countries (Lopes 1996; Valério 2002;

[20]Decree-law 42,656, 18 November 1959.

Nunes and Valério 2005). These steps led the country to join also the Bretton Woods institutions, i.e., the IMF and the World Bank, as well as to adopt their rules (the pegging of the currency to the US dollar—indirectly to gold, as the value of the dollar was defined in terms of gold), something that happened in 1960 (Macedo et al. 1988). Britain tried to join the EEC on different occasions (in 1961, in 1967, and in 1971) and, on each of them, Portugal looked for special trade conditions with the EEC. When Britain was finally accepted in 1972 (becoming a member in 1973, at the same time as Ireland and Denmark), Portugal signed a free trade agreement with the EEC. Conditions were more unfavorable to Portuguese exports (especially those involving tomato pulp, textiles, and wine) and implied lower protection of Portuguese manufacturing than in EFTA, but Portugal was allowed to increase duties on some goods by 20% at the time of the signing of the agreement, in order to dilute the impact of the new agreement (Macedo et al. 1988; Lopes 1996; Leitão 2007; Cunha 2015).

Despite its special status within EFTA, the opening of the economy from 1960 onward was unequivocal: by 1967, tariffs over 35% of the goods imported from EFTA countries had already been completely eliminated, and very low tariffs covered 15% of other goods; in what concerns the remaining 50% (those covered by Annex G), tariffs were reduced by half until 1970; additionally, the tariffs protecting infant industries could not exceed 20% and had to decline quickly (Lopes 1996). Figure 6 reveals precisely that not only the weight of tariffs over imports fell clearly from the beginning of Portugal's participation in EFTA but it also converged to the average of the EEC countries. The spikes in 1959 and 1970 visible in the figure are caused by the upward adjustment in the tariff schedule right before joining EFTA and right before the signing of the free trade agreement with the EEC. But none of these adjustments prevented a general declining trend. By 1974, the average tariff weight on Portuguese imports was virtually similar to the one existing in the EEC. Naturally, the share of trade in GDP expanded visibly, from around 7% in 1945 to 24% in 1973 (Fig. 7).

Free trade forced Portuguese authorities to change some of the most efficiency-hampering aspects of the existing institutional framework. Industrial conditioning had to be reformed: Portuguese firms should

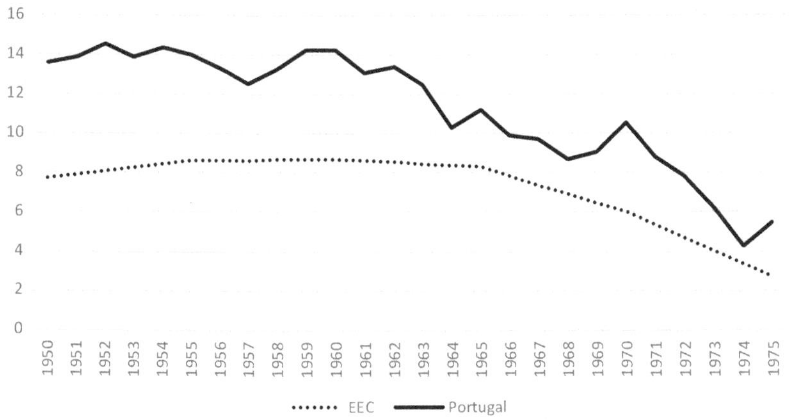

Fig. 6 Average tariffs % of imports, Portugal and EEC/EU, 1950–1975 (*Source* Portugal—Fontoura and Valério [2001]; EEC/EU: adapted from Dür [2008])

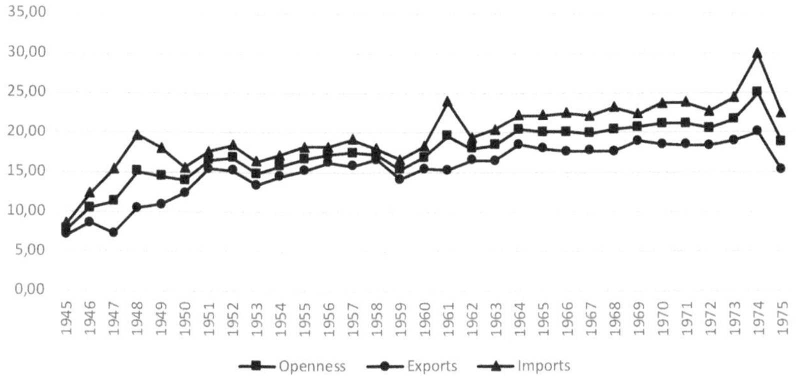

Fig. 7 Exports and imports, Portugal 1945–1975 (% GDP) Current prices; (Openness = 100 × [(Exports + Imports)/2]/GDP. *Source* Built by the author based on Fontoura and Valério [2001] for 1945–1947 and Pinheiro [1997] for 1948–1975)

not be forced to compete with those of more developed foreign countries while still be subject to the bureaucratic intricacies of industrial conditioning. The rules of this licensing scheme were, thus, transformed in 1965. From then on, industrial conditioning became more of a technical procedure, losing some of its most arbitrary aspects: from 1965

Table 4 GDP per capita annual growth rates, 1930–1950 (%)

1950–1959	3.88
1960–1973	6.54
1950–1973	5.38

Source 1950–1952—Batista et al. (1997); 1953–1973—Pinheiro (1997)

onward, it was simply necessary that the applications conformed to certain general rules for the Government to license them (Brito 1989, 1996; Confraria 1992, 1999; Lopes 1996). Finally, in 1970, a Law for the Defense of Competition closed the cycle, promising to combat situations of excessive market power.[21] The law started only to be applied in 1972, however, already a bit too close to the end of the regime. Also in 1970 the number of industries subject to industrial conditioning was reduced by two-thirds, being restricted only to defense industries and some "fundamental" sectors.[22] At this time, export-promoting policies gained preference over import-substitution ones (Confraria 2005).

Openness also changed the regime's approach to foreign investment. Until 1965, the rules applicable were those of a 1943 law: the Law of Capital Nationalization.[23] According to it, at least 60% of the capital in investments in public services, monopolies, and other activities deemed to be strategic had to be Portuguese. But in 1965 Portugal signed the OECD's Code for the Liberalization of Capital Movements, whose consequence was the drafting of new legislation liberalizing capital movements (Simões 1985).[24]

Economic growth under this institutional framework was very rapid: for the overall period between 1950 and 1973, the annual rate of growth of GDP per capita was 5.4%, but with an accelerating trend, from 3.9% in the 1950s to 6.5% in the 1960s and early 1970s (Table 4). High growth for such a long time was a novelty for

[21]Law 1/72, 24 March 1972.

[22]Decree 393/70, 19 August 1970.

[23]Law 1,994, 13 April 1943.

[24]Decree-law 46,312, 28 April 1965.

the Portuguese economy. Never had the Portuguese economy known previously in its history a process of the kind and never would it know another one again in the future. Contrary to what had happened in the first half of the century, industrial output grew much faster than agricultural output (eight times faster) and industrial productivity as well (two times faster) (Lains 1994).

Contrary to what happens in many countries subject to the same kind of episodes, industrialization and fast growth did not bring external imbalance (Fig. 1). Quite on the contrary, the current account remained roughly in balance for most of the period, displaying some surplus years in the second half of the 1960s and early 1970s. This was connected with two phenomena that had a large impact on the economy: emigration and tourism. Emigration accelerated in the 1960s, involving both rural and urban workers taking the direction of the then fast-growing North European economies, especially in France and Germany, in a clear reorientation from the traditional Brazilian destination of Portuguese emigrants: more than one million persons left the country between 1961 and 1974 (Baganha 1994) (Fig. 8). These emigrants were then responsible for an extraordinarily high influx of remittances, which grew in the late 1960s and early 1970s to reach a peak of 9% of GDP in 1972, as shown by the item transfers in the balance of payments (Fig. 1). Tourism also grew in the 1960s, as Portugal became

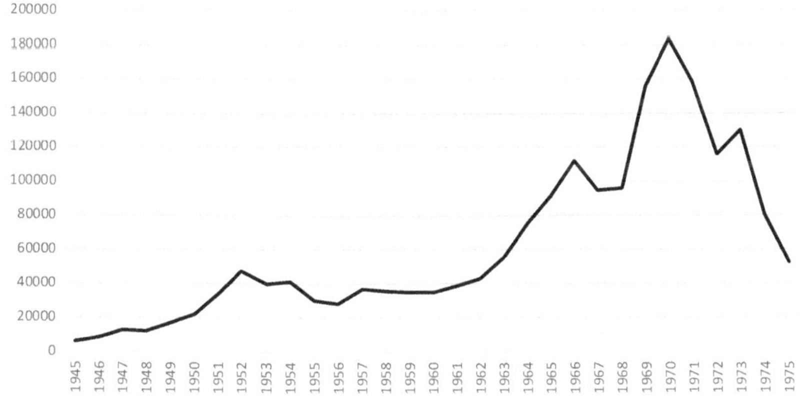

Fig. 8 Emigrants, Portugal, 1945–1975 (*Source* Baganha [1994])

a favorite beach destination for many North Europeans (mostly from the UK but also the Netherlands, Germany, or Scandinavia) and, in 1973, the number of tourists visiting Portugal reached the number of four million (Marques 2000). Foreign exchange originating in tourism grew in the 1960s until reaching a peak of 5% of GDP in 1966; it declined slightly afterward but still remained at a level of about 3% until 1973 (Fig. 1).

3 The Empire

The international environment after World War II continued to be hostile to the Portuguese Empire, but now for completely different reasons than in the past. Before the war, the Portuguese Empire was looked with contempt by the other imperial powers, which considered it to be ineffective at colonizing and developing African territories. Now, as they began decolonizing, they looked with hostility to the Portuguese Empire because it persisted in its intents on colonizing and developing African territories. The dominating international powers at the end of the war, the USA and the USSR, had a general stance against European empires. Also, whereas during the late 1940s and the 1950s the European colonial powers still had tried to resist independentist movements (the Netherlands in Indonesia, the UK in Malaya and Kenya, and France in Indochina and Algeria) (Holland 1994), their general attitude in the 1960s was of acceptance of independence, especially in sub-Saharan Africa. After the independence of Ghana in 1957, a stream of new countries appeared rather quickly in Africa: 18 new national units until 1960 plus 16 more from then until 1968 (Meredith 2005).

This international environment led to the birth of independentist movements within the Portuguese Empire, which initiated military activity in Angola, Guinea, and Mozambique between 1961 and 1964. The Portuguese authorities reacted to the attacks with a combination of military response and imperial reform. In fact, reform preceded the outbreak of the war. In the hostile international environment of the postwar period, even authoritarian Portugal felt "the political impossibility for a European State to continue to exercise trusteeship over an African territory" (Cooper 2015, p. 15).

The first reform was a relatively superficial one, although carrying with it a relevant symbolic dimension: in 1951 the *Estado Novo* promoted a constitutional amendment that changed the designation of the territories in Africa (and Asia) under Portuguese rule coming from the 1930 Colonial Act. From then on, they were no longer called "colonies" but rather "Overseas Provinces", and the empire was no longer the "Portuguese Colonial Empire" but the "Portuguese Overseas Empire". The Colonial Act was then abolished and inserted into the Constitution. This meant that, officially, the Portuguese state was no longer a European state with "colonies" outside of Europe but a multi-continental state with "provinces" spread around the world. This institutional change (analyzed in detail in Silva 1989) was accompanied by a first attempt at revising the relationship between the Portuguese authorities and the "indigenous" population. In 1953, a new Organic Law for the Portuguese Overseas Territories replaced the 1933 Organic Law, whereby the natives of São Tomé e Príncipe, and Timor lost their "indigenous" status and became full Portuguese citizens.[25] In 1954, a new Indigenous Statute was enacted, but applying only to the territories of Angola, Mozambique, and Guinea.[26]

All of this coincided with a new approach toward the empire: the *Estado Novo* passed in the second half of the 1950s from a "predatory" to a "modernizing" and "developmental" attitude in relation to Portuguese Africa (Castelo 2014, p. 513). Under the influence of the nascent field of "development studies", then also adopted in the British and French empires and transformed into a sort of official ideology of many international organizations such as the United Nations and its agencies, the regime started implementing pro-economic growth and pro-"native welfare" programs (Castelo 2012; Cooper 2015; Jerónimo and Pinto 2015). The development plans (*Planos de Fomento*)

[25]Law 2006, 27 July 1953.

[26]Decree-law 39,666, 20 May 1954.

used in the mainland had a large section dedicated to each of the overseas territories (Newitt 1981; Clarence-Smith 1985; Pereira 2012).

More thorough reform came with the actual beginning of the war in 1961. Reforms were felt on mostly two dimensions: on the relationship with the "natives" (in terms of welfare, labor conditions, or use of land) and on the relationship between the mainland economy and the colonial economies. The first substantial step concerning the first aspect was the revoking, in September 1961 (merely six months after the outbreak of hostilities in Angola), of the Indigenous Statute.[27] From then on, all persons living in the overseas provinces (native or not) could have the same rights and duties of the mainland Portuguese if they decided to, although they could keep living under local customary law if that was their decision. This was complemented with a new Code of Indigenous Labor in 1962 that was effectively able to suppress forced labor (circumscribed now truly to some residual instances)[28]: forced labor had already been forbidden in 1928, but in fact continued in practice, due to difficulties of enforcement (Bailey 1969), even if reduced to relatively small numbers—according to Wheeler and Pélissier (1972, p. 196), only 10% of the African male working population ran the risk of falling into it. Also of September 1961 was a new regulation of access to the land, with the purpose of preventing previous abuses, especially occupation by white settlers of land set to be toiled by natives.[29] This had been preceded by legislation ending with the system of "compulsory cultivation" (Oliveira 2014).[30]

The attempt at improving the relationship with the natives also coincided with a more determined policy of accelerating the migration of white settlers to the overseas provinces. The issue was an old one, and the Portuguese approach had never been clear. Up to the 1940s, the policy was essentially restrictive, controlling the number of Portuguese migrants (Castelo 2007). Now the idea was to promote a

[27]Decree-law 43,893, 6 September 1961.

[28]Decrees 44,309 and 44,310, 27 April 1962.

[29]Decree 43,894, 6 September 1961.

[30]Decree-law 43,875, 24 August 1961.

large movement. Government support would come both in a direct way, by setting actual rural colonies, and in an indirect way, by not restricting the migrants attracted by African economic development (Castelo 2007). In 1947, new legislation suspended emigration to foreign countries and promoted it to the overseas colonies, thanks to various support measures.[31] But this policy was still based on heavy administrative control, making migration dependent on arbitrary Government authorization. Definite change would only come in 1962, when circulation within the empire was made entirely free.[32]

The second dimension in which the *Estado Novo* implemented decisive reforms was at the macro-economic level. Until 1961, the main principles in the economic relationship between the mainland and the colonies were the following: the colonies should provide foreign exchange to help balance the mainland's balance of payments and also supply it with raw materials for manufacturing as well as agricultural and tropical goods; additionally, the economies of the mainland and of the colonies should be functionally integrated (Clarence-Smith 1985). The instruments to implement this policy were, on the hand, the administrative setting of prices and a system of preferences that was based on quotas and discriminatory tariffs, as well as exchange controls. As for industrialization of the colonies, the Portuguese traditional approach was ambiguous, sometimes fostering it, other times not (Clarence-Smith 1985). The instrument for this was the system of industrial licensing mentioned in the previous chapter.

The imperial preferential system was shattered by the introduction of the legislation creating the "Portuguese Economic Area" in 1961.[33] Quotas, tariff rebates, and exchange controls either disappeared or were heavily reduced (Clarence-Smith 1985). The introduction of this legislation was not exactly caused by the purpose to reform the economic relations of the empire but, instead, by the need to adapt to the principles of EFTA: being an EFTA member also implied signing the GATT,

[31]Decree 36,119, 29 March 1947.

[32]Decree 44,171, 1 February 1962.

[33]Decree-law 44,016, 8 November 1961.

according to which the system of imperial preferences had to be consolidated (i.e., not enlarged), unless the participants in such a system integrated a free trade area or a customs union. The Portuguese authorities decided to create a free trade area comprehending the mainland and the overseas provinces (Lopes 1996). As this was happening, the Portuguese Government also started using industrial conditioning to promote industrialization in the overseas provinces, a change that would become explicit in new legislation approved in 1965.[34] All this would be complemented with plans to expand education and health services (Bailey 1969; Paulo 1996). The Portuguese Economic Area allowed for increased trade between the territories but created major imbalances between them, as some (mostly the mainland) ran persistent payments surpluses while others ran deficits. In order to restore some balance, the Government reinstated tariffs within the empire in 1971, thus recognizing the failure of the experiment.[35]

Economic growth in the overseas territories was fast under this new institutional framework. This was visible since the 1950s, thanks to the continuation in the postwar period of the expansion of international demand for traditional African crops (especially coffee, sisal, palm oil, or beans) coming from World War II. But soon it was complemented with development in other sectors, including industry. Mining in Angola expanded quite fast, with the exploration of various minerals: iron, manganese, copper, and the first oil wells (with a refinery being built in the capital, Luanda, in 1958). As the mainland Government became less strict in the licensing of industrial projects in the overseas territories, a large number of new ones appeared, such as paper, textiles, tires, cement, fertilizer, aluminum, or petrochemicals. These projects were associated with both Portuguese and foreign capital (especially French, German, American, and South African), as the Government strategically tried to attract the latter, in order to gain international support during the Colonial War (Castro 1978; Newitt 1981; Clarence-Smith 1985).

[34]Decree-law 46,666, 24 November 1965.

[35]Decree-law 478/71, 6 November 1971.

The Colonial War did not interrupt the process. One reason for this was that, except in Guinea, the war only affected peripheral territories within each of the overseas provinces. In Angola, military activity was contained within the margins of the territory in very thinly populated areas. Most of the population never experienced war and life in the cities remained almost completely isolated from military activity (Wheeler and Pélissier 1972; McQueen 2015). In Mozambique, until 1968, action was contained in the northern region bordering Tanzania, in a relatively uninteresting area of the territory (Henriksen 1983). After 1968, activity expanded beyond the original area, but was never enough to put Portuguese control in danger. For the economic powerhouse of the south, one thousand kilometers away from the center of military activity, the war in Mozambique remained a remote reality until 1974 (Newitt 1995; McQueen 2015). Only in Guinea military action was always close to farms and cities from the beginning to the end of the war, but even there the Portuguese army continued to be effective enough to allow economic activity to continue at a fast pace (Newitt 1981).

Another reason for the rapid development of the Portuguese African territories related to the specific military strategy adopted by the Portuguese Armed Forces. The Colonial War was not a conventional war but rather one fought, on the side of Portugal, along counterinsurgency principles. In wars of this kind, there are practically no conventional battles and final victory is not expected to result from decisive military victories. The enemies rarely meet in open and direct confrontation, and military action is just a subset within a much larger range of activities. Among these activities, the economic and social acquire special preeminence. The counterinsurgency mindset is very clear in the famous phrase by Gerald Templer, British High Commissioner to Malaya, about the Malayan Emergency (1948–1960): success does not depend on "pouring more troops into the jungle, but in the hearts and minds of the people". The purpose of insurgency and counterinsurgency is not to physically annihilate the enemy but rather to win the allegiance of the population. The approach of trying to win the "hearts and minds" of the local population meant that the Colonial War, more than a military event, became a massive economic and social experiment.

Table 5 White population in Angola and Mozambique, 1940–1973 (%)

	Mozambique	Angola
1940	27,400	44,083
1950	48,200	78,826
1960	97,200	172,529
1970	150,000	290,000
1973	200,000	335,000

Source Newitt (1981)

The Portuguese Armed Forces tried to act mostly as agents of welfare, rather than a hostile force, running medical posts and schools for the population. This is why health and education indicators for the three overseas provinces increased significantly with a large contribution being given by military personnel (Cann 1997).

All sectors of the overseas territories' economies experienced growth, from agriculture, where there was a boom of coffee production, to different industrial and services activities. A growing native peasant and, increasingly, wage-earning urban class (with forced labor disappearing almost completely) was the reflection of this. The expansion of immigration of Portuguese white settlers also reflects it: for the first time in the history of the Portuguese African empire, the numbers were sizable (Table 5). Paradoxically, it was precisely when these territories were finally beginning to develop that they lost importance for the Portuguese economy: according to Clarence-Smith (1985, pp. 230–231), trade with them represented about 22% of all of the mainland's trade in 1950 but only about 14% in 1973. As the Portuguese economy opened and linked more with the West European economies, the overseas territories became less important for it. We could even ask one question: Were these territories becoming independent from Portugal or was Portugal becoming independent from them?

4 Economic Growth and Change

Economic growth was very fast in this period, the fastest ever in Portuguese economic history in such a consistent manner. Table 4 shows that the average annual growth rate between 1950 and 1973 was 5.4% but that it accelerated from the 1950s to the 1960s. Growth was so high that, even in the context of the "golden age" of economic growth, during which fast expansion included the already rich Western economies, Portugal converged consistently for the first time, during a period of more than twenty years. That is what Figs. 3 and 4 of the Introduction show. The GDP per capita level of Portugal was of about 33% of that of the average of richer countries but reached 55% in 1973. Comparing the behavior of the Portuguese economy with those of the Scandinavian countries does not make sense in this period, as they were already well within the core of rich economies, but it makes sense to do it with Finland, even if the latter's starting point was already higher. This time the performance of the Portuguese economy is comparable to the Finnish one, as it is also comparable to that of the southern peripheral countries, Spain and Greece. These two countries, after the respective collapses during the Spanish Civil War and World War II, reached a GDP per capita level similar to Portugal but much lower than their own prewar levels. From then on, the three countries grew at a similarly rapid pace. There is no doubt about the significance of this period for the development of the Portuguese economy.

Population continued to increase, from 7.8 million persons in 1940 to 8.7 million in 1970, even if declining mildly in the 1960s (8.9 million in 1960). This outcome was the result of the second phase of the demographic transition, when the birth rate falls, following the previous fall of the death rate. Population grew because life expectancy increased, from 50 years in 1940 to 68 in 1970. Infant mortality had a notable decrease, from 126‰ in 1940 to 55.5‰ in 1970 (Henriques and Rodrigues 2009). Such progress was impressive but still left Portugal distant from richer countries: infant mortality was one and a half times higher than in Italy, two than in France, and four than in the Netherlands or Sweden, and life expectancy was four years lower than in Italy and France, six than in the Netherlands, and seven than in Sweden (Campos 2000).

The structure of the economy changed drastically, both in terms of employment and structure of output. Agriculture still employed more than 50% of the active population in 1950 but, by 1973, it only employed 24% (Fig. 9) and it represented 30% of GDP in 1950 but only 12% in 1973 (Fig. 10). The sector that historically had been the largest employer became the smallest. On the contrary, industry only employed 21% of the active population in 1950 but jumped to 35% in 1973, and in terms of output, the figures were 31% in 1950 and 41% in 1973. Meanwhile the services sector became both the largest employer (from 27% in 1950 to 40% in 1973) and the largest contributor to GDP (from 40% in 1950 to 47% in 1973). With these changes, the Portuguese economy became an industrialized and urban one.

The best performing sector was industry, whose productivity grew at 5.8% per year between 1950 and 1973 (Lains 1994, p. 939). This was due not just to high productivity growth in all branches but also faster growth in some new ones. The largest branch in 1950, textiles, dropped from a weight in output of more than 30% to about 20% and was replaced as the largest industrial branch in 1973 by the metal transformation and equipment, which jumped from about 7 to 25%. The remaining traditional branches also lost importance: food and beverages declined from 18 to 15% between 1950 and 1973, and wood and cork from 10 to 9%. On the contrary, new sectors expanded: paper and paper pulp passed from 3 to 8%, cement from 5 to 8%, and basic

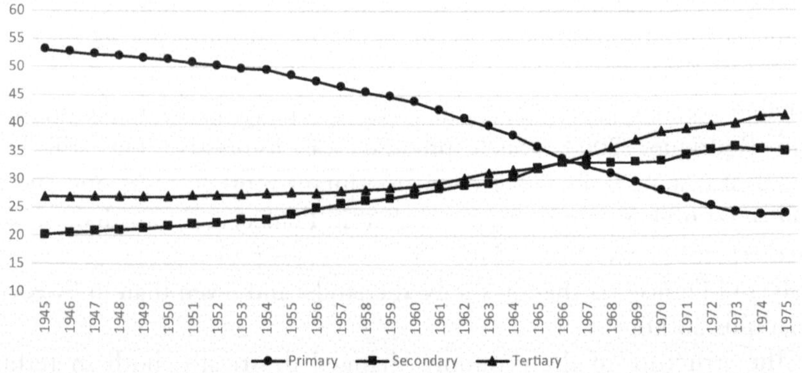

Fig. 9 Structure employment, Portugal, 1945–1975 (% overall employment) (*Source* Calculated by the author using Nunes [2001] and Pinheiro [1997] for the period 1953–1975)

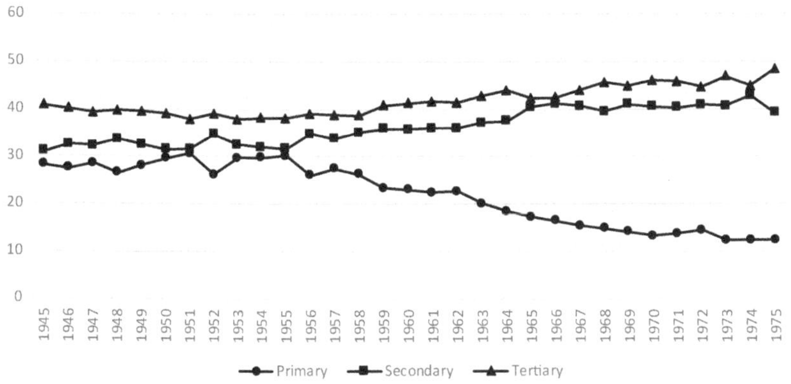

Fig. 10 Structure economy, Portugal, 1945–1975 (% GDP) (*Source* 1945–1952—Batista et al. [1997]; 1953–1975—Pinheiro [1997])

metals from 1 to 3%. The only relatively modern branch declining was chemicals and oil, from 20 to 15% (Aguiar and Martins 2005).

Even if it lost considerable weight in the economy, agriculture performed well in terms of labor productivity: 3.5% per year between 1950 and 1973 (Lains 1994, p. 939). Most crops increased their productivity, but a large part of the good behavior of the sector depended also on changes in structure: cereals declined in weight, from 30% of output in 1950 to 20% in 1973, losing its position as the most important agricultural branch, while meat became the largest, keeping its position at around 25%. Overall, vegetable production fell from a weight of 74% to one of 62%, whereas animal production jumped from 26 to 38%. And, within the vegetable part of the sector, more productive goods became more important while less productive ones declined: fruits and vegetables passed from 14% in 1950 to 18% in 1973, while olive oil fell from 8 to 5% and wine also declined mildly from 14 to 13%. Forest goods kept their relative position at about 17% of the sector's output, but there was some change in its composition, with an initial increase in pine trees and later of eucalyptus (Lains 2009; Lopes 1996). The growth of agricultural productivity is almost entirely explained by the substitution of labor with capital: as people moved from the sector into industry and services, they were replaced by various types of machines; the irrigation schemes promoted by the Government also gave a contribution (and they were also important to raise the share of fruits and vegetables). The increased use of other sophisticated inputs, such as chemical fertilizers, pesticides, selected seeds, or fodder, also supported by Government subsidies, gave a contribution too (Baptista 1993; Lains 2009; Amaral and Freire 2017). Another contribution to growing productivity came from the retraction in the use of marginal lands and concentration in better quality ones, as land under use declined quite fast (Soares 2005). Despite these changes, productivity growth in Portuguese agriculture was slower than in the already highly productive agricultural sectors of northwestern European countries (Federico 2005). Labor productivity in Portuguese agriculture declined from 45% of the average in the agricultural sectors of Western Europe in 1950 to 30% in 1973 (Amaral and Freire 2017, p. 250). And even if land productivity fared better, it also fell from 60 to 40% (Amaral and Freire 2017, p. 251).

The country abandoned finally its protectionist tradition, even if at a slower rate than its formal commitment to free trade in Europe might suggest: as we have seen above, Portugal was able to retain some selective protection while already participating in EFTA as well as a system of discretionary import licensing. Anyway, Portugal passed from being one of the most closed economies in Europe to one of the most open, as the share of exports in GDP passed from close to 10% in 1950 to 20% in 1973: in the latter year, this share was similar to those of Germany, Denmark, or Finland and clearly above those of Spain and France (or the United States, outside of Europe) (Fig. 11). The growth of openness did not allow the Portuguese economy to narrow, however, the gap between exports and imports, the latter's weight in GDP growing even faster than that of exports (Fig. 7). In order to cover this gap, the country relied increasingly on remittances and some services exports, especially tourism. Also of relevance was the change in the structure of foreign trade. Food products declined from a weight of 24% in exports in 1950 to one of 15% in the early 1970s, while non-food consumption goods passed from 7 to 10%. Capital goods also grew, although at very low levels, from 1 to 4%. Services as a whole passed from 24% of exports to 30%, and goods as a whole declined

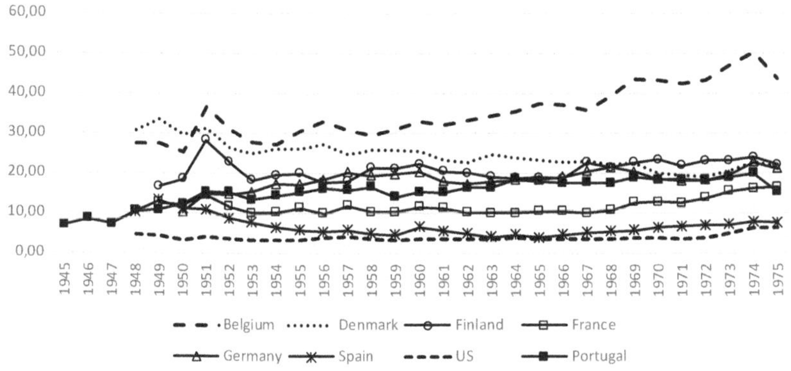

Fig. 11 Openness, various countries, 1945–1975 (exports % GDP) Current prices; (*Source* Federico and Tena-Junguito [2018], except Portugal: Fontoura and Valério [2001])

from 73 to 70% (Afonso and Aguiar 2005). As for imports, the structure remained roughly the same, with a slight increase of capital goods, from 17 to 19% and a slight decrease of intermediate goods, from 14 to 12%. Services kept a weight between 17 and 18% and goods as a whole between 82 and 83%. The largest weight was that of intermediate goods, mostly industrial ones for industrial use, staying between 29 and 30% throughout the period: if we add to them the roughly 12% of primary intermediate goods, the overall weight of intermediate goods in imports was 42% (Afonso and Aguiar 2005).

The change in the structure of exports was mostly due to the expansion of exports of textiles, footwear, and electrical equipment to the EFTA market. This represented a drastic transformation, for a country that had traditionally concentrated its exports on agricultural goods (mostly wine). In this period, the only semi-agricultural good also increasing its participation in exports was a new one, tomato pulp. As noted by Lopes (1996) and Afonso and Aguiar (2005), even if this transformation represented a switch in the direction of goods with higher value-added content, their technological level was still relatively low, and their ability to penetrate in the European markets was linked to the comparative advantages of the Portuguese economy in terms of relatively unskilled and low-wage labor. As for imports, their structure reveals the need in equipment and intermediate goods for a country still in the process of industrialization.

Did higher openness lead to higher economic growth? Economic theory posits that there are various efficiency gains to be obtained from openness, especially related to comparative advantages and increased competition. But most recent empirical works do not corroborate this idea in a clear way (Rodríguez and Rodrik 2000). In the case of Portugal, some recent econometric exercises show a negative relationship between the two variables for the second half of the twentieth century. They do not individualize the specific 1960s period, however, where the relationship might have been positive (Lampe and Sharp 2013; Federico et al. 2017).

In what concerns Portuguese banking, the sector was subject to a certain moderate reform in 1959, when the old 1925 legislation was replaced by a new one.[36] At the time, the Portuguese banking system comprised 24 incorporated commercial banks, 11 non-incorporated banking houses, and 20 savings banks, plus a few less important institutions (Amaral 2015). Incorporated commercial banks dominated the market, accounting for roughly 69% of all deposits (up from 40% in 1938). Non-incorporated banks were residual, with a market share of about 1.5%. Most of the 20 savings banks were small, with the exception of the National Savings Bank (*Caixa Geral de Depósitos*, CGD), which represented 90% of all deposits in savings banks and was the largest financial institution in the country.

Similarly to the situation existing in most other countries, the Portuguese legal framework included: (a) the principle of discretionary governmental authorization for the opening of banks and branches, and for mergers and acquisitions, to which was added an implicit freezing on the number of banks, something that prevented the appearance of new entrants (except in very special circumstances), (b) high capital requirements, (c) high liquidity requirements, (d) the establishment of interest rates by decree, and (e) some form of separation between the

---

[36]Decree-Law 42,641, 12 November 1959.

investment and commercial activities of banks, i.e., the refusal of the "universal bank" model, which Portuguese authorities believed had been at the origin of most of the banking crises from the second half of the nineteenth century until the 1920s (Reis 1995). Portuguese legislation did not impose a formal separation between investment and commercial banking, but severely limited the ability of commercial banks to engage in long-term ventures (further discussion can be found in Amaral 2013, 2015).

According to this institutional setting, banks had very limited freedom of action: quite restrained in their interest rate policy and forced to hold high cash reserves, they could not lend in the long run and could apply only a very limited portion of their resources in stocks or bonds. Also, if they wished to expand geographically by opening branches, the Government's authorization was needed. We must note that the market possessed some contestability: mergers, acquisitions, and entries depended on governmental authorization but were not forbidden. Thus, despite not being free, contestability existed, and the threat of exclusion, although not entirely determined by the market, was present. Amaral (2013) has also shown that, despite being forced by law to lend only short term, commercial banks had adopted the practice of renewing several times these loans, so that ultimately they functioned as long-term credit to the economy, giving a positive contribution to its growth (Amaral 2002).

There is no doubt about the exceptional nature of this period in terms of growth and catch-up. As for explanations for it, we can start by looking at some exercises measuring the proximate sources of growth (Silva and Lains 2013) (Table 6). All exercises point to a consistent picture: the largest contribution to growth came from capital but, this time, TFP gave a considerable contribution too. When the human capital variable is considered, which happens only in some of these exercises, its contribution is detectable but at a much lower level than the other two.

Existing calculations of the behavior of investment and of the capital stock in the Portuguese economy do show an acceleration in this period: the investment rate passed from roughly 10% in the 1930s and 1940s to close to 30% in the early 1970s (Freitas 2005, p. 93). Certainly, the

Table 6 Growth accounting, various studies, 1947–1975

		Annual growth rates			
References	Periods	Labor	Capital	Human capital	TFP
Lains (2003)	1947–1973	0.2	2.6	0.8	1.5
Silva and Lains (2013)	1947–1973	0.5	2.9	–	1.8
Amaral (2002)	1953–1973	−0.2	2.4	1.0	2.4
	1953–1959	−0.4	2.0	2.3	0.4
	1960–1964	−0.2	2.6	0.5	2.8
	1965–1973	−0.1	2.7	0.9	2.7
Mateus (2005)	1950–1975	0.3	2.5	0.6	2.1

Source Amaral (2002), Lains (2003), Silva and Lains (2013), and Mateus (2005)

institutional environment of the *Estado Novo* favored this result: the repression of labor and the organization of markets and sectors under the corporatist organizations continued to signal protection of the property rights of business. But other factors seem to have been at play too: one was the growing scarcity of labor, thanks to both emigration and mobilization for the Colonial War. These were massive shocks to the labor market, the first leading to the abandonment of the country of more than one million persons in the 1960s (even accounting for the return of some of them, whose figures are unknown, we are talking of the equivalent to more or less 10% of the country's population), the second involving 100,000 men from the mainland in the final years of the war (corresponding to about 1% of the population) (Amaral 2005, 2009). A natural consequence of this was a quick increase in wages, despite labor repression, leading to an incentive to substitute labor with capital. The data in Silva and Lains (2013) do show a faster growth of equipment than other components of the capital stock. Also important seems to have been the growth of household saving, which was essentially determined by emigrant remittances. These remittances reached very high proportions of GDP and were recycled into the banking system to be used in investment (Amaral 2002; Freitas 2005). Additionally, the abundance of reserves at the BoP allowed it to keep interest rates consistently low, something that, in turn, allowed the banking system to give credit at low cost (Amaral 2013, 2018). What is more, even if the banking system was highly regulated along lines similar to industrial conditioning (with a policy of control of the number of banks entering and leaving the market), the Government seems to have permitted the existence of a certain degree of competition in the market that also favored interest rates to remain low (Amaral 2013, 2015).

In what concerns the good behavior of TFP, the explanations for it seem to be varied. First, the change in industrial structure, favoring the growth of more complex branches, was certainly associated with many technological improvements. Second, there are reasons to believe that, despite its relatively high bureaucratic cost, industrial conditioning sometimes promoted the introduction of modern technology and methods of production. Loureiro (1991) and Confraria (1992) show that, depending on the markets and branches, industrial conditioning was sometimes efficiency-enhancing while sometimes had the opposite effect. We know of many cases of markets under monopoly or oligopoly (see examples in Loureiro 1991; Confraria 1992; Silva et al. 2016; Castaño et al. 2017), the question here being to know if these situations were inefficient or might have been necessary for the existing units to acquire some scale, but there are also examples of a much less protective approach (Loureiro 1991; Confraria 1992). One further point was the incentive given to the growth of very small firms, as "household industries" were exempted from the arbitrary rules of industrial conditioning: in order to dodge the system many entrepreneurs invested in firms having a sub-optimal scale (Loureiro 1991). In the current state of knowledge, it is not possible to assess what was the ultimate aggregate effect of industrial conditioning. A famous case where the conditions in the market seem to have fostered some form of national R&D is that of the paper and paper pulp industry, where the firms existing in the country were able to develop a new method to process wood from eucalyptus (rather than pine trees) which gave them an advantage in the world market (Branco and Neves 2018). A third explanation relates with structural change itself: the transfer of resources (labor and capital) from agriculture to industry and, within industry, to branches with a higher productivity level gave certainly a contribution to TFP; Aguiar and Martins (2005) show that the interplay between the growth of productivity internal to each sector and each branch and the growth of productivity resulting from the reallocation of resources to sectors and branches with higher productivity levels gave an unusually high contribution to the growth of overall productivity in the period 1950–1973.

A fourth reason for the growth of TFP relates to increased openness, which might have led to a better allocation of resources. According to Amaral (2002), most of the growth of TFP was concentrated in the period following the country's accession to EFTA in 1960 (Table 7). Openness is also related to the growth of foreign direct investment, especially after 1965, in the sequence of the adoption of the more welcoming policy referred above. For the first time in Portuguese economic history foreign direct investment acquired some significance, even if remaining below 1% of GDP (Silva 2016). But equally important as its value was its destination: whereas until the 1960s FDI had been mostly directed at activities such as mining, export-import, transport and communication or public utilities, now it was essentially directed at manufacturing, most of it in goods to export (textiles, electrical equipment, paper and paper pulp, or ship construction and repair) (Lopes 1996; Silva 2016); by 1973, 37% of exports originated in companies with foreign capital participation (Fernandes 1992). A fifth cause might be the appearance of new forms of business organization. Silva et al. (2016) show that business groups developed consistently throughout

Table 7 School enrollment (students enrolled in primary schools as a percentage of the 5–14 age group) (%)

	1940	1950	1960	1970
Portugal	32.34	36.73	53.17	56.44
Italy	59.43	57.36	53.83	55.01
Spain	43.81	44.58	62.98	75.86
Belgium		70.14	67.95	65.88
Denmark	65.12	62.48	77.97	77.97
Finland	73.10	69.26	67.24	59.18
France	84.07	75.37	69.68	61.86
Germany	71.65	73.64	69.91	73.40
The Netherlands	69.78	73.61	61.43	61.43
Norway	77.62	66.74	70.44	86.45
Sweden	62.85	62.48	68.01	58.84
Switzerland	71.00	68.10	64.17	–
UK		70.29	62.59	68.45

Source Amaral (2002)

this period. It is not clear, however, if they helped the economy become more efficient or the opposite: sometimes, groups grew as a consequence of protectionism and reserved markets under industrial conditioning, allowing for the creation of many instances of monopoly or oligopoly, but other times that was not the case. Again, a study is needed to assess the ultimate impact of these new forms of business organization.

Reis (1988) stresses some possible further reasons for relatively high TFP growth, namely a better use of natural resources. Whereas in previous periods natural resources seemed to have put a strict limit on the growth potential of the Portuguese economy (lack of coal or iron ore, technologically limited comparative advantages, such as in the case of cork or of tinned fish) (Reis 1984), now the opposite happened: thanks to the various hydro-electric projects promoted by the Government, the water resources of the country were used to enlarge the energy base of the economy. This seems to be confirmed by the figures presented in Henriques and Sharp (2019), although they also show that the true spectacular increase in energy use related to oil: the country finally began to approach the energy profile of the richest economies, even if still remaining at a long distance. A better use of natural resources was also visible in the case of the shipbuilding and repair industry, which was able to benefit from the good location of the Portuguese coast on the oil tankers route from the Middle East to Europe, in a period where most developed economies were switching their energy base from coal to oil (Reis 1988).

In what concerns human capital, the country seems to have continued to benefit from the Government's policies stimulating schooling and formal education, although some increased demand for skilled workers also played a role, as the economy got more complex and with a higher technological content (Amaral 2002). With both forces at play, there is no doubt that Portugal continued to converge to more educated countries (Table 7).

An interesting topic concerning the evolution of Portuguese society in this period taking into consideration the generic pro-business and anti-labor stance of the *Estado Novo*, with an additional little interest in social spending, is the evolution of income inequality. A close relationship between the Government and big business existed at various levels: in joint participations in industrial projects, in the process of industrial conditioning, or in simple private contacts (see examples in Loureiro 1991; Confraria 1992; Silva et al. 2016; Castaño et al. 2017). The relationship with labor, on the contrary, was much tenser. As we have seen in the previous chapter, labor regulation had the essential purpose of containing labor demands within a tight straightjacket. But changes favorable to labor did transform the framework designed in the 1930s, although only in the second half of the 1960s. In 1966, a new labor code (updated in 1969) reduced the number of instances for workers' dismissals (especially the more arbitrary ones) and increased their guarantees.[37] On the other hand, new union regulations increased the power of these institutions: no longer should their boards be arbitrarily approved by the Government and their professional and regional range was enlarged to give them a larger scale.[38] Adding to this, there was new legislation reducing working times: companies should start pointing to an eventual establishment of a 40-hour week, although in a progressive manner.[39] Finally, generalized unemployment benefits were introduced, although only for a few instances of unemployment.[40]

The existing data on income inequality are contradictory in many respects, but there is one in which they coincide: that inequality declined during the period, independently of the metric adopted, be it top income shares (Alvaredo 2009; Guilera 2010) or the wage gap between skilled and unskilled workers (Lains et al. 2013). Where the different authors disagree is in the chronology: according to Alvaredo (2009), decline started only in the late 1960s, whereas according to Guilera (2010) and Lains et al. (2013), it started in the early 1960s. Alvaredo (2009) and Guilera (2010), who provide international comparisons, also coincide in showing that inequality in Portugal, as measured by top

[37]Decree-law 47,032, 27 May 1966 and Decree-law 49,408, 21 November 1969.

[38]Decree-law 49,058, 14 June 1969.

[39]Decree-law 409/71, 27 September 1971.

[40]Decree-law 48,888, 1 March 1969.

income shares, followed the declining trend of other Western countries, even if remaining at a slightly higher level in the 1950s and part of the 1960s. They finally coincide in showing that, by the end of the regime, inequality in Portugal was well within the average of Western countries. This raises the question of the effectiveness of the mechanisms of labor repression and the absence of social programs in Portugal to keep inequality higher in Portugal than elsewhere. Lains et al. (2013) prefer other factors to explain the decline of income inequality: emigration and exports, from the early 1960s onward, leading to a contraction, at least, of the wage gap between skilled and unskilled workers.

References

Afonso, Óscar, and Álvaro Aguiar. 2005. A internacionalização da economia. In *História Económica de Portugal, 1700–2000, Vol. III, O Século XX,* ed. Pedro Lains and Álvaro Ferreira da Silva, 305–341. Lisbon: ICS.

Aguiar, Álvaro, and Manuel M.F. Martins. 2005. A indústria. In *História Económica de Portugal, 1700–2000, Vol. III, O Século XX,* ed. Pedro Lains and Álvaro Ferreira da Silva, 185–226. Lisbon: ICS.

Alvaredo, Facundo. 2009. Top Incomes and Earnings in Portugal, 1936–2004. *Explorations in Economic History* 46: 404–417.

Amaral, Luciano. 2002. *How a Country Catches-Up: Explaining Economic Growth in Portugal in the Postwar Period (1950s–1973)*. Florence, Doctoral dissertation European University Institute.

———. 2005. O trabalho. In *História Económica de Portugal, 1700–2000, Vol. III, O Século XX*, ed. Pedro Lains and Álvaro Ferreira da Silva, 65–90. Lisbon: ICS.

———. 2009. New Series of Portuguese Population and Employment, 1950–2007: Implications for GDP Per Capita and Labor Productivity. *Análise Social* XLIV (193): 767–791.

———. 2013. Imperfect But True Competition: Innovation and Profitability in Portuguese Banking During the Golden Age (1950–1973). *Financial History Review* 20 (3): 305–333.

———. 2015. Measuring Competition in Portuguese Commercial Banking During the Golden Age (1960–1973). *Business History* 57 (8): 1192–1218.

———. 2018. A Monetary Plethora and What to Do With It: The Bank of Portugal During the Second World War and the Postwar Period. *Economic History Review* 71 (3): 795–822.

Amaral, Luciano, and Dulce Freire. 2017. Economic Policy, Growth and the Demise, 1929–2000. In *An Agrarian History of Portugal, 1000–2000: Economic Development on the European Frontier*, ed. Dulce Freire and Pedro Lains, 245–276. Brill: Leiden.

Baganha, Maria Ioannis. 1994. As correntes emigratórias portuguesas no século XX e o seu impacto na economia nacional. *Análise Social* XXIX (128): 959–980.

Bailey, Norman F. 1969. Education, Health and Social Welfare. In *Portuguese Africa: A* Handbook, ed. David M. Abshire and Michael A. Samuels, 178–201. London: Pall Mall Press.

Baptista, Fernando Oliveira. 1993. *A Política Agrária do Estado Novo*. Porto: Afrontamento.

Bastien, Carlos. 2001. Preços e salários. In *Estatísticas Históricas* Portuguesas, ed. Nuno Valério, 615–655. Lisbon: INE.

Batista, Dina, et al. 1997. *New Estimates for Portugal's GDP: 1910–1958*. Lisbon: Bank of Portugal.

Battilossi, Stefano, James Foreman-Peck, and Gerhard Kling 2010. Business Cycles and Economic Policy. In *The Cambridge Economic History of Modern Europe, Vol II: 1870 to the Present*, ed. Stephen Broadberry and Kevin H. O'Rourke, 360–389. Cambridge: Cambridge University Press.

Beja, Filomena, Júlia Serra, Estella Machás, and Isabel Saldanha. 1996. *Muitos Anos de Escolas, Vol. II—Anos 40-Anos 70*. Lisbon: Ministério da Educação.

Bordo, Michael. 1993. The Gold Standard, Bretton Woods and Other Monetary Regimes: An Historical Appraisal. National Bureau of Economic Research Working Papers, No. 4310, April.

Branco, Amélia. 2011. El Plan de Repoblación Florestal (1938–1968): una medida del Estado Novo por evaluar. In *Agriculturas e Innovacíon Tecnológica en la Península Ibérica (1946–1975)*, ed. Daniel Lanero and Dulce Freire, 135–165. Madrid: Ministerio de Medio Ambiente y Medio Rural.

Branco, Amélia, and Pedro Neves. 2018. From Backward to Modern: The Adoption of Technology by the Pulp Industry in Portugal, 1891–2015. In *Technological Transformation in the Global Pulp and Paper Industry*, ed. Timo Särkkä, Miguel Gutiérrz-Poch, and Mark Kuhlberg, 1800–2018. Cham, Switzerland: Springer Nature.

Brito, José Maria Brandão de. 1989. *A Industrialização Portuguesa no Pós-Guerra (1948–1965)*. Lisbon: Publicações D. Quixote.

———. 1996. Condicionamento Industrial. In *Dicionário de História do Estado* Novo, ed. Fernando Rosas and José Maria Brandão de Brito. Lisbon: Círculo de Leitores.

Campos, António Correia de. 2000. Saúde Pública. In *Dicionário de História de Portugal. Suplemento P/Z, Vol.* XV, ed. António Barreto and Maria Filomena Mónica, 405–406. Porto: Editora Figueirinhas.

Campos, António Correia de, and Jorge Simões. 2011. *O Percurso da Saúde: Portugal na Europa*. Coimbra: Almedina.

Cann, John P. 1997. *Counterinsurgency in Africa: The Portuguese Way of War, 1961–1974*. Westport, CT: The Greenwood Press.

Cardoso, José Luís, and Manuela Rocha. 2003. Corporativismo e Estado-Providência (1933–1962). *Ler História* 45: 111–135.

Carolo, Daniel, and José A. Pereirinha. 2010. The Development of the Welfare State in Portugal: Trends in Social Expenditure Between 1938 and 2003. *Revista de História Económica—Journal of Iberian and Latin American Economic History* 28 (3): 469–501.

Carreira, Henrique Medina. 1996. As políticas sociais em Portugal. In *A Situação Social em Portugal*, ed. António Barreto, 1960–1995. Lisbon: ICS.

Castaño, David, Ana Mónica Fonseca, Pedro Lains, and Daniel Marcos. 2017. *Os Petróleos em Portugal: Do Estado à Privatização*. Lisbon: ICS.

Castelo, Cláudia. 2007. *Passagens para África: O Povoamento de Angola e Moçambique com Naturais da Metrópole (1920–1974)*. Porto: Afrontamento.

———. 2012. Ciência, Estado e desenvolvimento no colonialismo português tardio. In *O Império Colonial em questão (Séculos XIX–XX): Poderes, Saberes e* Instituições, ed. Miguel Bandeira Jerónimo, 350–379. Lisboa: Editora 70.

———. 2014. Developing 'Portuguese Africa' in Late Colonialism: Confronting Discourses. In *Developing Africa: Concepts and Practices in 20th Century Colonialism*, ed. Joseph Hodge, Gerald Hodl and Martina Kopf, 63–86. Manchester: Manchester University Press.

Castro, Armando. 1978. *O Sistema Colonial Português (Meados do Século XX)*. Lisbon: Editorial Caminho.

Clarence-Smith, Gervase. 1985. *The Third Portuguese Empire, 1825–1975: A Study in Economic Imperialism*. Manchester: Manchester University Press.

Confraria, João. 1992. *Condicionamento Industrial: Uma Análise Económica*. Lisbon: Direcção-Geral da Indústria.

———. 1999. Condicionamento Industrial (1). In *Dicionário de História de Portugal, Suplemento A/E, Vol. VII*, ed. António Barreto and Maria Filomena Mónica. Porto: Livraria Figueirinhas.

———. 2005. Política económica. In *História Económica de Portugal, 1700–2000, Vol. III, O Século XX*, ed. Pedro Lains and Álvaro Ferreira da Silva, 397–421. Lisbon: ICS.

Cooper, Frederick. 2015. Development, Modernization, and the Social Sciences in the Era of Decolonization: The Examples of British and French Africa. In *The Ends of European Colonial Empires: Cases and Comparisonsed*, ed. Miguel Bandeira Jerónimo and António Costa Pinto, 15–50. London: Palgrave.

Coppolaro, Lucia, and Pedro Lains. 2013. Portugal and European Integration, 1947–1992: An Essay on Protected Openness in the European Periphery. *E-Journal of Portuguese History* 11 (1): 61–81.

Cunha, Alice. 2015. Underwriting Democracy: Portugal and European Economic Community's Accession. *Cahiers de la Méditerranée* 90: 1–12.

Dür, Andreas. 2008. Bargaining Power and Trade Liberalization: European External Trade Policies in the 1960s. *European Journal of International Relations* 14 (4): 645–669.

Eichengreen, Barry. 1996. *Globalizing Capital: A History of the International Monetary System*. Princeton: Princeton University Press.

Faxén, Karl-Olof. 1982. Incomes Policy and Centralized Wage Formation. In *The European Economy: Growth and Crisis*, ed. Andrea Boltho, 365–389. Oxford: Oxford University Press.

Federico, Giovanni. 2005. *Feeding the World: An Economic History of Agriculture, 1800–2000*. Princeton: Princeton University Press.

Federico, Giovanni, and Antonio Tena-Junguito. 2018. Fedrico-Tena World Trade Historical Database. https://www.uc3m.es/ss/Satellite/UC3MInstitucional/es/TextoMixta/1371246237481/Federico-Tena_World_Trade_Historical_Database.

Federico, Giovanni, Paul Sharp, and Antonio Tena-Junguito. 2017. Openness and Growth in a Historical Perspective: A VECM Approach. EHES Working Papers in Economic History, No. 118.

Fernandes, Lino Gomes. 1992. *A Especialização da Economia Portuguesa*. Lisbon: Departamento Central de Planeamento.

Fontoura, Ana Paula, and Nuno Valério. 2001. Relações económicas externas. In *Estatísticas Históricas* Portuguesas, ed. Nuno Valério, 713–739. Lisbon: INE.

Freitas, Miguel Lebre de. 2005. O Capital. In *História Económica de Portugal, 1700–2000, Vol. III, O Século XX*, ed. Pedro Lains and Álvaro Ferreira da Silva, 91–124. Lisbon: ICS.

Gomes, Pedro, and Matilde Pinto Machado. 2019. Literacy and Primary School Expansion in Portugal, 1940–1962. Universidad Carlos III de Madrid Working Paper, 2019-07.

Guilera, Jordi. 2010. The Evolution of Top Incomes and Wealth Shares in Portugal Since 1936. *Revista de Historia Económica—Journal of Iberian and Latin American History* 21 (1): 139–171.

Henriksen, Thomas H. 1983. *Revolution and Counterrevolution: Mozambique's War of Independence (1960–1974)*. Westport, CT: Greenwood Press.

Henriques, Filipe Castro, and Teresa Ferreira Rodrigues. 2009. O século XX: a transição. In *História da População Portuguesa: Das Longas Permanências à Conquista da Modernidade*, ed. Teresa Ferreira Rodrigues, 417–513. Porto: Afrontamento e CEPESE.

Henriques, Sofia Teives, and Paul Sharp. 2019. Without Coal in the Age of Steam and Dams in the Age of Electricity: An Explanation for the Failure of Portugal to Industrialize Before the Second World War. EHES Working Paper, No. 148.

Holland, Robert. 1994. *Emergencies and Disorder in the European Empires After 1945*. London: Frank Cass.

Jerónimo, Miguel Bandeira, and António Costa Pinto. (eds.) 2015. *The Ends of European Colonial Empires: Cases and Comparisons*. London: Palgrave.

Lains, Pedro. 1994. O Estado e a industrialização em Portugal, 1945-1990. *Análise Social* XXIX (128): 923–958.

———. 2003. Catching Up to the European Core: Portuguese Economic Growth, 1910–1990. *Explorations in Economic History* 40: 369–386.

———. 2009. The Role of Agriculture in Portuguese Economic Development, 1870–1973. In *Agriculture and Economic Growth in Europe Since 1870*, ed. Pedro Lains and Vicente Pinilla, 333–352. London: Routledge.

Lains, Pedro, Ester Gomes da Silva, and Jordi Guilera. 2013. Wage Inequality in a Developing Open Economy: Portugal, 1944–1984. *Scandinavian Economic History Review* 61 (3): 287–311.

Lampe, Markus, and Paul Sharp. 2013. Tariffs and Income: A Time Series for 24 Countries. *Cliometrica* 7 (3): 207–235.

Leitão, Nicolau Andresen. 2007. *Estado Novo, Democracia e Europa, 1947–1986*. Lisbon: ICS.

Lopes, José da Silva. 1996. *A Economia Portuguesa desde 1960*. Lisboa: Gradiva.

Loureiro, João Adolfo. 1991. *Economia e Sociedade: A Indústria no Após-Guerra*. Lisbon: Edições Cosmos.

Macedo, Jorge Braga de, Cristina Corado, and Manuel Lopes Porto 1988. The Timing and Sequencing of Trade Liberalization Policies: Portugal 1948–1986. Faculdade de Economia da Universidade Nova de Lisboa Working Paper, 114.

Marques, Helena Torres. 2000. Turismo. In *Dicionário de História de Portugal. Suplemento P/Z, Vol. XV*, ed. António Barreto and Maria Filomena Mónica, 536–538. Porto: Editora Figueirinhas.

Mata, Maria Eugénia. 2001. Finanças públicas e dívida pública. In *Estatísticas Históricas Portuguesas*, ed. Nuno Valério, 657–712. Lisbon: INE.

Mateus, Abel. 2005. A tecnologia. In *História Económica de Portugal, 1700–2000, Vol. III, O Século XX*, ed. Pedro Lains and Álvaro Ferreira da Silva, 125–156. Lisbon: ICS.

McQueen, Norrie. 2015. O balanço militar nos três teatros de operações. In *O Adeus ao Império: 40 Anos de Descolonização Portuguesa*, ed. Fernando Rosas, Mário Machaqueiro, and Pedro Aires Oliveira. Lisbon: Nova vega.

Mendes, Fernando Ribeiro. 1983. O sector agrícola, a economia nacional e as relações de troca intersectoriais (1950–80). *Análise Social* XIX (77–78–79): 421–438.

Meredith, Martin. 2005. *The State of Africa: A History of Fifty Years of Independence*. London: Simon & Schuster.

Milward, Alan S. 1992. *The European Rescue of the Nation State*. London: Routledge.

Newitt, Malyn. 1981. *Portugal in Africa: The Last Hundred Years*. London: C. Hurst.

———. 1995. *A History of Mozambique*. Bloomington and Indianapolis: Indiana University Press.

Nunes, Ana Bela. 2001. Actividade económica da população. In *Estatísticas Históricas Portuguesas*, ed. Nuno Valério, 149–197. Lisbon: INE.

Nunes, Ana Bela, and Nuno Valério. 2005. Moeda e bancos. In *História Económica de Portugal, 1700–2000, Vol. III, O Século XX*, ed. Pedro Lains and Álvaro Ferreira da Silva, 227–263. Lisbon: ICS.

Oliveira, Pedro Aires. 2014. Uma descolonização fora de horas. In *História da Expansão e do Império Português*, ed. João Paulo Oliveira e Costa, 510–545. Lisbon: A Esfera dos Livros.

Paulo, João Carlos. 1996. Vantagens da instrução e do trabalho. 'Escola de massas' e imagens de uma 'educação colonial portuguesa'. *Educação, Sociedade e Culturas* 5: 99–128.

Pereira, Victor. 2012. A economia do Império e os Planos de Fomento. In *O Império Colonial em questão (Séculos XIX–XX): Poderes, Saberes e Instituições*, ed. Miguel Bandeira Jerónimo, 251–286. Lisboa: Editora 70.

Pinheiro, Maximiano. (ed.). 1997. *Séries Longas para a Economia Portuguesa, Pós-II Guerra Mundial, Vol. I—Séries Estatísticas*. Lisbon: Banco de Portugal.

Pinho, Ivo. 1976. Sector empresarial: antes e depois do 11 de Março. *Análise Social* XII (47): 733–747.

Ramos, Rui. 1999. Analfabetismo. In *Dicionário de História de Portugal, Suplemento A/E, Vol. VII*, ed. António Barreto and Maria Filomena Mónica, 95–100. Porto: Livraria Figueirinhas.

Ramos, Rui, Bernardo Vasconcelos e Sousa, and Nuno Gonçalo Monteiro. 2009. *História de Portugal*. Lisbon: A Esfera dos Livros.

Reis, Jaime. 1984. O atraso económico português em perspectiva histórica. *Análise Social* XX (80): 7–28.

———. 1988. The Historical Roots of the Modern Portuguese Economy: The First Century of Growth, 1850s to 1950s. In *The New Portugal: Democracy and Europe*, ed. Richard Herr, 126–148. Berkeley: University of California.

———. 1995. Portuguese Banking in the Inter-War Period. In *Banking, Currency and Finance in Europe Between the Wars*, ed. Charles H. Feinstein, 472–501. Oxford: Oxford University Press.

Rias, Ana Paula Lopes de Oliveira Andrade. 1997. *Regentes Escolares, 'Colaboradores Benévolos' ao Serviço da Educação Nacional*, Masters' thesis Presented at the Faculdade de Ciências Sociais e Humanas of the Universidade Nova de Lisboa, Lisbon.

Rodríguez, Francisco, and Dani Rodrik. 2000. Trade Policy and Economic Growth: A Sceptic's Guide to the Cross-National Evidence. *NBER Macroeconomics Annual* 15: 261–325.

Rollo, Maria Fernanda. 1994. *Portugal e o Plano Marshall: Da Rejeição à Solicitação da Ajuda Norte- Americana (1947–1952)*. Lisbon: Editorial Estampa.

Rosas, Fernando. 2000. Daniel Barbosa e a política de estabilização económica e social do pós-guerra. In *Salazarismo e Fomento Económico: O Primado do Político na História Económica do Estado Novo*. Lisbon: Editorial Notícias.

Sá, Isabel dos Guimarães, and Maria Antónia Lopes. 2008. *História Breve das Misericórdias Portuguesas*. Coimbra: Imprensa da Universidade de Coimbra.

Silva, Álvaro Ferreira da. 2016. Multinationals and Foreign Direct Investment: The Portuguese Experience (1900–2010). *Journal of Evolutionary Studies in Business* II (1): 40–68.

Silva, Álvaro Ferreira da, Luciano Amaral, and Pedro Neves. 2016. Business Groups in Portugal in the *Estado Novo* Period (1930–1974): Family, Power and Structural Change. *Business History* 58 (1): 49–68.

Silva, António E. Duarte. 1989. Salazar e a política colonial do Estado Novo: o Acto Colonial (1930–1951). In *Salazar e o Salazarismo*, ed. AAVV, 101–152. Lisbon: Publicações D. Quixote.

Silva, Ester Gomes da, and Pedro Lains. 2013. Capital Formation and Long-Run Growth: Evidence from Portuguese Data, 1910–2011. Paper Presented at Iberometrics III, Zaragoza University.

Simões, Vitor Corado. 1985. Portugal. In *Multinational Enterprises, Economic Structure and International Competitiveness*, ed. J. H. Dunning, 337–378. Chichester: John Wiley and Sons.

Soares, Fernando Brito. 2005. A agricultura. In *História Económica de Portugal, 1700–2000, Vol. III, O Século XX*, ed. Pedro Lains and Álvaro Ferreira da Silva, 157–183. Lisbon: ICS.

Valério, Nuno. 2002. A acessão de Portugal ao GATT. *Notas Económicas* (Novembro): 61–69.

———. 2006. Os debates das leis de autorização das receitas e despesas. In *Os Impostos no Parlamento Português: Sistemas Fiscais e Doutrinas Fiscais nos Séculos XIX e XX*, ed. Nuno Valério, 161–178. Lisbon: Publicações Dom Quixote.

Valério, Nuno, Ana Bela Nunes, Carlos Bastien, Rita Martins de Sousa, and Sandra Domingos Costa. 2010. *História do Sistema Bancário Português, Vol. II, Da Assunção pelo Banco de Portugal das Funções de Banco Central à União Monetária Europeia*. Lisbon: Banco de Portugal.

Van Der Wee, Herman. 1986. *Prosperity and Upheaval: The World Economy, 1945–1980*. London: Penguin Books.

Wheeler, Douglas L., and René Pélissier. 1972. *Angola*. New York: Praeger Publishers.

World Bank Open Data. https://data.worldbank.org/.

6

The 1973 Crisis, the 1974 Revolution, and Their Effects on the Portuguese Economy

Two main aspects mark the period covered in this chapter: (1) a strong slowdown in economic growth starting in 1974, enough to interrupt the previous catch-up process coming from the 1950–1973 period and (2) a political revolution, also starting in 1974, that had vast economic consequences. The two phenomena ended up by being connected, with the second affecting the first on many counts.

The revolution involved Portugal in a typical Cold War confrontation, the outcome of which, besides the strictly political dimension, would determine if the country's economy acquired socialist/communist features or remain a fundamentally capitalist one. Even within the last possibility, strong pressures existed for many of the institutional structures relevant to the economy to change: from labor law to fiscal or monetary policies, the distance between Portugal and the west European countries had increased during the postwar period. The institutional framework of the Portuguese economy was substantially transformed during the revolution but, in the end, the country remained within the capitalist side of the Cold War divide.

Besides the ideological confrontation, another issue was central to the revolution: the future of the Portuguese Empire. This was a process with

L. Amaral, *The Modern Portuguese Economy in the Twentieth and Twenty-First Centuries*, Palgrave Studies in Economic History,
https://doi.org/10.1007/978-3-030-24548-1_6

enormous economic consequences as well, essentially on two dimensions: trade, because the commercial connections between the mainland and the overseas territories were still intense by 1974; and labor, as the independence of these territories brought a massive influx of people into the mainland, corresponding to about 8% of its population, a human mass the country had to immediately accommodate in a time of crisis.

Once the most intense shock waves of the revolutionary period started receding, a challenge remained for the first democratic authorities: to garner the allegiance of the population to the new regime. The task was not easy, due to the international economic crisis. And, in fact, they adopted, after 1976, a series of expansionary policies that were responsible for two external payments crises, the first in 1977 and the second in 1982. The crises had to be settled with two interventions by the International Monetary Fund (IMF), with their typical contractionary measures; a new slowdown in economic growth ensued. The combination of all these politically induced reasons for turbulence meant that, one decade after the revolution, the Portuguese economy had stopped closing the gap to the richer ones.

1 The 1973 Crisis and the 1974 Revolution

The fact that the revolution affected the behavior of the economy does not mean that it was in itself the main cause of growth slowdown. Quite the contrary: the whole of Europe entered into a period of much poorer performance after the Golden Age of economic growth. Portugal was no exception (Table 1).

This means the Portuguese economy was affected by a set of forces much beyond the control of Portuguese economic or political agents. Two major shocks affected the world economy in the early 1970s: the end of the so-called Bretton Woods system (the fixed-exchange rate mechanism created in 1945), in the sequence of the Nixon administration's decision to terminate the convertibility of the US dollar into gold in August 1971; and the decision by the Arab countries of the Organization of Petroleum Exporting Countries (OPEC) to embargo oil exports to various Western countries in October 1973, leading to the

Table 1 GDP per capita, various European countries (average annual growth rates), 1950–1985

	1950–1973	1974–1985
Portugal	5.38	1.60
Austria	4.97	2.32
Belgium	3.56	1.77
Denmark	3.11	1.98
Finland	4.29	2.30
France	4.02	1.77
Germany	5.05	1.99
Greece	6.26	1.68
Ireland	3.06	2.59
Italy	4.97	2.40
Netherlands	3.48	1.32
Spain	5.66	2.02
Sweden	3.23	1.15
Switzerland	3.10	0.69
UK	2.43	1.75

Source The Conference Board, except Portugal: Amaral (2009)

quadrupling of oil prices in the world market in a matter of just a few months.

But these shocks were inserted in an economic environment that was already tense in most European countries: the notable growth process coming from the 1950s was showing some signs of stress, mostly reflected in wage pressures and inflation (Crafts and Toniolo 1996). Much of the 1950s–1973 growth was due to Europe catching-up to the US thanks to the import of American technology and methods of production. Room for exploration of this technological and management gap disappeared progressively during the 1960s and was virtually exhausted by the end of the decade. The relatively peaceful cooperation between capital and labor that had allowed for wage moderation until the late 1960s started cracking as a consequence (Crafts and Toniolo 1996; Eichengreen 2007). The European economies were already under stress since the late 1960s—the two shocks of the early 1970s just sealed the process.

Despite these general and external forces, internal ones contributed to the particular way in which slowdown took place in Portugal, especially in the short run. Table 2 shows the annual growth rates of

Table 2 GDP per capita, Portugal (annual growth rates), 1970–1985

1970	9.21
1971	11.07
1972	10.29
1973	4.87
1974	0.24
1975	−9.18
1976	−0.24
1977	7.18
1978	5.43
1979	6.71
1980	4.44
1981	2.39
1982	1.59
1983	0.61
1984	−1.45
1985	1.49

Source Amaral (2009)

GDP per capita in Portugal between 1970 and 1985. After spectacular growth in the early 1970s, the crash during the revolutionary years is unequivocal, especially in 1975 (with a fall of more than 9%). How this was different from the rest of Europe, including countries with a similar level of GDP per capita and also passing through political transition processes from authoritarianism to democracy of their own (Spain and Greece), is shown in the comparison displayed in Fig. 4 of the Introduction: while Portugal diverged noticeably from richer economies between 1974 and 1976, both Spain and Greece continued catching-up.

Understanding why the revolution had such an impact on the economy requires understanding also its main features. The events were initiated by a movement of junior military officers that gathered into an association to which they gave the name Armed Forces Movement (*Movimento das Forças Armadas*: MFA). Their starting point was a general dissatisfaction with their career prospects and combat conditions in the Colonial War and their main point was to terminate the war. But they associated it with the overthrowing of the authoritarian regime. On 25 April 1974, in association with some senior officers also involved in the war, MFA orchestrated a military coup that toppled the regime and initiated a process of transition to install a new one: according to their program, elections for a constituent assembly should take place one year from the coup. New legislation was drafted to operationalize those elections and, for the first time since the introduction of the electoral principle in the first half of the nineteenth century, the right to vote became truly universal, without income, wealth, or sex distinctions (Reis 1994; Ramos et al. 2009).[1] A true political landmark.

But there was no consensus among the revolutionaries over what the new regime should be. During the year preceding the elections, they split over the issue, together with the political agents and society in general. The division followed a typical Cold War pattern, with some favoring a liberal democracy of the Western type (even if admitting a significant role for Government intervention in the economy, as was the norm in postwar Europe, where social-democratic influences were very strong), while others favored an outright socialist/communist solution, even if differing over which version to adopt (Reis 1994; Ramos et al. 2009). Initially, significant importance (especially by the first provisional Governments) was given to the abolition of the most notable aspects of Government intervention during the *Estado Novo*. This is the case of industrial conditioning, which was abolished in October 1974 and replaced by an industrial licensing system, still discretionary, but based only on technical requisites.[2] It is also the case of the corporatist structure, which was abolished by several pieces of legislation referring to each type of organization during the years 1974 and 1975—the former corporatist organizations were replaced by new, fully public or private, institutions (Lucena and Gaspar 1991, 1992). None of this indicated a radical political course. But soon things started to change, in a highly complex process (Reis 1994; Ramos et al. 2009). Between September 1974 and March 1975, the groups committed to more radical Marxist interpretations of the future of the regime reached control of the political levers of the country.

Labor unrest gave a large contribution to the radicalization of the process, with the occurrence of various strikes and many episodes of occupation of firms by the workers. The purpose of much

---

[1] Law 3/74, 14 May 1974.

[2] Decree-law 553/74, 10 October.

of this activity was to obtain higher pay and shorter working time (Santos et al. 1976–1977). With the revolutionary authorities abstaining from repressing labor, workers were generally successful in their demands: wages increased 7 and 14% in real terms in 1974 and 1975, respectively (Mateus 2013). The various Governments approved legislation much favorable to labor: in May and June 1974, a national minimum wage was introduced[3]; in August, striking became legal[4]; in March 1975, a general system of unemployment benefit was created[5]; in April, the old corporatist unions were extinguished and unionization became free, although the various sectoral unions should belong to just one confederation (which happened to be the one dominated by the Communist Party)[6]; in July, a new labor code was approved, making individual firing almost impossible and collective firing also difficult: firing workers became possible only under the principle of "just cause", which was extremely difficult to prove.[7]

While this was taking place, the labor market was rocked by a massive shock deriving from the process of decolonization. Getting out of Africa was the main objective of the revolutionaries. So, negotiations between them and the African independentist movements started in 1974. In July, the second revolutionary Government admitted for the first time that independence should be granted to the overseas territories,[8] which would actually take place during 1974 and 1975, thus making the centuries-old Portuguese Empire disappear: Guinea-Bissau and Cape Verde became independent on 10 September 1974, Mozambique on 25 June 1975, São Tomé e Príncipe on 12 July, Angola, on 11 November, and Timor on 28 November. As a consequence, panic spread among the colonists of Angola and Mozambique (the two territories where sizable white populations existed). As their feeling of insecurity grew, they started an exodus in the direction of

[3]Decree-law 191/74, 6 May, and Decree-law 268/74, 21 June.

[4]Decree-law 392/74, 27 August.

[5]Decree-law 169-D/75, 31 March.

[6]Decrees-law 215-A/75 and 215-B/75, 30 April.

[7]Decree-law 372-A/75, 16 July.

[8]Law 7/24, 27 July.

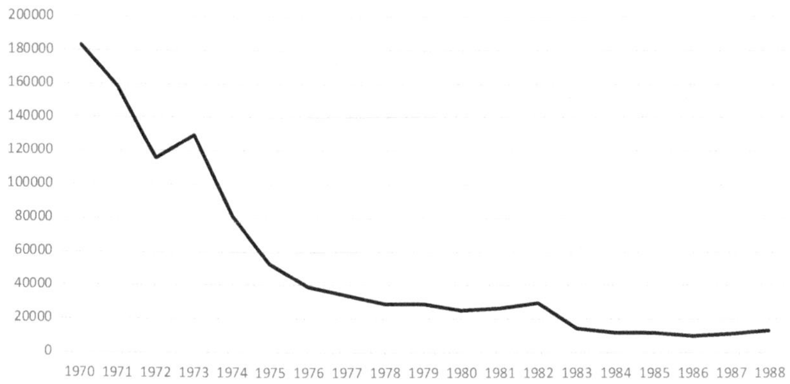

Fig. 1 Emigrants, Portugal, 1970–1988 (*Source* Baganha [1994])

mainland Portugal, in a process that corresponded to one of the largest population movements ever in Portuguese history: about 600,000–700,000 people (or something close to 8% of the mainland's population), most of them economically active, entered the mainland between late 1974 and early 1976 (Pires et al. 1984). Two European episodes of the same type provide us with benchmarks that put the Portuguese case in perspective: one is the case of France at the time of Algerian Independence in 1962, when 800,000 settlers (only slightly more than the Portuguese ones) were absorbed by a population 5 times larger (50 million as opposed to 9 million in Portugal): the proportion of the incoming settlers over the French resident population was of about 1.6%. Another case is that of the Dutch settlers fleeing from Indonesia at the time of independence in 1949 and returning to the Netherlands: in this case, about 250,000 persons entered a country with a resident population of 10 million; the proportion was of 2.5%. The magnitude of the Portuguese population movement was much larger than any of these examples, at least in relative terms. And the economic circumstances were also very different: whereas the French and Dutch episodes took place in a period of rapid growth, the Portuguese one happened in the middle of the hardest crisis since the 1930s. Besides the serious political problems brought by this movement, the social and economic consequences were outstanding.

The arrival of the mass of colonists from Africa was not the only shock to the labor market. The slowing down of emigration (Fig. 1), as the other European economies were also dealing at the time with the effects of the international crisis, and the demobilization of the soldiers involved in the Colonial War, were other major contributors. Labor supply expanded massively: active population grew by about 400,000 persons between 1973 and 1975, corresponding to growth rates of 3.08% in 1974 and 4.90% in 1975, spectacular figures by any standard (Amaral 2009). So, right when both the international crisis and the increase in the supply of labor should lead wages to fall, the exact opposite happened, thanks to the political environment of the country. Labor became a much dearer factor of production, not only because of wages but also the reduction of working time brought about by the new legislation mentioned above. Thus, firms, already threatened by the cost of energy (as well as of other imported goods) and the fall in national and international activity, felt straight-jacked by these unprecedented wage pressures. As a consequence, they tried reflecting them in prices.

One of the main instruments used by the revolutionary Governments to deal with the inflationary pressures thus created was to freeze prices of goods and services, a policy adopted in July 1974[9]—this means that price formation in the Portuguese economy continued to be, as during the *Estado Novo*, determined by the Government. The combination of exploding costs, frozen prices, and an overvalued exchange rate (as the revolutionary Governments shied away from depreciating the currency, mostly on account of prestige reasons) put firms in a very difficult situation. Capital flight started and unemployment, which was virtually inexistent in 1973 (1.7%), jumped to 6.2% (Amaral 2005, 2010; Franco 1994).

In the extremely volatile political environment of the period, the difficulties felt by firms to keep production levels were understood by the revolutionary authorities as "economic sabotage". Pressures started thus growing for many companies to be nationalized and taken away from their owners. Eventually, in March 1975, these pressures were translated

[9]Decree-law 329-A/74, 10 July.

into policy. The day 11 March marks the beginning of an eight-month period when the political process was clearly dominated by MFA (now considerably more radicalized), the Communist Party, and other radical left-wing political forces. One of the largest nationalization programs ever in modern European history unfolded: the move was directed at both the property of the large business groups and at those sectors the revolutionary authorities considered to be "strategic"—in reality, both categories coincided largely (Amaral 2015; Valério 2004). The process was quite rapid: the bulk of it occurred between March and September 1975. The first nationalizations had already taken place in 1974, affecting the three banks of issue of mainland Portugal and the Overseas Provinces: the BoP, the National Overseas Bank, and the Bank of Angola.[10] But these were still relatively conventional steps, as virtually all banks of issue in the West had been nationalized during the postwar period. What happened between March and November 1975 was a totally different affair. The first decision was taken by the "Revolutionary Council", a new institution, created in March, gathering the revolutionary officers. The Government, which by the time had become a sort of executive agency of the most radical political and military forces (namely those harbored by the Revolutionary Council), put in motion a sweeping nationalization wave: the first sector to be nationalized was Banking, on 14 March, immediately followed by Insurance, on 15 March.[11] These were still ad hoc nationalizations, but one month later, on 15 April, the Government approved a general program covering the "basic sectors" of the economy as well as the property of the business groups[12]: Electricity, Oil Production and Refining, Steel, Railways, Shipping and Air transportation were nationalized the next day. But this was not the end of it, as the process continued much beyond the already broad limits of the April program, following the radicalization of the political situation: cement and paper pulp on 9 May; tobacco on 13 May; coach companies and the Lisbon Underground

[10]Decrees-law 450/74, 451/74, and 452/74, all of 13 September.

[11]Banking: Decree-law 132-A/75, 14 March; Insurance: Decree-law 135-A/75, 15 March.

[12]Decree-law 203-C/75, 15 April.

on 5 June; the Lisbon bus system on 3 July; the agricultural areas irrigated under public or semi-public schemes on 30 July; glass and mining during the month of August; chemicals on 21 and 22 August; beer production on 30 August; naval construction and repair on 1 September, together with the companies dedicated to the assembling of transportation material; financial holdings were nationalized on 2 October; on 13 November it was the turn of *Companhia das Lezírias*, a large agricultural firm; radio and television on 2 December; various frozen fish companies on 20 July 1976; and, finally, on 29 July, the process touched some publishing houses.[13]

In the end, 250 firms or stock were directly nationalized. But, as many of these firms were banks, with significant shares in non-banking firms, these were also affected, implying the indirect nationalization of 1,300 firms. No compensation was given to the owners at this time, a reflection of the heightened radicalization of the political situation. Contrary to what had happened during the *Estado Novo*, the Portuguese entrepreneurial public sector became one of the largest in the Western world. By the end of it, the sector was responsible for about 20–25% of GDP, 30% of investment, and 8% of the workforce (Baklanoff 1996). To note is the fact that this vast expropriation process left foreign capital untouched, with the revolutionary authorities avoiding to hurt the interests of Western countries in a direct way, out of fear of a more forceful foreign reaction against the revolution. The owners of the business groups were either imprisoned or fled the country.

[13]The specific legislation referring to each sector is the following: Oil production and Refining, Railways, Steel, Shipping, Air Transportation, and Electricity: Decrees-law 205-A/75, 205-B/75, 205-C/75, 205-D/75, 205-E/75, and 205-G/75, all of 16 April; Cement, and Paper Pulp: Decrees-law 221-A/75 and 221-B/75, both 9 May; Tobacco: Decree-law 227-A/75, 13 May; Coaches and Lisbon Underground, Decrees-law 280-A/75 and 280-C/75, both 5 June; Carris (the Lisbon bus system): Decree-law 346/75, 3 July; Decree-law 407-A/75, 30 July; Glass and Mining: differentiated pieces of legislation for each firm; Chemicals: Decrees-law 453/75, 21 August, 457/75, 22 August, and 532/75, 25 September; Beer production: Decree-law 474/75, 30 August; Naval Construction and Repair, and Assemblage of Transportation Material: Decree-law 478/75, 1 September; Financial holdings: Decree-law 561/75, 2 October; Radio and Television: Decree-law 674-C/75, 2 December; *Companhia das Lezírias*, Decree-law 628/75, 13 November; Frozen Fish: Decree-law 572/76, 20 July 1976; Publishing: Decree-law 639/76, 29 July 1976.

Besides nationalization, two additional processes affected the property structure of the economy: one was a movement of occupation of factories by their workers. Since many of these experiences faced various difficulties to survive, control was transferred to the Government in a large number of cases: between 1974 and 1975, about 300 firms were passed into the hands of the Government, affecting roughly 100,000 workers (Lopes 1996). The other process was something the revolutionary authorities called an "Agrarian Reform". This was much different from the understanding of "agrarian reform" during the *Estado Novo*: it corresponded to the occupation by rural workers, small tenants, and small farmers of a great number of large farms in four Southern/Central regions of the country (Alentejo, Ribatejo, Beira Baixa, and Algarve), with Government support. The same 15 April program that had led to the nationalization of the "basic sectors" and the assets of the business groups also set the principles for expropriation of these farms: farms with more than 500 hectares in dry land or with more than 50 hectares in irrigated lands that were "underutilized" should be expropriated and handed into the workers, although the former owners would keep their property rights in a fraction of the expropriated farm (this fraction could go up to 50 hectares in irrigated lands and 500 hectares in drylands). Occupations started on 31 March 1975 and continued until the end of the year, with no compensation being given to the expropriated owners. In the Summer of 1975, the Government introduced new rules for expropriation: total area, quality of land, irrigated area and other criteria should be weighted into an index, which was then used to establish the threshold for expropriation; in practical terms this meant: (a) that the threshold for expropriation of irrigated lands was lowered to 30 hectares; (b) that expropriation could now include the entire farm and not just the land in excess of the threshold; and (c) that expropriation was no longer restricted to underutilized farms but included all farms with an area above the approved threshold.[14] At the beginning

[14]Decrees-law 406-A/75, 29 July.

of 1976, 1,200,000 hectares of land had been taken away from their former owners and appropriated by the workers, whom started running the farms in collectivist fashion. Roughly 13% of national territory, including about 4000 farms, 70,000 workers and 1000 owners, were affected by the process (Barreto 1987).

Alongside this set of revolutionary events, a simultaneous process of institutionalization of the new regime was also underway. On 25 April 1975, one year after the coup d'état, the promised elections for a constituent assembly took place and victory went to a set of forces favorable to moderation. A typical situation of dual power was thus created (with interesting parallels with revolutionary Russia in 1917): on one side, Governments invoked a revolutionary legitimacy and, on the other, the moderate parliament invoked electoral legitimacy. The new Constitution, approved on 2 April 1976, was the result of the clash between the two sides.

Although incorporating the most important elements of a liberal-democratic polity, the 1976 Constitution included also a vast socioeconomic section with a heavy socialist/communist penchant. According to its preamble, Portugal was now a country "opening the way to a socialist society". This meant that private property was recognized but should be seen as residual in relation to public property and co-operative property (Article 89). "Social property", which included both the public and the co-operative kinds, would "ultimately predominate" in the future (Article 90), for "the social and economic organization of the Portuguese Republic is based on the development of socialist production relations, to be actualized through the collective appropriation of the means of production, land, and natural resources, as well as on the democratic power of the working classes" (Article 80). A Plan encompassing the whole economy should be the fundamental instrument of economic policy (Articles 91–95). Article 10 made the 1975 and 1976 nationalizations and the Agrarian Reform irreversible (or "irreversible conquests of the working classes"). Additionally, the so-called basic sectors (i.e., those nationalized) were closed to private ownership. Also, the labor legislation approved in 1975, especially the "just cause" principle, became a constitutional matter, through Article 52, making change by regular legislative processes almost impossible.[15] The Constitution made the creation of a Welfare State compulsory, as Articles 63 and 64 determined public Social Security and Health systems should be installed. In an important compromise with revolutionary legitimacy, MFA and the Revolutionary Council were included among the political and judicial institutions of the country, alongside the President of the Republic, the Parliament, the Government, and the Courts (Articles 3 and 113). Perhaps the most important function of the Revolutionary Council was to verify the conformity of the laws with the Constitution, i.e., a sort of parallel Constitutional Court.

These developments explain why the revolution had such a large effect on the short-term behavior of the economy. Political agents, rather than trying to soften the impact of the 1973 crisis, were absorbed by the revolutionary changes. Many of the excesses of the revolution started being disciplined quite soon, from 1976 onward. But excesses of a different sort appeared then, leading to a very serious foreign imbalance crisis that had to be combatted with drastic methods.

2 Turning the Revolution Around (1976–1979)

If the main thrust of the course of the political process between September 1974 and November 1975 was radicalization, the opposite happened between November 1975 and April 1976. A failed coup d'état by radical forces on 25 November 1975 gave the upper hand to the moderates. The new Constitution was signed on 2 April 1976, and on 25 April elections took place, confirming the prevalence of centrist political parties. The first non-provisional parliament and Government were elected, marking the end of the revolutionary phase. However, the political process continued to follow convoluted paths, as the first constitutional parliaments and Governments proved to be fragile and unstable (details can be found in Reis 1994; Ramos et al. 2009).

[15] Translations by the author.

Still, the final result was a reversion of the most radical aspects of the revolutionary process.

The main purpose of the new authorities in what concerns the economy was to create a friendlier environment to private capital. This became immediately clear in the case of labor law, where some of the principles most protective of labor introduced in 1974 and 1975 were softened. Since labor law was a constitutional matter, changing it implied a lot of legislative ingenuity. In January 1976, a new piece of legislation reduced the threshold of collective firing to 2–5 workers in firms with less than 50 workers and to more than 5 in firms with more than 50 workers.[16] Even if firing individual workers continued to be almost impossible, under the protection of "just cause", the new thresholds made collective firing converge to individual firing, making of it a usable instrument for firm restructuring. Later in the year, in an another crucial legislative change, new short-term contracts were introduced, making it possible for firms to hire workers for any fixed period between one month and three years: for a firm to sever a working relationship it needed only not to renew the new short-term contracts.[17] Also of importance was the abolition of the principle of just one confederation for the various sectoral unions[18]: two months later a new confederation not dominated by the Communist Party was created.

Another aspect where reversion of the revolutionary inheritance was visible was in the introduction of limits to the intervention of the Government in private firms. In May 1976, it became no longer possible for the Government to take control of firms that had been occupied by workers, putting a halt to one of the most important vehicles of expropriation in 1974 and 1975.[19] And in July a new law defined the boundaries of the public entrepreneurial sector. The law received, in political discussion, the non-official name of "Law of Sector Delimitation", and its purpose was to define the economic sectors where

[16]Decree-law 84/76, 2 January 1976.

[17]Decree-law 781/76, 28 October 1976.

[18]Decree-law 773/76, 27 October 1976.

[19]Decree-law 422/76, 29 May 1976.

private ownership was authorized and those where it was not.[20] The 1976 Constitution prevented opening the sectors that had been nationalized to private ownership, but the new law found some shortcuts to it. Private ownership continued to be prohibited in banking, insurance, electricity, gas, water, communications, air transportation, railways, and cement. However, it became possible to create mixed firms (partly public, partly private) in Oil Refining, Petrochemicals, Steel, Chemicals, and the Armament Industry. Private management, although under public ownership, became possible in urban transportation, ports, and airports. Additionally, new kinds of financial institutions were created that did not fall under the category of "bank" as defined by the Constitution and which could, thus, according to the new law, be privately owned: "caixas económicas" (a new type of savings bank), regional development societies, and investment societies.

Still in one further reversion of the revolutionary inheritance, between 1976 and 1977, new criteria were adopted for Agrarian Reform. The ultimate consequence of the introduction of the new criteria was to put an end to the collectivist experience, by giving back the land that had been expropriated to the previous owners: in April 1976 an Agrarian Reform Zone was officially created ("*Zona de Intervenção da Reforma Agrária*"), limiting the expropriation process only to a certain geographical area of the country (which covered the four regions where the process had been more intense). Within that area new principles of expropriation were introduced, affecting the division between expropriated lands and those kept under private ownership: thanks to reclassification, many expropriated lands could be given back to the previous owners.[21] Then, in September 1977, a new law made the criteria for lawful expropriation much more restrictive (and, consequently, much more favorable to private ownership).[22] Significant amounts of land were reclassified under this law and given back to their previous owners. In the next few years, the whole Agrarian Reform had been completely

[20]Law 46/77, 8 July 1977.

[21]Decree-law 236-B/76, 5 April 1976.

[22]Law 77/77, 22 July 1977.

reverted. Since Agrarian Reform was a constitutional matter, reverting it implied again a lot of law-making ingenuity (Barreto 1987).

It was in 1977 that compensation was finally given to the former owners of the assets expropriated in 1974 and 1975, although with several limitations: the amounts were always set below the original value of the assets, most of the payment was done through (especially created) Government bonds that had below-market interest rates and could only be claimed for certain specific purposes prescribed by the law (Valério 2004).[23] Despite its limitations, there is no doubt that the law marked a new attitude of political authorities in relation to private entrepreneurs.

Part of the package of political moderation was Portugal's candidacy to join the European Economic Community (EEC). Until 1976, the member countries of the EEC were doubtful about inviting Portugal to join the club, essentially on account of the indeterminacy of the country's political evolution: the risk of it falling into the communist side of the Cold War had not disappeared yet. On the other hand, Portuguese politicians did not show much interest in membership either (Cunha 2015). But by late 1976 the ruling center-left Socialist Party, run by then Prime Minister Mário Soares, started associating membership with strengthening of democracy. In the following year, this idea had become common wisdom among both the Portuguese moderates and the EEC countries. On 28 March 1977, Portugal applied to become a member, initiating a long period of negotiations that only finished on 12 June 1985, when the country signed a treaty of accession with the EEC's member countries in Lisbon (in the same day as Spain, which had also applied in 1977), effective from 1 January onward (Cunha 2015).

3 International Payments Crises

Once the idea of keeping the Portuguese economy within the capitalist mold (although with a large Government intervention) prevailed among the political class, the various Governments from 1976 onward felt the

[23]Law 80/77, 28 October 1977.

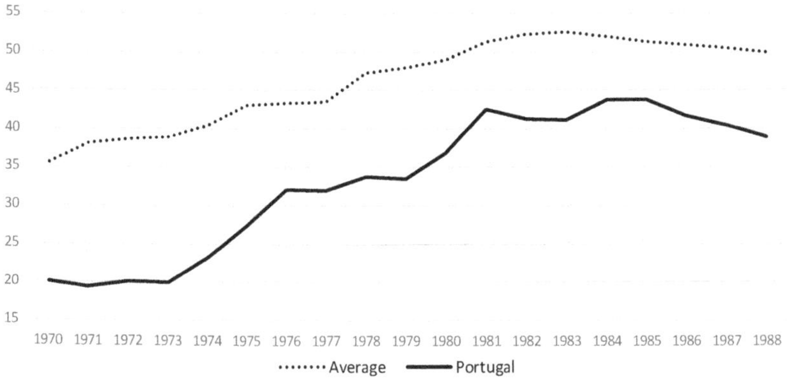

Fig. 2 Public spending (% GDP), Portugal and average European countries, 1970–1988 (*Note* The countries in the sample are the UK, Austria, Belgium, Denmark, France, Germany, Netherlands, Norway, and Sweden. *Source* Portugal: Pinheiro [1997]; other countries: Mauro et al. [2013])

need for two things: one was to fight the economic crash of the two previous years, the other was to provide the population with those sorts of social services that most European democracies had been developing since the end of World War II.

The essential instrument for both was public spending. This led to a radical transformation of the nature of fiscal policy, on various dimensions: the first was that of size; the *Estado Novo* had kept the Government small, as it equated the Welfare State with a form of disguised socialism. The revolution changed that for good: in three years, the 20% gap between Portugal and the European average was reduced by practically one half (to 10%), and the process would continue until a gap of just 5% was reached in the early 1980s (Fig. 2).

The change in size also meant change in structure. By comparison with European countries in the postwar period, the *Estado Novo* Governments spent very little on social items (education, health, social security). The revolution transformed this structure radically, as Fig. 3 shows. Spending on defense dropped suddenly after 1974, from around 6% of GDP to around 2% in 1977, reflecting the end of the Colonial War. Items concerning various dimensions of social policy grew instead: spending on Health, which corresponded to just 2% of GDP in 1970,

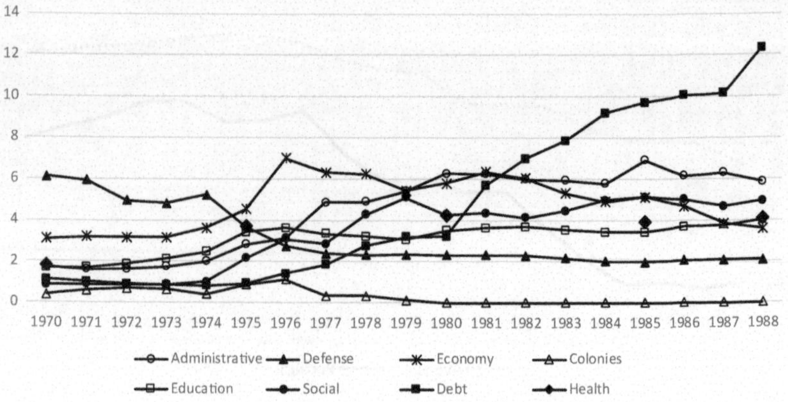

Fig. 3 Structure public spending, Portugal, 1970–1988 (% GDP) (*Source* Mata [2001], except Health: Carreira [1996]—in 1988 = 1990)

doubled to 4% in 1975 and was kept at that level until 1985; education had a similar evolution; as for pensions and unemployment benefits, the jump is equally clear, from roughly 1% of GDP in 1973 to close to 4% in 1976, and growing afterward to reach about 6% until 1985.

The new authorities were very quick in expanding the Government's grip over social services. Between 1974 and 1975, the national and local hospitals run by the *Misericórdias*, which corresponded to the largest hospital network in the country, were nationalized, something that explains the doubling of the Government's Health budget between 1970 and 1975.[24] Interestingly enough, the creation in 1979 of a National Health Service fully run by the Government did not immediately lead to an expansion of spending on Health (Fig. 3).[25] This seems to be related with a series of initial difficulties (among which the financial ones played a large role) faced by the Governments of the time to expand personnel and infrastructure (Mozzicafredo 2000; Campos and Simões 2011; Lima 2015).

A similar boost happened in education, where the number of public teachers and schools practically doubled between 1973 and 1976,

[24]Decree-law 704/74, 7 December 1974, and Decree-law 618/5, 11 November 1975.

[25]Law 56/79, 15 September 1979.

especially for the schooling cycles less developed during the *Estado Novo* (secondary and university education): the number of secondary teachers jumped from 10,879 in 1971 to 44,669 in 1976, and the number of secondary schools jumped in the same dates from 506 to 1661, while the number of university faculty passed from 2341 to 7206, and the number of university buildings from 42 to 109 (Carreira 1996). Again, and for similar reasons than in the Health sector, spending in education stalled from 1976 to 1977 until the mid-1980s (Fig. 3).

Pensions and unemployment benefits were also strongly affected, due to a series of innovations in policy: in 1974, the number of rural workers benefiting from pensions was enlarged[26]; in 1975, about 500,000 rural workers saw their pensions rise (not only old age but also disease and disability) and were included in programs that had only existed for industrial and services workers up to then (maternity pay and survivor pension)[27]; in 1977, social security was extended to independent workers, the same happening to domestic workers in 1978.[28] As a consequence, the number of social security beneficiaries passed from 187,300 in 1970 to 861,700 in 1975, and 1,656,200 in 1980. The creation of a national unemployment benefits program (previously only sectoral programs existed) also helps explaining the strong expansion of this budget item.[29] Such change corresponds to a clear institutional convergence in the structure of public spending with democratic Europe (Fig. 4).

One final dimension where change in fiscal policy was drastic was in the matter of balance. The *Estado Novo* had followed a very strict policy of budget balance. That definitely disappeared from 1974 onward, as Fig. 5 shows. The main reason for this was, precisely, the adoption of the new social responsibilities by the Government. Adequacy of the receipts to spending became difficult because of both the expansion of the new programs and the contraction of the value of taxes, thanks to the crisis.

---

[26]Decree-law 807/74, 31 December 1974.

[27]Decree 174-B/75, 1 April 1975.

[28]Ordinance 115/77, 9 March 1977, and Decree-law 180-C/78, 15 July 1978.

[29]Decree-law 169-D/75, 31 March 1975.

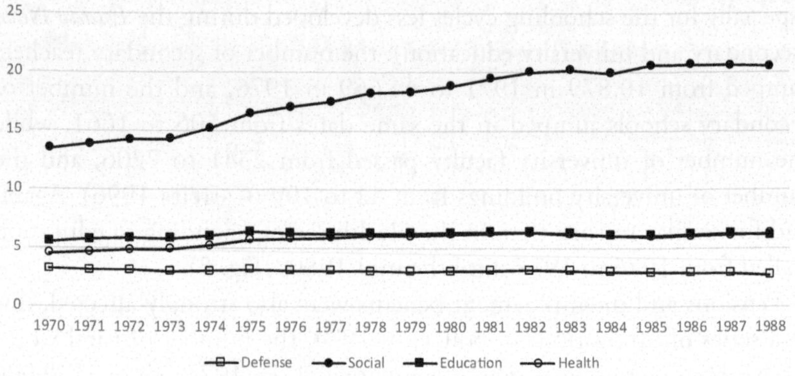

Fig. 4 Structure of public spending—average EU 15 (some items), 1970–1988 (% GDP) (*Note* Values for 1970–1975 are based on the values UK, Austria, Belgium, Denmark, France, Germany, Netherlands, Norway, and Sweden in order to splice the larger sample for 1975–1988. *Source* For social spending and health—Lindert data sets for *Growing Public* book; for education, and health 1970–1981—Lindert data sets for *Growing Public* book, chained with: for education 1982–1988—World Development Indicators—World Bank; Defense: Military Expenditure database, World Development Indicators, World Bank)

Fig. 5 Government budget deficit, Portugal, 1970–1988 (% GDP) (*Source* Pinheiro [1997])

In this respect, the fact that the tax structure remained largely unaltered in relation to the *Estado Novo* period made the whole process even more complicated. In 1974, there was a tax reform, but the only change introduced by it was more progressivity,[30] in fact extreme progressivity, with some marginal rates in certain brackets not too high in the income scale reaching 84%, something that led to an explosion of tax evasion (Franco 1994; Lopes 2005).

Another instrument used by the Governments to boost the economy was the now vast arsenal of public companies (including the banks). The nationalization process did not simply mean the passage of the assets of the business groups to Government property but also a profound reorganization of the nationalized firms. This reorganization was constantly biased in the direction of an increase in their size and market power. In the banking market, through various mergers, the number of banks was reduced by almost half between 1975 and 1977: from 14 to eight. In insurance, the number of companies was reduced from 40 to 27 in the same period. In oil refining, four companies were reunited in just one in 1976, which became a monopolist. In chemicals, three companies were merged into one also in 1976, which became the largest player in the market. In paper and paper pulp, five companies gave place to one, also with enormous market power. In electricity, 14 companies were replaced by just one in 1976, which became a monopolist. Seven cement firms were merged into one in 1977, acquiring also large market power. In beer production, five firms became one and in tobacco three were merged into one (Amaral 2015).

These new and much more powerful companies were used by the Government to expand investment. As private economic agents also became more confident after 1976, investment boomed in 1976 and 1977 (Fig. 6). The investment rate had reached unprecedented levels during the *Estado Novo*; a natural decline happened in 1975. But in 1977, the investment rate reached new heights, something that happened again in the early 1980s. One main link for this was the banking system: instrumentalized by Governments, the banks started practicing negative real interest rates; if this put them in serious solvability troubles, it also gave a strong push to investment

[30]Decree-law 375/74, 20 August 1974.

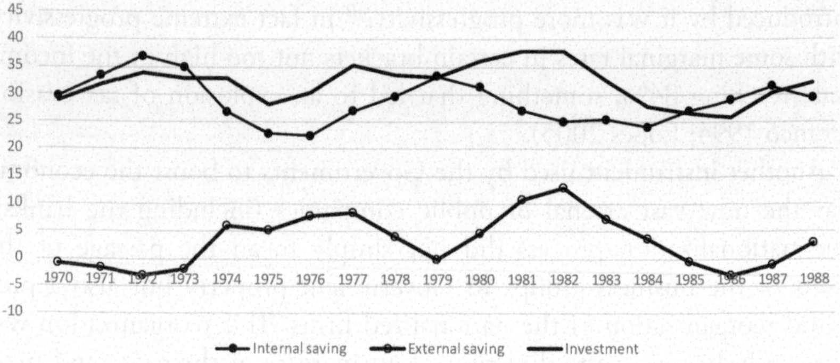

Fig. 6 Gross fixed capital formation, internal saving, and external saving, Portugal (1970–1988) (% of GDP) (*Source* Pinheiro [1997])

(Franco 1994; Lopes 1996). But the stimulus to investment came also from non-financial companies: there was in these years a spate of mega-projects, such as the installation of a new petrochemical plant in an industrial pole in Southern Portugal (in the town of Sines) that had been built in the final years of the *Estado Novo*, the expansion of the only steel plant existing in the country, the building of a new chemical plant or the reactivation of some mines (Lopes 1996). Small- and medium-sized private companies also gave a contribution in this context thanks to a more or less indiscriminate policy of Government and bank guarantee to their investments (Franco 1994). As Fig. 5 shows, a growing lack of match between investment and internal saving developed, something that helps to explain the international payments difficulties of the country.

This sort of approach to public spending and economic activity brought another fundamental transformation: that of monetary policy. Again, the break with the *Estado Novo* could not be clearer. The latter's approach to monetary policy was essentially anti-inflationary (even if inflation had started increasing in the final years of the regime). But the authorities of the new regime attributed only secondary importance to price stability. The link between the BoP's gold and currency reserves and money supply that defined the monetary system during the *Estado Novo* disappeared and was replaced by discretionary principles: the BoP acquired a series of new instruments to intervene in the money market,

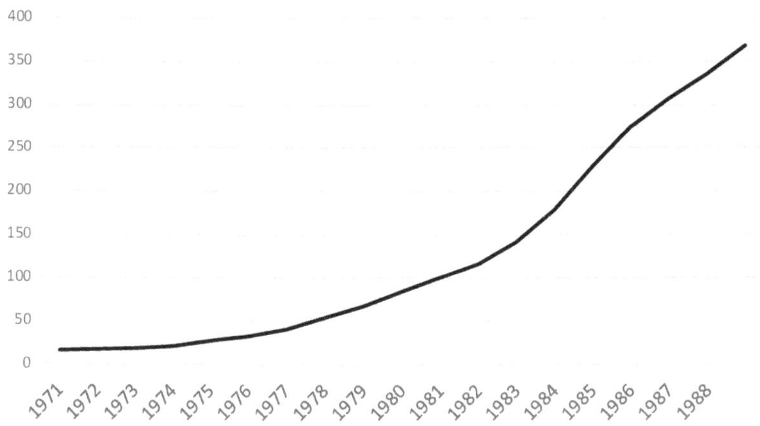

Fig. 7 Consumer price index, Portugal, 1971–1988 (1980 = 100) (*Source* Bastien [2001])

namely setting the interest rates practiced by banks and the level of their cash reserves.[31] The BoP also started to be concerned with the issue of short-run economic growth, besides being called to use money supply in order to finance the growing budget deficits. The inevitable consequence of this set of forces was an acceleration of inflation (Fig. 7).

It was the combination of all these factors that led to the appearance of serious problems of imbalance in international payments, so serious that they resulted in two IMF interventions, separated by just a few years. Everything started before 1976. The 1973 oil shock was the initial trigger, affecting more than just the price of oil: the price of many imported goods jumped as well. Economic activities had to deal immediately with an increase in costs as well as a decline in demand in foreign markets.

But we have to add to the exogenous shock the internal consequences of the 1974 revolution. One first consequence was the interruption of trade with the Overseas Provinces, as they entered into their

[31]Decree 644/75, 15 November 1975.

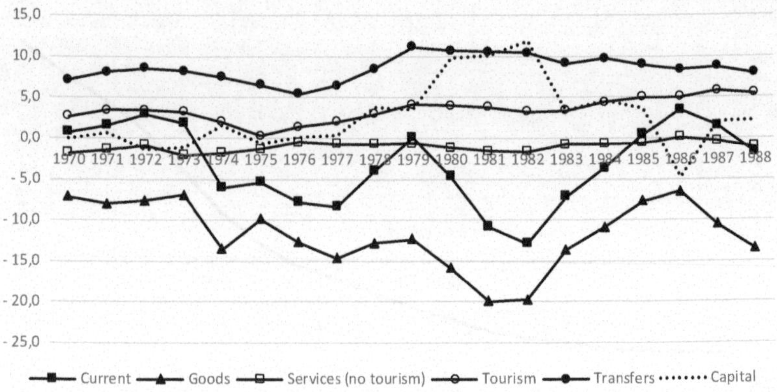

Fig. 8 Balance of payments, Portugal, 1970–1988 (% GDP) (*Source* Pinheiro [1997])

independentist processes. Since these transactions still represented 14% of the mainland's overall trade in 1973 (Clarence-Smith 1985), the impact was not negligible. Another consequence was the decline in tourism, with potential visitors avoiding Portugal, now seen as a risky destination, due to the revolutionary environment. A similar reasoning affected emigrants, who, fearing the destruction of their assets thanks to the volatile political situation, reduced the amount of remittances sent to Portugal. All of this can be seen in Fig. 8.

If these factors were roughly outside the control of Portuguese economic and social agents, the same cannot be said of other consequences of the revolution. One of the first reactions of the revolutionary authorities in order to try and control inflation was, as we have seen above, to set the prices of most goods and services by decree. At the same time, as strikes multiplied and labor unrest spread, the authorities accommodated most demands to increase wages, leading to a true wage explosion in 1974 and 1975. This created the perfect cocktail for difficulties in solvability of all kinds of firms, thus contributing to depress economic activity and to capital flight.

From this moment onward, the policies adopted followed a confusing path, some favoring the rebalance of international payments, others not. One of the first measures taken was a return to protectionism, something that had been in retraction since the 1940s. New tariffs

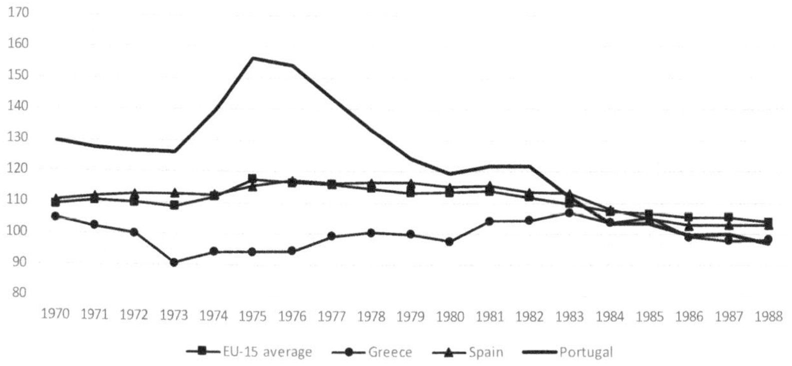

Fig. 9 Real unit labour costs; Portugal, Spain, Greece, and EU-15, 1970–1988 (2010 = 100) (*Source* AMECO)

were introduced in 1975, and a so-called sobretaxa (surcharge) of 20 and 30% over a vast and detailed array of imported goods was introduced in May 1975, and the system of discretionary licensing of imports was reinforced (Macedo et al. 1988).[32] The following year a protocol was signed with the EEC revising the conditions of the 1972 agreement: Portugal was allowed to increase by 20% the general tariff level in relation to imports from the EEC. Another measure was a depreciation of the escudo, although this was decided relatively late: it was only in the first half of 1976 that the monetary authorities started following this course of action, although not enough to accommodate the full explosion in costs (Macedo et al. 1988). At the same time, in 1976 and 1977, Governments became less tolerant of labor demands, something that, associated with the softening of the radicalization of workers and unions (thanks to unemployment), made wages decline. This time wages did not contribute to the deterioration of foreign imbalance, as their evolution from 1976 to 1978 completely offset the increase in the two previous years. The two movements in unit labor costs are clear in Fig. 9: the notable increase of 1974 and 1975 and the reversal of the next three years. If these aspects of the economic and social evolution of the period had a positive effect on the

[32]Decree-law 217-A/75, 31 May 1975.

international payments position of the country, the opposite happened with the many efforts to increase economic activity by banks and public companies. And the same can be said of fiscal policy, which became clearly expansionary. The net effect of such confusing measures was ultimately negative for the balance of payments (Fig. 8): a positive current account in the early 1970s was transformed into a negative one from 1974 onwards, reaching close to 8% of GDP in 1977.

The first reaction of the Governments to deal with these difficulties in international payments was to use the large amounts of reserves in foreign currency and gold at the BoP inherited from the previous regime (Lopes 1996). But as these reserves were eroded and the difficulties in payments got more serious in 1976 and 1977, other steps had to be taken. For a while it was possible to obtain loans from Western countries and institutions, bent on helping Portugal to remain within the "capitalist" side of the Cold War, such as EEC, EFTA, Bank of International Settlements, or Germany, Switzerland, and the US (Lopes 1996). But as the different steps taken by successive weak Governments were not enough to change the situation, a moment came when a more drastic recipe had to be used.

In 1977, two "austerity programs" were elaborated by the first non-provisional Government: the first in February, the other in August. Several prices were increased, interest rates too, bank credit was disciplined, taxes were raised and public investment reduced (Franco 1994; Mateus 2013). A policy of systematic currency depreciation was finally adopted, in order to compensate for the differential in inflation between Portugal and the other European countries: in February, the escudo was depreciated in 15% in relation to an average of reference currencies; in August, a new exchange rate policy was introduced: after one more ad hoc depreciation of 4%, the monetary authorities decided the escudo should depreciate 1% per month, a policy that received the name of crawling peg (Lopes 1996). This was accompanied by an increase in the BoP's discount rate to 6%, in August 1977, in order to avoid the most negative effects of depreciation in terms of capital flight and speculation against the currency (Mateus 2013). Protectionism was aggravated, through the introduction of quantitative restrictions on various imported goods, adding to the new tariffs coming from 1975 (Macedo et al. 1988).[33]

These measures had little effect, as can be seen in Fig. 8. Another large loan was then made to Portugal by a syndicate of countries led by the US, but now on one condition: that the country asked for IMF assistance (Lopes 1996). So, in May 1978, the Government signed a stand-by arrangement (SBA) with the IMF: the BoP was given the right to buy foreign currency from the IMF with no restrictions for the period of one year, but only insofar as a series of restrictive measures were adopted (Lopes 1982). The general thrust of the SBA was to contract internal demand: a ceiling was put on the credit to be granted by the banking system to economic activities in general and public companies in particular; interest rates, both of the BoP and the banking system, were raised; a ceiling was put on wage increase; the Government committed to a restrictive fiscal policy; and the prices set by the Government were increased, in order to avoid the scissors effect felt by firms between cost and revenue. The escudo was again depreciated by 6% in May 1978, at the time of the signing of the SBA (after another depreciation of 7% still in May, right before the SBA was signed), and the policy of monthly depreciation (the crawling peg) was reinforced, with the rate of depreciation increasing to 1.25% a month. Besides being an instrument to protect the economy from imports and stimulate exports, the aim of depreciation was to attract emigrant remittances again, something that the high-interest rates also sought to achieve (for all of this, see Lopes 1982, 1996; Mateus 2013). The Government also committed to phase out the various protectionist devices meanwhile that had meanwhile been put in place (Macedo et al. 1988).

The results of the program were very effective in terms of international balance, as Fig. 8 shows, and the worst fears concerning the deterioration of economic growth ended up by not materializing, as the economy kept on growing in a robust manner (Table 2). Some contribution for this joint positive result came from exports, whose share in GDP increased. But, as imports also grew, the contribution of

[33]Ordinance 51-D/77, 28 February 1977 and various legislative measures in August 1977.

the trade balance was only marginal. The essential contributions came from remittances, first, and tourism second, both returning in full force thanks to a new confidence in the stabilization of the country's political situation (Fig. 8). The Government, for instance, did not contribute to rebalance, as it did not comply with the reduction in the budget deficit negotiated with the IMF, on the contrary increasing it from 4% of GDP to 6% (Fig. 5). This was a problem the IMF allowed to be solved later, as well as the problem of inflation, which continued uncontrolled (Fig. 7).

But in 1979 and the early 1980s, a new combination of external and internal shocks reverted these positive steps. The trigger was again an oil shock, in 1979, in the sequence of the Iranian Revolution and the Iran–Iraq War. Terms of trade of the Portuguese economy deteriorated again (Lopes 1996). Much like the revolutionary Governments of 1974 and 1975, although now for electoral reasons, the Government in place took almost exactly the opposite steps it should have had in order to confront the external shock. Its objectives were two: to reduce inflation, first, and to spur economic growth, second. In 1980, the prices of the goods and services of public companies were freezed, and in May the gold reserves of the BoP were revalued, something that allowed for a appreciation of the escudo by 6%. At the same time, the monthly rate of the crawling peg was reduced to 0.5% (Franco 1994; Lopes 1996). The anti-inflationary effects of such policies were immediately visible—as a consequence, real wages improved substantially (Franco 1994). Meanwhile, the expansion of public spending continued. The largest contribution came from expenditure on the wages of civil servants' pay and from debt service (Fig. 3). The budget deficit reached 12% of GDP in 1982 (Fig. 5)—in reality the situation was even worse, as a hidden deficit had developed, resulting from delays in payment by the Government and public companies. According to the IMF, the overall budget deficit (including the hidden responsibilities) was of 18.5% of GDP in 1983 (Mateus 2013). Accompanying these developments there was also a new investment boom promoted by public companies: never had Portugal had such a high investment rate, with internal saving continuing not to be enough to finance it (Fig. 6).

As a consequence of the fact that these policies were adopted in a quite negative international context (with high import prices and most Western economies passing through a recession), the deterioration of foreign balance reached an unprecedented level: 12% of GDP in 1982. After two years of hesitant policies, there was no alternative but to ask for a new assistance program by the IMF. The new SBA was signed in September 1983, covering the period from October 1983 to February 1985: Portugal was given financial assistance but had again to comply with a series of contractionary measures. The aim of the program was the same as in the first case, although the measures were now more aggressive (as the situation was also more serious): reduce internal demand, increase external demand, attract foreign payments through interest rates and other instruments, and control the budget deficit. Consequently, the escudo depreciated 12% in June 1983 and the crawling peg rate was increased to 1% per month (before the program, some measures in the same direction had already been taken: the monthly rate of depreciation of the escudo under the crawling peg had been increased to 0.75% in December 1981 and an ad hoc depreciation of 9.4% had also been approved in June 1982) (Franco 1994). Credit ceilings to the economy were introduced again, as well as wage ceilings in the public sector. Investment programs by public companies were curtailed, controlled prices were liberalized, taxes were raised and public expenditure cut (Franco 1994). The Government committed again to suppress protectionist devices (Macedo et al. 1988).

As the initial measures taken under the SBA were not giving the expected results, especially in what concerns inflation and the budget deficit, the SBA was revised in 1984, with new objectives. The results of the program appeared quickly afterward, with foreign imbalance reducing rapidly: by 1984, the current account deficit had declined to just about 2% of GDP and in 1985 it had reached near balance (Fig. 8). The price in slower economic growth was now clear, however, contrary to what had happened during the first program. The secret to rebalancing this time was, precisely, the recession induced by the austerity measures, which improved the trade balance, as remittances and exchange brought in by tourists remained virtually at the same level: imports declined, as a consequence of reduction in demand, and exports as a share of GDP increased thanks to the fall of GDP itself (Fig. 8). The Government also gave some contribution, by reducing its deficit by two percentage points, but the figures continued extremely high, at 10% of GDP (Fig. 5). By 1985, when Portugal joined the EEC, fundamental external balance had been achieved, even if some problems were left unsolved, especially with respect to public finance (Fig. 5) and inflation (Fig. 7).

Besides their short-term impact, the interpretation of the revolutionary changes themselves is not a straightforward affair. Most of the changes represented little more than a process of convergence to the kind of institutions that had developed in Europe since the 1950s. This is clear in the case of the dismantling of the corporatist structure coming from the *Estado Novo*; it is also clear in what concerns the many changes in workers' rights (even if this meant that Portugal passed from being one of the countries where they were least protected into one where they were most protected); it is also clear in what respects the size and structure of public spending and nationalization, as most European countries had a large sector of public enterprises at the time, although the process went slightly beyond the European norm (Baklanoff 1996). Finally, the revolution went quite beyond traditional institutional changes in the case of "Agrarian Reform". So, to a certain extent, the revolutionary changes corresponded to a sort of delayed institutional convergence with the democratic regimes of Europe, especially when many of the revolutionary "exaggerations" were reverted after 1976.

4 Economic Growth and Change

The growth of the Portuguese economy was modest in this period: 1.6% per year between 1974 and 1985. But its main feature was volatility, oscillating between negative and positive periods (Table 2). This was reflected in its convergence path, which became erratic: the economy diverged abruptly, first, until 1976, and then converged strongly, until reaching the same comparative level ten years after the revolution, then it diverged suddenly again, during the second IMF intervention in the country. In the end, when the whole period is taken into consideration, the country was only able to keep the distance. During this faltering performance, the economy had to accommodate a true population shock, thanks to the arrival of the African colonists, the interruption of emigration and natural growth, so that resident population jumped practically 1 million between 1973 and 1976, from about 9 million to close to 10 million (Amaral 2009).

Structural change continued but took new directions. Employment in agriculture declined further, from 24% of overall employment in 1973 to 17.5% in 1985, but not in favor of industry, where the share of overall employment remained at 36% in the same period. Services were the sector where employment grew the most, with its share jumping from 38.5 to 46% (Fig. 10). The shares of output remained unaltered, however, despite these changes. Such behaviors reveal that productivity grew in agriculture but declined in the other sectors (Fig. 11). Indeed, the figures for sectoral productivity growth in the period 1973–1990 were 4% for agriculture, 0.7% for industry, and −0.1% for services (Lains 1994).

Most of the growth of agricultural productivity seems to have depended on the switch between branches rather than growth within branches (Soares 2005). Traditional crops as cereals fell from a share of

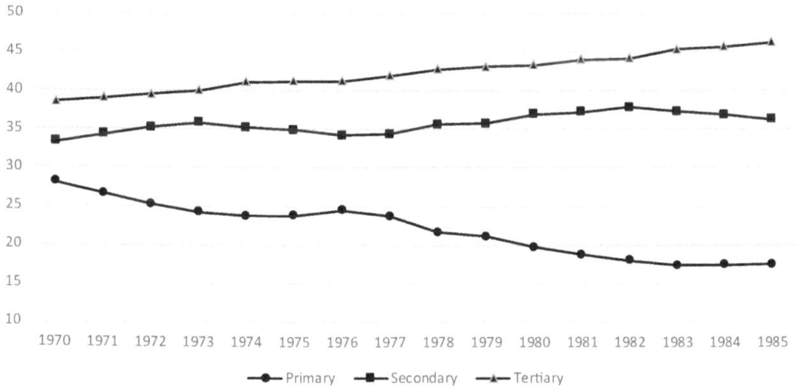

Fig. 10 Structure employment, Portugal, 1970–1985 (% overall employment) (*Source* Pinheiro [1997])

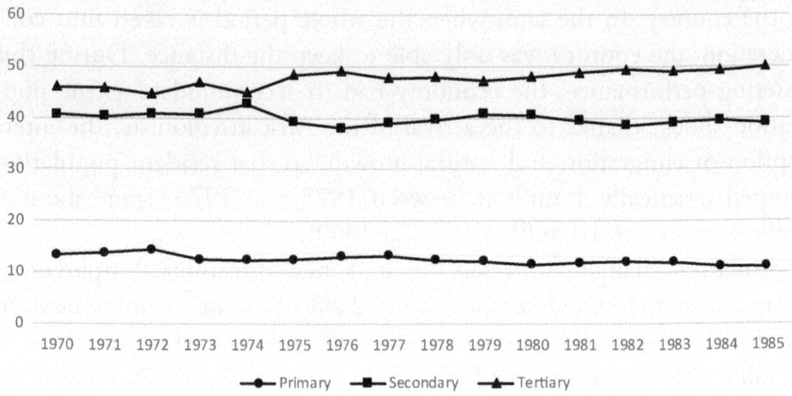

Fig. 11 Structure economy, Portugal, 1970–1985 (% GDP) (*Source* Pinheiro [1997])

agricultural output of 20 to 10% between 1970–1973 and 1987, wine from 13 to 5%, olive oil from 4.6 to 2%, and potatoes from 9.5 to 4.6%; on the contrary, more modern crops increased their share, such as fruits and vegetables, from 16.5 to 23.5%, becoming the largest branch, thus overtaking cereals; and the animal part of agricultural output also increased its share: meat, from 22 to 30%, and dairy, from 9 to 11.4% (Pinto et al. 1984; Lains 2009; Avillez et al. 2004). The beginning of the full operation of some irrigation schemes coming from the previous period certainly helped this result, but perhaps the most visible change in the Portuguese primary sector was the development of pig and chicken farming, activities of much higher capital-intensity and productivity. Additionally, the general process of factor substitution, with capital replacing an increasingly scarce labor factor, continued: tractors and various types of machines spread through the Portuguese countryside (Pinto et al. 1984).

In industry, a sort of opposite process happened, with more traditional branches recovering their importance and more modern ones declining: food and beverages passed from 15% of industrial output in 1973 to 20% in 1985, and textiles from 22 to 28%; on the contrary, metal products dropped their share from 25 to 19%. All other branches (wood and cork, paper and paper pulp, chemicals and oil, cement, and basic metals) kept their size (Aguiar and Martins 2005). Services also retained a traditional profile, essentially based on wholesale and retail trade (Pinheiro 1997). These movements in the structure of the sector reveal the incentives to exports after 1977, as a consequence of the adoption of a policy of continuous depreciation of the escudo, not only as a choice of Portuguese authorities but also advised by the IMF, under whose supervision the Portuguese economy remained for half of this period. In this respect, the crawling peg policy adopted from 1977 onwards must have had a particularly strong impact.

An initial inversion of the path coming from the last years of the *Estado Novo* respected protectionism, which increased, making the country diverge for a while in relation to Europe: as Fig. 12 shows the average weight of tariffs over imports passed from 4% in 1973 to 7% in 1977. The reversal was not complete, however, as there was no return to the tariff levels existing before participation in EFTA. This reflects the adoption of the surcharge and the revision of the tariff schedule mentioned above, to which must be added the return of quantitative restrictions, which are not reflected in these figures but survived well within the second half of the 1980s. We must also note that such kinds of restrictions were used at the time by European countries as well, as instruments to deal with the crisis, meaning that the picture arising

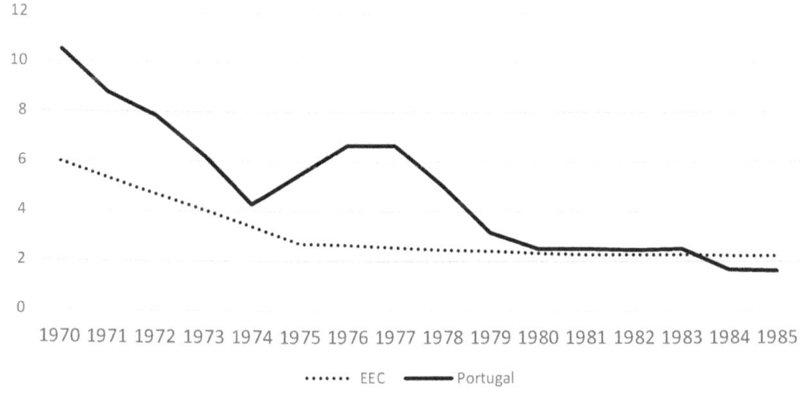

Fig. 12 Average tariffs % of imports, Portugal and EEC/EU, 1970–1985 (*Source* Portugal—Fontoura and Valério [2001]; EEC/EU: adapted from Dür [2008])

from Fig. 12 is incomplete (Van der Wee 1986). The decline in the Portuguese tariff level after 1977 reflects the impositions of the IMF under its 1978–1979 and 1983–1985 interventions.

Banking was very heavily affected by the revolution. Its institutional environment was radically altered in 1975, when the commercial banking sector was involved in the nationalization wave of that year. Despite a Government control that was stronger than in the previous regime, the number of operations open to banks was enlarged in this period: they were authorized to open foreign currency accounts, as long as they belonged to Portuguese emigrants (in 1975), to open accounts of non-residents, although only for time deposits (in 1977), and to give medium- to long-run credit (in 1977). All interest rates used by banks, rather than established by decree as in the *Estado Novo*, were set by the Bank of Portugal (BoP), which meanwhile had also been nationalized in 1974. The BoP was also given the power to set the ratio of commercial banks' currency reserves, which before had been set by decree. The population of commercial banks had important changes during this period. In 1974, the market was constituted by 16 commercial banks, which appropriated 80% of deposits. Virtually all the rest was appropriated by CGD, with a share of 18%. Between 1975 and 1976, all non-incorporated banks disappeared. Between 1976 and 1978, the Government (now the sole owner of commercial banks) promoted the merging of various banks thus reducing their number to eight (Martins and Rosa 1979; Valério et al. 2010). Under this framework, the banking system was largely manipulated by the Government both to stimulate economic activity, through various investment plans, or help the dwindling finances of the Government.

In order to explain the behavior of the Portuguese economy in this period, we can still rely on growth accounting. Several exercises of the kind exist for this period and, although their results diverge somehow, the overall picture is clear: capital continued to give a strong contribution to growth while TFP reduced its contribution or even gave a negative one (Silva and Lains 2013) (Table 3).

None of these features is exactly surprising, taking into consideration the institutional evolution described in this chapter. On the one

Table 3 Growth accounting, various studies, 1947–1975

		Annual growth rates			
References	Periods	Labor	Capital	Human capital	TFP
Afonso (1999)	1974–1985	0.7	1.5	–	0.2
Lains (2003)	1973–1990	0.1	1.7	1.6	0.6
Silva and Lains (2013)	1973–1991	0.2	2.1	–	1.0
Mateus (2005)	1975–1985	−0.1	1.7	1.4	0.7
Amador and Coimbra (2007)	1975–1985	0.2	3.3	–	−0.3

Source Afonso (1999), Lains (2003), Silva and Lains (2013), Mateus (2005), and Amador and Coimbra (2007)

hand, investment continued to expand quickly, although now for different reasons than in the *Estado Novo* period: then, it was essentially the protection of property rights stimulating private agents to invest; now, investment depended mostly on public companies, under governmental direction. And, as we have seen above, the Portuguese authorities adopted programs of mass investment in different moments after 1974, exerting their influence especially in favor of heavy industry ventures. It is again not surprising that the investment rate remained high throughout the period, at around 25% (Freitas 2005). Additionally, saving continued to be abundant, because emigrant remittances returned to high levels, after the initial reduction. As we have seen above, however, there was a growing mismatch between internal saving and internal investment, which was solved with the various international loans the country received, including IMF assistance. A problem of productivity of capital appeared, however: the governmental investment programs proved to be very inefficient, delivering erratic growth, and despite the large amounts involved; also, a lot of public investment was directed at equipment for public services that had been neglected by the authoritarian regime (schools, hospitals, social housing, sewage, telephone lines, electricity lines…): even if these investments had a long-run positive impact on the growth of the economy, initially they delivered very little return (Lopes 1996).

In what concerns reasons for the decline of TFP the causes were various. Clearly, the low productivity of investment just mentioned was one. Another was a decline of the capital-labor ratio in the sequence of the sudden abundance of labor resulting from the return of the colonists and of the demobilized soldiers, together with the slowing-down of emigration. The situation created incentives for the growth of labor-intensive activities, with lower technology and skill content. The expansion of the more traditional industrial sectors (and services) is certainly a reflection of this (Amaral 2010). Then, we have the effects of nationalization: although industrial conditioning was abolished, thus eliminating one possible source of inefficiency, a substantial fraction of the industrial sector started operating under public monopoly and oligopoly conditions without much consideration for the efficient use of resources.

Finally, we should consider the contribution from human capital, which, in the growth accounting exercises that considered it as a factor of production, gives a sizable contribution to growth, almost on a par with physical capital. This was certainly the result of the expansion of the means dedicated by the Government to education, as we have seen above, although the process was not as straightforward as it may seem. In the initial years after the revolution, there was a decline of the number of students in both secondary and university education, as a consequence of various effects of the economic crisis on the incentives of households to send their children to school. But from the late 1970s and early 1980s onwards, the picture changed completely and the number of students increased massively (Amaral 2005).

References

Afonso, Óscar. 1999. *Contributo do Comércio Externo para o Crescimento Económico Português, 1960–93*. Lisbon: Conselho Económico e Social.

Aguiar, Álvaro, and Manuel M.F. Martins. 2005. A indústria. In *História Económica de Portugal, 1700–2000, Vol. III, O Século XX*, ed. Pedro Lains and Álvaro Ferreira da Silva, 185–226. Lisbon: ICS.

Amador, João, and Carlos Coimbra. 2007. Characteristics of the Portuguese Economic Growth: What Has Been Missing? Banco de Portugal Working Paper, 8/2007.

Amaral, Luciano. 2005. O trabalho. In *História Económica de Portugal, 1700–2000, Vol. III, O Século XX*, ed. Pedro Lains and Álvaro Ferreira da Silva, 65–90. Lisbon: ICS.

———. 2009. New Series of Portuguese Population and Employment, 1950–2007: Implications for GDP Per Capita and Labor Productivity. *Análise Social* 44 (193): 767-791.

———. 2010. *Economia Portuguesa—As Últimas Décadas*. Lisbon: Relógio d'Água/FFMS.

———. 2015. *Em Nome do Pai e do Filho....* Lisbon: Publicações D. Quixote.

AMECO. https://ec.europa.eu/info/business-economy-euro/indicators-statistics/economic-databases/macro-economic-database-ameco/ameco-database_en.

Avillez, Francisco, et al. 2004. *Rendimento e Competitividade Agrícolas em Portugal. Evolução Recente. Situação Actual e Perspectivas Futuras*. Lisbon: Almedina.

Baganha, Maria Ioannis. 1994. As correntes emigratórias portuguesas no século XX e o seu impacto na economia nacional. *Análise Social* 29 (128): 959–980.

Baklanoff, Erik N. 1996. Breve experiência de socialismo em Portugal: o sector das empresas estatais. *Análise Social* 31 (138): 932–935.

Barreto, António. 1987. *Anatomia de uma Revolução. A Reforma Agrária em Portugal, 1974–1976*. Lisbon: Publicações Europa-América.

Bastien, Carlos. 2001. Preços e salários. In *Estatísticas Históricas Portuguesas*, ed. Nuno Valério, 615–655. Lisbon: INE.

Campos, António Correia de, and Jorge Simões. 2011. *O Percurso da Saúde: Portugal na Europa*. Coimbra: Almedina.

Carreira, Henrique Medina. 1996. As políticas sociais em Portugal. In *A Situação Social em Portugal, 1960–1995*, ed. António Barreto. Lisbon: ICS.

Clarence-Smith, Gervase. 1985. *The Third Portuguese Empire, 1825–1975: A Study in Economic Imperialism*. Manchester: Manchester University Press.

The Conference Board. https://www.conference-board.org/data/economydatabase/index.cfm?id=27762.

Crafts, Nicholas, and Gianni Toniolo (eds.). 1996. *Economic Growth in Europe Since 1945*. Cambridge: Cambridge University Press.

Cunha, Alice. 2015. Underwriting Democracy: Portugal and European Economic Community's Accession. *Cahiers de la Méditerranée* 90: 1–12.

Dür, Andreas. 2008. Bargaining Power and Trade Liberalization: European External Trade Policies in the 1960s. *European Journal of International Relations* 14 (4) (December): 645–669.

Eichengreen, Barry. 2007. *The European Economy Since 1945: Coordinated Capitalism and Beyond*. Princeton: Princeton University Press.

Fontoura, Ana Paula, and Nuno Valério. 2001. Relações económicas externas. In *Estatísticas Históricas Portuguesas*, ed. Nuno Valério, 713–739. Lisbon: INE.

Franco, António de Sousa. 1994. A economia. In *Portugal, 20 Anos de Democracia*, coord. António Reis, 170–293. Lisboa: Círculo de Leitores.

Freitas, Miguel Lebre de. 2005. O capital. In *História Económica de Portugal, 1700–2000, Vol. III, O Século XX*, ed. Pedro Lains and Álvaro Ferreira da Silva, 91–124. Lisbon: ICS.

Lains, Pedro. 1994. O Estado e a industrialização em Portugal, 1945–1990. *Análise Social* 29 (128): 923–958.

———. 2003. Catching up to the European Core: Portuguese Economic Growth, 1910–1990. *Explorations in Economic History* 40: 369–386.

———. 2009. The Role of Agriculture in Portuguese Economic Development, 1870–1973. In *Agriculture and Economic Growth in Europe since 1870*, ed. Pedro Lains and Vicente Pinilla, 333–352. London: Routledge.

Lima, Teresa Maneca. 2015. The History of Health Policies in Portugal: A Look at Recent Trends. *Research and Networks in Health* 1: 1–11.

Lindert data sets for *Growing Public* book. http://economics.ucdavis.edu/people/fzlinder/peter-linderts-webpage/data-and-estimates/lindert-data-for-cup-book.

Lopes, José da Silva. 1982. IMF Conditionality in the Stand-By Arrangement with Portugal of 1978. *Estudos de Economia* 3 (2) (January–March): 141–166.

———. 1996. *A Economia Portuguesa desde 1960*. Lisboa: Gradiva.

———. 2005. Finanças Públicas. In *História Económica de Portugal, 1700–2000, Vol. III, O Século XX*, ed. Pedro Lains and Álvaro Ferreira da Silva, 265–304. Lisbon: ICS.

Lucena, Manuel de, and Carlos Gaspar. 1991. Metamorfoses corporativas? Associações de interesses económicos e institucionalização da democracia em Portugal (I). *Análise Social* 26 (114): 847–903.

———. 1992. Metamorfoses corporativas? Associações de interesses económicos e institucionalização da democracia em Portugal (II). *Análise Social* 27 (115): 135–187.

Macedo, Jorge Braga de, Cristina Corado, and Manuel Lopes Porto. 1988. The Timing and Sequencing of Trade Liberalization Policies: Portugal 1948–1986. Faculdade de Economia da Universidade Nova de Lisboa Working Paper, 114.

Martins, Maria Belmira, and João Chaves Rosa. 1979. *O Grupo Estado: Análise e Listagem Completa das Sociedades do Sector Público Empresarial*. Lisbon: Jornal Expresso.

Mata, Maria Eugénia. 2001. Finanças públicas e dívida pública. In *Estatísticas Históricas Portuguesas*, ed. Nuno Valério, 657–712. Lisbon: INE.

Mateus, Abel. 2005. A tecnologia. In *História Económica de Portugal, 1700–2000, Vol. III, O Século XX*, ed. Pedro Lains and Álvaro Ferreira da Silva, 125–156. Lisbon: ICS.

———. 2013. *Economia Portuguesa: Evolução no Contexto Internacional (1910–2013)*. Lisbon: Principia.

Mauro, Paolo, Rafael Romeu, Ariel Binder, and Asad Zaman. 2013. *A Modern History of Fiscal Prudence and Profligacy*. IMF Working Paper, 13/5.

Mozzicafreddo, Juan. 2000. *Estado-Providência e Cidadania em Portugal*. Oeiras: Celta.

Pinheiro, Maximiano (ed.). 1997. *Séries Longas para a Economia Portuguesa, Pós-II Guerra Mundial, Vol. I - Séries Estatísticas*. Lisbon: Banco de Portugal.

Pinto, Armando Sevinate, Francisco Avillez, Luís Albuquerque, and Luís Frazão Gomes. 1984. *A Agricultura Portuguesa no Período 1950–1980*. Lisbon: IN-CM.

Pires, Rui Pena, Maria José Maranhão, João P. Quintela, Fernando Moniz, and Manuel Pisco. 1984. *Os Retornados. Um Estudo Sociográfico*. Lisbon: Instituto de Estudos para o Desenvolvimento.

Ramos, Rui, Bernardo Vasconcelos e Sousa, and Nuno Gonçalo Monteiro. 2009. *História de Portugal*. Lisbon: A Esfera dos Livros.

Reis, António. 1994. A política. In *Portugal, 20 Anos de Democracia*, coord. António Reis, 8–111. Lisboa: Círculo de Leitores.

Santos, Maria de Lurdes Lima dos, Marinús Pires de Lima, and Vítor Matias Ferreira. 1976–1977. *O 25 de Abril e as Lutas Sociais nas Empresas*. Porto: Afrontamento.

Silva, Ester Gomes da, and Pedro Lains. 2013. Capital Formation and Long-Run Growth: Evidence from Portuguese Data, 1910–2011. Paper Presented at Iberometrics III, Zaragoza University.

Soares, Fernando Brito. 2005. A agricultura. In *História Económica de Portugal, 1700–2000, Vol. III, O Século XX*, ed. Pedro Lains and Álvaro Ferreira da Silva, 157–183. Lisbon: ICS.

Valério, Nuno. 2004. Nationalizations and Privatizations in Portugal During the Last Quarter of the Twentieth Century: Were They Profitable to the State? *Revista de História Económica e Social* 7 (2ª série): 129–143.

Valério, Nuno, Ana Bela Nunes, Carlos Bastien, Rita Martins de Sousa, and Sandra Domingos Costa. 2010. *História do Sistema Bancário Português, Vol. II, Da Assunção pelo Banco de Portugal das Funções de Banco Central à União Monetária Europeia*. Lisbon: Banco de Portugal.

Van Der Wee, Herman. 1986. *Prosperity and Upheaval: The World Economy, 1945–1980*. London: Penguin Books.

World Development Indicators. http://datatopics.worldbank.org/world-development-indicators/.

7

The European Period (1986–2017)

This book ends almost in the same manner as it started: with a financial crisis. On 6 April 2011, the Portuguese Government requested international assistance in order to deal with its foreign financial commitments. This was the culmination of a crisis that had started in 2008, accompanying similar events around the world. But in the case of Portugal, this negative cycle was inserted into an already ongoing medium-run trend of mediocre growth. The crisis was not like in many other countries, a negative event (a "black swan") interrupting a phase of persistent and healthy growth. It was, rather, a sort of coda into an already worrying economic situation.

This chapter shows that the bad behavior of the Portuguese economy comes almost from the beginning of the participation of the country in the European Union (EU) in 1986, or the European Economic Community (EEC), as it was called in those days. These difficulties were not immediately visible from the start, thanks to an initial trajectory (between 1986 and 1992) of strong growth. But signs of stress were already visible then, namely in the deterioration of the trade and current accounts. Most of that stress had to do with the adoption of a monetary and exchange rate policy that led to real exchange rate appreciation

L. Amaral, *The Modern Portuguese Economy in the Twentieth and Twenty-First Centuries*, Palgrave Studies in Economic History,
https://doi.org/10.1007/978-3-030-24548-1_7

and, consequently, competitiveness decline. From 1977 to 1986, the economy got geared to the crawling peg, as we have seen in the previous chapter. This allowed for improved competitiveness, although one based on continuous exchange rate depreciation. But between 1986 and 1990, the rate of depreciation under the crawling peg regime slowed-down, and the regime was completely abandoned after 1990, as the Portuguese authorities adopted an exchange rate-based disinflation policy. Disinflation was successful but not enough to fully cover the inflation differential with the rest of the EEC/EU countries for a long time, meaning that real exchange rate appreciation was a hallmark of the economy until the early twenty-first century. A growing external imbalance developed, which could only be covered by an equivalent external indebtedness in relation to EU countries having external surpluses. Some literature links this process to the Economic and Monetary Union (EMU), starting in 1999. This chapter shows that, in reality, it started much before. The Portuguese economic troubles of the last quarter century result from a combination of a specific "Portuguese problem" with a wider "European problem", and the latter did not start with EMU but rather with the early efforts in the mid-1980s of increased economic integration within the EEC/EU.

1 European Misfit

Figure 4 in the Introduction shows that the difficulties of the Portuguese economy in inserting into the EU context were somehow masked by an extraordinary initial process of convergence: in a matter of six years (1986–1992), the Portuguese economy closed 15% of the gap differentiating it from the richest economies—in the case of the sample used for comparison in Fig. 4 of the Introduction, the gap passed from about 50% to about 35%. The explanation for this process lies in a set of very favorable circumstances in the second half of the 1980s. On the one hand, the price of oil fell by about 50% in world markets between 1984 and 1986. If, in 1973 and 1979, the increase in the price of oil had been the main trigger for the deterioration of external accounts, now the opposite happened. On the other hand,

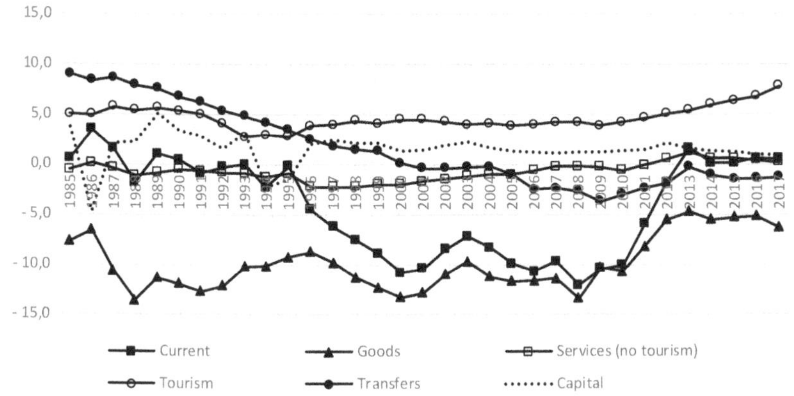

Fig. 1 Balance of payments, Portugal, 1985–2017 (% GDP) (*Source* 1985–1995—Pinheiro [1997]; 1996–2017—INE)

the period followed the successful rebalancing of external accounts in the sequence of the second IMF intervention. To this, we must add a short but ephemeral influx of FDI, which passed from a residual level to 4% of GDP in 1990 (Silva 2016). Finally, the EEC structural funds started entering the economy in the same period, in a proportion that reached about 1.5% of GDP per year until the 1990s—in some years reaching almost 4% (Amaral 2010).

Despite all these positive features, the process was also accompanied by many signs of external balance stress, as shown by the balance of payments in Fig. 1. We can extract many conclusions from this figure: first that, after the heavy effort to rebalance during the 1983–1985 IMF intervention, with the current account passing from −13% of GDP in 1982 to a 3.5% surplus in 1986, external imbalance threatened to return, thanks to the doubling of the size of the trade deficit. From the mid-1990s onward, the current account deficit did return and became a very serious problem. This deterioration was mostly determined by the trade deficit, which passed from −6.5% in 1986 to −13.5% in 1988, remaining at that level until 2010. The Portuguese trade deficit has historically been more than compensated by transfers, mostly emigrant remittances. The situation repeated after 1986 and until the early- to mid-1990s. But emigrant remittances started to decline, slowly but persistently, since the early 1980s (when they reached about 11% of GDP). In 1996, they had dropped to 3%. In the mid-1990s, the current account began a process of continuous deterioration, reaching levels around −10% of GDP during the first decade of the twenty-first century. EEC/EU transfers (classified in the capital account in Fig. 1) also helped to balance international payments. But they became increasingly less important and even residual since the beginning of the twenty-first century. In the first decades of the twenty-first century, the net balance of remittances became negative, an absolute novelty in modern Portuguese economic history. Emigration became a residual population movement and the amounts sent in the form of remittances by the communities of Portuguese emigrants became increasingly smaller. On the contrary, some immigration movements occurred in those years, leading to an outward flux of remittances. Consequently, the net effect of remittances has become negative since the first decade of the twenty-first century. Tourism kept its relative contribution at around 5% of GDP until the second decade of the twenty-first century, but then it has started increasing consistently, reaching in 2017 about the double of that value (8% of GDP). The recent overall rebalance of the Portuguese external accounts (from 2012 onward) has followed the pattern of the 1983–1985 external intervention: growth of imports halted thanks to the strong recession induced by the stabilization program accompanying foreign assistance.

The general message of the evolution of the Portuguese external accounts is that almost the entire "European period" (i.e., since the country joined the EEC) was one of external imbalance. This contradicts in part the idea that the responsibility for its recent difficulties lay only with EMU (as proposed, for instance, by Blanchard 2007; Holinski et al. 2012; Gros 2012). Figure 1 does show that EMU has not allowed for rebalancing, but it also shows that the deterioration of the external position of the economy started before, namely in the last decade of the twentieth century.

Figures 2, 3, and 4 add some more information: it is normally said that joining the EEC allowed for Portugal to increase openness; Fig. 2 shows that this is not exactly correct. The degree of openness of the economy increased rapidly between 1977 and 1985 and then stabilized

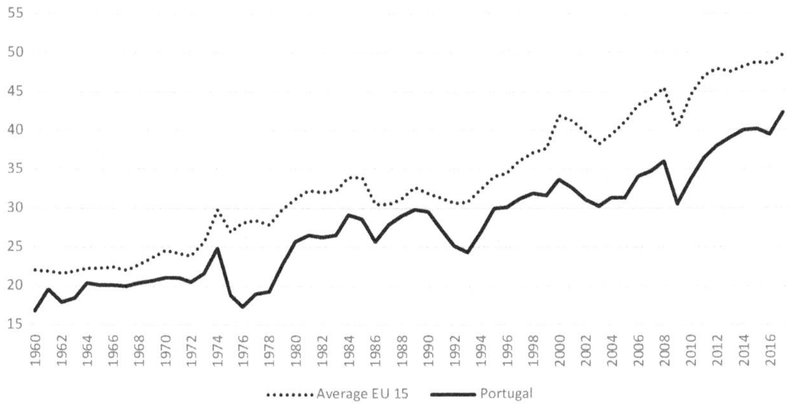

Fig. 2 Openness of the economy, Portugal and average EU-15, 1985–2017 (% GDP) Current prices; (*Note* Openness is measured as 1/2 × (exports + imports)/GDP. *Source* Portugal—Pinheiro [1997]; EU 15—AMECO)

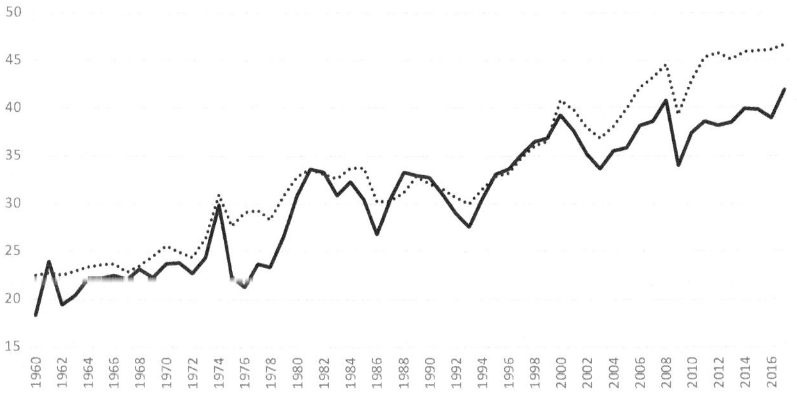

Fig. 3 Imports, Portugal and average EU-15, 1985–2017 (% GDP) Current prices; (*Source* Same as Fig. 2)

until the end of the first decade of the twenty-first century, expanding again only afterward (although most of the latest increase was due to the slowing down of GDP). When comparing the degree of openness of the Portuguese economy with the economies of the EU and EMU, as is done in Fig. 2, we get to interesting conclusions. First, that the

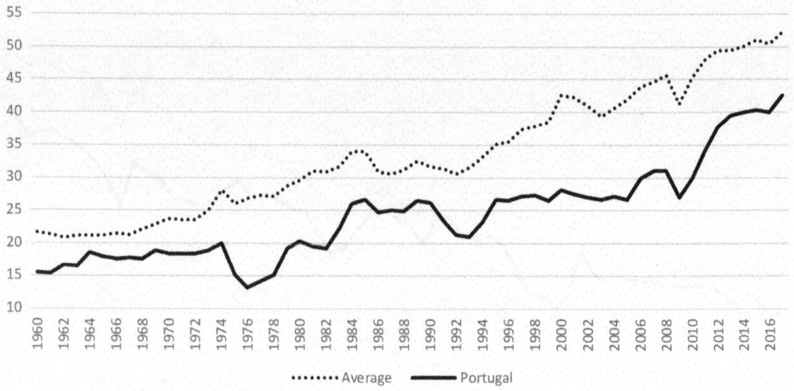

Fig. 4 Exports, Portugal and average EU-15, 1985–2017 (% GDP) Current prices; (*Source* Same as Fig. 2)

Portuguese economy increased openness between 1976 and 1984, allowing it to return to the comparative level of openness existing before the 1974 revolution. The gap between Portugal and the EU-15 countries was kept until the early twenty-first century, but then the trends changed completely, with the European economies increasing their openness, contrary to the Portuguese one. Portugal continues to be among the least open countries in the EU, especially taking into consideration its size (Amador and Cabral 2014).

More interesting still is the information obtained by decomposing openness into its constituent parts, imports and exports. When considering imports, its weight on Portuguese GDP has historically been within the European average. A slight change occurred in the early twenty-first century, when that weight increased in European countries but not in Portugal (Fig. 3). As for exports, the picture is completely different: Portuguese exports as a share of GDP have stayed persistently below the European average since the 1960s. Again the period of the second half of the 1970s stands out as one where the growth of this share was notable. Equally notable is the fact that the weight of exports remained virtually the same for almost the entirety of the period analyzed in this chapter: around 35% of GDP from 1986 to 2010, changing only from then on, and this last spurt is again explainable by the collapse of GDP during the crisis. Since the mid-1990s, that the Portuguese economy is among those where exports least weigh on GDP within Europe (Fig. 4).

What the set of information just presented reveals is a structural difficulty of the Portuguese economy to cope with the integration brought by both the EEC/EU and EMU. The question arises naturally: was this an exclusively Portuguese problem or was it a problem of the whole European project? Figure 5 illustrates the process of convergence of GDP per capita among the participating countries of the EU and shows that, independently of the chosen group of countries, convergence stopped after the 1980s and 1990s. The largest group is that of the EU 28 (or the form the union takes currently). Strikingly, considering that this group includes a large number of former Eastern Bloc countries, convergence was faster between 1950 and the 1980s. Then it stopped and even turned into divergence for a while (although in the special period of disaggregation of communist Europe). In the early twenty-first century, convergence returned but only recently has the gap returned to the same level of the early 1980s. The other group

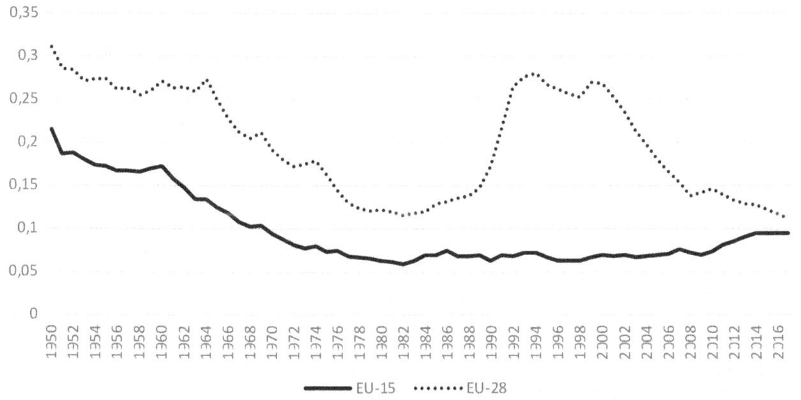

Fig. 5 Convergence in the EU, 1950–2017, GDP per capita (*Note* The information in the graph refers to σ-convergence, which is measured as: $\sigma_t = \left[\frac{1}{n}\sum_{i=1}^{n}(\ln y_{it} - \ln \bar{y}t)^2\right]^{1/2}$, where $\ln y_{it}$ is the natural logarithm of GDP per capita in country i at time t and $\ln \bar{y}t$ is the natural logarithm of the average of GDP per capita in the sample under consideration, constituted of n observations. GDP=GDP per capita in 2017 US$ [converted to 2017 price level with updated 2011 PPPs]. *Source* The Conference Board)

considered is that of the EU-15: here again, convergence halted from the 1980s onward. All of this shows that the EU has stopped being a convergence engine since the 1980s, precisely when Portugal joined the club. It is very interesting to verify that convergence was much stronger in the period when Europe was divided into three different blocs (EFTA, the EEC, and the communist bloc), one of them not even sharing the same market mechanisms as the other two. It was when integration got stronger that convergence stopped. The problem of the Portuguese economy within the EU cannot, thus, be seen in isolation from a wider European problem.

2 Institutional Convergence

The most notable feature of Portuguese society and its political system in the period following the country's accession to EEC was its institutional convergence with the more developed countries. This was especially visible in an increased role taken by the Government, mostly associated with the construction of what we might call the Portuguese version of the modern Welfare State. In 1974, public spending weighted about 23% of GDP, much below what was already common in Western Europe at the time (when the average was 40%); in 1985, the figure was practically the double, at around 45%, but still below the European average (then at about 50%); in the early twenty-first century, the level of public spending in Portugal overtook that of the most developed European countries, with a 55% level (50% on average in the EU-15) (Fig. 6). Financing this growth has not always been easy, however, due to the relatively slow performance of the Portuguese economy since the 1970s (Lopes 2005).

The new role of the Government has been translated not only into an increase of size but also a transformation of the structure of spending. Military expenditure converged to the levels that became common in Europe after World War II, between 1 and 2% of GDP. On the contrary, social items grew steadily. Adding social security expenditure to expenditure on health care and education gives a weight of about 30% of GDP in the second decade of the twenty-first century for these social

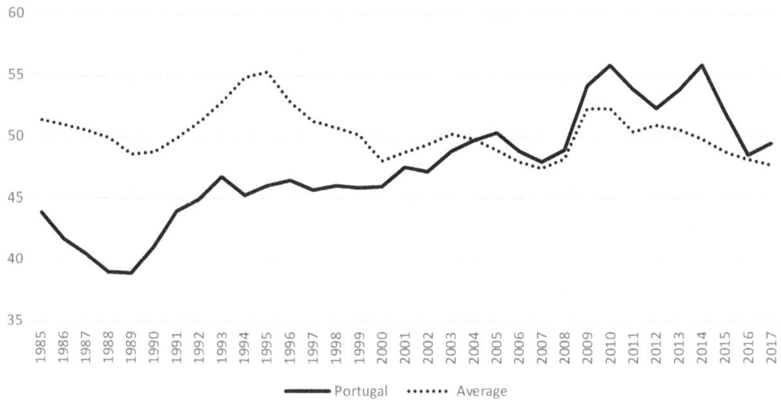

Fig. 6 Public spending (% GDP), Portugal and average European countries, 1985–2017 (*Source* Same as Fig. 2)

items, with health care and education reaching a proportion between 6 and 7% each (Fig. 7). All these proportions are well within the European average (Lopes 2005; Cunha and Braz 2006, 2009) (Fig. 8). For a while, new resources coming from the decline of debt service and large amounts resulting from a privatization program implemented in the 1990s were available to finance these expenditures. But when those resources were exhausted and economic growth started to falter, difficulties appeared.

Social spending grew mostly because of social security, as it transitioned from the corporatist model of the *Estado Novo* into a fully governmentalized one. The hallmark in this respect was the approval of a General Social Security Law (*Lei de Bases da Segurança Social*) in 1984.[1] Thanks to it, many of the different corporatist subsystems inherited from the previous regime were integrated into a single public one—even if some of the old corporatist schemes have still survived. The item weighing the most on social security spending is pensions (mostly old age, but also disability and survival). Pensions have grown due to various reasons: because of increases in value many times above inflation rates, because of an

[1]Law 28/84, 14 August 1984.

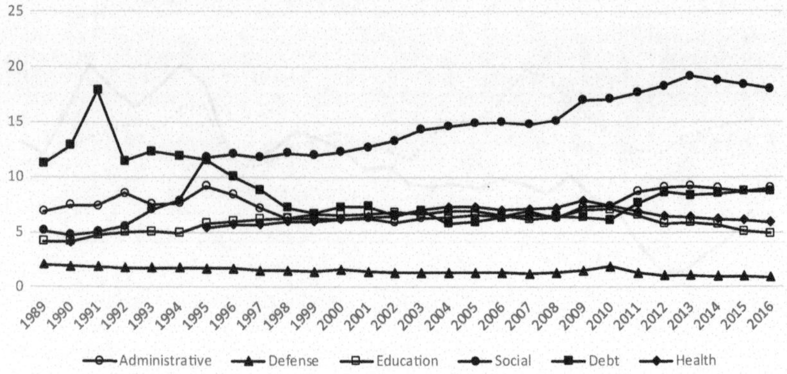

Fig. 7 Structure public spending, Portugal, 1988–2016 (% GDP) (*Source* 1989–1994—Mata [2001]; 1995–2016— Eurostat; except Health 1990—Carreira [1996])

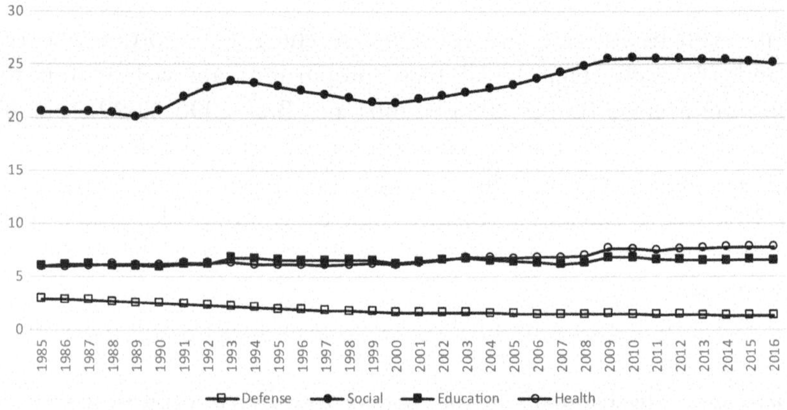

Fig. 8 Structure of public spending—average EU 15 (some items), 1985–2016 (% GDP) (*Source* Social Spending—OECD Social Expenditure database; Health 1985–1994—Lindert data sets for Growing Public book chained for 1995–2016 with General Government expenditure by function—Eurostat; Education 1985–1994—World Development Indicators—World Bank chained with General Government expenditure by function—Eurostat; for Defense: Military Expenditure database, World Development Indicators, and World Bank)

expanding number of pensioners, because of the growth of the value of average pensions (as the Portuguese workforce gets more qualified), and, essentially, because of population aging (Silva et al. 2014).

The growth of expenditure in Health Care has been determined by the expansion of the National Health Service. As the population uses more health services, in a process also not independent from aging, the amounts spent by the Government have expanded vastly (Campos and Simões 2011). The growth in expenditure in education has been determined by a consistent policy of growth of the public education system. As most of the effort to spread primary education had already been done by the *Estado Novo* (see Chapters 4 and 5), the democratic regime put most of its effort in the growth of both the secondary and university levels: a large number of schools were built and of professors recruited; the levels of compulsory schooling were increased throughout time, passing from eight years at the end of the authoritarian regime to nine, in 1986,[2] and 12, in 2009 (Teixeira et al. 2014).[3]

The Government has also been responsible for significant modernization of infrastructure, especially roads, something that has made Portugal acquire one of the best road networks in the world (Amaral 2010). Many of the financial difficulties that the construction of the Portuguese Welfare State has faced result from the circumstances in which the process took place. Most Western countries built their welfare states during the period of the golden age of economic growth: in those days, it was not difficult to raise public spending in a rapid fashion. By the 1970s, the countries of Western Europe had reached a level of public spending that Portugal would only reach in the early twenty-first century (Fig. 6). This means that Portugal started the process precisely when slow growth became the norm in the Western world, something that led to many sustainability problems.

If the structure of spending changed, some innovations appeared also on the side of receipts: a tax reform was implemented between 1984 and 1988, altering in a definite manner the tax structure still coming from the *Estado Novo*. The first crucial change was the introduction of a value-added tax (VAT) in 1984 (becoming operative on 1 January 1986), replacing the Transactions Tax that had been created in the

[2]Law 46/86, 14 October 1986.

[3]Law 85/2009, 27 August 2009.

mid-1960s, a fundamental step in the modernization of the Portuguese tax system.[4] And in 1989, two new taxes (created in 1988) replaced the various existing taxes on different sorts of incomes: the new general income tax (*Imposto sobre o Rendimento das Pessoas Singulares* [IRS])[5] and the new capital tax (*Imposto sobre o Rendimento das Pessoas Colectivas* [IRC])[6] replaced the real estate tax (*contribuição predial*), the industrial tax (*contribuição industrial*), the wage tax (*imposto professional*), the old capital tax (*imposto sobre a aplicação de capitais*), and the tax on overall income (*imposto complementar*). With this reform, finally, real income substituted presumed income as the basis for taxation, a principle introduced in 1928 and only partially abandoned in the 1950s and 1960s. The tax simplification brought by the reform was real but incomplete, however, as integration into one full income tax was not really achieved. Also, special difficulties existed in the collection of the new capital tax, as evasion became rife (Lopes 1996, 2005).

Another problem the governments of the period tried to deal with was that of the constitutional conditions for economic activity. After the 1982 constitutional amendment of the Constitution, that abolished the Revolutionary Council, in 1983 the "Law of Sector Delimiting", mentioned in the previous chapter, was revised in order to increase the number of activities open to private agents, including now banking and insurance.[7] The effects of this revision were rapid: the first private bank started operating in 1984 and was followed by many others (Amaral 2015). But only in 1989, the Constitution was amended in order to revoke the principle of collective appropriation of the means of production, to extirpate the Agrarian Reform from the Constitution and to establish the reversibility of the nationalizations. Immediately afterward, a vast privatizing program was initiated (Franco 1994; Lopes 1996).

This process of institutional change was much helped by the international environment. As we have seen in the previous chapter,

---

[4]Decree-law 394/84, 26 December 1984.

[5]Decree-law 442-A/88, 30 December 1988.

[6]Decree-law 442-B/88, 30 December 1988.

[7]Decree-law 406/83, 18 November 1988.

nationalizations like the ones operated during the revolution were not an aberration in postwar Europe. More likely, Portugal was the aberration, with its virtually non-existent public company sector. The revolutionary nationalizations corresponded to a process of delayed institutional convergence, whereby Portugal got closer to what was already common in Europe since a few decades. But right when this was happening, the international political and ideological environment was changing. The great turn came between 1979, when Margaret Thatcher was elected prime minister in the UK, and 1980, when Ronald Reagan was elected president in the United States, both putting forward a "free market" agenda for the economies of their countries. Similar principles spread from then on through most Western countries. This time, Portugal followed the trend on time. If in 1975 it passed from having one of the smallest public company sectors in Europe into having one of the largest, during the 1990s it went in the opposite direction.

A new law was drafted to frame the privatization process.[8] Among the most important ideas inserted in it were those dedicated to create (or re-create) national business groups and those limiting access to foreign capital in the privatization operations. In the latter case, the generic principle was given a precise content in 1994, when the limit to foreign capital participation in each privatization operation was set at 25%.[9] Between 1989 and 2010, 118 privatization operations were implemented, making practically all the assets that had been nationalized during the revolution to return to private hands. The methods used to put those assets in the market did indeed favor their acquisition by Portuguese business groups (Alpalhão 2011; Amaral 2015). It is not yet entirely clear if the way the privatization process unfolded has contributed or not to improve the efficiency of the Portuguese economy. First, we must note that the companies that were privatized were not the same that had been nationalized. As we saw in the previous chapter, the nationalized companies were subject to drastic processes of restructuring, normally making them monopolist or oligopolist agents

[8]Law 11/90, 5 April 1990.

[9]Decree-law 65/94, 28 February 1994.

in reserved markets. This has allowed the Portuguese business groups acquiring them at the time of privatization to shelter from both national and foreign competition. With the crisis starting in 2008, most of these groups could not survive, something that raises the doubt if they were ever viable without the special conditions granted to them in the 1990s. In the latest years, they have simply been wiped away from the Portuguese economy (with a few exceptions) and replaced by foreign capital (Amaral 2015).

3 How to Integrate

The central issue for the Portuguese economy in the period analyzed in this chapter was its relationship with the EU. This relationship has become increasingly complex in large part due to changes in the EU itself, not just in Portugal. Joining the EEC opened new opportunities for the Portuguese economy, after the recovery from external imbalance in the late 1970s and early 1980s, as described in the previous chapter. These new opportunities led to a period of strong, albeit brief, growth between 1986 and 1992 (Amaral 2010) (Table 1). However, all of this growth happened in a new context, mainly due to changes in the EEC project. As a matter of fact, when Portugal joined, the EEC was entering into a crucial new phase, marked by the adoption of both the Single Market and monetary union programs. The Single Market program was adopted by the EEC in 1986, in the sequence of the signing of the Single European Act by the European Council. The idea was to fight what was then called "Eurosclerosis", i.e., the low growth and high unemployment plaguing European economies. A recipe of competition, by making truly effective the principle of the abolition of protectionism embodied in the Treaty of Rome, was seen as the most adequate method to do it: a Single European Market should be created, preventing all forms of non-tariff protectionism between member-states, such as discriminatory taxes on both imported and exported goods and services, Government subsidies, legal access to activities and technical standards, and allowing for the free circulation not just of goods but also of capital and labor (Vetter 2013). Cecchini et al. (1988), in a study commissioned by the

Table 1 Growth rate of GDP per capita, Portugal, 1986–2017

1986–1992	5.42
1993–1994	0.18
1995–2000	3.06
2000–2007	0.45
2008–2010	−0.31
2011–2013	−1.97
2014–2017	2.15

Source The Conference Board

European Commission, expressed the vast optimism prevalent in EEC circles: the wealth effect generated by the Single Market could reach 6.5% of GDP for all member countries on aggregate, and dynamic growth effects could reach 0.9% of GDP per year. A natural complement to the Single Market was monetary union, as exchange rate devaluations were also a form of covert protectionism.

In 1989, the Delors Report, a document produced by a commission of experts led by President of the European Commission Jacques Delors, was accepted by the European Council. Its most important proposal was, precisely, the creation of a monetary union. The idea of unifying the currencies of the countries belonging to the EEC was a rather old one. Hints at it had even been present in the founding treaty of 1957 (the Treaty of Rome), and since 1969, there was a plan (the Barre Plan, from the French politician Raymond Barre) for its implementation (Dinan 2004). In 1971, the Council of Ministers adopted the Werner Report (from the Prime Minister and Minister of Finance of Luxembourg, Pierre Werner), a blueprint for monetary union to be achieved until 1980 (Magnusson and Stråth 2002). In 1972, the so-called currency snake was created, whereby the European currencies had to contain their value within a ±2.25% band in relation to the US dollar (James 2012). The collapse of the Bretton Woods system in that year and a series of disagreements on sovereignty issues killed the Werner Plan, but not the idea of monetary union: Europeans felt vulnerable in relation to the power the United States could exert thanks to the reserve currency role played by the dollar (Eichengreen 1996). In 1979, the European Monetary System was created, where the currencies of the member-states were allowed to float only within a narrow band of ±2.25% and a wide band of ±6%—the Exchange Rate Mechanism (ERM) was the technical device used to keep the system functioning (James 2012).

In December 1990, the European Council gathered in Maastricht, in the Netherlands, to sign a treaty which not only created the European Union (in place of the EEC) but also set a blueprint for the birth of the single currency (James 2012). The process should go by stages: in Stage I, starting in late 1990, countries should remove capital controls (with the exception of Greece, Ireland, Portugal, and Spain, which were given more time due to their still higher inflation and interest rate levels) and make their central banks independent from the Government; in Stage II, starting in 1994, there should be further convergence of national macroeconomic policies; and in Stage III, starting in January 1999, full monetary union should be achieved. Countries could be part of it by fulfilling four criteria: having been able to keep the value of their currency within the normal ERM fluctuation bands for at least two years before entry; having had an inflation rate in the year before 1999 no higher than that of the three lowest-inflation member-states by 1.5%; and having a public debt no higher than 60% of GDP and a budget deficit no higher than 3% of GDP in 1999 (Eichengreen 1996).

EMU was the natural conclusion of the integrative effort initiated with the Single European Market. There was much political voluntarism in putting it forward, as decision-makers chose not to heed to many reservations then raised from many quarters (James 2012). The optimist case for monetary union had its foundations in the "optimal currency area" theory of Mundell (1961). Some authors even suggested that the conditions for such an area were so good in the EU that EMU was an endogenous result of those conditions (Frankel and Rose 1998). The growth impact of EMU would be large, according to many, thanks mostly to trade expansion, generated by the disappearance of exchange rate frictions (Rose 2000; Rose and Wincoop 2001). The doubts raised by many over if the EU was an optimal currency area were not enough to stop the process, even if sometimes they anticipated the issues that became evident to all after 2010 (James 2012).

Since the Portuguese Government decided to participate in this new integration leap, including monetary union, the control of inflation became a central policy objective (Abreu 2001). The crawling peg exchange rate regime had been designed as an instrument to keep competitiveness in a context of high inflation. But that was something that could not continue in a currency common to different countries. The objective of controlling inflation was also an autonomous one of Portuguese authorities, besides participating in the common currency. The two things combined to make the Government adopt a hard exchange rate policy from 1986 onward. The pace of depreciation of the crawling peg's monthly exchange rate was reduced in 1986. The consequence of this was that, as depreciation no longer compensated the inflation rate, there was a real appreciation of the escudo. As the pace of the crawling peg was successively reduced until 1990, real appreciation continued (Abreu 2001) (Fig. 9).

As these partial measures did not seem to be enough to control inflation, which started increasing again in 1988 and 1989, the Government decided to take the more radical step of completely ending with crawling peg and pegging the escudo to a basket of five currencies participating in EMS (the Deutsche mark, the pound, the French franc, the lira, and the peseta). The purpose was not only to control inflation but also to prepare the escudo to enter EMS and ERM, a necessary previous step to be a founding member of the

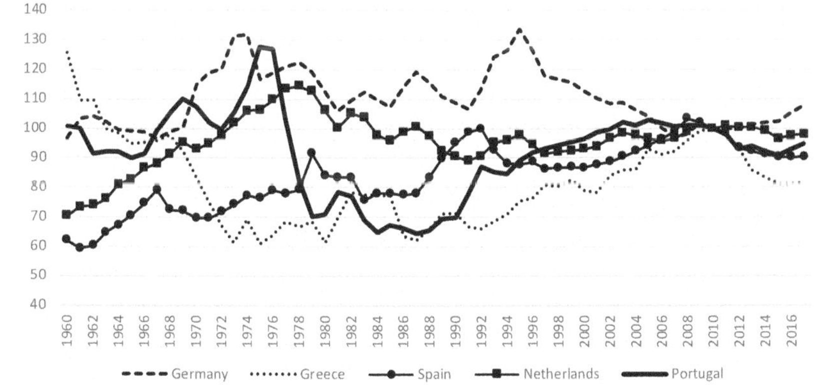

Fig. 9 Real exchange rate in eurozone countries (201 = 100), 1960–2017 (*Note* Based on unit labor costs. *Source* AMECO)

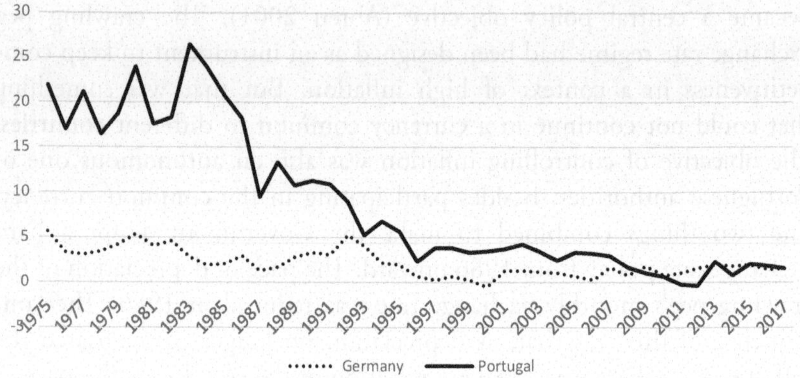

Fig. 10 Annual inflation rates, Portugal and Germany (based on Consumer Price Indices), 1975–2017 (%) (*Source* AMECO)

common currency. The nominal value of the escudo remained stable until 1992, thus making Portugal qualify to join EMS (Detragiache and Hamann 1997). However, as the inflation differential continued to be substantial (Fig. 10), real appreciation suffered a dramatic increase until 1992: 30% in three years, from 1990 to 1992 (Fig. 9). The loss of competitiveness was sudden and strong.

In 1992, the escudo did enter ERM. ERM was, however, passing through a complex period at the time, as doubts arose that EMU would ever become a reality, in the sequence of a referendum in Denmark in December 1992 in which the vote was against the participation of the country in it (Detragiache and Hamann 1997; Abreu 2001). Various currencies were put under pressure. The pressure was so strong that the pound and the lira abandoned ERM in September 1993. This happened despite the fact that the wide fluctuation bands of ERM changed from±6% to±15%. Portugal remained in it but depreciated twice, in 1992 and 1993, although by relatively small amounts (6% in November 1992 and 6.5% in May 1993) (Abreu 2001). In order to demonstrate its commitment to disinflation, the Portuguese authorities chose not to use the 15% margin given by the new ERM rules. Consequently, competitiveness improved only slightly until 1993, as there was only a mild decline of real appreciation, but started deteriorating again immediately afterward, a process that has stopped only in 2002 (Fig. 9). The anti-inflationary success of this policy had, hence, consequences for competitiveness.

Certainly in connection with the process just described, economic growth slowed-down and became even negative in 1992–1994, putting an end to the "mini golden age" of the 1986–1992 period (Amaral 2010) (Table 1). From 1995 to 1999, growth returned, but slower than between 1986 and 1992. The big stimulus came now from internal demand, mostly thanks to the expansion of certain budget items, such as social expenditure and public servants' recruitment and pay (Braz et al. 2009). Not by chance, this was the period of higher growth of external indebtedness (Fig. 1). For Portugal to enter EMU, it had to qualify on the basis of the inflation, budget deficit, and public debt criteria. Thanks to the disinflation process, the inflation criterion was achieved. As for the budget and debt criteria, they were also achieved but in a less straightforward way. Fiscal policy was ambiguous: it was expansionary, mostly through the increase in the number of public servants and of their wages; but this did not imperil the reaching of the Maastricht criteria thanks to two concurrent phenomena: the steep decline in interest rates, allowing for an equally pronounced decrease in debt service, and the income stream coming from the privatization program (then in full force), which was used by the Government to reduce public debt (Braz et al. 2009; Amaral 2010). Thus, by 1998, the budget deficit was within the 3% of GDP limit (Fig. 11) and public debt within the 60% one (Fig. 12). Portugal became a founding member of EMU.

EMU began its existence on 1 January 1999, with eleven countries (Austria, Belgium, Finland, France, Germany, Ireland, Italy Luxembourg, Netherlands, Spain, and Portugal) sharing the same currency, the euro. National central banks delegated their authority in a new institution, the European Central Bank (ECB), which was given the strict mandate of keeping price stability. A Stability and Growth Pact was signed concomitantly, in which countries committed to keep their budget deficits within the limit of 3% of GDP and public debt within 60% (James 2012). In the EMU period, from 1999 onward, growth in Portugal has been persistently low. The culmination of this bad performance came with the 2007–2008 crisis and the subsequent request for foreign assistance.

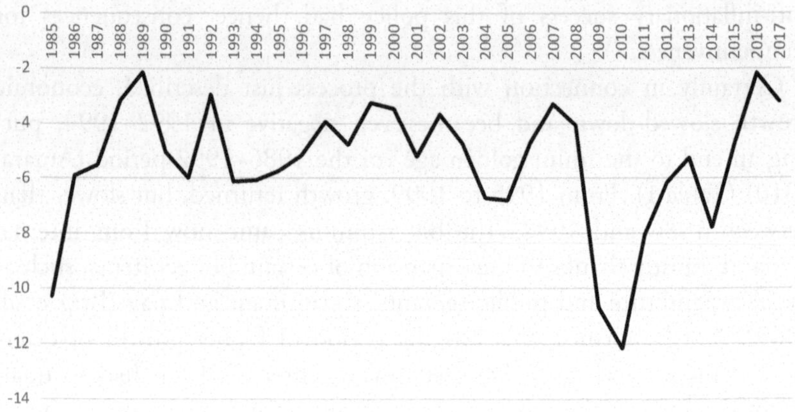

Fig. 11 Government budget deficit, Portugal, 1985–2017 (% GDP) (*Source* Same as Fig. 2)

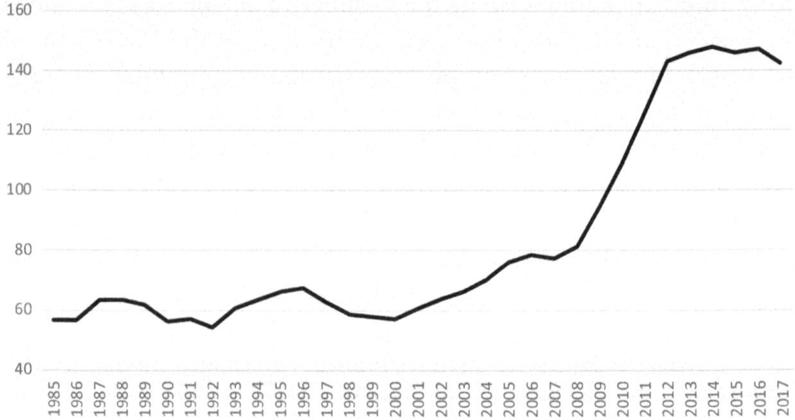

Fig. 12 Public debt, Portugal, 1985–2017 (% GDP) (*Source* Same as Fig. 2)

4 Consequences of Integration

In assessing the impact of this policy evolution, one thing is clear: Portugal was the country in Southern Europe with the largest swings in competitiveness between 1974 and 2017. As we can see in Fig. 9, it was the country where the real exchange rate most declined in the decade preceding accession to the EEC. Nothing similar is visible in the cases of Spain or Greece, also peripheral economies. This is a demonstration of the success of the crawling peg policy in managing the competitiveness of the economy.

But Portugal was also the country where the real exchange rate most increased after 1985 and until the beginning of the twenty-first century. The increase was especially steep between 1988 and 1992, although then the country was accompanied by Spain. This was a consequence of the radical disinflationary policy followed by Portuguese authorities and described above. As we have seen, Portugal adopted an exchange rate-based disinflationary program. When the variable chosen to control inflation is the exchange rate, it stops being a discretionary policy instrument. The credibility of the policy depends on the currency's peg. This leaves the authorities with only the interest rate to manipulate in order to stabilize the peg. That was what the Portuguese authorities did. Interest rates had an important increase from 1988 until 1991 (Fig. 13) and started declining only then, although still keeping a significant differential to Germany until 1997. The escudo depreciated three times between 1992 and 1994, but the Portuguese authorities chose not to use all the margin of depreciation the ERM range gave them. This implied keeping a hard monetary policy, with high interest rates. The

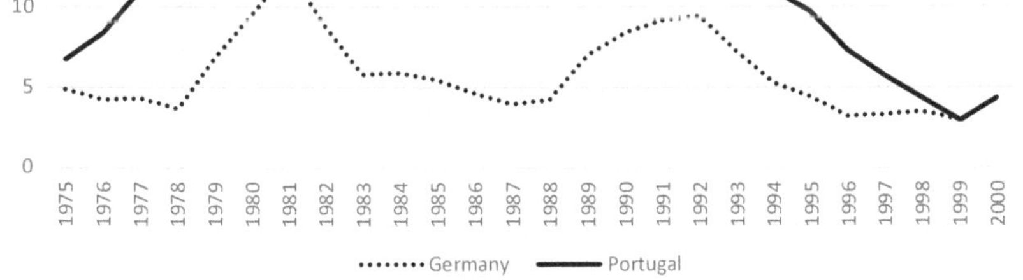

Fig. 13 Nominal short-term interest rates (three months), Portugal and Germany, 1975–2000 (%) (*Source* AMECO)

impact of such high rates on credit for investment was dramatic and many firms could not survive (Lopes 1996). A severe crisis hit the economy between 1992 and 1994.

Because of this monetary policy, from then on until today, a set of incentives has been created in favor of the non-tradable sector of the economy and of the contraction of the tradable one. The strong exchange rate policy meant that only an increasingly lower number of firms could cope with external competition. As noted by Abreu (2001), a substantial differential between the prices of tradable goods and non-tradable goods was then created, persisting well into the twenty-first century. From 1995 until the early twenty-first century, growth came mostly from an expansionary fiscal policy, which the Government could follow without many serious consequences as interest rates started finally to decline (after the early 1990s' depreciations and the success of disinflation) and public debt could be covered with income resulting from the privatization program then underway (Amaral 2006, 2010; Bento 2009; Alexandre and Bação 2012; Bação and Duarte 2014; Alexandre et al. 2016). Not only the number of public servants and of their pay increased but also a series of public projects were launched using mostly EU structural funds (Braz et al. 2009; Bento 2009; Amaral 2010). This was what Alexandre and Bação (2014) called a "public sector 'bubble'", which they insert within a larger "non-tradable 'bubble'" (see also Alexandre et al. 2016). Inevitably, external balance deteriorated even more: the current account imbalance grew to reach around −10% of GDP in 2000 (Fig. 1).

The imbalances developed in the 1990s became clear by the beginning of the twenty-first century, when budget deficits were shown to be unacceptable under EMU rules. From then on (with the exception of 2009), governments adopted contractionary fiscal policies. The last available growth engine disappeared thus. With the exchange rate (or the implicit exchange rate within the euro) punishing exports and fiscal policy moderating internal demand, the economy entered into a period of sluggish growth (Blanchard 2007). By then convergence of interest rates had been achieved. Capital circulation was now free within the EU and financial integration had never been as high (Blanchard and Giavazzi 2002). All this was a stimulus for debt, to compensate for slow growth. Consequently, the current account deficit remained at 10% of

GDP until 2010 (Fig. 1). Reis (2013) called this process and the subsequent crisis the "Portuguese Slump and Crash".

Between 2007 and 2008, a world financial and economic crisis erupted. At first, the Portuguese Government did not react. In this, it followed most other European Governments, for whom, between the Summer of 2007 and the Summer of 2008, the crisis was still only an American phenomenon. The first reactions of the Portuguese Government came in October 2008 and centered first on the threats to the financial and banking system. This priority was similar in the rest of the Western world and was closely connected to the turbulence arising from the failure of the bank Lehman Brothers in the United States. A second phase of measures opened in December 2008, when the Government adopted a stimulus package. There was again a European dimension in this reaction, as it followed the adoption of the self-styled European Economic Recovery Plan, proposed by the European Commission in late November. Thanks to the stimulus package, the Portuguese deficit deteriorated in 2009, reaching 10% of GDP.

A budget deficit of such size was impossible to sustain, particularly in the context of increasing threats to Portuguese debt that developed during the year. The Portuguese Government entered, thus, into a new phase, generally marked by austerity. But all efforts made in 2010 proved to be futile. In March 2011, a new austerity package was proposed by the Government, but the parliament did not lend its support to it. As a consequence, the Government resigned. Even if it first tried to delay formal acceptance of a rescue plan from the European Commission (EC), the International Monetary Fund (IMF) and the ECB (the so-called troika), mounting political and public opinion pressure, led it to do so. On 6 April 2011, the Government acknowledged the need of foreign assistance. After a series of negotiations, a document was produced with a vast set of measures to be applied between 2011 and 2014. The program was centered on three main areas: fiscal consolidation, the solidity of the Portuguese banking system, and a set of "structural reforms" pointing at the improvement of Portugal's potential economic growth, enabling it to overcome the lack of competitiveness that had fed its increasing external indebtedness in the previous decade.

The rebalancing effect of the troika program has been clear: the current account passed from −10% of GDP in 2011 to balance from 2013 onward (Fig. 1). But so have its punishing growth effects (Table 1). The question is to know if this rebalancing has been enough to put the economy on a new growth path and compensate for the dysfunctionality of monetary integration. The differential impact EMU had from its inception between competitive and less competitive countries that are part of it has lately become accepted wisdom. Cumulative current account deficits are a demonstration that structural macroeconomic imbalances exist within the euro area, separating mostly the "northern" countries (essentially Germany, Austria, the Netherlands, and Luxembourg) from the "southern" ones (mostly Portugal, Greece, and Spain, with Ireland also sometimes thrown into the bunch) and the remaining countries somewhere in between. The former have accumulated persistent current account surpluses while the latter have accumulated deficits. Such differential behavior has led to a complementary problem of growing debt in the "South" with money borrowed from the "North" (see, for instance, Holinski et al. 2012; Gros 2012) (Fig. 14 documents this process).

Portugal, together with Greece, was the country with the worst current account deterioration since the late 1980s and early 1990s until

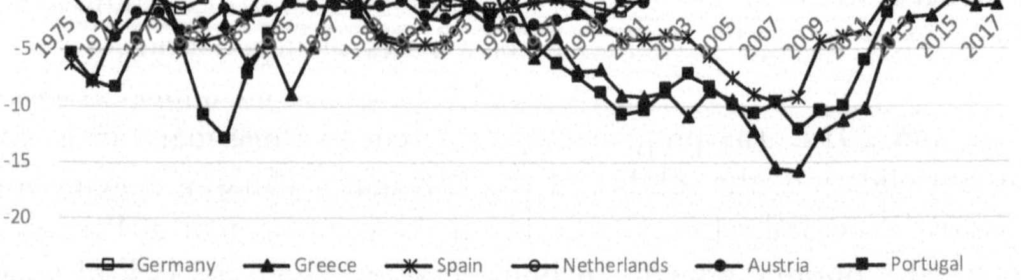

Fig. 14 Current account in Eurozone countries (% GDP), 1975–2017 (*Source* AMECO, except Portugal: 1975–1995—Pinheiro [1997]; 1996–2017—INE)

the recent improvement dictated by the austerity policies under the troika program. Spain also followed an equivalent path, but later and in a less pronounced way. So, no doubt a large part of the problem of the Portuguese economy is connected with EMU or, perhaps more correctly, with EMU and the preparations for joining it. All Southern European countries suffered from the pegging of exchange rates under conditions of lack of competitiveness. But there was also something specific to Portugal. The question is to know if it was the result of the forceful way with which the Portuguese authorities tried to comply with the requirements of EMU or the lack of initial conditions to be part of it, or a combination of the two.

According to recent estimates, the implementation of the Single European Market has increased GDP in the EU by about 2 or 3%, a figure much below the early optimistic projections. Furthermore, the impact has not been homogeneous between the countries. Countries with larger foreign trade shares and higher competitiveness have been positively affected but not countries in opposite circumstances. The most important effect has been on trade, with its importance growing in the economies participating in the Single Market and EMU (Vetter 2013). According to Vetter (2013), intra-EU trade intensity increased between 1992 and 2012 from 12 to 22% of GDP. Figures 2, 3, and 4 illustrate this process. But they also illustrate how the same effect did not occur in Portugal: in Portugal's case, as soon as there was a moderation of the depreciation rate of the escudo in 1986, the trade balance deteriorated (Fig. 1). Precisely at the time when restrictions to trade within the EEC ended, the competitiveness of the Portuguese economy got worse. And this was much before EMU. A fundamental problem for the Portuguese economy was the structural decline of emigrant remittances (transfers in Fig. 1), which started then, as remittances had been the historical instrument to keep the current account balanced. The situation got even worse after 1994, when the escudo's exchange rate was kept stable within the ERM, and competitiveness deteriorated at the pace of the inflation differential between Portugal and EMS partners. All of this means that Portugal was under EMU conditions much before EMU and, consequently, that the real appreciation and competitiveness problems started before EMU, being masked by the growth of borrowing from surplus countries. Real appreciation only improved when austerity started in 2002.

What the Portuguese case shows is that there is indeed a "Portuguese problem" but also that such a problem is part of a wider "EU problem". Visibly, not all economies belonging to the EU dealt well with the harder integrative effort starting in the 1980s. The fact that GDP per capita convergence stopped in the EEC/EU from the 1980s onward reveals it. Portugal was one of the countries worst prepared for it, but this does not mean that its preparedness was and is the only problem of EMU and of the EU.

5 Economic Growth and Change

The growth of the Portuguese economy during the European period was far from spectacular: for the overall period 1986–2017, the average growth rate was 1.96% per year. This was only slightly faster than the richer economies of the world, something that had as a consequence a relatively slow pace of convergence, as shown in Fig. 4 of the Introduction: the level of Portuguese GDP per capita passed from 56% of GDP per capita in richer economies to 62%. This is not what was expectable of the Portuguese economy. What was expectable was a strong process of catch-up, especially after the country joined one of the clubs with best institutions in the world, the EEC/EU. Without institutional obstacles, the country should have been ready to profit from the advantages of relative backwardness. But that was not what happened.

The behavior of the Portuguese economy varied substantially between different sub-periods (Table 1): between 1986 and 1992, the average rate was 5.42%, a fast pace that has allowed it to converge strongly to those richer economies; the 1990s were still a period of relatively quick growth (after the 1992–1994 crisis, during which rates were negative or only marginally positive), but this was not enough for catch-up; as for the period since the beginning of the twenty-first century, growth has been dismal, with an average growth rate between 2000 and 2017 of only 0.26% per year. The consequence of this mediocre performance was the longest divergence period since the nineteenth century, even if some mild catch-up has reappeared in the last few years. Growth was very slow until the 2008 crisis, was negative during the period of the crisis and of the troika intervention, and became positive, although far from spectacular, from the end of the troika intervention in 2013 until 2017.

Population continued to increase, from 10 million in 1985 to 10,300 million in 2017, but now, as the demographic transition was completed, due to the growth of life expectancy, as both birth and death rates dropped to very low levels. In fact, resident population declined from 2011 onward, thanks to a combination of extremely low birth rates and a new emigration bout, coinciding with the most recent economic crisis, thanks to which about 500,000 people emigrated between 2011 and 2017. The birth rate in Portugal is one of the lowest in Europe (and the world), only surpassed by Greece and Italy. Life expectancy has passed from 67 years in 1970 to 80 in 2016, putting Portugal within the average of developed countries (80 years in the EU-15). Equally spectacular results have been achieved with respect to infant mortality, which has dropped from 51‰ in 1970 to 2.7‰ in 2016, one of the lowest in the world (3.3‰ in the EU-15).

Structural change continued but took a different path now, with deindustrialization and tertiarization taking place, as is expected in later stages of development. Although employment in agriculture continued to decline, from 17% of overall employment in 1983 to 6% in 2017, this time employment in industry declined too and at a similar proportion, from 37 to 23% in the same dates (Fig. 15). But the most spectacular process was the increase in employment in services, which passed from 45% in 1983 to 70% in 2017: the sector just captured all employment moving out of the other two. The trends were similar in output: agriculture dropped its weight from 12% in 1983 to 3% in 2017, industry from 40 to 25% in the same dates, and services increased from 50 to 70%. The process was particularly pronounced from the late 1980/early 1990s onward, most probably reflecting the incentives to replace tradables by non-tradables (Fig. 16).

Portuguese agriculture was deeply affected by membership of EEC. The sector is the only one for which there is a truly coordinated European policy, the Common Agricultural Policy (CAP). Support to

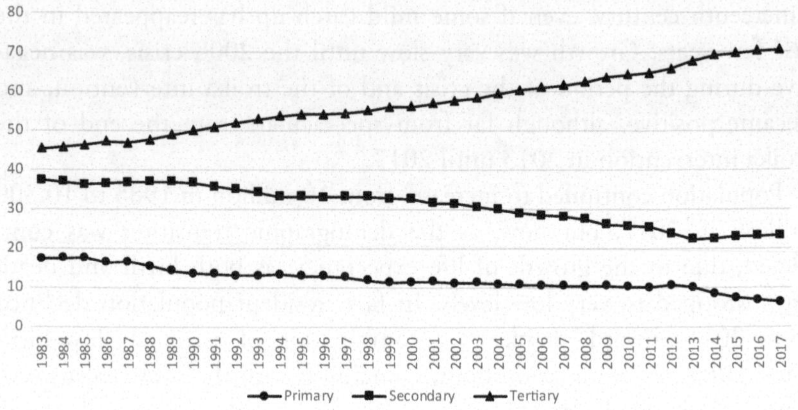

Fig. 15 Structure employment, Portugal, 1983–2017 (% overall employment) (*Source* 1983–1995: Pinheiro [1997], corrected with Amaral [2009], extrapolated forward using AMECO)

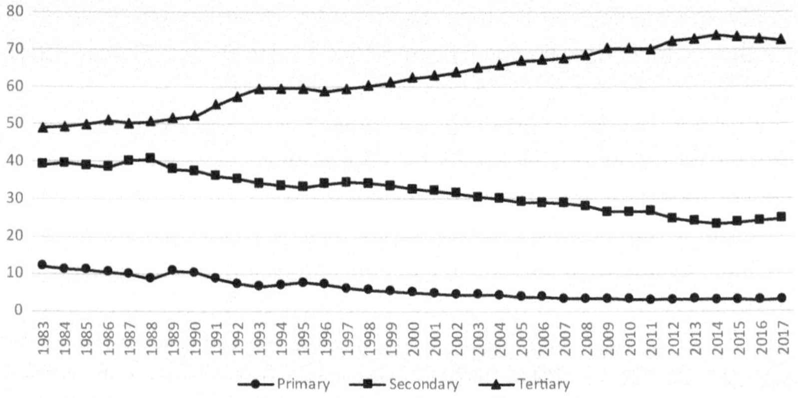

Fig. 16 Structure economy, Portugal, 1983–2017 (% GDP) (*Source* Same as Fig. 15)

prices has been the essential instrument of the CAP, as structural reform has received much less attention. In the negotiations pertaining to Portuguese agriculture, a double transition process on prices was established. One was a classical transition, lasting seven years (1986–1993) and applying to products where no major difficulties existed in terms of price harmonization between Portuguese agricultural policy and the CAP. The second type of transition affected the remaining products and lasted for 10 years (1986–1996). In this transition, no price harmonization would take place in the first five years, and Portuguese agriculture would benefit from funds for the reorganization of marketing schemes. In the second half of the period, prices would converge along lines similar to the classical transition. The process of price harmonization was accompanied by a 10-year "structural reform" program. Together with these policies, a "pre-accession package" was signed, according to which Portugal benefited from two payments devoted to the modernization of various aspects of Portuguese agriculture. However, the transition period was also the one of most pronounced reform of the CAP itself. The main objective of reform was to lower guaranteed prices, increase direct payments, and promote structural change. A very important principle of the CAP, most strongly adopted after 2003, was that of the so-called decoupling or the dissociation between direct payments and production (Amaral and Freire 2017).

According to Avillez et al. (2004), Portuguese agriculture suffered in the CAP a stronger decline in price support than most EU-15 countries. This was only partially offset by an increase in direct support to production and in "decoupled" support. Support through prices and direct support to production were much lower in Portugal than in the rest of the member-states on average, the opposite occurring with "decoupled" support. In the expression of Baptista (1994), Portuguese agriculture became a "subsidized" sector rather than a "productive" one, meaning that support to Portuguese agriculture was not essentially directed at improving the productive conditions of the sector but rather at keeping its income without structural transformation. This does not mean that structural change did not occur, but rather that it occurred independently of a deliberate policy to force it. The performance of agriculture was very poor: labor productivity grew, but not as quickly as in the already more productive agricultural sectors of the EU, and land productivity did not even grow. As a consequence, the productivity level of the labor used in Portuguese agriculture, measured as a percentage of labor productivity of the agricultural sectors of Western Europe, declined from 30% in 1992 to 20% in 2005 (Amaral and Freire 2017, p. 250). The ultimate result of the CAP was to create a sort of dual agricultural sector: a set of modern and efficient farms able to compete within the conditions of the European market sprout alongside vast stretches of land not used or converted to extensive farming or forest. The impact on the product mix of Portuguese agriculture was vast: cereals and wine, followed by olive oil and fruits, which had been the traditional and most important Portuguese crops, lost their importance. Milk and dairy products have become the undoubted front-runners, with a relevant increase in beef and other meats as well (Avillez et al. 2004; Amaral and Freire 2017).

The main effect of EEC/EU membership on Portuguese industry was to make the sector much less competitive than in the period from the 1960s until the late 1980s, again as a consequence of real appreciation of the exchange rate. The economy deindustrialized and the branch most negatively affected by it was textiles and footwear, precisely the one that had been at the basis of the "export miracle" of the period between the 1960s and the 1980s. The branch's share in industrial output declined from about 25% in the mid-1980s to about 20% in 2017. One further reason for this decline was the end of the multi-fiber agreement, which governed world trade on textiles from 1974 to 2005 (phasing out since 1994) and protected the textile industries of developed countries from imports originating in developing countries. The Portuguese textile industry seems to have had difficulties in adapting to the new environment. Food and beverages, on the contrary, increased its share, from about 12% to about 20% in the same dates. The remaining branches kept their relative importance: wood and paper and paper pulp at around 20%, chemicals at about 10%, cement at about 11%, machines and equipment at about 20%, and base metals at about 7% (Aguiar and Martins 2005; Eurostat). This means that, besides deindustrialization, EEC/EU membership has not contributed to change much the structure of the industrial sector.

For the first time in its history, the Portuguese economy had to live without any major differential protection in relation to external markets (except the one resulting from the EEC/EU's common tariff). The adaptation has not been easy, as we have seen above: the country remained persistently one of the lowest exporters in the EU (as a percentage of GDP) and a lot of its economy's troubles were related with this difficulty. But the pattern of trade has changed very clearly throughout this period, making it approach what is common in the most developed economies. The branch that had defined Portuguese exports since joining EFTA in the 1960s, textiles and footwear, stagnated its relative weight at around 40% of overall exports in the first decade of EEC membership and then declined persistently, until reaching a weight close to 10% in the second decade of the twenty-first century. The decline was so strong that nowadays paper pulp and cork exports weight more in overall exports (around 20%). This relatively low-skill and low-technology branch was overtaken by a medium-skill and medium-technology one, the metal transformation and equipment one, which increased from 15% of exports in the beginning of EEC membership to 35% in the early twentieth century; then it has started to decline, reaching about 25% of exports in the second decade of the twenty-first century (Amador and Cabral 2014; Afonso and Aguiar 2005). This sector had also given an important contribution in the first period of European integration in the 1960s, although at a lower level than textiles and footwear, but its composition changed in time: until the early 1990s, electrical equipment was the largest contributor, but from the late 1980s and early 1990s car assemblage took the baton, thanks to a series of high-profile investment projects in the country.

Nowadays, the Portuguese export profile is more diverse, without a dominant branch, distributed between the three branches just mentioned plus some, also diverse, novelties of the first decades of the twenty-first century: agricultural goods, manufactured food products, oil products, or pharmaceuticals. At the same time, services have increased their share in exports, especially tourism (Amador and Cabral 2014). With this transformation, the Portuguese export sector has lost two of its most important features of the past: concentration in low-tech branches and excessive concentration in one or two branches (agricultural goods up to the 1960s, textiles and footwear from then until the 1990s). Now, Portuguese exports have a medium-technology content and are relatively diverse. On the other hand, the pattern of imports has also changed and is no longer so concentrated in intermediate goods, as is typical of industrializing countries. Now, the country also imports a high volume of goods from its most traditional exporting branches, such as textiles and footwear. In the early twenty-first century, 70% of Portuguese trade corresponds to exchanges within each branch, and Portuguese firms compete in branches where the country is both an importer and an exporter. Competitiveness does not depend so much anymore on low wages (although it still does) but on other factors such as technological content or product differentiation (Amador and Cabral 2014). In this sense, the pattern of Portuguese exports has approached that of richer countries. The real appreciation of the Portuguese exchange rate, which has defined the economy since the early 1990s, contributed to this result: thanks to such appreciation, it was no longer possible for the country to rely on the traditional advantage of the low cost of labor. But with another consequence, not too dissimilar with what has happened in agriculture: the export sector is small, as only a relatively small number of very efficient firms can compete in the European market, and is accompanied by a vast multitude of low-tech and low-productivity activities that, thanks to being non-tradable, survive without major threats from external competition.

The banking sector suffered a big transformation thanks to the legislative changes of the period. When the 1983 revision of the "Law of Delimiting Sectors" opened commercial banking to private investors, it did not mean yet that the banks that had been nationalized could now be privatized—these were still under the irreversibility constitutional norm. But it meant that new private banks could open. The new institutions were regulated in 1984:[10] new private banks had to be incorporated and have a minimum capital of 1.5 billion escudos and their opening was dependent on authorization by the Government—the same happened with mergers and acquisitions and the opening of branches. New kinds of financial institutions were also authorized: investment funds (for stock and bonds and for real estate) (in 1985), factoring companies (in 1986), venture capital companies (in 1986), and credit companies (i.e., companies for consumption credit) (in 1989). By 1989, the number of Portuguese banks had jumped back to

[10]Decree-Law 51/84, 11 February 1984.

14, more or less the same as in 1974. Adding the foreign ones, however, the number passed to 23, more or less the same as in 1960.

The situation of banks would change further with the 1989 constitutional amendment that abolished the principle of irreversibility of the revolutionary nationalizations. Three years later, the legal framework for banking also changed.[11] The new legislation was a watershed for Portuguese banking. An important purpose of it was to make Portuguese legislation converge with that of other countries participating in the European Union (EU), especially in the European Monetary Union (EMU). The new legislation incorporated the basic principles of the first three EU banking directives.[12] Since EMU presupposed freedom of circulation of capital, the legislation incorporated the principles of freedom of establishment and of supplying of services by foreign banks. The Bank of Portugal (BoP) retained a series of important powers that limited the impact of such principles, especially with respect to the installation of foreign banks. In what concerns entry in the market, the Government was for the first time in Portuguese history stripped of its powers to authorize the opening of banks or mergers and acquisitions. These powers were now attributed to the BoP, which in principle should follow strictly technical and prudential criteria, rather than political ones. The only power left to the Government was that of setting the minimum capital requirement for opening a bank. The legislation adopted the principles of universal banking, something completely opposite to the spirit of the Portuguese legislation since the 1920s. The nature and the number of operations banks could now perform increased thus significantly. Limits to these operations became residual. Banks were now given a large margin of action.

All of this was accompanied by the process of progressive liberalization of banks' interest rates: between 1988 and 1993, all limits to interest rates were abolished and banks became for the first time entirely free to set the level of their rates (rather than the Government or the

[11] Decree-Law 298/92, 31 December 1992.

[12] Directives 77/780/EEC, 12 December 1977, 89/646/EEC, 15 December 1989, and 92/30/EEC, 15 April 1992.

BoP). In 1993, CGD was transformed into a universal bank, subject to the same regulations as all other universal banks (although exclusively owned by the State), thus ending with another tradition.[13]

The period from 1989 onward was perhaps the most lively in Portuguese banking history since the late nineteenth century and the first decades of the twentieth century. This had fundamentally to do with two processes, separated by about twenty years: the privatization program of the 1990s and the financial crisis of the years 2008–2015. The first process led all banks that had been nationalized in 1975 to be re-privatized between 1989 and 1999 (with one exception). Legal conditions for banking competition improved massively in this period. It is not surprising that there was then a flourishing of new banks. Between 1992 and 2004, the market went through a hectic phase, with banks opening, closing, and merging at notable rates (Valério, et al. 2010). By 1997, the number of Portuguese banks had multiplied to 27 and that of foreign ones to 13—the overall number being, thus, 40 (Amaral and Machado, forthcoming). In the late 1990s and the early twenty-first century, there was a very important process of consolidation, with a series of quite spectacular merging and acquisitions episodes involving the largest banks (Amaral 2015). The second process, the 2008–2015 financial crisis, led to the disappearance of a few banks, some counting among the most important (Amaral 2015). These movements were reflected in a concentration of the market. The big mergers and acquisitions of the late twentieth century led to a massive increase in market concentration and the crisis reinforced the trend: the Portuguese market has become the most concentrated in Europe (Costa 2014; Amaral 2015). Some authors believe the banking sector did not give a relevant contribution to the growth of the economy, as it concentrated its credit activity in protected markets (Amaral 2015; Alexandre et al. 2016).

As for explanations for the behavior of the economy, growth accounting is always a good starting point. According to most existing exercises, the largest contributor to growth in this period was the factor capital. One of those exercises, however, points to human capital as being the

[13]Decree-Law 287/93, 20 August 1993.

Table 2 Growth accounting, various studies, 1947–1975

		Annual growth rates			
References	Periods	Labor	Capital	Human capital	TFP
Amador and Coimbra (2007)	1985–1995	0.3	2.5	–	1.1
	1995–2005	0.0	3.4	–	−1.0
Afonso (1999)	1986–1993	0.2	1.5	–	1.3
Mateus (2005)	1985–2000	0.2	1.4	1.6	0.9
Silva and Lains (2013)	1991–2011	0.2	2.1	–	−0.6

Source Afonso (1999), Lains (2003), Silva and Lains (2013), Mateus (2005), and Amador and Coimbra (2007)

largest contributor. In all the exercises, TFP gives a low to negative contribution (Table 2). Despite its high contribution, capital displayed an ambivalent behavior: it grew strongly between the mid-1980s and the early twenty-first century but then declined in the following two decades. Both are understandable: in the first period, the new institutional environment provided by EEC membership and by political stability gave confidence to investors; not surprisingly, the investment rate continued to be high, at around 25% of GDP (Freitas 2005). In the second period, with the progressive disappointment with the growth performance of the Portuguese economy and the actual (and long) crisis between 2008 and 2014, the investment rate fell to quite low rates, similar only to those existing in the 1940s and early 1950s (Fig. 17). A large part of what happened with investment is related to the disappearance of funds for investment, i.e., internal saving, which declined to very low levels by historical standards in a process starting in the early 1990s. This is mostly explained by the waning of remittances, which, although originating externally were included in the national saving pool. As this led to a growing current imbalance, external savings took the position of internal saving, being essentially composed of debt to the European credit market by both the Government and private agents.

The high contribution from human capital is explainable by the persistent efforts of the successive democratic governments to foster public schooling as well as by the existence of very high returns to education (Teixeira et al. 2014). Thanks to both, student enrollment in the first

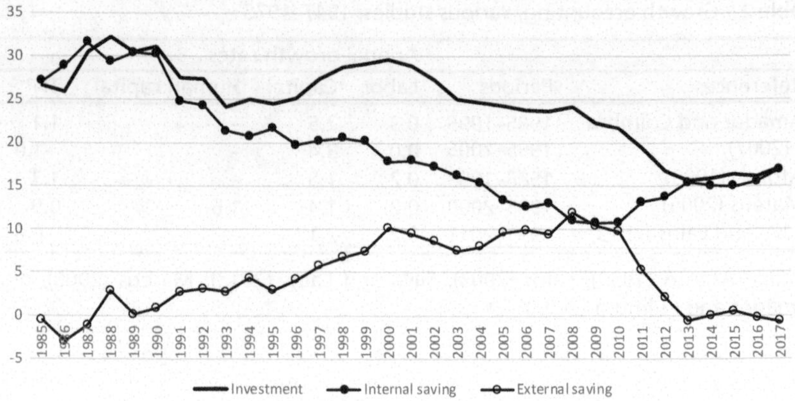

Fig. 17 Gross fixed capital formation, internal saving and external saving, 1985–2017 (% GDP) (*Source* 1985–1995—Pinheiro [1997] and 1996–2017—AMECO)

two years of secondary education (for the relevant age group) has passed from 26% in 1974 to 57%, in 1985 and 87% in 2000, stalling at that level until 2017; enrollment in the second cycle of secondary education has risen from 18% in 1974 to 38% in 1986, 84% in 2000, and 88% in 2017; and in what concerns the last three years of secondary education, it has passed from 5% in 1974 to 16% in 1986, 59% in 2000, and 78% in 2017. University education has expanded vigorously as well, especially after 1985: school enrollment of the relevant age group was 1.5% in 1974, 6% in 1985, 23% in 2000, and 34% in 2017. Despite these impressive figures, the comparative results have not exactly been outstanding: Portugal continues to be, among developed countries, the country with the lowest-skilled workforce, as workers with secondary and university education correspond to 15 and 14% of all workers, whereas in the EU-15, they correspond to 45 and 24%. This is what explains the fact that Portugal is still one of the European countries with higher returns to education (Varejão et al. 2014).

In what concerns the bad performance of TFP, there seem to be various reasons explaining it. First, there are the strictly technological factors: despite impressive growth, Portugal continues to have very low levels of R&D in the European context, as well as an unimpressive patent registration record (Simões et al. 2014; Alves 2017).

But non-strictly technological factors must have played an even more important role, one of them being the pattern of structural change followed by the Portuguese economy from the late 1980s and early 1990s onward, which, in turn was a consequence of the real appreciation policy adopted then and of some aspects of policy, such as those resulting from the CAP in agriculture. This led, for instance, to a slower pace of movement of labor out of agriculture into other sectors: as farmers were offered income in exchange for reducing production, many remained in the sector without contributing to output (Amaral and Freire 2017). On the other hand, the growth in services was done in favor of relatively low-productivity branches, such as public administration, education, and health care, in order to accommodate the expansion of social services promoted by the Government, but also in favor of hostelry, in this case as a consequence of the growing importance of tourism (Alves 2017). Some growth in more productive branches, such as R&D and ICT, does not seem to have been enough to compensate the other movements. This pattern of structural change has made Portugal converge to the structure typical of more advanced economies, but the question is if this has not been too precocious, i.e., the Portuguese economy has acquired a structure close to that of those economies while still having only little more than half of their GDP per capita. One further possible reason for low TFP growth relates to the process of privatization from the 1990s onward, as the newly privatized companies were given special conditions, through monopolies, oligopolies, and reserved markets. Amador and Soares (2012) show how activities in the non-tradable sector, where those companies were inserted, had higher profits and lower competition in the first decade of the twenty-first century: all these aspects seem to be associated with a massive decline in capital productivity, a particularly worrying aspect in a country still with only half of the capital-labor ratio of the EU-15 (Alves 2017).

One final topic worth mention is that of income inequality. If the previous authoritarian regime repressed labor and paid little attention to social programs, Portuguese democracy has done the opposite. Labor is duly represented in a large number of powerful unions and legislation has been generous to labor. Portuguese labor law continues to be the most protective of individual dismissals within OECD, despite a recent revision (during the troika intervention) making firing easier (OECD 2017).[14] But such protection has been essentially responsible for the appearance of legislative schemes to facilitate short-term contracts, with the consequence of Portugal being the country where this sort of labor relations is more widespread, except Spain and Poland. Formal rigidity has, thus, allowed for actual flexibility, through a process of segmentation: on the one hand, a declining share of workers is fully protected within the rules of labor law, on the other, a growing share has virtually no protection, running the risk of being dismissed at any time by simple non-renewing of their short-term contracts (Blanchard and Portugal 2001). This, in turn, has led to wage flexibility: throughout the period of the Portuguese democracy, wages have adapted with large swings to the business cycle (with good consequences for unemployment, which has been persistently low, even through the worst periods of crisis) (Lopes 1996; Blanchard and Portugal 2001; Amaral 2005). The evolution of real exchange rates shown in Fig. 9 is a reflection of this wage flexibility. Not only the regime is generally friendly to labor but also its governments have been able to implement quite comprehensive social programs.

These should be good institutional conditions to reduce income inequality. But that is not what has happened: Alvaredo (2009) and Guilera (2010) have shown that top income shares in Portugal declined immediately after the revolution, something that is explainable by the expropriation of business groups and the massive redistribution of income implied by the explosion of wages, but also that those shares increased persistently until the early twenty-first century and remained at a high level until 2010. According to this measure, income inequality is now at the same level as in the 1950s or 1960s. The evolution of the Gini coefficient in Portugal points in the same direction: this indicator remained at a level of 37 between 1994 and 2006, corresponding to one of the highest in Europe (only surpassed by a few countries of Eastern Europe, Spain, and Greece) (Rodrigues et al. 2012). Even if, from 2006 on, it has declined in a pronounced manner, reaching a value of 32 in 2017, Portugal remains within the group of most unequal European countries (Rodrigues et al. 2016).

---

[14] Law 47/2012, 29 August 2012.

References

Abreu, Marta. 2001. Da adesão à Comunidade Económica Europeia à participação na União Económica e Monetária: a experiência portuguesa de desinflação no período 1984–1998. *Boletim Económico do Banco de Portugal*, Vol. 7, nº 4 (December): 17–38.

Afonso, Óscar. 1999. *Contributo do Comércio Externo para o Crescimento Económico Português, 1960–93*. Lisbon: Conselho Económico e Social.

Afonso, Óscar, and Álvaro Aguiar. 2005. A internacionalização da economia. In *História Económica de Portugal, 1700–2000, Vol. III, O Século XX*, ed. Pedro Lains and Álvaro Ferreira da Silva, 305–341. Lisbon: ICS.

Aguiar, Álvaro, and Manuel M.F. Martins. 2005. A indústria. In *História Económica de Portugal, 1700–2000, Vol. III, O Século XX*, ed. Pedro Lains and Álvaro Ferreira da Silva, 185–226. Lisbon: ICS.

Alexandre, Fernando, and Pedro Bação. 2012. Portugal Before and After the European Union: Facts on Nontradables. Núcleo de Investigação em Políticas Económicas, Working Paper, No. 15.

———. 2014. A História de uma economia desequilibrada. In *A Economia Portuguesa na União Europeia: 1986–2010*, ed. Fernando Alexandre et al. (orgs.), 77–103. Coimbra: Actual.

Alexandre, Fernando, Luís Aguiar-Conraria, and Pedro Bação. 2016. *Crise e Castigo. Os Desequilíbrios e o Resgate da Economia Portuguesa*. Lisbon: Fundação Francisco Manuel dos Santos.

Alpalhão, Rui. 2011. *SARL, EP, SA. O Percurso das Empresas Portuguesas entre Mercado e Estado*. Lisboa: Rei dos Livros.

Alves, Ricardo Pinheiro. 2017. Portugal: A Paradox in Productivity. GEE Working Papers, No. 70.

Amador, João, and Carlos Coimbra. 2007. Characteristics of the Portuguese Economic Growth: What Has Been Missing? Banco de Portugal Working Paper, No. 8.

Amador, João, and Ana Cristina Soares. 2012. A concorrência na economia portuguesa medida através da elasticidade dos lucros. *Boletim Económico. Banco de Portugal* 18 (3): 95–109.

Amador, João, and Manuel Caldeira Cabral. 2014. A economia Portuguesa no contexto global. In *A Economia Portuguesa na União Europeia: 1986–2010*, orgs. Fernando Alexandre et al., 183–228. Coimbra: Actual.

Amaral, João Ferreira do. 2006. O impacto económico da integração de Portugal na Europa. *Nação e Defesa*, 3rd Series (115): 113–128.

Amaral, Luciano. 2005. O trabalho. In *História Económica de Portugal, 1700–2000, Vol. III, O Século XX*, ed. Pedro Lains and Álvaro Ferreira da Silva, 65–90. Lisbon: ICS.

———. 2009. Portuguese Population and Employment, 1950–2007: Implications for GDP Per Capita and Labor Productivity. *Análise Social* (193): 767–791.

———. 2010. *Economia Portuguesa – As Últimas Décadas*. Lisbon: Relógio d'Água/FFMS.

———. 2015. *Em Nome do Pai e do Filho…* Lisbon: Publicações D. Quixote.

Amaral, Luciano, and Dulce Freire. 2017. Economic Policy, Growth and the Demise, 1929–2000. In *An Agrarian History of Portugal, 1000–2000: Economic Development on the European Frontier*, ed. Dulce Freire and Pedro Lains, 245–276. Leiden: Brill.

Amaral, Luciano, and Filipa Santos Machado. 2019. *Institutional Shocks and Competition in Portuguese Commercial Banking in the Long Run, 1960–2015*. Dactil.

AMECO. http://ec.europa.eu/economy_finance/ameco/user/serie/SelectSerie.cfm.

Avillez, Francisco, M.N. Jorge, C.P. Trindade, N. Pereira, P. Serrano, and I. Ribeiro. 2004. *Rendimento e Competitividade Agrícolas em Portugal. Evolução Recente. Situação Actual e Perspectivas Futuras*. Lisbon: Almedina.

Bação, Pedro, and António Portugal Duarte. 2014. Taxas de inflação, de juro e de câmbio e o processo de convergência nominal. In *A Economia Portuguesa na União Europeia: 1986–2010*, ed. Fernando Alexandre et al. (orgs.), 155–172. Coimbra: Actual.

Baklanoff, Eric N. 1996. Breve experiência de socialismo em Portugal: o sector das empresas estatais. *Análise Social* XXXI (138): 925–947.

Baptista, Fernando Oliveira. 1994. A agricultura e a questão da terra – do Estado Novo à Comunidade Europeia. *Análise Social* XXIX (128): 907–921.

Batista, Dina, et al. 1997. *New Estimates of Portugal's GDP: 1910–1958*. Lisbon: Banco de Portugal.

Bento, Vítor. 2009. *Perceber a Crise para Encontrar o Caminho*. Lisbon: Bnomics.

Blanchard, Olivier. 2007. Adjustment Within the Euro: The Difficult Case of Portugal. *Portuguese Economic Journal* 6 (1): 1–21.

Blanchard, Olivier, and Francesco Giavazzi. 2002. Current Account Deficits in the Euro Area: The End of the Feldstein-Horioka Puzzle? *Brookings Papers on Economic Activity* 2: 147–209.

Blanchard, Olivier, and Pedro Portugal. 2001. What Hides Behind an Unemployment Rate: Comparing Portuguese and U.S. Labor Markets. *American Economic Review* 91 (1): 187–207.

Braz, Cláudia et al. 2009. Finanças públicas em Portugal: tendências e desafios. In *A Economia Portuguesa no Contexto da Integração Económica, Financeira e Monetária*, ed. AAVV. Lisbon: Bank of Portugal.

Campos, António Correia de, and Jorge Simões. 2011. *O Percurso da Saúde: Portugal na Europa*. Coimbra: Almedina.

Carreira, Henrique Medina. 1996. As políticas sociais em Portugal. In *A Situação Social em Portugal, 1960–1995*, ed. António Barreto, 365–498. Lisbon: ICS.

Cecchini, Paolo, Michel Cainat, and Alexis Jacquemin. 1988. *The European Challenge 1992: The Benefits of a Single Market*. Aldershot: Wildwood House.

The Conference Board. https://www.conference-board.org/data/economydatabase/index.cfm?id=27762.

Costa, Sílvio Domingues. 2014. Concentração Bancária em Portugal, Uma Análise de Performance do Sector Bancário. Masters dissertation at Faculdade de Economia—Universidade de Coimbra, Coimbra.

Cunha, João Correia da, and Cláudia Braz. 2006. Public Expenditure and Fiscal Consolidation in Portugal. *OECD Journal on Budgeting* 6 (4): 103–121.

———. 2009. The Main Trends in Public Finance Developments in Portugal: 1986–2008. Banco de Portugal Occasional Papers, No. 1.

Detragiache, Enrica, and Alfonso J. Hamann. 1997. Exchange-Rate Based Stabilization in Western Europe: Greece, Ireland, Italy and Portugal. IMF Working Papers, No. 97/75.

Dinan, Desmond. 2004. *Europe Recast: A History of the European Union*. Basingstoke: Palgrave Macmillan.

Dür, Andreas. 2008. Bargaining Power and Trade Liberalization: European External Trade Policies in the 1960s. *European Journal of International Relations* 14 (4): 645–669.

Eichengreen, Barry. 1996. *Globalizing Capital: A History of the International Monetary System*. Princeton, NJ: Princeton University Press.

Eurostat. https://ec.europa.eu/eurostat/home?.

Fankel, Jeffrey A., and Andrew K. Rose. 1998. The Endogeneity of the Optimum Currency Criteria. *Economic Journal* 108: 1009–1025.

Franco, António de Sousa. 1994. A economia. In *Portugal, 20 Anos de Democracia*, coord. António Reis, 170–293. Lisbon: Círculo de Leitores.

Franco, Francesco (org.). 2008. *Challenges Ahead for the Portuguese Economy*. Lisbon: ICS.

Freitas, Miguel Lebre de. 2005. O Capital. In *História Económica de Portugal, 1700–2000, Vol. III, O Século XX*, ed. Pedro Lains and Álvaro Ferreira da Silva, 91–124. Lisbon: ICS.

Fontoura, Ana Paula, and Nuno Valério. 2001. Relações económicas externas. In *Estatísticas Históricas Portuguesas*, ed. Nuno Valério, 713–739. Lisbon: INE.

Gros, Daniel. 2012. Macroeconomic Imbalances in the Euro Area: Symptom or Cause of the Crisis? CEPS Policy Brief, No. 266, April.

Guilera, Jordi. 2010. The Evolution of Top Income and Wealth Shares in Portugal Since 1936. *Revista Historia Economica—Journal of Iberian and Latin American Economic History* 28: 139–171.

Holinski, Nils,Clemens Kool, and Joan Muysken. 2012. Persistent Macroeconomic Imbalances in the Euro Area: Causes and Consequences. *Federal Reserve Bank of St. Louis Review* 94 (1): 1–20.

INE (Instituto Nacional de Estatística). https://ine.pt/xportal/xmain?xpgid=ine_main&xpid=INE.

James, Harold. 2012. *Making the European Monetary Union: The Role of the Committee of Central Bank Governors and the Origins of the European Central Bank*. Cambridge, MA: The Belknap Press of Harvard University Press.

Lains, Pedro. 2003. Catching Up to the European Core: Portuguese Economic Growth, 1910–1990. *Explorations in Economic History* 40: 369–386.

Lindert Data Sets for *Growing Public* Book. http://economics.ucdavis.edu/people/fzlinder/peter-linderts-webpage/data-and-estimates/lindert-data-for-cup-book.

Lopes, José da Silva. 1996. *A Economia Portuguesa desde 1960*. Lisbon: Gradiva.

———. 2005. Finanças Públicas. In *História Económica de Portugal, 1700–2000, Vol. III, O Século XX*, ed. Pedro Lains and Álvaro Ferreira da Silva, 265–304. Lisbon: ICS.

Magnusson, Lars, and Bo Stråth (eds.). 2002. *From the Werner Plan to the EMU: In search of a Political Economy for Europe*. Brussels: Peter Lang.

Mata, Maria Eugénia. 2001. Finanças públicas e dívida pública. In *Estatísticas Históricas Portuguesas*, ed. Nuno Valério, 657–712. Lisbon: INE.

Mateus, Abel. 2005. A tecnologia. In *História Económica de Portugal, 1700–2000, Vol. III, O Século XX*, ed. Pedro Lains and Álvaro Ferreira da Silva, 125–156. Lisbon: ICS.

———. 2013. *Economia Portuguesa: Evolução no Contexto Internacional (1910–2013)*. Lisbon: Principia.

Moravksic, Andrew. 1991. Negotiating the Single European Act: National Interests and Conventional Statecraft in the European Community. *International Organization* 45 (1): 20–56.

Mundell, Robert. 1961. A Theory of Optimum Currency Areas. *American Economic Review* 51 (4): 657–665.

OECD. 2017. *Economic Survey of Portugal*. Paris: OECD.

OECD Social Expenditure Database. http://www.oecd.org/social/expenditure.htm.

Pinheiro, Maximiano (ed.). 1997. *Séries Longas para a Economia Portuguesa, Pós-II Guerra Mundial, Vol. I - Séries Estatísticas*. Lisbon: Banco de Portugal.

Reis, Ricardo. 2013. The Portuguese Slump and Crash and the Euro Crisis. *Brookings Papers on Economic Activity* 1: 143–210.

Rodrigues, Carlos Farinha, Rita Figueiras, and Vítor Junqueira. 2012. *Desigualdade Económica em Portugal*. Lisbon: Fundação Francisco Manuel dos Santos.

———. 2016. *Desigualdade do Rendimento e Pobreza em Portugal. As Consequências Sociais do Programa de Ajustamento*. Lisbon: Fundação Francisco Manuel dos Santos.

Rose, Andrew K. 2000. One Money, One Market: The Effect of Common Currencies on Trade. *Economic Policy* 30: 7–45.

Rose, Andrew K., and Eric van Wincoop. 2001. National Money as a Barrier to International Trade: The Real Case for Currency Union. *American Economic Review* 91 (2): 386–390.

Silva, Álvaro Ferreira da. 2016. Multinationals and Foreign Direct Investment: the Portuguese Experience (1900–2010). *Journal of Evolutionary Studies in Business* II (1): 40–68.

Silva, Ester Gomes da, and Pedro Lains. 2013. Capital Formation and Long-Run Growth: Evidence from Portuguese Data, 1910–2011. Paper Presented at Iberometrics III, Zaragoza University.

Silva, Pedro Adão, Sílvia Sousa, and Mariana Trigo Pereira. 2014. Maturação e convergência: a evolução da proteção social. In *A Economia Portuguesa na União Europeia: 1986–2010*, orgs. Fernando Alexandre et al., 375–419. Coimbra: Actual.

Simões, Marta, João Sousa Andrade, and Adelaide Duarte. 2014. Crescimento e convergência. In *A Economia Portuguesa na União Europeia: 1986–2010*, orgs. Fernando Alexandre et al., 105–123. Coimbra: Actual.

Teixeira, Pedro, João Cerejeira, Marta Simões, Carla Sá, and Miguel Portela. 2014. Educação, economia e capital humano – notas sobre um paradoxo. In *A Economia Portuguesa na União Europeia: 1986–2010*, orgs. Fernando Alexandre et al., 329–355. Coimbra: Actual.

Valério, Nuno, Ana Bela Nunes, Carlos Bastien, Rita Martins de Sousa, and Sandra Domingos Costa. 2010. *História do Sistema Bancário Português, Vol. II, Da Assunção pelo Banco de Portugal das Funções de Banco Central à União Monetária Europeia*. Lisbon: Banco de Portugal.

Varejão, João Cerejeira, and Miguel Portela. 2014. O mercado de trabalho. In *A Economia Portuguesa na União Europeia: 1986–2010*, orgs. Fernando Alexandre et al., 233–268. Coimbra: Actual.

Vetter, Stefan. 2013. The Single European Market 20 Years On. *Deutsche Bank Research—EU Monitor*, 1–20. European Integration, October.

World Development Indicators. http://datatopics.worldbank.org/world-development-indicators/.

8

Conclusion: Some General Topics—Government, Openness and External Imbalance

Some general topics concerning the evolution of the Portuguese economy during the twentieth century and the first two decades of the twenty-first century arise out of the analysis provided in the previous chapters. Besides long-run growth and structural change, issues that were dealt with in the introduction, there are perhaps three topics worth some more attention: the size of Government, the openness of the economy, and its external balance, the latter impinging on the issue of the sustainability of the growth path of the Portuguese economy. As we have seen in the previous chapters and will see again next, Government acquired an increasingly larger role in Portugal throughout the period analyzed in this book. The Portuguese Government started by being one of the smallest in the European context and is nowadays one of the largest. Also, the economy started by being one of the most protected and least open and ranks now among the least protected and most open. Finally, the Portuguese economy seems to have had from a certain moment onward persistent problems of external balance, that have been solved in different manners, raising questions about sustainability of growth.

L. Amaral, *The Modern Portuguese Economy in the Twentieth and Twenty-First Centuries*, Palgrave Studies in Economic History,
https://doi.org/10.1007/978-3-030-24548-1_8

1 The Growth of Government

Figure 1 shows the evolution of the size of Government in relation to GDP, from the mid-nineteenth century until 2017. The picture could not be clearer: the size of Government was very small in the nineteenth century and in the beginning of the twentieth century (at around 5% of GDP), had one first jump during World War I (doubling in dimension, to 10%) and remained at the same level until the 1950s. It entered then into a path of persistent growth, although passing through three main phases: in the first, from the 1950s to the mid-1970s, expansion was moderate, even if doubling in size again at the end of the period, from 10% of GDP to 20%; in the second, from the mid-1970s to the early 1980s, expansion was very rapid, doubling its size once again in a very short time span, reaching a weight of 40% of GDP at the end of the period; in the third, corresponding to the last thirty years, growth has been constant, even if at a slower pace than in the previous five years, reaching nowadays a dimension of around 50% of GDP.

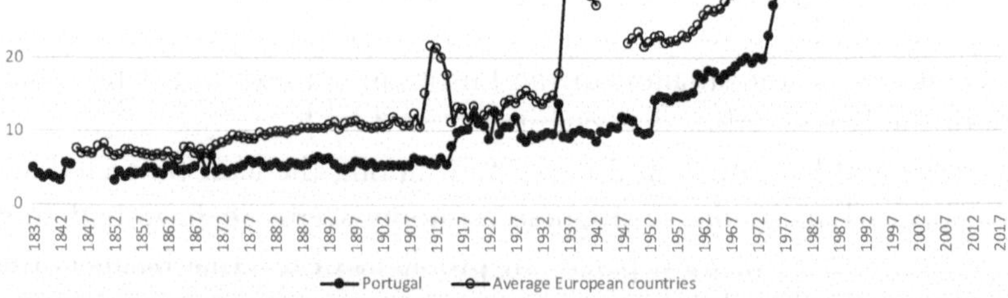

Fig. 1 Public spending, Portugal and average European countries, 1837–2017 (% GDP) (*Source* Portugal: Mata [2001] until 1953; Pinheiro [1997] for 1953–1995; AMECO for 1995–2017; European countries: 1850–1970—Mauro et al. [2013] [average of Austria, Belgium, Denmark, France, Germany, Netherlands, Norway, Sweden, and UK]; 1971–2017: AMECO, average of the countries part of EU-15)

The comparison provided in the figure with the average of European countries reveals two more interesting features: the first is that the growth in its size was something that Portugal shared with the remaining European countries. All Governments started by being very small until reaching nowadays a dimension of about 50% of GDP. The second is that the Portuguese Government kept a smaller dimension than most other European ones practically for the totality of the period, except from the beginning of the twenty-first century until today. But there were different moments in this comparative behavior as well. In the nineteenth century, Portugal diverged from the European average, as Governments started growing across Europe while left at the same dimension in Portugal. Then, Portugal converged briefly to the European average during World War I only to start diverging again from the 1920s to the 1950s. From the 1950s to the mid-1970s, the distance was kept and was followed then by rapid convergence.

The description above tells us that the Portuguese Government was subject to similar forces than in most of Europe, contributing to a long-run expansion of its size. But it tells also that the differentiated way in which those forces were felt in Portugal created a persistent lag in relation to most European countries. The most common explanations for the growth of Government in modern economies derive from the suggestion of German economist Adolph Wagner, according to whom, as economies grow and industrialize, Governments grow more than proportionality, mostly as a consequence of social programs. The Portuguese case seems to confirm this idea (commonly known as Wagner's law). While the economy was poor and growth was small, in the nineteenth century and early twentieth century, the Government kept a low dimension. The liberal revolution of the nineteenth century was responsible for creating the modern Government (in Portugal and elsewhere), but the liberal regime had many difficulties in spreading the grip of the Government over society. Also, the first embryonic social programs started appearing in the more industrialized economies of Europe in the second half of the nineteenth century. But Portugal remained outside of that process. Then, from the 1930s onwards, European Governments, first spurred by the 1930s crisis and then by the destruction caused by World War II, started building their welfare states, and Portugal remained again outside of the trend, at least until the mid-1970s, thanks to a political regime that did not give voice to the population in general and labor in particular. But once the country acquired a modern Western-style democracy, in the mid-1970s, a national version of the Welfare State was built in a very thorough manner.

2 Openness

Figure 2 shows the evolution of the degree of openness of the Portuguese economy since the mid-nineteenth century until 2017. Again the picture could not be clearer: Portugal had a very low degree of openness in the nineteenth century and in the beginning of the twentieth century, with exports and imports (divided by two) weighting around 2–3% of GDP. Then, there was one slight increase during the 1920s, to 5%, which was, however, followed by some decline, making

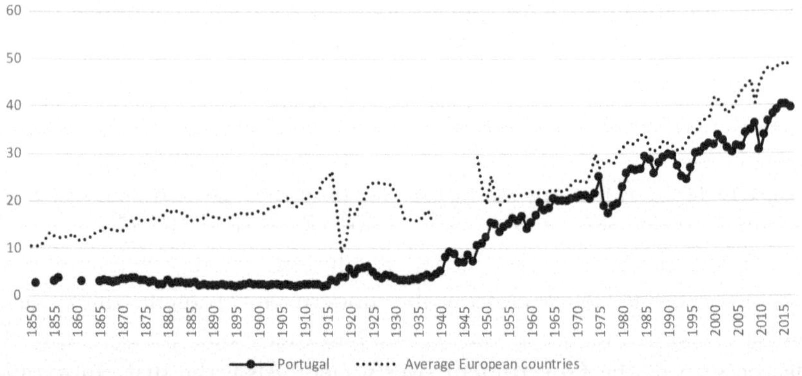

Fig. 2 Openness, Portugal and average European countries, 1850–2017 (exports and imports % GDP) Current prices; (*Source* Portugal: 1996–2017: AMECO, extrapolated backwards with Pinheiro [1997] for 1948–1995, and with Fontoura and Valério [2001] for 1851–1947 [only exports between 1850 and 1959]; European countries: 1850–1959: Federico and Antonio Tena [2018]; 1960–2017: AMECO—average EU-15 [only exports until 1959])

the economy remain extremely closed until World War II. From then on openness grew visibly, in a process that continues today: the weight of exports and imports on GDP as of 2017 is 40%.

The comparison provided in the figure with the average of west European countries shows that Portugal had a consistently divergent behavior until World War II but that it closed the gap very quickly from then on. The Portuguese economy has become as open as the average of the countries of Western Europe since the 1960s. A somewhat worrying feature seems to have appeared, however, from the mid-1980s onward: an inability to keep the same pace of opening as the one verified in Western countries. The explanation for the long-run comparative behavior in openness is relatively simple: the country missed the first age of globalization, in the second half of the nineteenth century, by keeping a protectionist stance when protectionism was being abandoned in the Western world; then, during the period covering World War I, the 1930s crisis and World War II it continued to be protectionist, but now it was accompanied by most other Western countries; after World War II, Portugal became a full participant in the process of European integration, even during the period when it was ruled by an authoritarian regime. This regime has many times been associated with autarkic policies. In fact, autarkic policies were followed by the *Estado Novo*, but when most of the world was following them too. When protectionism was abandoned in Western countries, the regime seems to have been quite eager to go along with the trend. Figure 3 shows the degree of protectionism of the Portuguese economy and of the richest European economies, from the mid-nineteenth century until the mid-1980s, as measured by the average weight of tariffs over imports. Even if this measure has a series of problems, at least the comparison with other parts of the world gives an idea of the order of grandeur of Portuguese protectionism. The country was much more protectionist than the advanced European economies during the nineteenth century and the beginning of the twentieth century. Then, the period of World War I, the 1930s crisis and World War II made all countries resort to protectionism. But once that phase of radical closing passed, we can see that Portugal had, at the end of World War II, an already lower degree of protection than its historical tradition, and then converged

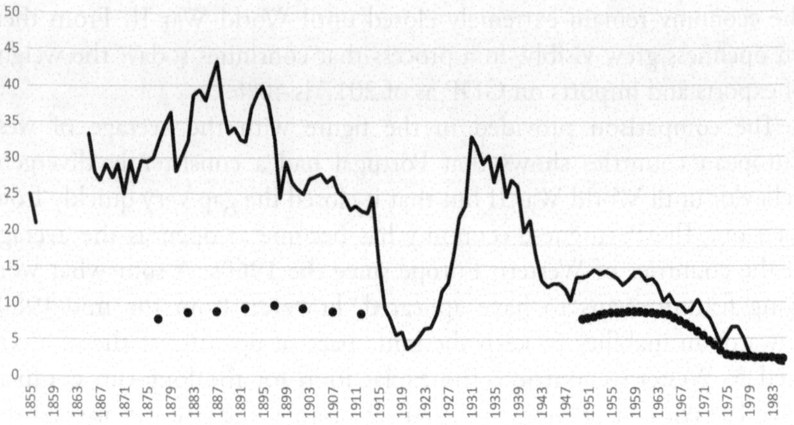

Fig. 3 Average tariffs % of imports, Portugal and European countries, 1855–1985 (*Source* Portugal: Fontoura and Valério [2001]; European countries: 1877–1912: O'Rourke [2000] [average of Denmark, France, Germany, Italy, Norway, Sweden, and UK; 1950–1985]: adapted from Dür [2008])

rapidly to what was common in Western Europe, especially from the 1960s onwards. The democratic regime installed in the country in the mid-1970s only picked-up from the inheritance left by its predecessor (although with some initial hesitations) and developed it. By the 1970s and 1980s, the country had inverted completely its protectionist tradition.

3 External Balance

Figure 4 shows that the country has never been able in the last two centuries to rely simply on its exports to keep external balance. The trade balance has been consistently negative, with very few exceptions: the period of World War II, whose special features were analyzed in Chapter 4, and the last few years, since 2012, and only if we classify tourism among exports. In order to balance its external accounts, the country has had to take hand of other influxes: for a long time, emigrant remittances were their main source. This started with

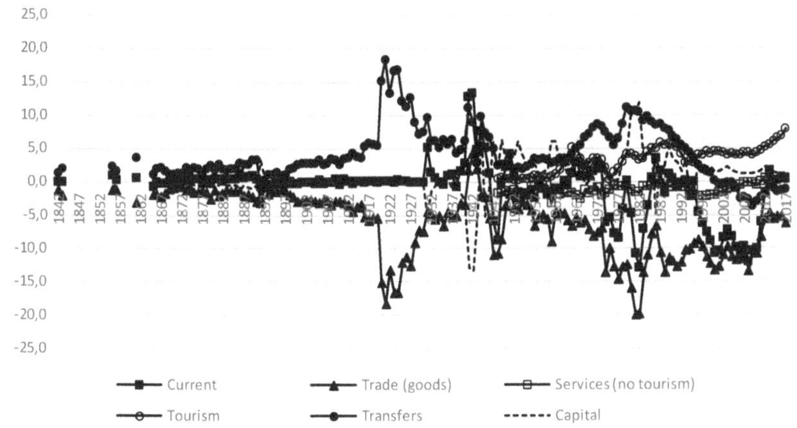

Fig. 4 Balance of payments, Portugal, 1842–2017 (% GDP) (*Source* 1842–1947—Fontoura and Valério [2001]; 1948–1995—Pinheiro [1997]; 1996–2017—INE)

the movement of mass migration in the direction of Brazil in the second half of the nineteenth century, which was interrupted with the outbreak of World War I, and continued with another movement of the sort between the 1950s and the 1970s, now in the direction of the fast-growing European economies. The movement has been interrupted then and this has had an impact on remittances: they reached the highest point in Portuguese economic history during the second half of the 1970s and then started declining consistently, becoming negative from 2005 onward, thanks to an outgoing flux generated by immigrant communities that started arriving in the country in the 1990s. Tourism also started giving an important contribution in the 1960s and has recently become the key to external balance, reaching in 2017 an importance to GDP similar to the one remittances had in the 1970s and early 1980s.

The seriousness of the problem has depended on the degree of openness of the economy: until the first decade of the twentieth century, as trade represented only a small fraction of GDP, a relatively small amount of transfers was enough to cover its deficit. But as the economy increased in openness the problem became more serious: from

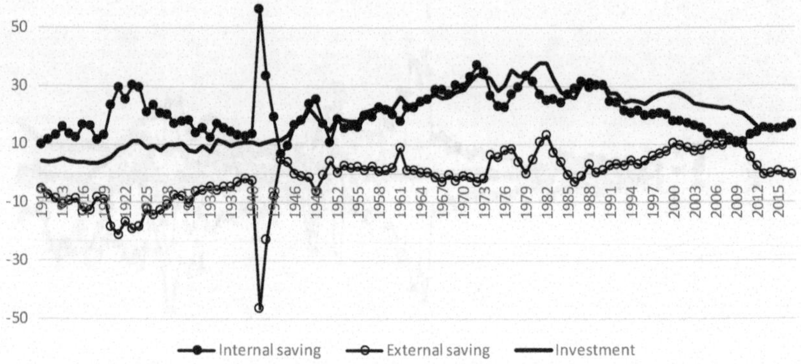

Fig. 5 Gross fixed capital formation, internal saving, and external saving, Portugal (1910–2017) (% of GDP) (*Source* 1910–1952—own calculations based on Batista et al. [1997] and Valério [2001]; 1953–1995—Pinheiro [1997]; 1996–2017—AMECO)

the 1920s and 1930s onwards the trade deficit has remained at high levels, always between 5% and 10% of GDP (with some peak years at higher values). While both remittances and tourism gave a simultaneous contribution, the problems of balance of the economy were not visible. But when remittances shrank, until becoming a negative contributor to external balance recently, those problems have become more acute.

Another way of looking into the issue is by assessing how much internal and external saving the country needs to pay for its investment. That is what Fig. 5 shows for the Portuguese economy between 1910 and 2017. Although some doubts exist concerning the quality of the data for the period between 1910 and the 1950s (see Freitas 2005), we can see there that the country was an international creditor, mostly on account of an extremely low investment rate. Opportunities for investment were very few in the country and savers must have preferred to use their resources especially in such objects as foreign bonds (again, much caution must be used in the interpretation of this period, due to the low quality of data). After a temporary peak during World War II, national saving increased consistently until the early 1970s, accompanying the expansion of the investment rate. This is the period of the golden age of economic growth, during which the savings pool grew thanks to many sources: firms' saving, due to good economic results; households' savings, mostly due to the incorporation of remittances into the income of the households remaining in the country; and public saving, due to the "orthodox" approach to public finance by the authoritarian regime ruling the country between the 1930s and the 1970s. From then on both investment and savings declined, but savings more so than investment. The decline in savings results mostly from the decline in remittances, but also from consistent public dissaving and a higher reliance of firms on debt. This decline made national saving insufficient to pay for investment and in a growing manner from the late 1980s until 2011. Then, there was a sudden correction, as the economy collapsed during the troika intervention in the country.

The problem just described can be best understood through a famous macroeconomic expression. An economy's GDP can be decomposed in the following manner:

$$Y = C + I + G + NX$$

where Y is GDP, C is consumption, I is investment, G is Government spending and NX is net exports. We can rearrange the identity in order to obtain an expression for saving:

$$Y - C - G = I + NX$$

or

$$S = I + NX$$

Since net exports equal net foreign investment, then:

$$S = I + NFI$$

where NFI is net foreign investment.

If we look at Portugal through the lens of this expression, we can see that the Portuguese economy has developed recently a problem of saving which is ultimately a problem of ability to export and be competitive in the world market. A declining national saving rate was covered by external saving in order to keep investment at the level desired by

Portuguese economic agents. Or, which is the same thing, by a growing external indebtedness. This was not a problem when foreign savers believed in the Portuguese capacity to repay. But once it became clear that the economy was growing too slowly and that the payment of that debt was at risk, foreign saving withdrew from the country at the end of the first decade of the twenty-first century. A balance has been reestablished in the last five years, but investment remains at a very low level. In fact, the investment rate is now at roughly the same level as in the 1930s and 1940s (15%), which is very low for an economy still with a capital-labor of about half of the richer countries. There is only one way of increasing it, and consequently increasing also the growth potential of the economy, and that is by making the Portuguese economy more competitive in order to rely more on exports.

References

AMECO. http://ec.europa.eu/economy_finance/ameco/user/serie/SelectSerie.cfm.

Batista, Dina et al. 1997. *New Estimates of Portugal's GDP: 1910–1958*. Lisbon: Banco de Portugal.

The Conference Board. https://www.conference-board.org/data/economydatabase/index.cfm?id=27762.

Dür, Andreas. 2008. Bargaining Power and Trade Liberalization: European External Trade Policies in the 1960s. *European Journal of International Relations* 14 (4): 645–669.

Federico, Giovanni, and Antonio Tena-Junguito. 2018. Federico-Tena World Trade Historical Database. https://www.uc3m.es/ss/Satellite/UC3MInstitucional/es/TextoMixta/1371246237481/Federico-Tena_World_Trade_Historical_Database.

Fontoura, Ana Paula, and Nuno Valério. 2001. Relações económicas externas. In *Estatísticas Históricas Portuguesas*, ed. Nuno Valério, 713–739. Lisbon: INE.

Freitas, Miguel Lebre de. 2005. O Capital. In *História Económica de Portugal, 1700–2000, Vol. III, O Século XX*, ed. Pedro Lains and Álvaro Ferreira da Silva, 91–124. Lisbon: ICS.

Mata, Maria Eugénia. 2001. Finanças públicas e dívida pública. In *Estatísticas Históricas Portuguesas*, ed. Nuno Valério, 657–712. Lisbon: INE.

Mauro, Paolo, Rafael Romeu, Ariel Binder, and Asad Zaman. 2013. A Modern History of Fiscal Prudence and Profligacy. IMF Working Paper, 13/5.

O'Rourke, Kevin H. 2000. Tariffs and Growth in the Late Nineteenth Century. *Economic Journal* 110: 456–483.

Pinheiro, Maximiano. (ed.). 1997. *Séries Longas para a Economia Portuguesa, Pós-II Guerra Mundial, Vol. I—Séries Estatísticas*. Lisbon: Banco de Portugal.

Valério, Nuno. 2001. Contas nacionais. In *Estatísticas Históricas Portuguesas*, ed. Nuno Valério, 505–535. Lisbon: INE.

Correction to: Introduction

Correction to:
Chapter 1 in: L. Amaral, *The Modern Portuguese Economy in the Twentieth and Twenty-First Centuries*, Palgrave Studies in Economic History, https://doi.org/10.1007/978-3-030-24548-1_1

The original version of this chapter was inadvertently published with the incorrect numerical information about the Size of Portuguese economy in 2017 in text and Figure 1. The corrections to the chapter have been updated with the changes.

The updated version of this chapter can be found at
https://doi.org/10.1007/978-3-030-24548-1_1

L. Amaral, *The Modern Portuguese Economy in the Twentieth and Twenty-First Centuries*, Palgrave Studies in Economic History,
https://doi.org/10.1007/978-3-030-24548-1_9

Index

L. Amaral, *The Modern Portuguese Economy in the Twentieth and Twenty-First Centuries*, Palgrave Studies in Economic History,
https://doi.org/10.1007/978-3-030-24548-1

E

Z

The manufacturer's authorised representative in the EU is Springer Nature Customer Service Centre GmbH, Europaplatz 3, 69115 Heidelberg, Germany. If you have any concerns regarding our products, please contact ProductSafety@springernature.com

Printed and bound by CPI Group (UK) Ltd, Croydon, CR0 4YY

30/09/2026

02225661-0010